C000011211

THE PHOENIX

CHRISTOPHER JOHN REASON

Paperback edition first published in the United Kingdom in 2019
by aSys Publishing

Copyright © Christopher John Reason 2019

Christopher John Reason has asserted his rights under the Copyright
Designs and Patents Act 1988 to be identified as the author of this work.

All rights reserved

No part of this book may be reproduced or transmitted in any form or by
any means, electronic, mechanical, photocopying, recording, or otherwise,
without prior written permission from the author.

A CIP catalogue record for this book is available from
the British Library.

ISBN: 978-1-913438-06-7

aSys Publishing 2019

http://www.asys-publishing.co.uk

INTRODUCTION

Hi there, my name's Chris Reason, and I'm writing this book, some seventeen years after the event, from the comfort of the little 3-bed semi in Fishponds, Bristol, that both myself and my wonderful wife Helen both still occupy. I probably would've written it a little sooner, but essentially, as is generally the case with most ordinary folk, work has always got in the way, and I've simply never managed to find the time. However, now that I'm semi-retired, thanks to my amazing daughter Michelle, coupled with the fact that Helen is still currently working, albeit in the same stuffy old high-rise office block in the centre of town, it seems that finally I have managed to find the time. So now I no longer have any excuse not to.

So here goes then:-

My earlier years never proved to be quite as laid back as I seem to find them these days. In fact, it has to be said, precisely the opposite! Firstly, because my father and I started our own Blinds & Awnings manufacturing business together back in 1979, which had kept me busily grafting away pretty much 24/7 for at least the first twenty-odd years of its existence, *such is an absolute MUST if you're seriously determined to make a true success of something worthwhile!* And secondly, because I hadn't managed to be overly successful on the female relationship front. Although I will add, in my clearly biased opinion, that the one most definitely does not encourage the other! Not that I have any regrets whatsoever in that respect, mainly because I have three of the most fabulous children that anyone could ever wish for, from the two failed marriages of my younger days. Thankfully too, after all this time, I've still managed to remain friends with both Caroline, the mother of my eldest daughter Michelle, as well as Rachel, the mother of my other two considerably younger offspring, Tori and Alex.

In between marriages however, now that's a different kettle of fish altogether! My father was the leader of 1st Batchworth Sea Scouts near

1

Rickmansworth when I was born, and consequently introduced me and both of my two younger brothers to sailing at very early ages. Nick and I both went on to become highly competitive canoeists, whereas Julian's natural-born talent led him into more of a musical hobby instead. Both during and following my own education, my apprenticeship, as well as my business, social and family life, the simple fact was, *and still is to this day,* that the obsession with boating never ever left me, and I'm pretty damned sure it never ever will.

One day, I was chugging around Brunel's infamous '*Floating Harbour',* otherwise known as Bristol City Docks, in a tatty old Fletcher speedboat that I'd acquired for next to nothing. '*Look at what you could've won!'* springs to mind. Anyway, I met a wonderfully charismatic guy called Tony, who not only became a very close friend, he changed my perception of life, and my views on the value of materialism altogether. At the time he was living aboard a scruffy old Second World War American PT boat called Gallipoli, whose engines, amongst other things, had ceased to function some considerable years previously. However, one way or another, by hook *AND* by crook, he'd managed to continue living aboard for a full ten years, before the Harbour Authority demanded he remove all eighty feet of its rotting marine-ply hull from their respectable waterways, before it sank altogether, a feat that I was more than happy to assist him with, and thank God I did when I did too! *Some joker had already chalked a line through the name Gallipoli on her stern transom, and scribbled the name TITANIC underneath instead!*

Sadly, due mainly to the pressures of trying my damnedest to get our new business off the ground, my first marriage failed whilst Michelle was just a three-year-old. Some six months after that I'd met Tony at a party aboard Gallipoli, and a further six months later I bought the good ship Bettola. I moved her from one end of Bristol Harbour to the other, moored her right behind Gallipoli, gave up my rented flat in Fishponds, and moved aboard. Bettola was a 1970's Colvic Norseman, a 38ft twin diesel engined heavy fibreglass cabin-cruiser, and unlike Gallipoli, far from being simply a static liveaboard, I used to love taking her out sailing as often as I could manage. Caroline and I had amicably agreed that Michelle would alternate her weekends between the two of us, and to this day I still have many fond memories of her running around and exploring the beaches of both Ilfracombe and Barry Island, both locations easily reachable from Bristol on just the one tide, as a precocious little six, seven and eight-year-old bundle of fun. On other occasions, without my young daughter's most enjoyable company, although often with my dear old mentor Alf aboard, I'd sailed longer voyages on Bettola, such as down to St Mary's in the Scilly Isles, as well as up to Tewkesbury on the River Severn.

The years marched forward, the business steadily grew, and after five years of living aboard Bettola, through a mutual friend late one evening, I met the young girl who was to become my second wife, namely Rachel. Following much soul-searching, with the deliberate intention of having two more children, I then sold the boat and moved back to suburbia. A year or so afterwards my second daughter Victoria was born, followed precisely eighteen months later by my first and only son Alexander. *'Happy days are here again...'* I hear you all singing. Until, once again, it all went horribly pear-shaped! I walked away from the house that I'd bought in Fishponds, leaving a very capable Rachel with the two youngsters, and spent the next six months sofa-surfing. Thankfully, Rachel and I reached the same amicable agreement with regard to child access that Caroline and I had also reached together, and some months later, whilst giving Tori and Alex a guided tour of Exeter Maritime Museum one sunny Sunday afternoon, I stumbled across the good ship Marovonne, laid up in Exeter's inner harbour. The minute I laid eyes on the Marovonne, the first thought that immediately sprang to mind was, *'Oh dear, here we go; another divorce, another boat! Hey ho, such is life!'* Some six months later, following my long trek back to Bristol aboard the Marovonne, via Turf, Plymouth, Penzance and Padstow, due to certain adverse weather conditions along the way, I moored her immediately outside the Arnolfini Art Gallery right in the city centre, and much to the harbourmaster's annoyance, immediately moved aboard right there and then; still with a couple of years left to go before catching the city harbour's spectacular Millennium celebrations from my significantly advantageous viewpoint. Just another one of my cunning little *'Chrissy-plans'* that I'd dreamt up well in advance.

The Marovonne was a beautiful old girl, a 65ft converted MFV, built in 1944 by Curtis & Pape of Looe, Cornwall, as a navy supply ship. She was originally commissioned Marazan, HMS MFV 88, heavily larch-planked over massive oak frames, and powered by a gorgeous single Gardner 8L3 diesel engine. Ironically she was decommissioned the same year I was born, and following her no expense spared conversion shortly afterwards, her new owner spent some twenty years running charters with her off the coast of East Africa. I bought her shortly after her return to the UK, via Suez, the

Med, and then Brest in France, and with her huge saloon, self-contained galley and three double cabins, two for'ard and one aft, each one with its own en-suite, I felt more than comfortable aboard. As indeed did both Tori and Alex every other weekend. Whether they were simply lazing in the hammocks slung across the aft deck on a sunny summer's day, watching the world and the ferryboats go by. Or sometimes feeding their leftover breakfast cornflakes to the young swans through the porthole in their twin-bunked cabin, before setting off for school early on a Monday morning. Or indeed whether we were actually off sailing somewhere together, which I tried to do as often as possible, especially during the school summer holidays. Either way they were both always as happy as Larry, as indeed was Michelle if ever she chose to join us. I had my Day Skipper's ticket by then, and I always planned and logged each and every voyage meticulously, both before and during our sailings. Despite its world-renowned reputation for being somewhat dangerous, albeit justifiably, the Bristol Channel had simply become my weekend playground. *(Ooh, I think I feel another episode brewing here, Kevin!)* I spent many a wonderful hour plying its often lumpy seas back and forth between Bristol and Padstow, with my varying assortment of wonderful children, friends and crew aboard. Well before the turn of the Millennium, Lundy Island had become one of the whole family's *'favouritest'* places in the whole wide world.

And then I met Helen! One night in the Shakespeare Tavern, just a stone's throw from the Marovonne's mooring. After far too many pints of Abbot Ale I'd asked her if she fancied spending Christmas with me in Sharm el-Sheikh, Egypt. She'd said thanks, but no thanks, but I took her with me anyway! It was my turn for a kid-free X-word, so I needed to leave the UK, and I didn't really fancy going away on my own. Hey ho! Some months earlier, during the late summer of that same year, I'd taken Helen with me down to Portishead Harbour Regatta aboard the Marovonne, and a great weekend was had by one and all. Upon our return to Bristol, Helen had gone back to her mum's house in Bath, where she lived at the time, and when we flew back from our week in Egypt together, she went straight back to her mum's house yet again. Sadly, in the March of 1998, Helen's mum passed away, *at far too young an age,* and having lost her dad some few years before I'd even met her, *also at far too young an age,* she decided at this point to move aboard the Marovonne with me. The summer of '98, I'll never forget, was simply wonderful! In between the usual stresses and strains of running one's own business, we sailed here, there and everywhere, through good weather and bad, both with and without the kids. We made many, many friends together, and threw just as many parties, much to the frustration of more than one harbour authority. We anchored off Lundy's south-eastern lee shore on several occasions that year, before climbing the steep path up to the Marisco Tavern for both lunch and dinner, then sleeping aboard before moving ever onwards with our nautical travels. The photos that still adorn the walls of our little home here in Fishponds, some twenty-one years later are a testimony to how fabulous a year we'd spent together, as well as how much by then we'd quite clearly fallen in love with each other. Then, all too suddenly, before we even knew it, that summer was gone, and now I was forever attempting to keep the dodgy old 1944 diesel-fired central-heating boiler down in the Marovonne's engine room alight, in order to provide us both with at least some form of intermittent warmth. I don't care what anyone says, winters in the UK are never easy onboard ship.

1999 was just as wonderful a year, with just as much sailing, possibly even more, and just as much fun with the kids, possibly even more too! There were even more parties, we made even more friends, and generally there was much more upsetting of various harbour authorities all-round *(Rick & Dave!)* Getting towed into Appledore by lifeboat late one night, due to unmarked lobster pot lines getting tangled around the prop, and stalling the engine some five miles north of Bull Point, didn't help! Neither did it help towards the end of that summer when I'd had to tell Helen one evening that I'd accidentally left her *home* down in Padstow. I believe her words to me at the time went along the lines of *'Well best you go buy me a bloody house somewhere then!'* So I did! As we'd already discussed getting married at some point in the near future by then, it seemed to make eminent sense at the time anyway. *Fingers crossed, third time lucky. And as its turned out, thankfully, I was right!* Coupled with the fact that Helen didn't really fancy spending yet another winter on an old navy supply ship, on an ice-covered harbour in chilly old Bristol, with only intermittent heating working at its very best to keep the pair of us just barely warm enough. So, ever grateful for the opportunity, I'd taken an interest-free loan from the business, in order to cover the deposit, and purchased this ever so slightly above average little house tucked away in a quiet little Fishponds backstreet, a place that we both still call home to this very day. Whilst the Marovonne was stuck down in Padstow, owing mainly to adverse weather conditions at the time, Helen and I holidayed together in Menorca for a week, an island that she'd visited many times before, and one that I immediately fell in love with myself too. On our return to the UK I found the weather conditions to have settled sufficiently, and sailed the Marovonne once again back to her home port of Bristol. Some few weeks later, before the winter really began to bite, we took possession of the house and moved in together, leaving the Marovonne in the highly *incapable* charge of my dear old liveaboard lodger-buddy Nik.

I now found myself well and truly multi-tasking! Not only did I have an ever-expanding business to manage, I also had two young children to look after, bring up and educate, albeit only on a part-time basis; a new house that was in need of partially decorating and fully furnishing, along with an extra-large corner plot garden, that required some fairly urgent attention; plus a sixty-five foot ex-luxury yacht down in the harbour, that firstly needed regular general maintenance, secondly needed a constant eye kept on her, mainly due to Nik's excellent mastery of the *'art of irresponsibility'*, and thirdly I could ill afford to keep up the mooring fees for, on top of my new mortgage repayments. Shortly after that I put the Marovonne on the market, but not before holding one final huge party aboard. This time it wasn't just our friends that attended, it was the whole family. My father and his friends, Helen's relatives and their friends, and all my kids and all their friends too! Far too many folk to squeeze aboard in total. But hey, no matter, those that didn't make it aboard simply crowded around the quayside, and late into the night, with one of the most magnificent firework displays that I've ever had the pleasure of witnessing, Bristol City Council's long-awaited Millennium celebrations more than lived up to all our expectations.

After entertaining a plethora of time-wasters with brief but enjoyable little jaunts down the Avon to Portishead and back, the Marovonne was finally sold, oddly enough for exactly the same figure that I'd bought her for some four years previously. Nik moved back to his mum and dad's pub, the Railway Tavern in Fishponds, and although I shed a tear as I watched her sail off into the sunset from some 250 feet high above, stood right in the middle of the Clifton Suspension Bridge, I felt comforted by the fact that I knew she was moving on to yet another good home. Her new owner was taking her to Hayling Island for a full refit, following which he'd be running dive charters with her off the west coast of Scotland, or so I was given to understand. It took me a long, long time to get over the sale of the Marovonne, however, not only did it allow me to repay the loan I'd taken from the business for the deposit on the new house, it also afforded me the time to concentrate on everything that needed doing to the house itself, a welcome distraction indeed.

Moreover, there was sufficient cash left over for Helen and I to pool our resources and buy a very small 2-bed holiday apartment in Menorca. We holidayed there once again in the early summer of 2000, just for a week on our own, and accidentally stumbled across a pretty little place that we absolutely fell in love with, so we paid a small deposit and set the wheels in motion. We then followed it up with a full two-week family holiday with Tori and Alex later that summer, during which I concluded the bargain purchase, and we took possession of our new holiday home in Playa de Fornells.

Immediately upon my return to our wonderfully efficient '*production mill*', where production had evidently ceased, due to the occurrence of several calamitous errors in the midst of my absence, I was forced into making some critical and substantial decisions towards the company's future. Firstly, from now on, with the exception of Christmas, I would restrict all my own holidays to just one week only. Secondly, in order to facilitate one decent two-week holiday per year for all employees, not just for myself, we'd instigate an annual company shut down for the whole of the Christmas period, this making eminent sense, given the depths of winter historically being our quietest season. Thirdly, and most importantly, I'd ask my now-qualified daughter Michelle if she might have any kind of interest in becoming my partner in the business. Partly because I desperately needed more help with managing the company's gradual but steady growth and expansion, and partly in order to facilitate my father taking more of a back seat position, given that he was by now seventy-six years old, and whilst still mentally energetic and fighting fit, was also clearly looking towards some form of retirement. Shortly before Michelle's twentieth birthday she came round to our house one sunny Sunday afternoon. After helping me trim the boundary hedges around the back garden, she happily announced that she'd be absolutely delighted to come and join me, and furthermore she'd already given notice to the firm of solicitors that she'd learnt everything from over the previous two years. Marvellous! Amongst her many other suitable talents, the company now gets its very own legal department! So here I sit today, some nineteen years later, extremely proud in the knowledge that my eldest daughter is now '*The Boss!*' What more could a man ask for?

However, at the time there was more! Something was missing! It took me a while to put my finger on it, because I was happy with my new life in suburbia. I loved everything about it. Helen's wonderful company, *and cooking,* the house, the garden, the kids, the kittens, the Koi carp. Even work was going extremely well. But something was missing. And then it hit me! For probably one of the first times in my entire life, I found myself oddly, sadly and utterly *'boatless!'* This was a situation that I felt neither familiar nor comfortable with. A bit like a cyclist not owning a bicycle I suppose, or a hundred other analogies I could think of right now. Anyway, needless to say, I found it entirely unacceptable. Not that I was yearning for yet another liveaboard, far from it in fact. Trying to maintain a boat of that kind of size on top of all my other commitments would prove entirely impractical. However, another little toy boat, now that would be a different matter altogether. It was all very well most of the family living in Fishponds, me working in Fishponds, the kids going to school in Fishponds, that was all fine and dandy. Plus I knew Helen and I had our new little holiday escape abroad. But I really felt I needed more of a local escape, more of a weekend hobby so to speak. Or more to the point, to put it bluntly, I just wanted yet another boat to go play with.

So one day, during the late autumn of 2000, purely on a whim, I'd bought this rather old but sound little fishing tub from a boatyard near Weston-Super-Mare, and dragged it somewhat gingerly, on its decrepit old yard trailer, back to my old stomping ground of Bristol City Docks. I launched it single-handedly under the cover of darkness from Bristol Marina's slipway, then moored it to a secure pontoon in St Augustine's Reach, paperwork and payment for which would inevitably follow in due course. The boat didn't have a name at the time, but after I'd launched and secured her I named her Phoenix. *The reason behind that will provide sufficient content for a whole new book in itself!* She was actually a rather beautiful, classic 23-foot Norwegian fjord fishing boat, built entirely from GRP, with a solid heavy keel, and an imitation clinker-style hull with a canoe-stern. She had a large 2-berth forecabin, with separate toilet cubicle, and a wonderful little 4-cylinder 1.6 litre marinised Ford diesel engine centred between the seating area around the open aft deck. Her bilges had been ballasted to an initial dry-weight of 3,650 kilograms, or so I'd been informed, thus making her somewhat heavy for her length, but also exceptionally stable. She was in extremely good condition for her age, and that little Ford engine was right on the button every single time. In fact, it just purred away to me like a sweet little pussycat every time I started it. She was safe, she was sound, she was economical, and I couldn't wait to take her out somewhere. I wanted to take her down through the Avon Gorge and out into the Severn with a couple of mates on a fishing trip, and I wanted to take her up the river with the kids aboard, all the way to The Lock & Weir pub at Hanham, where we'd have lunch outdoors in the summer sunshine. 2001 was going to be a great year, the whole family was going to have so much fun on the Phoenix. I paid some £300 to insure her fully comp., then I paid the harbour authority around £600 for a secure annual pontoon mooring. I then set to work on her, scrubbing, cleaning, polishing, new decals, new bedding and curtains. I even changed the engine oil, and fitted new anodes to her perfect little phosphor-bronze rudder. Yes indeed, although the winter of 2000 was fast approaching, the summer of 2001 was most definitely going to be a good one!

And a good one it most certainly was too! In fact, I'd go as far as to say probably one of the best years I've had in the whole of my lifetime. Not that it was connected in any way with the aforementioned thoughts and aspirations that I'd had in relation to the Phoenix, or anything even remotely connected with the Phoenix whatsoever. No, it was all simply down to the fact that Helen and I had got married. It was a pretty damned spectacular wedding mind you, even if I do say so myself! Saturday the 16th of June, on-stage in the Landmark Theatre, Ilfracombe, in front of a hundred and eighty invited guests. Brother Julian's new band played afterwards, with me as surprise guest vocalist for one particular song, which I'd sung as a complete surprise specifically to Helen, and thanks to my dear old mate Mike, the night culminated in a magnificent firework display right over the seafront. Hotels for most folk for the two nights. Then on Sunday the 17th the MV Oldenburg took a hundred and twenty of us over to Lundy Island for our blessing in the Church of St Helena, closely followed by my mum, the vicar, and the photographer, by helicopter. After being piped both in and out of the church, then celebrating to excess in The Marisco Tavern, we danced our way back towards Ilfracombe to an excellent Irish band aboard the Oldenburg once again. Despite some fairly rough weather during the two-hour outbound voyage, with just a modicum of *'vomitage'* from all those unaccustomed to sailing, yet again a fabulous weekend was had by one and all. Following which, after the huge amount of effort and organisation that putting that kind of show together inevitably involves, thanks once again to Michelle's capability and willingness to hold the fort for me at work, Helen and I took a well-earned honeymoon in the Maldives. *(There's more than sufficient content in all of this for yet another whole new book! Maybe one day, we'll see!)* Needless to say that both before, during and after the wedding, for one reason and another, or should I say '*for one Reason PLUS another!*', very little attention had been paid to the poor old Phoenix that particular year.

Very little attention indeed! Something would definitely have to be done about that! Somehow I'd have to put yet another cunning little '*Chrissy-plan*' together. Hmmm ... let me think now ...

PROLOGUE

T'was early spring 2002, and the dear old Phoenix was still lying idle at her secure pontoon mooring in Bristol Harbour. The previous year hadn't proved manic solely because of everything involved in putting the wedding together. The business had played a significant role too, particularly as Michelle and I were attempting to relocate our steadily expanding little success story into far larger and more suitable premises, whilst at the same time continually pushing to grow and expand our client portfolio. In addition to that I also had Tori and Alex to educate and entertain, however every time I asked them if they'd like to come out somewhere nice with me aboard the Phoenix, they simply said no thanks, they'd much rather go to Menorca instead.

Of course, the word *'instead'* couldn't always apply! One spring weekend Helen and I took the kids up the river to Bath and back, stopping at several pubs along the way for lunch, tea and dinner, and they had an absolutely wonderful time. Unlike myself! I'd begun to grow somewhat tiresome of never ending lock gates by the time we'd finished! During the following Easter school holidays we took them to Menorca for a week, and they both had an even better time! After recovering from the summer wedding celebrations I tried on a couple of occasions to take the Phoenix out into the Bristol Channel for a spot of sea fishing, but both times the weather forecast put paid to that idea, and I ended up just pottering around the harbour, every inch of which I knew by then like the back of my hand. Towards the end of the school summer holidays I asked Tori and Alex where they'd most like to go for a week, and guess what they both said? Yep, you guessed it, another week in Menorca, and a very hot one at that!

We were all having a fabulous time together, especially whilst enjoying our wonderful little holiday home, but I was beginning to wonder to myself just why I'd bought the Phoenix in the first place. A week or so after that particular holiday, one Sunday morning when the kids were at

11

their mother's, I found myself once again sat aboard the Phoenix, not going anywhere, just contemplating life, the universe and things in general. I no longer wanted to live my life as a *water-gypsy!* I was perfectly happy with being a simple suburban landlubber, and I was also most certainly very happily married. No more liveaboards for this old kiddy, *no siree!* Work, home, the wife, the kids, holidays too, everything was all good. I just wasn't getting the use out of the poor old Phoenix that I'd initially intended, that was all. And with that, all of a sudden, the heavens opened, and it began to pour with rain.

We took the kids to Menorca for a third visit that particular year. It was the autumn half term at school, and they both wanted to take friends over with them. After sorting out the costs and insurances with their friends' parents, Helen and I took Tori and Leah with Alex and Tom up to Bristol Airport, and boarded yet another flight to Mahon. I remember buying the four kids a giant yellow inflatable octopus to play with in the pool, and as the weather was glorious yet again, this afforded me the opportunity to leave Helen supervising them for an afternoon whilst she relaxed, read her book, and topped up her tan on the sun-terrace. I myself chose to go off and explore a little more of the area surrounding our relatively new Spanish home town of Fornells. We'd certainly chosen a very beautiful place to buy. The surrounding rocky countryside was spectacular, with Fornells Bay itself simply an amazing and very special sight to behold. There were countless little yachts sailing its expansive and well-protected inshore waters, along with many small fishing boats both entering and leaving the sanctuary of Fornells Town's pretty little inner harbour. Out in the middle of the bay there were also several larger boats laying at anchor, their tenders in the water alongside them. Whilst standing there alone at the very end of the harbour wall, in the beautifully warm sunshine, lost somewhere deep within my own imagination, whilst surveying all that I saw before me, I couldn't help but feel just the tiniest little twinge of envy . . .

The Phoenix at her mooring in Bristol Harbour

CHAPTER ONE

O kay, so its still early spring 2002. Helen's best friend, who also happened to be called Helen, had married her new found hero Steve some eighteen months previously, conceived during their exotic honeymoon to Bali, and now Helen and I had been requested to attend little Keelin's christening ceremony. Essentially this being on account of Helen agreeing, sometime shortly before Keelin was born, to becoming her godmother. Well that was all well and good, but there were two slight issues here. Firstly, it was scheduled to be a three kid fully Catholic religious ceremonial event in an old-fashioned traditional Catholic church. So, whilst I have no particular religious views either way on this, I knew that it meant it was going to drag on for at least half a day. Yes, that's a whole half a day sat perfectly still and completely silent, without so much as a single tea break, on an uncomfortable old wooden church pew. Not exactly my idea of fun. And secondly, it was in Halifax! Which meant we'd have to stay over. And guess what? We'd ail been requested to attend the after-christening party too, and make the subsequent stay over at Steve's parents' house, meaning that yours truly got to bagsy the sofa! *Whoopee-do!* So, off we both trekked to Halifax, by car, by motorway, making sure we left plenty early enough to avoid any possible delays along the way; of which, quite obviously, there weren't any! We subsequently arrived in Halifax town centre, fully togged up to the nines, ready for the 1pm start, at 10am in the morning! *'Hmm, three hours to kill. Where's the nearest Wetherspoons?'* I thought to myself. 'Tis a strange old place, that there Halifax. Everything in the High Street appeared to be either shut down for good, or not yet open, even at 10am on a Saturday morning. The only place we did find open was, yep, you guessed it, a Wetherspoons! Hey ho, Eggy McMuffins and a pint of slosh for breakfast it was then. So with those three hours to kill, and nothing more than a pack of cards and a cribbage board between us, I began to run these rapidly developing thoughts of mine past my dear lovely young wife.

15

They were essentially a culmination of the thoughts that had already been running through my mind, partly whilst sat idly twiddling my thumbs aboard the Phoenix back in Bristol Harbour, and partly, thanks to Helen's questionable taste in music on that particular day, whilst being subjected to some dreadful Daniel O'Donnell music on the car stereo during the three hour drive to Halifax.

"Helen," I began to suggest, "you know our lovely little holiday apartment that we now own, down by the seaside in sunny old Menorca . . . ?"

"Yes . . . ," she replied, rather slowly and somewhat warily.

So therein, I suppose, begins the very start of this amazing little adventure of ours. The start of yet another fun and exciting episode of our marital lives together, and essentially, having hopefully now explained and justified the reasoning behind it, the beginnings of this little book that I'm now attempting to write. The pretty little 2-bed holiday apartment that we'd bought together in Playa de Fornells was on the far north-eastern coast of the quiet and beautiful little Mediterranean island of Menorca. It was situated within a lovely community complex of 28 apartments in total, each of which fronted on to our own wonderful communal swimming pool, with a sun terrace that looked directly over the rocky shoreline, and far, far out to sea. The little community was named *Tamarindos* after the tree lined boulevard that ran around the entire estate. Around past the two little beach shops, and on down towards a couple of wonderfully located restaurants, sited along the rocky shores, with exceptional patio-fronted views across the mile long golden sandy beach. All the apartments throughout the complex were painted in brilliant white, and most were adorned with a gorgeous array of bougainvillea, with spectacular pink, white and lilac flowers that bloomed for the majority of the year. It was absolute heaven, and the kids loved it to pieces. It had always been our intention to take them over there as often as we could possibly manage, however, by 2002 we'd all come to know and love pretty much the whole of the island quite intimately anyway. On-site in Tamarindos, Helen and the kids had absolutely everything they needed, they couldn't wish for more. However, in my own mind, something was very obviously missing . . .

"Well," I continued, "you know I've always wanted to have a little boat over in Menorca?"

"Yes . . . ," she replied, still slowly and warily.

"And you know the Phoenix is sat in Bristol Docks doing absolutely nothing?"

"Yes . . . ," she replied, even more slowly this time.

"Well, why don't we just take the Phoenix over to Menorca? *Simples!*"

"Oh yes, of course," she said. "Simples! Just like that! What could possibly go wrong? So how then exactly, oh clever husband of mine, are you proposing to achieve this little exercise?"

"Just thinking aloud," I muttered.

However, a cunning little *Chrissy-plan* was already beginning to formulate itself in my mind.

"Well I wouldn't sail that old tub any further than Watchet," she scowled, "let alone around Land's End! And all the way across Biscay would simply be impossible! So what's Plan B exactly?"

"Well of course not babe, I wouldn't even dream of sailing her there," I retorted. "It would have to be by road."

"Well that scabby old yard trailer, the one that's currently cluttering up my front drive as we speak, that wouldn't even make it one junction down the motorway without collapsing, and that's just on its own, let alone with a 4-ton boat loaded on top of it. And there's no way that you're ever going to find a suitable new trailer for it, not one that'll safely carry that particular weight and hull-shape anyway. Let alone afford something half decent that's capable of towing it. And that's saying nothing about dragging the whole lot some thousand odd miles across four countries! The whole idea is simply preposterous!" she scolded.

"Firstly," I said, "she's not just an old tub, she's sound, solid, safe and reliable. Secondly, I'm not going to just sell her, even if she is worth somewhere in the region of six grand; and especially now that I've done all that work to her. So I'm keeping her, and I'm taking her to Menorca, and I'm going to keep her and use her in and around Fornells Bay, walking distance from our lovely little apartment. The kids can even sleep aboard for the odd night every now and then, if ever they want, and I'm going to take her out fishing and catch mackerel and squid and octopus, which you can cook for us for our tea, and, and, and, and . . . trust me, where there's a will there's a way. *I'll go buy a lorry!*"

CHAPTER TWO

The christening had gone entirely according to plan. None of the kids had got dropped in the font, Keelin was now officially called '*Keelin*', and much Catholicism was had by all. Even the after-show party had gone swimmingly well too, and much to our enjoyment, Steve's parents had laid on an exceptional spread of first class buffet-style food, which was extremely welcomed, as we'd eaten absolutely zilch since our eggy brekkie in the 'Spoons earlier that morning. And so, much later on that evening, I gradually drifted off to sleep, half wrapped in an old sleeping-bag, whilst half-heartedly attempting to count how many empty bottles of Prosecco were dotted around various parts of the lounge. Helen had retired slightly earlier to a very similar situation in the drawing room, although I suspected she'd far more likely be counting empty bottles of baby milk, rather than those of Prosecco. The following morning I slowly and delicately peeled my aching body off the sofa, and headed straight for the kitchen kettle. Coffee was desperately needed. Helen had beaten me to it however, as her sofa had apparently turned out to be considerably less comfortable than mine. No matter. We sat and drank coffee together until Steve and his mum quietly tiptoed into the kitchen, begging us to stay sufficiently quiet so as not to wake baby Keelin from her delicate slumber. So we politely expressed our gratitudes for a splendid and successful event, bid fond farewells all round, jumped purposefully into the car, and headed back down south post haste. The journey home was equally as uneventful as the drive up there, and shortly before arriving I stopped off at a newsagent's and bought the latest edition of the commercial Auto-Trade-It. *The seed had been sown!* During our many visits to our little holiday home in Menorca over the previous couple of years, I'd often strolled along the rugged rocky coastline from Tamarindos into Fornells Town itself. It was only about a mile, but it could take up to an hour, as there was no real path, and the footing could be quite unstable in places. So much so that, if I had the kids tagging along with me, it often took up to two hours. But it was always warm, interesting and fun, and occasionally, if wearing our cossies and the appropriate submersible footwear, we'd stop off for a welcome swim along the way. Tori would always step really gingerly down the flattest series of rocks she could find, and gently lower herself into the sea, whereas Alex would throw himself backwards off the highest rock available, in a vain attempt to splash her as much as possible before she got herself all the way in. After making sure both where and what they were doing was entirely safe, I just sat there and laughed. They were such happy times. Anyway, the beautiful little town of Fornells only had a population of around one thousand, a few back street shops and boutiques, and the most wonderful array of waterfront restaurants, particularly famous for their fresh lobster. We ate there often, and spent many an evening just strolling along the waterfront and around the harbour, always marvelling at how very picturesque everything was. Menorca really was a very beautiful place indeed, and to us Fornells was the jewel in the crown. It was very special in all of our hearts. Fornells harbour itself, perfectly safe and protected from the elements from all angles due to its ideal location well inside Fornells Bay, was a traditional little Spanish fishing port, within which sheltered a little fleet of small, white painted, locally built Menorquin fishing smacks. They all had little putt-putt engines, open decks, single foresails, blue and white canvas sun canopies, and the obligatory lobster pot bracket and winch bolted to their stern transoms. Oh, how I would've loved to have kept my own little boat moored up somewhere amongst them, in pretty little Fornells harbour. I honestly felt that the Phoenix was stylish and pretty enough to blend in perfectly with them, without looking the slightest bit out of place. Sadly though, I knew this was never going to happen, as moorings there were only allowed for the local resident fishermen and their own little fishing boats, with which they operated their own locally licensed commercial businesses, supplying all manner of fresh fish and seafood, but especially freshly caught lobster, to the local restaurants. Mind you, what a wonderful way to earn a living! Spending your days toiling on the beautiful, warm, calm, azure blue Mediterranean Sea. I so wanted my own boat out there, somehow, someday, one way or another. By hook or by crook! So I checked with the local harbourmaster, and I treble-checked with the local harbourmaster, but it was always a big, fat, stubborn '*NO!*'

'*There are no permanent moorings available within Fornells inner harbour for private leisure craft, and no amount of bribery will persuade me otherwise!*

Our inner harbour here is solely for the use of our own local fishing fleet, and I'm very sorry señor, but its as simple as that! Just outside of the inner harbour we have the public slipway, which is free of charge for anyone to use at any time. To one side of the slipway we have the fuel pontoon, with both gasolina and gasoleo always available by prior notification. On the other side there is the longer run of pontoons which are available for the short-term use of small visiting craft, such as the tenders to larger craft. Large yachts are welcome to anchor anywhere within the bay, but the pontoons are strictly for embarkation and disembarkation only, NOT for permanent mooring. So those are your options Señor Reason. Alternatively you can use one of the private marinas, either in Addaia or in Mahon!"

Both of which were much too far away, way too expensive, and totally impractical. The Phoenix didn't carry a tender anyway, she simply wasn't big enough to accommodate one. Oh, what to do, what to do? *Surely there's a way?* Shortly afterwards, one warm and sunny lunchtime, following my early morning stroll along the rocky shoreline into Fornells, I was ambling back towards Tamarindos with an old local farmer. He was a chap whom I'd met in the local butcher's shop, and who happened, surprisingly enough, to speak far better English than I did Spanish. I never did quite catch his name, but I'd gleaned that he was a Menorcan, born and bred, and had farmed some of the hillsides around Fornells bay, mainly for olives and oranges I seem to recall, for the past fifty years or more.

He'd looked up and asked me, roughly speaking, "D'you see that very large, white painted, Spanish castle-style house over there, nestled secludedly amongst the trees on that pretty little hillside overlooking the bay?"

"Indeed I do," I replied. "I've noticed it on many a walk into town."

"And d'you have any idea who it is that owns said house?" he continued.

"No," I admitted, "although it looks quite spectacular, if a little austere."

"That there house," he replied in his very best *Spanglish*, "is the country residence and holiday home belonging to one King Juan Carlos of Spain. And, I will add, although it is supposed to be kept a muy, muy gran secreto, that our King he comes here for two weeks every year for his holidays."

"Hmm, very interesting," I said.

"And did you know," he continued, "that when he first starts to come to Menorca for his holidays, some twenty years before, at first he is coming here by boat. And he sails his muy gran yacht into the Fornells Bay, and drops his anchor. And then he comes up here to buy this beautiful house."

"Yes, very interesting," I repeated.

"And what's more," he continued, "because not always, but sometimes, he still arrives with his big yacht, so he has now officially declared, by Royal Decree, that for a period of at least the next one hundred years from this time, all moorings and anchorages within the whole of the protection of the Fornells Bay itself, with the exception of the inner fishing harbour, whether temporary or permanent, both for locals and visitors alike, shall be granted to all and sundry *entirely free of charge!*"

"*WOW*", I exclaimed, "that's *EXTREMELY* interesting! *I feel a plan coming together!*"

Tamarindos Apartments, Playa de Fornells, Menorca

CHAPTER THREE

I sat on my sofa back home in sunny old Bristol, where it wasn't sunny at all. It was cold, dark and drizzling, and I began looking through the Trade-It. I knew roughly what I was going to start looking for. I'd kind of formulated a plan, based upon the practicalities of what I needed to achieve, coupled with the limitations of the machinery that I was working with. I also had to balance that with the somewhat limited amount of financial resources that I had access to at the time, which realistically weren't exactly huge. So I had a pretty good image in my mind of exactly what kind of transportation I was going to need. Basically, an old car transporter! Loading the Phoenix on to some kind of flatbed truck wouldn't be a problem, because I knew I had access to the travel hoist in Bristol Marina, which had a lift capacity of fifty tons, and I only needed to lift a little over four. Launching the Phoenix back off the vehicle, an operation that I planned to execute on the concrete slipway just outside the entrance to Fornells inner harbour, was not going to prove anywhere near as simple. It was a gently sloping, safe and expansive slipway, always open and available for public use, or so I'd been told. However, other than the fuel pontoon, and a simple toilet block with a fresh water supply nearby, there were no other marine amenities available in Fornells. More specifically, there were no craning facilities within the area whatsoever. More importantly too, due to the timescale that I'd allowed myself to plan and achieve this little exercise, I'd most likely be launching the Phoenix into Fornells Bay somewhere during the depths of the forthcoming winter months, and Menorca, to all intents and purposes, shuts down for the winter. Due to ninety percent of the island's economy being based around tourism, with the exception of Mahon, the capital city, the majority of the remaining residents of the island tended to shut up shop out of season, and take an extended winter holiday. This was often away from the island, and included the majority of the residents of Fornells Town itself. This meant that I would more than likely be executing this tricky little operation entirely on my own, just as I had previously in Bristol. No help, no witnesses! I just prayed that the term '*execute*' wouldn't somehow end up as the word of the day! So, what I had in mind was a car transporter. It would have to be quite old, because I didn't exactly have a huge amount of spare cash at the time. Equally it would have to be up to making the whole round-trip journey; some two and a half thousand miles or so, fully loaded for half of it, legally and in one piece. More to the point, it would need to have a sloping, ramp-style back section, known apparently as a '*beaver-tail*', with a pair of those pull-out, clip-on ramp extensions. Plus some kind of powerful hydraulic winch mechanism, with an extra long, tough steel cable. This would enable me to slowly winch the Phoenix, whilst sat securely attached to her scruffy old yard trailer, backwards down the slope of the flatbed, across the extensions, and onto the concrete slipway apron, then on down into the water. I had it all perfectly pictured in my mind. As for the old boat trailer itself, it was far from being roadworthy, however it would suffice for this particular purpose. Plus I had a another cunning little *Chrissy-plan* in mind for it immediately afterwards. So that's how we'd get the Phoenix off and floating. How exactly do we get her '*unfloated*', and back on to her trailer in the first place? Especially bearing in mind the old trailer itself has no winch. Due to the Phoenix's almost three foot draft it would prove virtually impossible attempting to position the boat onto the trailer by simply backing the trailer down a slipway into the water, whilst securely attached to the back of a vehicle. The depths and weights and angles involved simply didn't add up. The trailer would need to go much further out than the towing vehicle would allow. Getting her launched and afloat was one thing. I'd already done this once previously, on the basis that recovering an empty trailer from deep water with the aid of an extra long tow rope was a relatively simple operation. However, even if I were to manage to correctly position the boat back onto its trailer, whilst standing waist deep in cold grubby dockwater, attempting to drag it up fully loaded, again with the aid of an extra long tow rope connecting the front of the trailer to the tow bar of the vehicle? Well again, what could possibly go wrong? Even with a long wheelbase 4x4 Land Rover? Nope, sorry, just ain't gonna happen! Especially with this particular boat, and this particular trailer. No, there would be a much easier way, as well I already knew. As I mentioned earlier, providing I managed to buy exactly the right type of lorry that I was looking for, I'd use its own cable winch to haul the scruffy old yard trailer up the ramps and onto the flatbed, secure it firmly into place, and then lift the Phoenix from the water using Bristol Marina's travel hoist. Then I'd gently lower her down into position onto her trailer, and secure the whole load down with the appropriate ratchet straps. Again, simples! And although I say so myself, bordering on what might possibly even appear to be semi-professional. I slowly became more deeply engrossed in my latest edition of the Trade-It. 1988 Renault hydraulic-back 2-car transporter, only 186,000 miles, £4995ono. Too big, too expensive. 1992 Leyland Daf single car ex-break-down truck, low mileage, tax and MoT, only £4000, no offers. Right idea, still too much money. *Ah, looky here!* 1977 Foden single car transporter, 3-litre straight six diesel engine, only 260,000 miles, good runner, economical and reliable, only £2000. Any trial welcome. Hmm, outskirts of Bath eh? Trial welcome eh? Let's go trial her then! The following morning, two phone calls and two hours later, I pulled into the front yard of what appeared to be a relatively decent breakdown repair operation. I parked the car over in a corner, well out of harm's way, strolled meaningfully into their office, and asked to see Dave. Whilst crossing the yard I'd noticed two fairly new looking breakdown trucks, parked up, but obviously being used quite regularly. Over in another corner I then caught my first glimpse of the old Foden, and to coin a corny old phrase, it was love at first sight. Well not quite, but almost, if you know what I mean. So, Dave introduced himself to me, and then introduced me to the old Foden. He then asked me if I'd ever driven a lorry before. I told him that I'd driven all sorts of vehicles all of my life, from tractors to trailers, from bikes to boats. I drove for a living, and one of the first jobs I'd had after leaving school was driving a seven and a half tonner for Lloyd Maunders in Willand, running multi drop meat deliveries around Exeter.

"Cool," he said. "She's only three and a half tons unladen, starts first time every time, bang on the nail. Why don't you go take her for a spin. Don't be doing more than a couple or three miles mind, she's very low on fuel."

I climbed up into the cab, turned the key, and sure enough, she fired straight up, and sounded great. No knocking, no rumbling, and after driving her up over Odd Down and back, I had already decided that this was exactly the one for the job. Three things I did notice on the way back to Dave's yard however. Firstly, she seemed to struggle just a little on steep uphill gradients. Secondly, she had a massively powerful *HIAB* hydraulic crane mounted directly behind the cab, just in front of the cable winch mechanism, which I was never going to need. And thirdly, the tax had run out some six months previous. *'Hey ho, what d'you get for your money these days?'* I thought to myself. I was greeted by Dave's beaming smile as I jumped back down from the cab.

I asked him the obvious question, "How long's the MoT?"

"Oh, no, no, no," he said, "there's no MoT I'm afraid. But we've had her looked at, and we know she'll sail straight through one, no problem."

"Oh," I said, "and how much d'you estimate that's likely to cost?" I asked dubiously.

"We've been told around £400," he stated convincingly.

"Ok," I said, "well in that case I'll give you £1,600 cash for her right now, sold as seen, and I'll take her away with me right now too. No comebacks, other than returning to pick my car up within the next few days. How does that sound?"

"Deal!" said Dave gladly.

We shook hands, and he handed me over the keys and the log book. I then drove the old girl straight to the nearest fuel station, poured in around a dozen gallons of diesel, and then drove her home. I had to park her on the road immediately outside the house, as there wasn't enough room on the drive, due to an old yard trailer that was still standing there, dropping bits of rust everywhere and forever getting in Helen's way. Helen would be home from work shortly though, I'd explain to her then that everything was going to work out just fine. "Hi honey," I hailed, as she backed her little Vauxhall Astra into what remained of the front drive. "Look what I've bought for us. We're going on a road trip together."

As she got out of the car she exclaimed, "What idiot parked that heap of junk over there. Don't they realise that's completely in our way? Where's your car gone anyway?"

"That's it babe, that's ours," I replied proudly. "We're taking the Phoenix to Menorca."

"You don't really expect me to spend two thousand odd miles sat in the passenger seat of that scruffy old thing do you?"

"Yes, I do!" I said quite firmly. "Once its passed its MoT, and once we've properly route planned the journey, you'll love it!" I squawked optimistically. "And don't worry, I'll find plenty of interesting things to break the journey up with along the way. It'll be a proper mini adventure!"

"Oh dear, not another one!" she muttered, and disappeared off indoors.

Earlier that afternoon I'd asked my own car mechanic if he knew of a relatively cheap but reliable garage that carried out commercial MoT's, and he'd highly recommended an associate of his who ran an operation in Keynsham, Paul's Commercial Vehicle Services. I telephoned Paul right away, explained exactly what the vehicle was, and asked if I could book it in for an inspection, a full service, an MoT, plus whatever else he felt might need doing, bearing in mind our proposed journey with her. He told me that he was extremely busy, and could it wait for a couple of weeks? I said the MoT itself could wait, at least until he could fit it in, but I needed to get her off the road somewhere asap, as she wasn't currently taxed. Obviously I couldn't tax her until she'd passed her MoT, so did he have a yard that was large enough to accommodate her in the meantime, whilst awaiting an inspection? Luckily for me he said he would shift things around a little and find the space for the dear little old Foden, and the following morning I dropped her straight over to Paul's yard in Keynsham. I explained to him that I was flying back to Menorca any day, just for a week or so, but I'd be straight back to Keynsham upon my return to see how things were coming along. After looking over the old girl for a few minutes he stated that all was good, she should be done and sorted alright by then. I handed him the keys, then called a taxi to take me back to Dave's yard near Bath to pick up my car. I then drove home, and proceeded to book a one-way ticket on the next available flight to Mahon.

I had a sinker mooring to lay in Fornells Bay!

CHAPTER FOUR

Over the previous couple of years I'd grown to know and love Fornells Bay immensely. As well as being officially classified as an '*Area Of Outstanding Natural Beauty*', its also listed worldwide in nautical almanacs as a '*safe haven*' for yachts, hence why King Juan Carlos had chosen the area for his holiday home location. Just over a mile wide and a little over three miles long, its situated on the north-east coast of Menorca, the wild and rocky side of the island, where the deep, harsh, open waters of the Mediterranean Sea often tend to be much rougher than Menorca's far calmer and more sheltered southern shores. Menorca's prevailing winds generally tend to be northerlies, originating from way back beyond Barcelona, and high up above the mountains of the Pyrenees. The inlet itself runs north to south, and after negotiating the often heavy swells whilst passing between the steep rocky cliffs either side of the northern entrance, with just over a quarter of a mile separating them, the bay opens out, the land flattens considerably, and the waters calm, almost to the point of resembling a large, flat, shimmering lake. To the north-west shore lies the little town of Fornells itself, with its inner fisherman's harbour, and a couple of pretty little coves with sandy beaches to either side; both considered excellent locations for a spot of sea fishing. Roughly halfway down the bay, set over towards its eastern shoreline, lies a small group of islands, by far the largest one of which, Lizard Island, has the ruins of a couple of old farming buildings on it. However, they remain unused to this day, and entirely purposeless, other than providing a point of reference for the bay's numerous wind-surfers to navigate around. The eastern shores of the bay, whilst containing many pretty little coves and beaches, tend to remain entirely deserted. Although proving vaguely accessible to the most ardent of hikers, with the exception of the odd farm dotted around here and there, these barren but beautiful shores have absolutely no settlements. There's no roads, no infrastructure, and they're renowned for being accessible solely by boat.

Absolutely ideal if you're looking to spend the day relaxing on a little beach in total seclusion and isolation. To the far southern end the bay shallows significantly, sand becomes mud, and reed beds grow in abundance. Whilst providing a perfect haven for wildlife, this renders the extreme southern marshes of Fornells Bay entirely inaccessible. Beyond the reed beds, evaporation, caused by year upon year of extreme summer heat, has created salt flats, some of which are still mined to this day, and the salt refined and sold locally. And beyond the salt flats, and another couple of old rural farms, lies the main road that takes you across country to Mahon, Menorca's wonderful capital city, and its one and only airport just a little further beyond. I stepped off the EasyJet Airbus A319, and after satisfying passport control I headed straight for the car rental offices. I knew exactly what I had in mind for the sinker, and I needed a 5-seater hatchback to achieve it. As you round the southern end of Fornells Bay, just as you begin to head due north towards Fornells Town itself, there's a small lane that dives off to the right, and takes you down to a quiet little village, situated right at the water's edge, called Ses Salines; its name derived from the Spanish for '*the salts*'. One of the nicest things about Ses Salines was its one and only high-class restaurant, perched atop a small promontory, with spectacular views across the bay from its surrounding sun terraces set amongst the pine trees. There was always that wonderful aroma of wild pinewood in the air, coupled with the constant background buzzing of cicadas late into the evenings. The other great thing about Ses Salines was its easy access to the water. You could park on the road right next to its long shingly beach, which was relatively narrow, and easily walk straight down into the water. It was quiet, secluded, calm and safe, and about three miles inshore from the open sea. If you waded about fifty metres out from the shore, you'd just about be up to your neck in flat calm non-tidal waters, with a bottom of firm-ish muddy silt. It had seemed to me to be the absolute *perfect* place to lay a sinker mooring. Clearly it had seemed so too to several other folk, most likely locals I'd guessed, as there were around half a dozen other small fishing boats attached to sinkers within the immediate vicinity. To the northern end of the tiny village there was an old wooden jetty, that projected some ninety metres or so out to sea, and more often than not there was a thirty-eight foot sailing yacht moored alongside the far end of it. I had been informed by the owner, who happened to be English, that the jetty was privately owned, and that he paid the land owner to moor his yacht there for the summer, living aboard as often as he could, whenever he managed to get away from his family responsibilities back in the UK. He'd also told me that laying a sinker precisely where I'd intended would be absolutely fine, and we could even use the jetty for dropping off or picking up crew, passengers, and/or equipment, providing we were extremely careful, as the wooden jetty itself was very old, and somewhat dilapidated. It was great to know that we could use it though, and I mentally picked a spot for my sinker, just slightly away from all the others, so as not to cause any interference or consternation amongst the locals. After all, at twenty-three feet, the Phoenix was just a little larger than the other boats sitting there at their moorings. Before driving up to Fornells however, once I'd picked up the hire car, I first needed to pay a visit to a very special man that I'd met on several previous occasions. The infamous Pedro, of '*Pedro's Boat Centre, Mahon, Menorca, Baleares*'. Mahon is the second deepest natural harbour in the world, second only to Pearl Harbour. its about three miles long by a mile wide, which is roughly the same size as Fornells Bay. I'd always got the impression that Pedro owned about half of it! That obviously wasn't entirely true. It was just that everywhere you looked around Mahon harbour there seemed to be yet another offshoot of Pedro's Boat Centre. The chandlery, the new boat sales, the brokerage sales, the permanent moorings, the visitors pontoons, the service yard, the cranage facilities, the winter storage yard, shrink wrap facility, travel hoist, slipway, and so on. Pedro ran quite an operation, and he was quite a guy too. He was well known and highly respected by everyone across the island, and I really do mean everyone! The particular one of his facilities that I was after rummaging around was his scrap yard. It was just across the other side of the harbour, adjacent to Mahon's famous gin factory. I told Pedro roughly what I needed, and exactly what I had planned for it, and he called his man on yard security and told him to expect me.

He also said, in his wonderfully charismatic broken Spanglish, words to the effect of, "Good plan, I am hoping it is working for you, but come to talk me about it in more details por favor, after you have fixing it, but before you are leaving back on plane."

I said '*gracias*', and I'd arrange to talk with him further when I came back to pay him for whatever I managed to salvage from the scrap yard, which I assured him really wasn't going to amount to very much. But I'd definitely be back before flying home. I drove around to the opposite side of the harbour, and after only about thirty minutes or so of searching around the far reaches of the expansive scrap yard, I'd managed to find pretty much everything I was looking for. A decent length of old, heavy, but liftable, ship's anchor chain. A large, old, heavy duty, round, red plastic mooring buoy, with a steel ring fixed and sealed both top and bottom, which appeared to still be in perfectly serviceable order. And forty large Spanish concrete building blocks, the type with two square holes through the centre, which had once formed part of an old wall, that had either fallen or been knocked down, and I'd reckoned probably weighed a little over twenty kilos each. All in all, by my estimation, around one ton in total. I proceeded to load it all into the back of the poor little hatchback hire car, and then drove, rather slowly and gingerly, the sixteen miles or so to Ses Salines. There'd always seemed to have been this very old, upturned little wooden dingy laid up on the shingly beach of Ses Salines. I'd noticed it there on several previous occasions. It wasn't locked or tied up even. It certainly didn't appear to belong to anyone, and it just looked like it might even still float. So I'd borrowed it. Just for the day of course! And float it certainly did. I'd offloaded the concrete blocks, chain and buoy from the car down onto the beach, and whilst I'd waded the fifty metres out from the shore myself, I'd used the little old dingy to ferry the rest of the stuff to where I'd wanted it laid. Standing neck-deep in around five feet of warm salty water, I'd slipped the long heavy length of anchor chain over the side of the dingy, with both ends attached by shackles to the lower ring of the floating buoy. I'd then forced the buoy under the water, as far as I could manage, to test it for leaking air bubbles. There weren't any! It was absolutely fine, and the stainless steel rings, fixed and sealed to the top and bottom of the buoy, and connected through its centre by their adjoining threaded steel bar, seemed more than adequate for the purpose. I then waded back ashore for the blocks, and ferried these out on the little dingy four at a time. Disconnecting one end of the chain from the underside of the buoy, I passed it through one of the holes in the centre of a block, and then slid each of the blocks in turn down the chain and onto the seabed, where they settled comfortably into the soft silt. Back to the shore for the next set of four heavy concrete blocks, wade back out to sea, dragging the dingy along behind me, whilst stumbling occasionally over the odd rock now and again, which couldn't be foreseen due to the cloudy waters at this end of the bay having virtually zero visibility. This was turning out to be pretty exhausting work, but it absolutely had to be done, and I knew it'd be well worth it in the end. I'd allowed myself a whole day to achieve this mission, but that wasn't going to work. It was way too tiring! Ten trips, four blocks at a time? Three trips and I was well and truly knackered! It sure as hell wasn't easy lifting those kind of weights around whilst standing up to your neck in muddy, salty seawater!

So I took a break. Back to the apartment in Tamarindos, just the other side of the hills by Playa de Fornells. I took a quick shower and a fresh-en-up, pulled on some tidy togs, then walked the rocky coastal path into Fornells Town for some fresh lobster and a large jug of sangria, whilst sat outside one of the pretty little waterfront restaurants. First thing the following morning I resumed the work detail. I'd reckoned on a day; it actually took me three! Actually, to be fair, one and two halves. So once I'd slid the very last block down the chain to the seabed, I secured both ends of the steel chain to the underside ring of the buoy using a pair of heavy duty shackles that I'd bought the previous day from Pedro's Boat Chandlery. I'd then tugged at everything, really good and hard, just to make sure it was all firm and secure, and Hey Presto! There we go then, one perfectly laid one ton sinker mooring! In approximately five feet of perfectly calm and sheltered waters, just fifty metres off Ses Salines beach, in Fornells Bay, three miles inshore from the open sea; safe and secure, with absolutely no fees to pay. *For the next one hundred years!* What more could a man want for? Absolutely bloody marvellous!

On my way back to the airport I stopped off at Pedro's, and we agreed on a hundred euros for the rubbish that I'd salvaged from his scrap yard, which I duly paid him for there and then. I apologised for not being able to find the time to meet up with him to discuss my plans in more detail, but I had an imminent flight to catch, and I'd make a point of doing so next time I was over. He shook my hand somewhat vigorously, said '*adios mi amigo*', then I dropped the rental car back to Autos Victoria at Mahon airport, and jumped aboard my EasyJet flight back to Bristol.

CHAPTER FIVE

I needed to curtail some of my galavanting, and stay back home for a bit. Mainly for three reasons. Firstly, I had a transport lorry to sort out and prepare. Secondly, if I didn't start paying just a tad more attention to my dear wife Helen, toiling away for forty hours a week in a stuffy old office block in the centre of Bristol, where both the air-conditioning and the heating only ever worked intermittently, then I was starting to feel the beginnings of yet another divorce potentially looming on the horizon. That would inevitably result in me taking to the water for a third time. '*Yet another divorce, yet another houseboat!*' Not that they would ever actually be just '*house*'-boats of course! But neither, on any level whatsoever, was I relishing that horrendous thought anyway. And thirdly, and probably most importantly, I had to get back to work! The summer was fast approaching, and I had a business to run, and not an easy business at that!

Whilst '*toldos*' may indeed sell themselves en España, trying to flog '*sunblinds*' to the UK market, for obvious reasons, took considerably more effort. Therefore sales strategies and planning for the forthcoming summer season had to be thought through, constructed and put into place, and that involved careful budgeting, as well as partnership discussions. My partners being my family of course. Although I've always been the main driving force behind our little company, I've also always very much appreciated the freedom that simply having them around, sharing the burdens and the highs and lows of self-employment, has often afforded me. Whether indeed that's to allow me to travel far further afield on spec, in search of new contracts, or whether its to allow me the opportunity to take off whatever time necessary, as I was now planning to do, in an attempt to relocate my little fishing boat from Bristol to Fornells. Plus, I was doing this so that *hopefully*, fingers crossed, the whole family could enjoy the wonderful pleasures of using our pretty little fishing boat out in the beautiful calm seas of the sunny Mediterranean, on the odd occasion, whenever they should choose to take their holidays over there.

[Therefore, to my dear father John, who by this time had reached the proud old age of seventy-eight, had started the business together with me back in 1979, and still played an active role in sales and marketing. And to my clever and enthusiastic young daughter Michelle, my eldest offspring from my first marriage, and the light of my life; by now aged just twenty-two, and essentially thrown in at the deep end just a couple of years previously. Regardless of any past, present or future outcomes, to both of them, I was, I am, and I forever will be eternally grateful.]

So it was back to the office; phone calls, meetings, travelling, more meetings; sell, manufacture, install; sell, manufacture, install; and so on. Building, hopefully, success upon success. *Until Friday!* We never stopped for lunch, we never managed to find the time. But the following Friday I did. Just briefly. Following a complex but successful installation, I shook hands with a highly satisfied customer, and accepted their offer to join them for coffee and sandwiches, whilst sat on their new patio furniture underneath their very expensive, but spectacularly colourful, new sun awning. Just as I was finishing my second coffee, the wind got up, the awning automatically retracted into its very expensive housing, and it started to rain, quite heavily.

"Nice to do business with you sir, madam. Don't you just love England's green and pleasant land?"

I then took my leave somewhat rapidly, jumped back in the car, and immediately dialled Paul's number in Keynsham.

One of his mechanics answered, and informed me that Paul was lying flat on his back, somewhere in the depths of the workshop, underneath an old Foden transporter.

"Oh, cool," I said, "how's the old girl coming along?"

There was a brief, somewhat disconcerting pause. However, once the mechanic realised that I wasn't actually referring to Paul himself, I heard a brief snigger on the other end of the line.

He then simply replied, "I'll get him to call you back when he's done."

An hour later Paul called me back.

"A little more work than I was expecting I'm afraid, especially with the brakes. Had to fit new shoes all round, bit of a job really. But she's basically sound; tyres are all good, a couple of new bulbs and all the lights are now working, including the twin-revolving yellows on the cab roof. Horn, wipers, all good, she should fly through her MoT tomorrow morning. Nice HIAB by the way, three-tonner that is, decent bit of kit."

"I won't be using the HIAB," I said, "but how's the cable winch? That's most important to me."

"Sound as a pound," he replied. "Give me a call first, just in case anything untoward crops up, but all being well you should be able to come pick her up whenever it suits on Monday."

"Thanks a lot Paul," I said, and hung up with a big smile on my face. I also needed to start paying just a tad more attention to my poor lonely wife, so I took her to a spa resort in the Cotswolds for the weekend. Lots of hills and trees and greenery everywhere. Total peace, quiet and relaxation, and not a single boat to be seen, not anywhere! It was absolute bliss, and it made her very, very happy indeed.

First thing Monday morning I called Paul from my office.

"All done!" he announced. "Full check over and a full service, including the hydraulics, and an oil and filter change. New brake shoes all round, plus a new MoT. You can come collect her anytime, but preferably today please, I'm running out of space yet again."

I managed to get out of the office by 3pm, drove across to Keynsham and walked into Paul's office, where he sat wearily in a torn and battered old leather swivel chair, heaps of paperwork strewn across all three of his desks, coffee in one hand, cigarette in the other. He looked up at me and smiled.

"Keys, MoT, invoice," he announced. "Cash or card?"

I picked up the invoice, ran through the itemised list of works, and then stared, somewhat incredulously, at the bottom line:

"*WELL KNOCK ME DOWN WITH A FEATHER!*" I exclaimed, *or words to that effect!!*

"*£1,600!* How the heck did you get to that figure exactly? Dave said he'd been quoted something in the region of £400!"

"Who's Dave?" he asked innocently. "Anyway, its £400 just for a commercial MoT! Then there's £500 in parts, and £500 in labour, give or take, and then there's the VAT. £1,600 please Mr Chris!"

"Can't you at least knock the VAT off, if I go get you the cash?" I enquired hopefully.

"Nope, sorry," he replied, "we're a bona fide commercial operation, and I've already run the invoice through the books. Sixteen hundred quid please Mr Chris; and trust me, you wouldn't have got it done any cheaper anywhere else. And that's even if you'd managed to get it done anywhere else at all. Bloody thing's almost past its sell-by date!"

"American Express?" I suggested.

"Ha, we'd never deal with that shoddy old Mickey Mouse outfit, not in a month of Sundays!"

"MasterCard?" I continued.

"That'll do nicely," he answered smugly.

His secretary duly processed my card, and I shook hands with Paul, thanking him profusely for an extremely first class excellent service. I'd arrange to come pick my car up sometime the following day. I then climbed up into the cab of my dear little red and white Foden, with its brand sparkly new MoT document, and drove carefully out of his yard onto the main road, knowing full well that precisely where I'd parked my old Shogun would completely prevent him from getting back into his brand new gleaming little Porsche. Unless he were to try and break in through its sun roof that was! Hey ho, I'd move it out of his way tomorrow. Which is precisely what I did. First thing, very early, as soon as someone unlocked the gates to Paul's yard, but before Paul himself arrived. *'Sneaky',* I thought to myself, although I'm sure he'd have had the use of numerous other vehicles whenever he'd wanted. Mind you, I had to admit, the way the old Foden had driven on the way back to Bristol, I couldn't fault Paul's efforts. She seemed to be vastly improved from when I took her out on that initial test drive. Not that there are any steep hills between Keynsham and Fishponds, at least not like the two up over Odd Down, but everything about her seemed to be far more positive. Especially the brakes, which was a great comfort, as I had this sneaky suspicion that I was going to have to rely on them quite heavily at some point during this epic journey. I drove the Shogun home from Keynsham, having got an early cab over there, and parked it somewhere well out of sight, mainly due to Helen's continual moaning about my ever increasing pile of scrap cluttering up our front drive. *'Time to remedy that'*, I thought to myself. Time to check out my newly acquired equipment for real.

So here was the plan. The Foden had a three-ton HIAB crane, which I was never going to use, but because of the vehicle's complex hydraulic set-up it would prove far too difficult simply to remove it from the truck's flatbed, so I'd swung it as far out of the way as its reach would allow, and strapped it firmly to the crash rail behind the cab so that it couldn't work its way loose in transit. Bolted down securely to the flatbed, adjacent to the HIAB's main pillar, was a one ton cable winch, with an extra long steel cable, and a cable wired remote control handset. This allowed the operator to stand at a completely safe distance away from whatever he or she was operating, should anything happen to fail, or not go entirely according to plan. Or worse still, decide to break! I'd already guessed that the old trailer weighed around half a ton, so there would be no problem winching that up onto the flatbed. And whilst it was more than obvious that it wouldn't cope with winching the trailer all the way up once laden with four tons of boat, I felt perfectly confident that the breaking strain of the cable itself would be sufficient to winch the fully loaded trailer back *off* the flatbed, and down onto the concrete apron of the Fornells slipway, providing that everything was sitting on an adequately acceptable slope, which I believed the continued slipway on the outskirts of Fornells inner harbour to be. And so began phase one of my cunning little *Chrissy-plan.* I backed the lorry up close to the front of our drive, slid the ramp's extension boards out, and clipped them into position. Then I connected the winch cable hook to the ball hitch at the front of the trailer, pressed '*UP*' on the cable remote, and up she went, all the way, sweet as a nut. I knew I'd have to make some adjustments before aligning, lowering and securing the Phoenix onto her old yard trailer, but I felt perfectly happy with the positioning of it for the time being, and I securely strapped the rusty old bird to the flatbed with a pair of heavy duty ratchet straps. I then drove *'phase one'* down to Bristol Marina's yard, parked her up well out of anyone's way, then called Helen at work to ask her if she wouldn't mind picking me up from the Orchard pub when she'd finished. And with that, and two or three very satisfying pints of ale later, for me that was, not for her, she very obligingly did so.

Upon our return home to Fishponds she looked over at me, raised her eyebrows and exclaimed, "Wow, great to see you've finally got that rusting old pile of crap out of our front drive at last!"

I just smiled and left it at that.

CHAPTER SIX

I felt it was time to pause and take stock of my situation, particularly when it came down to the finances. We were now well and truly into the summer, and although work had become pretty manic, demanding more and more of my time on an ever increasing daily basis, we were actually doing okay. In fact, according to our accountant, we were probably doing significantly better than just okay, but the fact of the matter was we never really saw very much in the way of the company's profits. Apart from drawing a relatively modest monthly dividend, the majority of any profits that the company generated were simply ploughed straight back into the business again, mostly in the form of stock purchases, for the purpose of both future trading, as well as hopefully, *forever hopefully,* further profitability. It was just a never ending cycle. But we did okay. Whilst fully accepting many moons ago that I'd never even come close to becoming a millionaire, I was always personally very comfortable with the fact that I could manage to afford a little above the average amount of holidays per year. Some years previously I'd learnt to restrict all of my holidays to a maximum of just one week at a time. I'd found that being away from the business for any longer period than that was simply far too stressful. As with any business, things would sometimes go wrong, but Sod's Law always dictated that such occasions inevitably occurred when I wasn't around to put them right, the consequences of which could sometimes prove to be quite disastrous. Plus it had actually happened too, on more than one occasion; so as with most things in life, I'd learnt the hard way. So just one week's holiday at a time, that was plenty enough for me and my delicate stress levels.

Having said that, providing Michelle was in the office to cover for my absences, presuming that she wasn't actually on holiday herself at any given time, I pretty much had the freedom to take a week whenever I felt like it. Not that I often did, but it was always good to know that the opportunity was afforded me if ever I wanted or needed it. Plus occasionally, very occasionally that is, providing everything was completely under control work-wise, then for the sake of Tori and Alex during their long school summer holidays, I might, *just might,* manage to squeeze a whole fortnight in. Providing I felt it was sufficiently important of course, and also providing Michelle was in full agreement. Two week summer holidays though, solely for Michelle and myself I might add, were generally exceptionally rare. Christmas time, however, was always different. I'm generally not a very Christmassy sort of person. I've always said that Christmas is for kids, and I stand by that to this day. So if I had my kids with me for Christmas, whether that be the younger ones or the older one, or indeed all three of them together, as was generally the case, by way of careful pre-planning, then I'd organise a whole fully traditional family Christmas around them. Put the trimmings up, decorate the tree, dress up as Santa, eat too many mince pies and drink my way through far too much sherry. Open pressies in the morning, roast turkey dinner, Xmas pud, *Chitty Chitty Bang Bang* on the telly at teatime, bubble and squeak on Boxing Day. *Yes of course with Brussels sprouts in, it'd be sacrilege not to!* And so forth. Having previously gone through two marital failures, quite successfully I might add, whatever you might take that to mean, I'd always had an amicable agreement between myself and their mothers for our children to share their time evenly between us. Unless I was away, as a general rule they'd always spend every other weekend with me, and nowadays with both Helen and me, and each year their mothers and I would take it in turns to spend Christmas with them. Which meant that every other year I got to spend a traditional family Christmas at home having fun with the kids, and on the years in between I'd have a completely 'non-Christmas', and go off travelling somewhere. I always went somewhere different each time; an island in the Caribbean, a tour around Scandinavia, skiing in the Alps, fell-walking in the Lake District, and so on. The essential point being, however, that these were proper, decent, extended two week holidays. And that was simply because, some years previously, whilst starting to collect employees, and subsequently being forced to learn the art of delegation, I'd taken the decision to shut the company down completely for a full two weeks over Christmas and New Year. The big advantage to this was that everyone got the whole sixteen days off in a row, with full pay. The only one disadvantage was that it made both December and January just three week months, which wasn't good in terms of the company's production and invoicing. The knock-on cash-flow effect of which was often felt towards the end of February, and even into the beginning of March. But as they were generally the quietest times of the year anyway, I'd always felt it was well worth it, even if purely for the sake of our own sanity. Somehow we'd always managed to get through it though, generally by working hard and putting in those extra hours, both leading up to and immediately after our two week Xmas shutdown. Somehow, thankfully, we always seemed to make it through. We'd always survived. As it so happened it was Rachel's turn to have Tori and Alex with her for the next upcoming Christmas, plus, as carefully planned as ever, it was Caroline's turn to spend the festive period with Michelle. Which perfectly suited my plans right down to the ground. I'd estimated it would take a little over a week to drive an overloaded lorry all the way from Bristol to Menorca, a couple of days to offload the Phoenix and secure her to her new sinker mooring, then probably significantly less time to drive back home again. All in all I reckoned I needed to allow roughly a fortnight to complete the mission. So what better time to undertake it than over the forthcoming Christmas break. Where firstly, I wouldn't have to worry about being away from work, or from the family, and secondly, it still gave me plenty more time to properly prepare for the journey. Oh yes, and not forgetting one other extremely important factor of course! Could I really expect my poor dear wife to sit in the passenger seat of this dear old jalopy for two weeks, and two thousand miles non-stop, without so much as a single break, and turn around afterwards and say that she'd had an extremely pleasant and enjoyable Christmas break? No, I feared probably not! Some form of bribery was required here. Some kind of ulterior incentive. Something to make her feel enthusiastic enough about making the trip with me in the first place. Otherwise, after all, why the heck didn't I just go do it on my own? Which, to be honest, was the last thing I wanted. I wanted my wife with me for company, especially with it being Christmas and all. However, I had a little trick up my sleeve, and I knew that the upcoming Christmas hols would prove to be the perfect time to play my trump card. So I made an elicit phone call and sowed a seed, which generated a highly successful and enthusiastic response the other end, and consequently I'd set a few more wheels into motion. All I needed to do now was run this additional little diversionary plan past Helen and gauge her reaction, which, I had my fingers crossed, all eight of them, would be met with an equal amount of enthusiasm. I'd wait for her to get home from work, chill for a bit first, pour her a nice cold G&T, and then I'd broach the subject with her that very evening. In the meantime, as I believe I may have mentioned earlier, I still needed to take stock, and in particular with regard to the financial implications of this proposed little expedition of ours. I still had a fair few quid in the bank, but I wasn't exactly made of money, and I wasn't prepared to simply jaunt off half cocked either. I was more than happy with the arrangements I'd made with Davina, the owner of Bristol Marina. I'd spoken with her when I'd dropped the truck down to her yard, and she'd said that, providing I didn't leave it there for too long, then on the basis that I'd be paying her to use the travel hoist to lift the Phoenix up onto it anyway, it could stay parked up there for the time being free of charge. Which was great, because the yard was always locked up at night. And as for the cost of the cranage, providing I had my own insurance in place, she'd only be charging me a hundred quid for the lift. If I had no insurance it would cost me a further hundred quid for a specific one-off lift policy. I'd explained that I had my own fully comprehensive insurance for the Phoenix, and provided her with a copy of the policy document. She'd said *great, all good to go, whenever you're ready then*. To which I'd simply lied and said hopefully one day the following week. To be honest, I knew full well that once the Phoenix was loaded onto the Foden, Davina would be asking me to vacate the yard, and I didn't really want the whole shooting match parked up on my own front drive in Fishponds, probably sticking out into the road somewhat, causing a minor obstruction for the neighbours, as well as preventing Helen and I from getting either of our cars onto the drive for the next couple of months! So I thought I'd try and stall dear old Davina for as long as possible. Plus I still had more equipment that I needed to load aboard the boat before the trip, and it would be far easier to do that whilst she was moored up at her pontoon in the harbour, than it would be by having to climb a ladder to get aboard her, and a pretty long ladder at that. At least Davina seemed sympathetic towards that little plight, and asked me politely to *'please try not to leave it for too long then'*. I told her I'd crack on asap. Meantime I was beginning to count the costs to date in my head. I'd initially paid just £4,000 for the Phoenix, but I'd done quite a bit of work to her, as well as adding a significant amount of new equipment, such as warps, fenders, VHF, GPS, a new anchor with chain, and new curtains in the little forecabin, and I still had a little more to add yet, so I'd valued her at around £6,000, and that's exactly what I'd insured her for. The insurance had cost me nigh on £300. Then there's £1,600 for the Foden, and a further unexpected £1,600 for its MoT. I was hoping to recover a significant amount of that when I eventually sold the truck after we got back. Then €100 to Pedro, plus £100 to

Davina. its a damned expensive game this boating lark, and I hadn't even properly started with her yet! As for the cost of the pontoon mooring in Bristol, well I'm not going to bother counting that in. And the cost of the flights back and forth to Menorca; no, not really, I probably would've been going that way anyway. Oh yeah, and then there's the . . .

Ah, that sounds like Helen's car pulling into the drive.

CHAPTER SEVEN

I was sat out in the back garden when Helen walked in, looking as weary as ever from yet another long day of dullness and drudgery working in a city centre office for a top notch firm of solicitors. I wasn't exactly sunning myself either, it was dull and drizzling as per usual. Still, at least I had a nice big retractable awning to sit under, with integral lighting I might add, that covered the majority of the patio. She said a quick hello, then disappeared upstairs to change into something a little more comfy. So sit there I did, waiting patiently for her to come back down and sit with me, so that I could impart my good news to her, of which she new absolutely nothing about as yet; and hoping beyond hope that I didn't finish off the whole jug of sangria that I'd made especially for her as a nice little surprise, shortly before she'd arrived. I'd shelved the G&T idea on the basis that I personally hate gin, but also that we both loved sangria. Anyway, I was already on my second glass. By the time she came back down I was on my third! However, there was plenty left, it was an extremely large jug! So I simply asked her to sit. I poured her a nice glass of the chilled claret nectar, and prepared to attempt to put her mind at rest over our forthcoming expedition.

"D'you know, I've been thinking an awful lot about this trip to Spain in that little old lorry," she began, before I could even get a word out myself, "and I'm really beginning to come to terms with the idea. In fact I'm actually really looking forward to it, I've never travelled right the way across France before, so I think its probably going to be really quite exciting, as well as very interesting."

Well, that was a massive relief to hear, I can tell you!

"Actually," I replied, gulping down my fourth glass of sangria, and almost choking on it due to the size of the smile that had suddenly spread across my face, "its going to be more than just interesting, its going to be fun too. And not only am I going to make it fun for us, but I'm going to break the whole trip up halfway through with an exciting little diversion. You know our dear old mate Mandy who lives in Benalmadena, whom we've not seen for almost a year?" I questioned, carefully gauging her attention. "Well I spoke to her on the phone the other day, and apparently she's going to spend the Christmas break with her dad and his wife in Malaga for a few days, and she said it would be absolutely fabulous if we could join her for a day or two. She's checked it out with her dad, and not only do we get a bedroom to ourselves, we're personally invited to join them for a full-on roast turkey dinner on Christmas day, trimmings and all."

I sat there and watched Helen's eyes light up like main beam headlamps.

"There's just one tiny caveat though," I continued. "She's demanding that we bring a box of Xmas crackers over with us; apparently they don't sell them over there."

"Blimey! Just perfect!" Helen retorted, "I'll go buy a luxury box from John Lewis myself, especially for them. I can't wait!"

"So, what I thought we'd do is this. We drive the truck to Barcelona airport, park it up somewhere safe and then take an internal flight down to Malaga. Spend the X-word with our Mand, a couple of days maybe, depending on flights, fly back to Barca, then drive the truck to the ferry terminal and catch the Trasmediterranea across to Mahon. Mand says she's all good to use her dad's car to pick us up and drop us back to Malaga airport. How does that all sound?"

"Absolutely bloody marvellous," was Helen's enthusiastic response, and knowing me the way she does, finished the sentence with *"What could POSSIBLY go wrong?!!?"*

We sat there together, light-heartedly pondering the possibilities of that particular favourite saying of mine, and promptly finished off the last two glasses of sangria.

I was now feeling far more comfortable with the fact that we were both going to make the most of this mini adventure to the very best of our abilities. I ceased stressing about whatever Helen might be thinking about it all, and continued to concentrate on some of the finer details of the task in hand, of which there were a great many, and put my mind at rest in regard to the overall concept. Enjoyment was the order of the day, and enjoy it we jolly well would! Next on the list; RAC cover for the Foden.

"UK commercial roadside assistance sir? Ninety-five pounds for the year, how would you like to pay?"

"Actually", I replied, "I need European cover please, specifically for France and Spain."

"Yes sir", the telesales girl read back off her crib sheet, "that'll be just an extra forty-five pounds for the roadside guaranteed immediate call-out assistance, but you'll have to pay additionally for any specific on-site assistance that may have to be given, including parts and labour. Or alternatively, for total and complete peace of mind, you can select our 5-star European Commercial Policy, which includes overnight hotel expenses too if necessary, as well as getting you as efficiently as possible to your onward destination, for the one-off cost of only six hundred and ninety-five pounds."

As quickly as I could possibly manage it, I forced the scary image of a boat, on a trailer, on a lorry, on another lorry, on a hard shoulder, with way too many flashing lights going on, in the dark, in the middle of nowhere, entirely out of my mind altogether.

I simply replied, "I'll just go for the standard cover at one-forty please."

I gave the nice girl my credit card details over the phone.

After all, 2,500 miles isn't exactly a huge distance in the overall scheme of things, and following her recent MoT and minor service our little Foden was running as sweet as a nut, whatever that should happen to mean!

Insurance? I rang my broker. Actually, after a considerable amount of shopping around they came back to me with what I felt was a very reasonable offer, mainly due to the relatively low value of the vehicle, coupled with the fact that I wouldn't be using it for any kind of commercial gain. Although it was technically a commercial vehicle, as I would only be using it solely for private use, and I was only looking for a third party, fire and theft policy, the lowest premium they could come up with was four hundred and twenty-five pounds, which, given that up to thirty days of European cover in any one visit was automatically included within that cost, I was more than happy to accept. I instructed them to proceed immediately. That put a little spring in my step, I was expecting significantly more than that.

Good stuff! What's next? Oh yes, road fund licence, or to use what I'd come to consider to be just another swear word, *TAX!* So, as my car at the time was costing a hundred and twenty-five quid for the year, I wondered just how much a seven-and-a-half ton commercial vehicle was likely to set me back. As it turned out, four hundred and twenty-five quid, exactly the same as the figure I'd paid for the insurance. I can't honestly remember whether I was surprised, disappointed or pleased, but at the end of the day it was what it was, and I had no choice but to pay it. So pay it I did, in full, and because a first time commercial application couldn't be done through the Post Office back then I had to post a cheque to DVLA in Swansea. Oh, how technology's moved on nowadays! A week or so later my pretty little purple tax disc arrived in the post, and I proudly stuck it to the windscreen in the Foden's cab using one of our company's latest Xmas giveaways, a printed tax disc holder.

So there she was, up and running! Taxed and insured, tested and MoT'd, breakdown cover, fully road-legal, and no further excuse to keep her parked off-road in Davina's yard. *'I suppose I'd best start considering my next move then',* I'd thought absentmindedly to myself, whilst mixing up yet another jug of sangria. Time was marching inexorably onwards, with our all too short two week Xmas break soon to be upon us, and still a whole host of things to do before we'd be ready to leave. Shopping list; write it all down Chris! I was just *so, so* busy at work! But I'd already rung Davina and booked the travel hoist for the next upcoming Friday morning. Which gave me the rest of the week, in between being manic at work, to get everything loaded into the Phoenix that we wanted to take away with us. That would have to include our suitcases, albeit I'd be loading them at the very last minute. However, other than the empty third seat in the centre of the Foden's cab, there was no other covered space anywhere else whatsoever to store anything. So everything we wanted to take along with us had to go in the boat; with the exception of the ladder! I was going to need a ladder to reach the gunwales of the boat from the ground, but at least I could easily strap the ladder to the flatbed underneath the trailer. Straps! Six heavy duty ratchet straps to be precise. And a separate plug-in yellow flashing light with extension lead. It was all very well having a twin revolving yellow light unit mounted on the roof of the cab, but I'd just had this sneaky suspicion, some kind of subconscious intuition, that at some point I might need one mounted at the very rear end of the load, as well as at the front. Tools! Yes indeed, a visit to Halfords was very much in order. Essential foreign driver's kit; headlamp deflectors, two red triangles, hi-vis jacket, spare bulbs, first aid kit, torch and GB sticker. Plus I thought it not a bad idea to keep a fire extinguisher aboard, even though both the boat and the lorry only ran on diesel, so there was neither gas nor petrol anywhere to be seen. Even so, for the sake of a tenner, better to be safe than sorry!

Talking of which, some three hundred quid later, I reckoned we were sufficiently kitted out to take on all eventualities. The Foden only had a single rear axle, but she had two wheels at each side, so altogether she was a six wheeler; plus there was a brand new spare bolted to the crash rail mounted between the HIAB and the back of the cab. I also had a foot pump, an extra-strong jack, and a whole host of other emergency kit, and I just hoped to God that I wouldn't be needing any of it. I'd also bought some extra long coils of rope, having a multitude of uses, and being significantly cheaper at Halfords than they would've been at a marine chandlery. As would virtually anything to be honest, hence why I always tried my best to avoid such places like the plague. However, for certain necessities, such as lifejackets and fenders, etc, sometimes, sadly, needs must. But I'm pleased to say that all that kind of essential marine equipment was already safely stored aboard, and had been for some considerable time. And that included my fully immersible grab bag containing my marine essentials; flare kit, VHF, GPS, assorted charts, compass and plotter, torch and whistle, etc, etc. That little lot was very safely hidden from view, right out of the way at the very bottom of one of the forecabin seat lockers. Everything else that we considered non-essential for the journey would be locked away in the forecabin, and stuff that we would, or might, be needing would be placed strategically around the aft deck, and covered over with the securely fastened tonneau. Our suitcases, a five gallon can of spare diesel, and the ladder, would be the last things to load, so all I had to do now was wait, with a certain amount of trepidation, until Friday morning. I awoke at 6am on the Friday morning, an hour before my alarm was due to go off. I showered, dressed, and drove down to the Little Buttery by the dockside steam cranes, alongside Bristol Industrial Museum, for a mug of tea, and what was undoubtedly one of the best bacon sarnies anywhere in the world. I sat at an outside table in the early morning late autumn sunshine, savouring the moment, whilst fending off the seagulls that continually dive bombed everyone in an attempt to ravage their breakfast platters, and at the same time constantly trying to avoid getting shat on from a great height by the half dozen cormorants that resided atop the steam cranes. To this day I still love Bristol to pieces! So, time to cast the Phoenix off for one final time then. Time to leave my safe, secure pontoon mooring within the safe haven of Bristol City Docks, and head for cruising grounds anew. Time to set sail for the travel hoist down at the marina, and Davina's expert ability at craning a vessel onto its awaiting transportation. Time to wave bye bye to my beloved old Floating Harbour for one last time! Time to . . . oh enough already Chris! Just go get the hell on with it! '*Time is money*', as Davina would say, as she stood there waiting impatiently for me, with nothing else whatsoever to do for the rest of the day! So I cast off, chugged on down to the marina, tied up alongside the pontoon in the travel hoist berthing area, then climbed the walkway ashore, to be greeted by precisely no one! In my haste and enthusiasm, or so it would appear, I'd arrived just a little early. I checked my watch; 8.30am. The hoist was booked for 10.00am. Hey ho, at least that would give me plenty of time to position the lorry correctly, and to get the ratchet straps ready for safely securing the load. The little Foden fired up first flick of the key, and I steadily backed her into such a position that I knew was perfectly aligned for the hoist to lower the Phoenix directly onto her rusty but solid old trailer. I'd winched the trailer as far forward as it would go, so that the ball hitch was resting firmly on a solid piece of eight-by-two timber on top of the cable winch housing. Firstly, this was so that the wheels of the trailer had ended up on the flat section of the flatbed, rather than the initial rear sloping section, and could therefore be more easily chocked. But mainly it was because I wanted the whole load as far forward on the lorry as possible, partly for the sake of even weight distribution, and partly so that I had as little as possible of the stern of the boat overhanging the rear of the flatbed. I've always known that a one metre overhang, either front or back or both, is the legal maximum, because of the nature of the work that I'd been doing all my life; and also that any given overhang must be clearly flagged. I also knew by now that I would end up with a certain overhang at least, having worked all of this out by Pythagoras, as well as with a tape measure, even before purchasing the lorry. But I'd kept the trailer as far forward as possible anyway. In fact I'd go as far as to say perfectly positioned, specifically for these reasons.

Davina hailed me from her office window, and politely gesticulated at me to produce my credit card, to which I duly obliged. We then approached the travel hoist together, and following her approval of my correct positioning of the lorry she drove the hoist forward directly over the top of the Phoenix. As she slowly lowered the hoist's straps into the water, I cast the Phoenix off from the pontoon, and held her close against the small amount of breeze that was present, until the straps were correctly positioned underneath her keel, roughly the correct distance apart, and clearly avoiding any mechanical components, such as the prop shaft, etc. Once we were both confident that everything was correctly aligned, Davina hit the '*UP*' button. The Phoenix rose smoothly and gracefully from the water, high into the arms of the hoist, and when the hull was somewhat higher than the bed of the trailer Davina hit the '*STOP*' button. That was the first time I'd seen the hull of the Phoenix for a number of years, and I have to say she was as clean as a whistle. Oh, the joys of mooring a GRP boat in fresh water! All she needed was a quick hosing off with the yard's pressure wash, which I'd do myself whilst she was still wet, just as soon as she was secured to her trailer on the back of the dear old Foden. Inch by inch Davina steadily drove the travel hoist away from the basin, and when the wheel booms straddled the Foden to the point where the Phoenix was perfectly positioned above the trailer, again she hit yet another '*STOP*' button.

The moment of truth! The time had finally come, after many months of meticulous planning, to sit the Phoenix down on to her perfectly positioned cradle; ready hopefully for the long journey south. Davina hit the '*DOWN*' button, and inch by inch the Phoenix was lowered towards her trailer. However, two or three moments and as many inches later Davina suddenly hit the '*STOP*' button, and muttered the words that summed up something we'd both noticed at exactly the same time,

"*I think we've got ourselves a very slight little problem here ya know!*"

"Hmm, so it would appear!" I replied in a mildly disappointed tone. "No matter," I then piped up in a more positive manner, "I'll just shift the trailer back a tad, that'll fix it."

The problem itself had immediately become apparent to both of us. If we hoisted her all the way down as she was, because of the curvature of the bow, the very front of the boat would be hitting the top of the HIAB crane's fully retracted hydraulic boom. *Bugger!* I was fully aware that the front of the Phoenix slightly overhung the front of the trailer, but I thought I'd positioned the HIAB in such a way as to avoid this from happening. I certainly couldn't position it any better, and owing to the complexity of the way its hydraulics and electrics had been integrated with the rest of the old Foden's workings, removing it altogether was entirely out of the question.

"Don't worry, I've got it." I announced cheerfully. "I'll unstrap the trailer and pull it backwards a little. Then we'll lower the Phoenix on to it, and then I'll just winch it back as far forwards as it'll go with the cable winch. its bound to be powerful enough to pull the whole load that very short distance."

I unstrapped the trailer from the Foden's flatbed, and with the winch cable still attached to the trailer's ball hitch, dropped it back so that the wheels were halfway down the rear sloping section of the bed. Davina then carefully repositioned the travel hoist somewhat, hit the '*DOWN*' button again, and a few moments later the Phoenix was sat nice and snugly on the bed of her trailer. Exactly as she had been when I'd first bought her and towed her, very slowly, from Weston-Super-Mare back to Bristol. I must say that although the trailer was rather old and decrepit, it had been adapted and adjusted to suit the Phoenix just perfectly, and providing the trailer didn't move anywhere, then neither would its safe and secure load. Suffice to say however, I'd bought enough ratchet straps to lash both the trailer and the boat to the lorry's flatbed completely independently of each other. After Davina had removed the lifting stops from under the Phoenix, and wheeled the travel hoist slowly back to its parking bay straddling the cranage basin, all that remained for me to do was winch the trailer as far forward as possible, until the bow of the Phoenix was touching the flat face of the HIAB's lower boom cowling. Should be a piece of cake!

I rummaged around the marina yard's scrap pile until I found a very small, worn out old trailer tyre. I lashed it securely to the front of the Phoenix's bow, so that it would provide an adequate cushion between the boat and the cowling of the HIAB. I then hit the *'UP'* button on my own cable remote, and gradually inched the whole load forwards. The cable winch appeared to be coping with the strain okay, there was no sign of it being underpowered, and certainly no blue smoke coming out of it anywhere. I kept it pulling the trailer forward until the little black tyre squashed itself tightly up against the HIAB's cowling, and there she stopped, that was as far forward as she was ever going to go. I coiled the cable remote back into its locked security box beside the winch, then looked up at the Phoenix's bow. Her chrome pulpit rails, that extended some foot or so beyond the front of the bow, were overhanging the top of the HIAB just perfectly, precisely as planned. The squashed rubber tyre would prevent any undue travel vibration, as well as acting as a buffer in the event of any sudden braking. God forbid! All in all, perfect positioning I'd reckoned.

Until, that was, I walked towards the back of the truck to look at where the trailer's wheels had ended up. *'Oh dear,'* I thought to myself. Actually, under the circumstances, *'Oh shit!'* would've been far more appropriate. I'd always reckoned on the wheels of the trailer pulling all the way up to the flat section of the flatbed. *They hadn't!* They were still some quarter of the way down the sloping section, they hadn't quite made it all the way to the top. *'Hmm, maybe not exactly perfectly positioned after all,'* I muttered to myself. Hey ho, it was what it was, just get on and deal with it Chris! I found some bigger lumps of timber to chock the trailer wheels with, then repositioned the ratchet straps that secured the trailer to the flatbed in such a way that it couldn't possibly shift in any direction whatsoever. I'd even restrained it perfectly from bouncing up and down. Happy with that! Sorted!

I spent the next hour jet washing what little grime there was off the hull of the Phoenix, then before lashing the boat itself independently to the flatbed, I stood back at a reasonable distance to admire my handiwork. That's when I noticed, for the very first time, what could potentially prove to be a *MASSIVE* problem! *'Bollocks!',* I immediately thought to myself. Essentially, the stern of the Phoenix was now overhanging the rear of the flatbed by significantly more than I'd bargained on. I dropped a plumb line down from the very back of her stern, then ran a tape measure from that to the tow bar fixed to the back of the flatbed. *Fifty-one inches!* That's one-point-three metres, which is exactly a foot over the legal overhang limit. Technically that one foot was above car windscreen height, which I knew could potentially make a difference to the view that English traffic cops might take on such things. But French and Spanish? Who knows? However, that one little foot over the limit wasn't actually the biggest problem. No, the biggest problem was simply the way that it looked! Because the Foden's beaver-tail sloped downwards, and the Phoenix's curved hull sloped upwards, the overall impression that this gave was probably significantly worse than it actually was in reality. In fact, I'd go as far as to say that, to the casual observer, it created a little bit of an optical illusion. But hey, that was just an illusion, right? The reality was far less than it actually appeared. Even if it was just the very tiniest bit illegal. Hey ho! I felt pretty confident I could wing it. I'd carried far longer loads than that the length and breadth of the UK on the roof racks of Transit vans for many a year 'til now, with little or no intervention from the authorities whatsoever. *(Well, apart from just once, but that's another story altogether, maybe for another time!)* Anyway, this wasn't a commercial load, for hire or reward, it was purely my own private vehicle, which to the best of my knowledge also makes a difference in the eyes of the law. Plus, first and foremost, I personally felt 100% confident that the whole load would be safe, secure and roadworthy. And what's more I had yellow flashing lights both front and rear, although I had no intention of using them, except in the case of a real emergency, *God forbid!*

Luckily I'd bought more ratchet straps than I thought I'd need whilst in Halfords, and I lashed the Phoenix securely to the flatbed completely independently of the trailer. And finally, I secured a diagonally red and white striped reflective safety board to the very back end of the Phoenix's stern. So there she was, finally all securely loaded, cleaned and ready to go. I stood back at a distance once again, partly admiring my handiwork, partly stressing about what it actually looked like, and just how many miles I was going to attempt to drive it without attracting too much attention, and partly wondering when the hell it was going to stop raining. Davina sidled up to me and asked me one simple but rather poignant question,

"Any idea what she weighs?" she whispered, with just a modicum of sarcasm.

Well now there's a thing! I knew the travel hoist had a weight gauge, but in some ways I'd been somewhat reluctant to even peek at it. I'd kept the overall load down to what I'd considered to be basic requirements only. The water tank was almost empty, the diesel tank was only about a quarter full, and most of the extras that I'd loaded aboard didn't really amount to very much weight-wise. And I knew I was going to be carrying technically a little more than the dear old Foden's maximum limit, but I'd estimated it wouldn't prove to be a significant amount. Anyway, the powerful old girl would cope admirably with a load such as this. I had every confidence in her.

I crossed my fingers behind my back whilst asking, "Go on then, pray tell?"

"Pretty much spot on four-and-a-half tons," she said flatly.

Then she kind of almost giggled at me, took one morlook at the rear of the load, smirked almost imperceptibly, turned on her heels and strolled back towards her office.

The Foden was commercially plated, its unladen weight stamped on an aluminium plaque which was securely fastened to the face of the first step up into the driver's side of the cab. It was clearly visible to anyone who might decide to take a look. The truck itself was rated at 3,800 kilograms. That gave it a maximum carrying capacity of 3,820 kilograms. I'd reckoned on the Phoenix coming in at somewhere under four tons, with virtually no water and little fuel aboard, plus the trailer at an estimated half a ton. So now I'm told I'm carrying around five imperial tons in total. Which is 5,080 kilograms. Which is 1,260 kilograms over and above our maximum legal limit. *A ton and a quarter!* So, I'm a metre and a quarter overhanging the back of the truck, and I'm a ton and a quarter overloaded by weight. Oh well, what more could I do? It all looked good enough and perfectly safe to me, I'll just wing it! *What could possibly go wrong?* Anyway, I've got to this point so far, and at just how much expense exactly? So there's no going back now, *no way Jose!* Plus, its the first of December tomorrow, and Helen's booked a couple of extra days off work, a bit earlier than their normal Xmas holiday period would be starting. Plus I've already set everything up at work so that I can be away for however long it takes, and so that's it! We're leaving in two weeks time! Ish! Subject to pre-booking our outbound crossing via the Channel Tunnel.

I double checked all around the Foden and its carefully strapped-down load, backed it over into a corner of the yard that I knew wasn't being used, but one that was well overlooked by a couple of old mates of mine that had their boats out of the water for the winter, in order to carry out essential maintenance works. Or in other words to stop them from sinking! I knew she'd be perfectly safe where she was parked up, so I locked her up and headed over to Davina's office once again.

"Sorry my dear," I genuinely-ish apologised, "but with that ridiculous load aboard I'm afraid this old truck simply isn't going to fit on my driveway, and I have no other options available to me. Would you mind awfully if I left her parked up where she is right now for the time being? She's not in anyone's way, and we'll be off to Spain with her in a couple of weeks anyway?"

"Blimey," she exclaimed semi-dramatically, "you really do want jam on it, don't ya?"

"Oh, yes please!" I retorted eagerly.

"Huh? Oh, okay, just give us another fifty notes and I'll make sure she's safely locked away in the yard every night. Two weeks mind, not a day more, or it goes up."

I gave her the fifty quid and said thanks a lot, and as I wandered off to grab a quick pint in the Orchard, whilst waiting for a cab, I just hoped that she'd meant the cost would be going up, as opposed to the whole lot would be going up! I was pretty sure I knew her better than that by then though. So, homeward bound for my gorgeous wife's wonderful home cooking, followed by some brief online research into commercial Chunnel costs, before collapsing tired and exhausted into bed.

All loaded and ready to go

CHAPTER EIGHT

The basic outline plan was this. Bristol to Folkestone, commercial Chunnel-train to Calais, then just see how it goes. Take it however it comes, checking into cheap hotels along the way, but aiming for Barcelona in time to catch a flight down to Malaga to spend Xmas with Mandy and her folks. After which we'd fly back to Barca, catch the Trasmed ferry over to Mahon, drive to Fornells and launch the Phoenix. What could possibly go wrong? Just in case anything did go wrong though, we'd make a point of checking into hotels as and when we came across them, rather than attempting to book something in advance, and then find ourselves running to a strict daily schedule. Not that booking in advance was particularly easy back in 2002, unless you already knew the name of the hotel that you were specifically aiming for. Which we clearly didn't. So, other than the outbound Chunnel crossing, and Malaga for the X-word, we had nothing else pre-booked whatsoever. The only other specific deadline we both had was getting the job done, then getting back to Bristol in time to go back to work at the beginning of the new year. I'd taken the train through the Channel Tunnel from Folkestone to Calais on many previous occasions, as I'd worked for a few years on fit-out projects for Center Parcs all over Europe, but that always involved taking either a car or a Transit van, so I'd never before used the commercial lorry aspect of the Chunnel. I was sure it would prove to be a bit of an eye opener, and right from the offset the cost certainly was! Previously I'd always simply turned up at the toll, in a Transit van let's say, paid fifty pounds for a one way trip, waited in the queue for some fifteen minutes, or maybe even gone and grabbed a quick bite to eat in the cafeteria if the next train wasn't due for another thirty minutes or so. Back then it was just drive straight onto the train carriage, sit in the van in the dark for twenty-three minutes, then drive off the other side straight onto the French AutoRoute, heading due east from Calais towards Belgium. Pretty much the same thing on the way back, it was that simple. However, as I was going to be driving nearly nine tons worth of seven-and-a-half tonner, I thought I'd best pre-book on this occasion.

The next morning, after boiled eggs, tea and toast, I sat at the breakfast bar in the kitchen at home in Fishponds, with my phone and credit card at the ready, and called the Channel Tunnel commercial '*hotline*' number. After ten minutes of listening to music on hold I was then able to describe my requirements to the nice gentleman, who, after a brief pause whilst he pressed a few keys on his computer, came back to me with,

"That'll be £249.95 please sir, that's including the VAT."

"Huh?" I retorted, "I assume that's return?"

"No sir," he grunted in a disinterested but slightly impatient manner, "that'll just be the one way. The return cost will depend again on the weight and dimensions of the vehicle."

I told him to forget about the return, I'd cross that bridge when I came to it, and gave him the registration number and my credit card details to cover the one way trip only.

"*Two hundred and fifty bloody quid!*" I muttered to Helen, who was in the middle of washing up. "£250! That's five times the cost of a Transit van, overloaded with rolls of canvas *and* with three blokes in it! And there's only the *two* of us!"

"Oh, stop moaning," she retorted, "that's nothing in the overall scheme of things, compared to what this whole project has cost so far. And God only knows what it'll be likely to have set us back in total, by the time its all done and dusted. And anyway, its done, the crossing's paid for, everything's accounted for, sorted and loaded, and other than packing our bags at the last minute we're now good to go. Am I not right?"

I put my arms around her and gave here a big hug.

"Yes honey," I replied softly, "we're good to go. its just that . . . well, as I'm sure you're well aware, I've been trying to pull this whole plan together on what effectively amounts to a shoestring budget, and so far, or so it would seem, its cost me around half an arm and half a leg. Although I have to say, if we manage to achieve it all successfully, and get ourselves safely back home to Bristol in one piece, if by then its cost me a whole arm and a whole leg, well hey, so be it. That'll be mission accomplished, I'll still have one more arm and one more leg, and I'll be happy to get by with just them. Until such time as my wallet recovers sufficiently to be able to afford a new arm and a new leg that is. And also, just knowing that our pretty little

Phoenix is sat there afloat, safe and sound on her new sinker mooring in Ses Salines, waiting for us to take her out for a day's jaunt around gorgeous Fornells Bay, in the beautiful Mediterranean Sea, anytime we wish at the drop of a hat, that'll put a big smile on my face for many a year to come. So yeah, you're right babe, its all good."

Saturday morning, one week before departure, and after hurriedly downing some coffee and toast I caught the bus from Fishponds to the Centre, then took a stroll along the harbourside towards the marina. It was dull and drizzling again, so I was carrying a brolly, and I politely said good morning to the two or three friends that I saw and knew along the way. They were generally tending to minor on-deck issues on their own liveaboards, and I'd said sorry, I couldn't stop to chat, I was on a mission! Just before reaching the marina I remembered that I'd forgotten something. It wasn't of great importance, it was more of a courtesy issue really. I stopped briefly at the marina office to let Davina know that I'd be back very shortly to take the truck away, and thanks for all her kind help and patience, etc, and continued on along the harbourside, past the pretty little Cottage Inn, through the Underfall Boatyard, and walked into the ground floor Harbourmaster's office and said good morning to Sophie, the boss.

She wasn't the Harbourmaster as such, although she may just have well have been on weekends, when Geoff wasn't around. So I said to Sophie, kind of jokingly really,

"You may have noticed that the Phoenix has disappeared from her mooring. Don't worry, she hasn't been stolen or anything, I've taken her out of the water, loaded her on to a truck, and I'm taking her over to Spain with me."

Sophie didn't do joking!

"I know," she replied, "David told me. I noticed Phoenix sitting awkwardly on a scruffy old lorry when I was passing, so I asked him, and he just said he wished you'd hurry up and get the whole shooting match the hell out of his yard. I wasn't worried anyway, I never worry about old vessels leaving the harbour, I'd just prefer it if there weren't any new ones coming in, that's all."

"Oh, ok. Well in that case I guess I'm kind of doing you a favour then," was my lighthearted response. "And by the way, you do know you're not supposed to be calling her David anymore, don't you? She's been called Davina for at least a couple of years now. Not that there's any mistaking it mind you! Anyway, any chance I could get a refund on my mooring fees for the unused period please?"

"Nope!" she replied firmly. "You've got nine weeks remaining until they'd be due for renewal anyway, and we only issue refunds on a quarterly basis, and only then providing you've supplied adequate prior notice. So no, you don't qualify for any refund. But I'm happy to confirm that you don't owe anything, and therefore you're free to leave the harbour with no fear of repercussion."

'Wow!' I thought to myself. 'How polite and welcoming. NOT!' But hey, I guess that's the difference you can expect between a privately run marina, operating purely for profit, and a local authority run, not-for-profit operation, whereby the 'Harbourmaster' isn't actually a qualified Harbourmaster anyway, his official title within the council is simply 'Head of Leisure Services'. So in essence, to a private marina, the more boats, the more work, the better. And to a council run harbour, the less boats, the less work, the better. Now don't get me wrong here folks, I'm not singling Bristol out with this ethic. I've travelled extensively by water, and in my experience this kind of attitude appears to apply the world over. Or at least, if not the whole world, as I haven't as yet actually travelled the whole world, then certainly the whole of the UK, as well as many other parts of Europe. Hey ho, at the end of the day I guess ya gets what ya pays for. And rules is rules. Although in my humble opinion, 'rules is for fools!'

So, I'm not getting back any of what I've paid for but haven't yet used? Oh well, no matter, it was worth a try I suppose!

"Just thought I'd ask Soph," I responded. "No harm in asking, eh? Anyway, thanks for all you've done for me during this latest stop over."

Which, in reality, other than what I'd had to pay for, was virtually nothing!

"So, I shall be off now then. Maybe at some point in the future I'll be back up into Bristol with a nice, new, big flashy yacht, you never know. If work picks up amazingly, or if I win the lottery one day, or something like that."

"Its no problem if you're not," she mumbled back at me.

I muttered a faint 'bye for now' under my breath, turned and walked back through the Underfall Yard towards Davina's office in the Marina. At least Bristol Marina was run privately, separately from the remainder of the council run harbour, and therefore I found Davina and her staff far more helpful, and certainly more accessible than anyone within Leisure Services.

Apart from Sophie of course, who always appeared to be somewhere around the docks 24/7. Not so much to help mind you, more just to tell everyone, *'you can't do this, and you mustn't do that!'* But really though, at the end of the day, she was basically a kind-hearted old soul, and strange though it may seem I'd actually grown quite fond of her over the years.

"Ah!" Davina chirped up. "Thank God you're removing that bloody eyesore from my yard at long last!"

I winked back at her, smiled cheekily, climbed up into the cab, and yet again the dear little Foden fired up first flick of the key.

Well, this was going to be a first! Other than parking her up in the yard I'd not driven the lorry anywhere yet with the boat loaded aboard. It was three and a half miles from the marina to our little home in Fishponds, half of it flat, then a little bit of uphill, but nothing steep, so it should be a walk in the park. Let's see how she goes. I called Helen and asked her to make sure that both of our cars were moved out of the driveway, could she please park them just a short way down our little road, outside a couple of other peoples houses please. She said she would just as soon as she'd got herself dressed. I backed the truck around in the yard, shoved the gear stick into first gear, one of only four I might add, and drove her slowly out of the yard. I turned left onto Cumberland Road and drove towards the City Centre. She seemed to drive absolutely fine; 10mph in first, 20mph in second, and after driving slowly through the Centre and on towards the M32, she seemed to be perfectly comfortable at 30mph in either third or fourth gear. I pushed her up to 45mph on the M32 before taking the turn off for Fishponds, and after negotiating the roundabout at the bottom of the slip road, we came across our first minor little uphill gradient, Muller Road, which runs up to the top corner of Eastville Park. 25mph in third, no struggle, no problem, then 30mph in third and fourth as we negotiated Fishponds Road. Then Lodge Causeway, and back to the front driveway of our little 3-bed semi. All good, I was more than happy with that first little run. She'd be absolutely fine, I was convinced of it.

I pulled her as far into the front driveway as she could possibly go, leaving the front bumper just touching the wall at the very end, switched off the engine and climbed down out of the cab. Helen was waiting for me outside the front door, and immediately asked how well she'd driven, and whether I was totally happy with everything. I said *'yes, more than'*, and she threw her arms around me and gave me a great big hug.

"So, we're all set then?" she queried.

"Yep," I replied, "all you've got to do is pack your bags. Enough clothes, etc, for a fortnight's holiday, like as if we were going somewhere cold and damp for a while, which we probably are to be fair, and that's it. One more week of work, and we're ready for the off. And everything's sorted and all working perfectly."

She gave me another big hug, then disappeared back indoors and left me to check things over for the hundredth time. Of course, the first thing I noticed, needless to say, was just how far the back of the boat was sticking out of the driveway. The back wheels of the lorry hadn't even made it onto the drive, they were firmly planted halfway across the pavement, and the very stern end of the Phoenix was literally halfway out into the middle of the road. Luckily our little road is generally very quiet. its a side street that very little traffic uses, and our house is the corner house, on the outside corner of a right-angle bend. Because the back of the boat was so high off the ground, any cars driving around the corner would easily fit underneath it. And I wasn't worried about the dustcart, the refuse collection, which, due to local authority cutbacks, now only happened once a fortnight. It wasn't due until the Monday after we were due to leave. If any other large delivery lorries happened to come along, such as the likes of Argos or Homebase, etc, well I'm sorry but they'd just have to reverse back down to the bottom and go around the other way. It wasn't like that was a massive inconvenience or anything.

I've no idea whether that had happened or not, because I was up to my eyes in it over the following week, finishing everything up at work in time for the imminent Xmas break. Completion dates! Oh my God! How many?!!? But we got them all done. Between myself, my wonderful daughter Michelle and our excellent team of staff, with a significant amount of overtime, we managed to get every single job completed, in time and on time. As we always did, that's the way it worked. That's what made the company tick. I took one short amount of time out on the Wednesday morning, and drove the loaded little Foden down to Morrison's fuel station. I filled her up with diesel, three quarters of a tank costing me a hundred and twenty quid, although I still had no idea whatsoever how many miles per gallon she'd be capable of with this kind of load onboard! I double checked the oil level. Spot on! Water level in the radiator. Spot on! The twin batteries. Spot on! I then drove her round the corner to Britannia Tyres, who kindly checked the tyre pressures for me in all nine tyres. Two at the front, four on the rear axle, one spare, and two on the trailer. All seven of the Foden's tyres were spot on, even given the weight she'd been loaded with, but apparently the old yard trailer's tyres were dreadfully low, as well as bordering on illegal. I said it didn't matter, it was never going to get used on the road, but Tony pumped them up to the correct pressure anyway, just to make sure the overall load was a little more stable. I bumped into my old mate Mark briefly, and he asked me where I was going exactly with this dodgy-looking load? *'Menorca!'* I'd replied casually, *'by road!'* His typically dry-witted response being simply, *'Blimey, that takes some balls!'* I then drove her home, parked her back on the drive, went back to work, and both Helen and I waited patiently for Saturday to arrive.

I'd booked the Chunnel for a lunchtime crossing on Saturday 17th December, although the guy in the booking office had said it didn't really matter what time we turned up, the trains ran every hour on the hour, and they'd just get us on the next available one, just as soon as we'd been scanned. *Scanned??* Anyway, I'd figured four hours to drive from Bristol to Folkestone, an hour or so for the crossing, then that would allow us adequate time to get ourselves some way down towards Paris before looking for a hotel for the night. Bearing in mind there was no such thing as '*Booking. Com'* back in those days, but I had heaps of experience, not just in the UK, but all over Europe, of just walking into hotels and asking if they had a room available. '*S'il vous plaît? Por favor? Pretty please?'* In mid-December in Northern France I wasn't exactly envisaging any problems with this, so I was happy to just wing it. Neither, at that particular time, did either of us have any such thing as SatNav. What's more, believe it or not, a mobile phone was simply that, and nothing more. Mine didn't even have a camera built in to it, although I would be taking my little portable Olympus Digital along with me.

As for finding our way to where we were going? Well again, believe it or not, what we actually used to do back in those days was to follow these things called '*signposts*!' To be honest, I'd driven across France several times before, even all the way down to Barcelona on more than one occasion, so I was pretty confident about what I was doing, where I was going, and which route I knew we were going to be taking. Needless to say however, I'd invested in a new version of the '*RAC Concise European Roadmap*', and one of the first things that I'd checked when I'd first bought the little old Foden was that there was a cigarette lighter in the cab. Not for smoking of course. Far more importantly than that, for keeping our phones fully charged, just in case of emergency. Not that we were going to be having any emergencies of course! Helen wasn't really supposed to be finishing work until the 21st, which, coincidentally, happens to be my birthday, but as I've already mentioned her boss had very kindly given her leave to take the few extra days too. Unpaid of course! So I'd figured on the 17th as being pretty much the best day to leave, to safely allow us to arrive at Barcelona Airport in plenty of time to catch a flight down to Malaga. Not only that, but we'd be spending the first couple of days travelling over a weekend, thus hopefully avoiding as much commercial traffic, and as many potential snarl-ups, as possible. So basically, that was it. One more week and then we were off. Off on our fun little mini adventure. *'To boldly go where no boldly man has boldly gone before boldly . . .' Oh Chris, stop! Please!!* I knew it was winter. I knew half the time it would be dark, but I also knew, because my teacher in nursery school had taught me, that, *'If you want to head south, all you gotta do is follow the sun.'* I never could get that out of my head.

So I'd drawn a little picture of the sun on a piece of card, coloured it in bright yellow with a felt pen, cut it out and stuck it on the face of the sun visor in the cab of the Foden, right above the steering wheel. So if I didn't have the sun in my eyes for real, then I'd still be following the sun. Right? Seemed logical enough to me! And just to give it a slightly more purposeful meaning I'd measured the overall height of our load, and as a constant reminder I'd written it in black ink across the centre of the little yellow cardboard sun, *'Height 4.1 metres'*, just in case we unexpectedly came across any low bridges along the way.

So that was it then. The Phoenix, the Foden, and the pair of us, all sorted and ready to rock 'n' roll.

CHAPTER NINE

All of a sudden, there it was! Saturday the 17th of December! No excuses now then! We both awoke to the clanging of the alarm, I quickly showered, and whilst Helen was showering I knocked up a quick breakfast of bacon and eggs, tea and toast. Two suitcases had been packed the night before, and carefully stowed securely in the front section of the Phoenix's aft deck, which was protected from the elements by the extended coach roof that covered the helm seating, and was covered in behind that with a secure blue PVC tonneau cover. We then had a large canvas hold-all each, basically our overnight bags, which would sit on top of each other on the cab's central third seat. The foreign travel essentials, red triangles, spare bulbs and jump-leads, etc, and any other stuff that we hoped wouldn't be needed along the way, had all been stashed in a separate bag just forward of the boat's aft deck. This would be easily accessible if necessary using the ladder, which itself had been securely lashed to the truck's flatbed underneath the trailer. I had one additional kit-bag, which sat neatly on top of our hold-alls, containing all of our most important essentials. Passports, Chunnel tickets, English and European cash, credit cards, torch, camera, multi-tools, phones, etc; and more obviously, of course, some chocolate! There was a reasonably extensive dash area, on which could comfortably sit the RAC road map, along with Helen's small selection of paperback novels, and a small portable radio and CD player, which also plugged into the cigarette lighter socket. Plus, of course, any food and drink that we might happen to accumulate along the way. However, one factor that I'd become very mindful of was the fact that, in order to access the engine, including the gearbox, as well as all the rest of the Foden's mechanical components, the whole cab itself needed to be cantilevered forwards, and in order for the counter-balance to make this easy to do, we'd first have to remove all of our kit entirely from the cab. So firstly, we'd try and keep the contents of the cab to a minimum, and not clutter it up, just in case. And secondly, we'd just keep our fingers *and toes* crossed that we wouldn't need to be pivoting the cab forwards in any event, for whatever reason.

As it turned out, the weather that morning was reasonably good, at least for that time of year. It was dry, the sun was shining, and there was very little wind; other than my own! I blamed the eggs, although Helen blamed the way I'd cooked them! The temperature was a balmy nine degrees centigrade, not at all bad for mid-December. Regardless of that, we'd dressed as hikers. Several thin layers, followed by a fleece, then a warm ski jacket, with our *'Pac-a-Mac'* rain gear stowed in our overnight bags. Jeans, thick socks, and decent walking boots. It had become apparent that the cab's heating wasn't particularly efficient, so I'd slung a couple of sleeping bags into the forecabin of the Phoenix at the last minute, just to be on the safe side.

"Ready?" I asked Helen.

"Yep, ready and raring to go!" she replied excitedly.

"Ok baby, let's hit the road!" I said, and we both climbed up into the cab and settled into our comfy faux-leather seats.

Last minute thoughts; house double locked, work all completed, family all accounted for, and fully aware of our intentions; oh dear, this could go on and on and on, and already had done for over nine months, *and almost nine sodding chapters!* Start the bloody engine Chris, *let's just go!* We reversed out of the driveway, then headed off through Downend and Hambrook towards the M4. It was 185 miles from Bristol to the Chunnel, and I'd allowed four hours. That's averaging 50mph, and reckoning on one or maybe even two service station stops along the way. I was hoping to God that we wouldn't need any fuel before Folkestone, because I was reckoning on 35 gallons of diesel onboard getting us at least twice that far, even fully loaded, as well we most certainly were! Still, all seemed well, and we'd managed to leave, exactly as planned, bang on 8am. We hit the M4, and here, straight away, was about to prove to be our little Foden's first real test. The hill that runs from the M32 junction up to junction 18 for Bath at Tormarton is probably about eight miles long at a rough guess. This was undoubtedly going to be the steepest hill we'd encounter throughout the whole of the first leg of our journey. Let's see just how she copes with it then. Initially it runs pretty flat, and we topped her out along there at 65mph. Smooth, stable and comfortable. Very happy with that. Then a bit of an incline for a mile or so, over which she slowed to around 55mph. Still happy. Then another mile of flat, back up to 65mph, all good. Then we hit the start of a two and a half mile long relatively steep gradient, at the top of which lies the Stroud/Bath junction, and just as we passed underneath the junction flyover the speedometer read exactly 45mph. I couldn't grumble at that, no complaints whatsoever. We'd even managed to overtake a slightly slower lorry halfway up the hill, albeit that took a scarily long amount of time to achieve, but we were flashed back in to the inside lane some way before reaching the summit. So all was good in the land of Chris and Helen, and their cute little Foden with the wonderful Phoenix loaded aboard. We were both very excited, and really looking forward to yet another one of our mini adventures, and whatever surprises it may hold in store for us both along the way.

At long last, after all these months of planning, here we were, on our way, trundling eastwards along the M4 averaging 55mph, perfectly as planned. And so it continued; 50mph uphill, 60mph down dale, foot eased off the gas as much as possible, conserving both energy and fuel, happy as pigs in the proverbial; but with one exception. *Helen had bloody Daniel O'Donnell playing on the stereo again!* However, just as we pulled off the M4 onto the M25, Helen asked if we could pull into the next service station so that she could use the toilets, and grab a take-away coffee. A few miles and as many minutes later I pulled the truck off the motorway into Cobham Services, and as she hopped down from the cab she asked me if I wanted anything.

"Just a small bottle of water please love," I answered.

Some ten minutes later, as she climbed back up into the cab clutching a Starbucks, and passing me my water, I don't think she was overly surprised to note that Daniel O'What's-his-face had been switched for Pink Floyd. Not only that, but the volume had increased just a tad; plus the sun was still shining, and life was all good. We hit the road again, and before we knew it, in fact, before the album '*The Wall'* had even finished, we were pulling into the lorry park at the commercial terminal of the Channel Tunnel. Well, much to my surprise, as well as pleasure, that first 185 miles had proved to be an entirely uneventful journey. And long may it continue. This next bit was all going to be entirely new to me though. I'd not done the Chunnel this way before, and I kept my eyes peeled for all or any relevant signage.

The first thing we encountered was effectively a toll booth, or more accurately, as we'd already pre-booked, a check-in booth. There was no queue as yet, and the young chap in his smart black uniform checked our ticket and passports, told us that we'd be getting on the next available train, *whatever the heck that meant,* raised the barrier, and told us to join the back of the queue in lane number twelve. We did as instructed, and pulled up neatly behind a stationary, half empty articulated car transporter. As I turned the ignition key to switch off the engine I glanced across at the fuel gauge, and was very pleasantly surprised to see that it was still reading a little over half full. Of course, I had no way of knowing how accurate the gauge was, but my gut instinct told me that, even overloaded though we were, 35 gallons at just twelve miles to the gallon should get us some considerable way towards Paris. Plus I was well aware of the fact that, generally, fuel was somewhat cheaper abroad than it was in the UK, so I'd aim to fill her up again somewhere around halfway between Calais and Paris. Let's say then, for the sake of decision, somewhere near Amiens. Good plan, very happy with that.

One by one the lorries in front of us were starting their engines, moving forward just a single lorry length, and then stopping again. However, within about half an hour we were at the front of the queue in lane number twelve. We'd made such good time on the motorway, in fact just under three and a half hours, as opposed to the four that I'd allowed, that even now it was only just on twelve noon. That made it 1pm French time. *1300hrs CET, or Central European Time, as its correctly referred to.* Which meant that we should get to somewhere around Amiens shortly before dark, then find a hotel there or thereabouts, as well as a fuel stop, and keep our driving as much as possible to daylight hours only. That would make eminent sense. With that, another uniformed Customs official stepped up to the drivers window of the cab, frowned almost imperceptibly at the somewhat over-sized load on the flatbed of the Foden, and then said,

"Follow the black and yellow arrows please sir, as you drive your vehicle into the scanner. Stop when instructed to do so, apply the handbrake, switch the engine off and leave the keys in the ignition. You will then both exit the vehicle, ensuring, *PLEASE,* that you take any and all photographic equipment with you, and leave the vehicle X-Ray Department via the clearly marked door. Your photographic equipment, along with your jackets, will be searched individually by one of our uniformed officers in the waiting room. Once your vehicle has cleared X-Ray, you'll be free to re-join it using the same door, and when ready, drive out of the Scanning Department by again following the black and yellow arrows. These will lead you directly back to your position in the queue awaiting boarding the next train. Do you have any questions?"

"Yes," I said immediately. "Do you X-Ray every single lorry that boards the commercial crossing?"

"No sir," he replied politely, "its purely random; EU International Customs and Excise Policy."

'Purely random my arse!' I muttered to myself, as we followed his every instruction to the absolute letter. I'd never even heard of vehicle X-Ray checks before, let alone been put through one. But hey, there's a first time for everything, and probably lots more *firsts* to come too, I felt sure. As it happened, by the time the uniformed lady Customs Officer had quickly looked at my little portable *digital* Olympus camera, *without opening it, so as not to expose the film roll that it DIDN'T contain,* and briefly searched the pockets and linings of our jackets, she said we were free to return to our vehicle, start the engine, drive out of the Department, and re-join the queue. The whole process had taken somewhere in the region of fifteen minutes, so clearly the X-Ray machine hadn't spotted anything suspicious within our load. There again, we had nothing whatsoever to hide anyway, so that didn't exactly surprise me. Neither, however, did it surprise me that it was us that got picked on. Firstly, I must admit, the fact that the boat was basically just a tad too big for the lorry certainly did make the whole load look just a wee bit *'iffy',* even though I was 100% confident of its safety. And secondly, its just me! Everywhere I go, no matter how I'm travelling, I *ALWAYS* get picked on by Customs and Excise. So although I had nothing to hide, neither should I have had anything to moan about I suppose. I'd just come to expect it by then. And anyway, its always a different and somewhat amusing experience, even if more often than not considerably time-wasting. We re-joined our little truck, fired her up, and followed the arrows out of the scanner, which directed us quite clearly to the back of the queue; which, as had now become perfectly apparent, was the queue for train carriage number twelve. One by one, and, I must add, most efficiently too, we all drove along what appeared to be an extra wide platform, then swung our vehicles in through a wide opening, and drove them a short way along what appeared to be a massive, open-sided car transporter. We pulled up tightly behind a different lorry this time, a Spanish 12-ton Pantechnicon, or so it had appeared. As we'd already been requested so to do, after again switching off the engine and applying the brake, we climbed down from the cab, and walked carefully along the steel walkways located either side of the long row of vehicles, then through a doorway into what appeared to be a very small, transport-caff-style lounge carriage. I always knew that people using the Chunnel by car had to remain inside their vehicles. But the carriages, as well as the engines themselves, are much larger ones for lorries, and drivers

and passengers are not allowed to stay with their vehicles for the short duration of the ride. They all have to take a seat in the lounge carriage, of which there is one for every pair of rolling-stock. We took our seats accordingly, and surprisingly the travel time was exactly the same for that of domestic cars. Within exactly twenty-three underground minutes of gentle, low lit '*bumpety-bumpeting*,' the train pulled back uphill into daylight, gently rolled to a halt at what was clearly the end of the line, and over the tannoy system we were politely asked, in both English and French, to rejoin our vehicles, and exit the train once the vehicle in front of us has moved away by a clear and safe distance. We climbed back into the cab of the Foden, and within five minutes we were on our way, driving off the train carriage, along another long wide '*platform*', and then immediately onto the main dual carriageway that heads southwards towards a huge roundabout on the outskirts of Calais. It was all extremely efficient, including, I have to say, the '*stop-and-search*'. We were even shepherded automatically into driving on the right-hand side of the road, so there was no possibility of getting that bit wrong, and just as it is in an ordinary car, once you're off, you're off, and your onward travelling route begins immediately. Ours began, there and then, at the French time on my newly adjusted watch of roughly 2.45pm, which gave us, at a rough guess, around two hours before it began to get dark.

CHAPTER TEN

I'd thought over and over about the approximate route we were going to take, especially having travelled it on several previous occasions. If I was just driving a car from Calais to Barcelona, I'd most likely take the mountain roads up through the Pyrenees, through Andorra, then drop straight back down into Catalonia. But there was no way this big old load was going up through those mountains, so the only other sensible route was straight across the Massif Central through the middle of France, via Clermont-Ferrand, and down towards Montpellier, then take the flatter coastal route via Perpignan, and on down across the border into Spain just south of there. Initially though, given the way the load was apparently attracting much attention from onlookers, I'd decided it might prove wise just to stay off the motorways for a bit, at least until we'd got someway south of Paris. Partly because of the expensive French toll costs, partly because of our rather slow speed, but mainly because we blatantly stood out like a sore thumb! And so, after leaving the Calais Channel Tunnel Terminal behind us, instead of taking the A16 directly to Amiens we simply headed due south along some of the smaller '*B*'-roads. Clearly, however, this was to prove to be entirely the wrong decision.

We were just entering a very small village called Landrethun-le-Nord, approaching a simple three exit roundabout, when I noticed, parked in the most ridiculous position possible, and very clearly obstructing every car drivers' clear view, a very large blue and white police van, with a whole array of assorted flashing lights on its roof. Three uniformed and armed Gendarmes were walking around in the middle of the approach roads leading up to the roundabout, gesticulating wildly in all directions, and waving their batons in what appeared to be a totally meaningless manner. '*Blimey,*' I thought to myself, '*has there been an accident or something?*' And with that, just as we approached the broken white lines at the entrance to the roundabout, one of the Gendarmes stepped right out in front of us, holding up his hand in such a way that demanded we stop, which, quite obviously, we did. He then instructed me to wind my window down, and motioned for me to turn the engine off. *'Well,'* I thought, *'how bloody ridiculous is that?!!? If you want to talk to me, at least let's go park up somewhere sensible and talk!'* But no, clearly the idea of *'sensible'* wasn't present within any of their simple little minds. By now there must have been at least a dozen cars pulled up behind us, none of which could move anywhere, they were simply stuck there.

"How do you do officer?" I said in my perfectly poshest, politest English accent, "And what exactly can I do to help you today?"

The fact was, I *could* actually speak a reasonable amount of French, but I could never understand what anyone was saying back at me, especially when they gabbled it back at high speed, and so basically that made any two-way conversation in French pretty much impossible for me. So I tended to stick to English and simply plead ignorance. One of the Gendarmes was now stopping all the traffic on both of the other two approach lanes, whilst another was waving his arms wildly towards the Phoenix and the back of the truck, and the third was attempting to ask me a multitude of questions. Not one of which did I even remotely understand, let alone have any kind of clue where any of them were coming from exactly! He asked me to step down from the cab, which I immediately did, whereupon, firstly, I'd noticed that there were now at least forty or more cars jammed up behind us. More to the point, secondly, *he'd* noticed the 3,800kg plated weight sign fastened to the cab's step, and began tapping it smartly with his baton, whilst pushing his face a little closer to mine. *'Oh dear, oh dear,'* I thought to myself, *'please let's not let this get totally out of hand! He obviously thinks I'm way overloaded!'* Which, to be fair, we were somewhat, maybe just a little. But I wasn't about to entertain fighting over it, and I certainly wasn't going to let a simple French copper spoil any of my fun. *No sirree!!*

"3,800kg, 3,800kg," he shouted at me in angry French.

"Come here," I said, and forced him to look again at the plating, this time a little closer. "You see that word there, that word says *'unladen'.* And yes its hanging out over the back a bit, but its very clearly flagged with a big red and white safety board, and I can assure you, it is *NOT* overweight. Take me to a weighbridge if you like, if you don't believe me, but for God's sake, can we not just go and park up somewhere sensible to do this, and stop jamming up all this traffic?"

By now the whole village had ground to a halt. It was totally gridlocked, and I don't think the daft copper had understood a single word I'd said. So I thought I'd give it another go in my very best French,

"Monsieur, ce bateau, c'est mon bateau, ce n'est pas une charge commerciale. Et aussi, ce camion, c'est mon camion, le mien seul, ce n'est pas un camion commerciale. Donc, toute cette charge, c'est tout à moi, et le tout est non commerciale! Et aussi, donc, vous n'avez pas toute juridiction ici, alors s'il vous plaît, LAISSEZ-NOUS PARTIR!!"

I'd found myself raising my voice at him considerably towards the end of that little tirade, and Monsieur Gendarme, the one that was stood closest to me, backed off a little. He then grabbed his radio from his lapel and started gabbling in to it; to whom I had no idea, but I'd guessed it might be his supervisor. In my considered opinion, he definitely needed one! They all did! After a few minutes of gabbling, and a few more cars stacked up behind us, he walked back over to me, radio still in hand and asked firmly,

"Où allez vous?"

"Where am I taking it?" I repeated, with a minor alteration. *"Mahon, via Barcelona!"* I stated proudly.

"Oh, *merde*!" was his blatantly simple reply. "Continuez, enculez, sois parti avec toi!"

Essentially, 'Oh shit, go on, be off with you!'

I climbed back into the cab, started the engine, the three Gendarmes reluctantly stepped to one side, and we continued on our way. What a complete bloody waste of time that was. Probably twenty minutes in total, and the whole town had become gridlocked. And for what? Simple basic stupidity on their part, along with their inability to park their van up sensibly, and do their jobs properly by simply controlling the flow of the local traffic. *Blithering idiots!* So anyway, I'd decided there and then, let's go find the A16, and sod the cost of the tolls, we'll stick to the motorways from now on.

Onwards! With an old Wishbone Ash album playing quietly on the little CD player as we trundled on along the relatively traffic-free B-road through the pretty Northern France countryside towards the A16. I'd found it somewhat ironic that the song 'Phoenix' had come on, and I happily sung along with it. We hit the A16 just outside Marquise, and were immediately confronted with a *Péage*, or toll booth. As I'd already decided by then to ignore the toll costs from now on, Helen reached down from her passenger side window and took a ticket from the automatic machine. Maybe, in some weird, spooky kind of way, this was to prove to be our '*fine*' for upsetting the stupid traffic cops back in the village! Who knows? Anyway, as we steadily picked our speed up to a far more practical level along the triple-laned *AutoRoute*, it was not only beginning to get dark, it was also starting to rain. I suggested to Helen that maybe we should stop off before reaching Amiens, like maybe Abbeville for example, and she looked down briefly at the opened page in the RAC roadmap and wholeheartedly agreed with me.

"It'll be getting towards dinner time by then anyway," she said. "Hopefully we'll be able to find a relatively nice hotel that has its own restaurant."

"Let's hope so," I replied, "but we've still got around fifty miles to go yet."

And with that, as I'd suddenly come to realise, not only had it become *VERY* dark, but it was also chucking it down cats and dogs! Although the roads through Northern France are relatively flat, I'd had to slow our speed to a little under 50mph due to the *extremely* heavy rain and poor visibility, even though other cars were recklessly passing us in the outer lanes as though it were a normal summer's day. Quite clearly, it was very much exactly the opposite, and getting steadily worse to boot. Suddenly Helen said she was beginning to get cold, and as she zipped up her fur-lined ski jacket I noticed that the cab's warm-air fan had stopped working.

"Well ain't that just what we bloody well need, and just when we want it the most too." I muttered, and swore under my breath as I zipped my own ski jacket up as well.

Our jackets would've proved perfectly adequate until we'd found some place to stop for the night, however, a couple miles further down the road and the music stopped playing too. And it wasn't like it had reached the end of the album exactly, it had just stopped, mid-track. '*Bad Weather Blues*', hah, it doesn't get much more ironic than that!

"Now what?" I tutted.

Little did I know at that point exactly what was to follow. The windscreen wipers were two-speed, and they were already working on '*fast*', the rain was that bad. We'd passed Boulogne, still heading for Abbeville, when suddenly they stopped working altogether.

"*Oh shit!*" I exclaimed, "We've got ourselves a serious problem here! How far is it to the next turn-off babe?"

Helen flicked on the interior light, but that wasn't working either. As she rummaged through the kit-bag for the torch I slowed the old Foden down to around 30mph. I still couldn't see through the windscreen properly, but any slower on the AutoRoute would simply have proved too dangerous, and I didn't want to turn any of the yellow flashing lights on either, just in case they caused something else to fail as well. Suddenly though, as I urged Helen to hurry with the torch, something else *did* fail! She switched the torch on, looked down at the map and then joyfully exclaimed,

"It looks like there's a junction coming up in a couple of miles, as best as I can make out."

And with that, *the headlights went out!* I had no idea about the remainder of the lights; sides, rears, brakes, etc. But I'd've put money, there and then, on the fact that they'd all packed up too.

"*Two miles!*" I muttered, "Two bloody miles; pissing down with rain, pitch black, no wipers, no sodding lights! *Well ain't this just bloody wonderful! Welcome to France Chris and Helen!*"

I kept her sitting at 30mph, whilst doing my damnedest to follow the solid white line that divided the slow lane from the hard shoulder. Which just happened to be right underneath my right elbow as it was resting over the fully opened driver's side window, which I was leaning out of, and getting absolutely soaked. I needed it there as a point of reference though, as I could see nothing through the front screen whatsoever, other than the blurred tail lights of other vehicles speeding past us. Luckily, so far, nothing had run into the back of us. *Yet!* Oh God, just imagine . . . *NO CHRIS, don't imagine!!! Just concentrate!* After about two and a half miles of this awful nightmare, and what seemed like an eternity, I began to see the faint blur of overhead lights some way ahead of us, and gradually they started getting brighter.

"*Its a junction!*" I shouted above the noise of the rain spattering over my face as I hung out of the driver's side window, as well as splashing halfway across the inside of the back windows of the cab.

And sure enough, there was the 300m countdown marker, and the overheads above the flyover steadily got even brighter. The 200m marker appeared out of the wet gloom, and through my rain sodden eyes I could just about make out, off across to the right a little, the brighter still lights of the Péage toll booths. '*Thank God no one has run into the back of us yet!*', was still all I could think about at the time. Suddenly the 100m marker appeared, and that's when I noticed, just a little further on past the Péage, a much bigger and brighter light altogether. Now I'd seen these signs on many previous occasions, all across the whole of France, and I'd always avoided them like the plague. Seeing this one, however, had warmed the cockles of my heart, and as I carefully rounded the bend off the AutoRoute, and up onto the well-lit slip road that led down to the Péage just a couple hundred metres ahead, I turned to Helen, smiled a little crookedly, and said gleefully,

"*Honey, we're home!*"

I'm not entirely sure she'd understood, but anyway, as we pulled up at the Péage pay booth, she handed the concerned looking operator our ticket and simply said to him,

"*Casse!*"

Meaning broken! I guess he'd understood, because he just pointed at the little screen, which clearly read €3.25. She handed him the cash, and we drove on, slowly and carefully, and approached a well-lit T-junction.

"What d'you mean, we're home?" Helen asked, a little bewildered.

"Well," I replied, "you see that huge illuminated chequered flag a hundred metres off to our left?"

"Yes," she replied, "what is it?"

"Its an F1, a *Formule Un,*" I replied. "A simple-to-use, *or so the ads say,* coin-operated hotel. The cheapest hotel chain in the whole of France, and if you're to believe the ads, the whole of the world. Let's go see, shall we?" The F1 had a small car park in front of it, just off the road and through a rough gravel drive, which just happened to be not only well-lit, but also totally empty. This was a great help, as I was able to swing the old Foden all the way around and bring her to a halt right underneath an overhead light, whilst directly facing the exit, which might prove extremely handy if she were, *God forbid,* in need of being towed somewhere. I pulled on the air-assisted parking brake, the compressor for which still appeared to be working perfectly, wound my side window back up, pulled my jacket hood up over my head, and jumped down out of the cab without switching anything off. To be honest I was pretty worried about switching the engine off, just in case it wouldn't start again, but I certainly couldn't leave her running all night, so really I had no choice. But I wanted to check her all round first before doing so, and so I left her running whilst I took a walk around. Unsurprisingly I have to say, nothing at all was working. I got Helen to move across to the driver's seat and press the brake pedal, *nothing!* Indicators, *nothing!* Horn, *not even a squeak!* Hey ho, RAC here we go then! But first, let's get settled, cleaned up, warmed up, and hopefully find something somewhere to eat. I turned off the engine, switched everything else off that wasn't working anyway, and grabbed our overnight bags. We both climbed down from the cab, locked her up, and walked briskly through the pouring rain into the sheltered entrance porch of the F1 hotel, whereupon I breathed a massive sigh of relief. That chequered flag sign may well have been one of the biggest, brightest signs I'd seen in many a year, but there were certainly no lights on inside, and judging by the state of the car park, I'd guessed no one in residence either. There was, however, a small illuminated console within the porch, a bit like a mini cashpoint machine, which was flashing '*Entré – €10*'. I shoved a ten euro note in, and the front door clicked open. We both walked through into a small foyer, which contained two coin-operated vending machines, one for hot drinks, the other containing cold snacks; crisps, chocolate, etc. There was also a small and simple reception counter, with a stool behind it, but nothing else, and certainly no person anywhere to be seen. Far more noticeable than that however, was the large, complex and quite obviously active CCTV camera pointing directly at us. Below that was another entrance door, to one side of which was another small illuminated machine. its orange illuminated letters were flashing, '*Une chambre, deux lits, €10 par nuit*'. One room, two beds, €10 per night. I pushed in another ten euro note, and the little machine kindly spat a small card out at me, with a whole load of incomprehensible small print on one side, and the number 12 clearly printed on the other. I stuck the card in the little slot on the face of the door and it clicked open. We carried our bags along a narrow corridor, with motion-activated lights mounted within the suspended ceiling, and stopped outside room number 12. Again I slotted the card into its little receiver on the face of the door, which again clicked open, and as we entered the lights automatically came on.

There were two single beds, neatly made up with clean white bed-linen, and barely enough room to squeeze between the two of them. A small, white plastic table with a pair of matching chairs, and a pair of coat hooks fixed to the back of the door. It was also good to see that there was a door handle on the inside of the door, and a light switch on the wall just above it, but most important of all was the large printed sign attached firmly to the back of the door. It read, quite clearly, in six different languages,

'*Your Key card Will Expire At 12 Noon On Your Day Of Departure*'

I guess it had said that somewhere on the back of the card too, but it was comforting to see it written in plain English. There was also a small bathroom, with a toilet, sink and shower cubicle, and two white bath towels, with two matching hand towels, hung neatly on a white plastic towel rail. There was a mirror above the sink, and securely fixed to the wall between the mirror and the shower was another sign, this one a little smaller, but again reading in six different languages,

'*Hot Water Maximum 20 Minutes Per Day*'

We felt sure that would prove to be plenty, agreed that the accommodation, given the circumstances, was entirely adequate, and we dumped our bags on the beds and proceeded to wash, change, freshen up, and then head off out to look for somewhere to eat. Immediately before that however, I double checked the key card, just to make sure it would let us back in okay, but all was well, the tacky little F1 appeared to do exactly what it said on the tin, and we wandered across the car park out to the main road.

Luckily, or just bloody typically, depending on how you looked at it, the rain had considerably eased up, and the horrible, nasty looking black clouds appeared to be clearing a little too. Look right, look left, look right again; it seems we weren't even in a village, we were pretty much in the middle of nowhere. A road sign opposite pointed towards '*Nouvion – 2 Km*', so we weren't going to try and walk *there*, or anywhere else very far for that matter. As it turned out, luckily for us, we didn't need to. In the opposite direction, back behind us and directly behind the F1, was another B-road, and situated more or less adjoining the back of the F1 was a Chevron fuel station, which, as it happened, was not only manned, but came complete with its own truck-stop café. It was open, apparently, from 6am until midnight. *Marvellous!* Just exactly what we needed. I glanced at my watch. It was almost 8pm. '*Food* and *rest first*', I thought to myself, '*must keep the missus happy at all times*'. Not that I'd made a very good job of that on our first day out. But hey, it had been different, certainly interesting, and so far neither of us had but a single blister, let alone a minor scratch, so we couldn't have be trekking along all that badly!

"So, let's eat babe", I said calmly, after we'd walked in and sat at a table, and pointed to exactly what I fancied on the simple little picture menu. "Order me a rare sirloin with mushrooms and French fries please, and you order yourself whatever you fancy; plus, dare I suggest, a bottle of house red?"

"I'll certainly try my best," she said with a happy little grin, which I was very pleased to see, "and what are you about to get up to exactly?"

"I need to call the RAC babe. I need to try and get a mechanic out to us as soon as possible. I've already checked the fuse box up under the dash with the torch, looked at every single one of 'em, they're all absolutely fine. So God knows what the problem is, but we obviously need a well-trained auto electrician to fix it, and hopefully the RAC can get one here fairly quickly."

I went and stood outside, away from the noise of the jukebox, which was playing on auto as there were no other customers in the café whatsoever. As it had now stopped raining altogether, I wandered around under the street lights whilst dialling the 24hr UK emergency RAC breakdown number. A lady answered immediately, took my membership number, registered all the other relevant details, and advised me that, under the circumstances, she wouldn't be able to action anything whatsoever that same night, but that either she or a colleague would call me back on this number at 9am in the morning French time, and let me know exactly what they'd managed to organise. And if I hadn't heard anything by 9.30am I was to call again.

"Thank you very much for your kind assistance," I said, hung up, and rejoined Helen at the dinner table, where my steak was already sat there waiting for me.

And I have to say, it was just as delicious as it was cheap, and the cheap red plonk wasn't half bad either. *But I was knackered!* And even if I do say so myself, it had been, for me at least, a pretty strenuous and stressful day. We finished up our meals, paid the nice attendant man behind the counter, and retired to our tiny little white plastic bedroom for an early night. I kissed Helen goodnight, jumped into bed and immediately fell asleep, telephone in hand.

CHAPTER ELEVEN

I'm pretty sure Helen slept like a log that night. *I didn't!* Apart from the cheap nasty mattress being far from comfortable, I kept dreaming that my phone was ringing. And every time the dream woke me up, *it wasn't!* But I felt confident that it would. By 8am I was up, showered, dressed, and checking the lorry over yet again, out in the car park during the chilly French winter's first light of day. I'd left Helen asleep. There was no need for her to be up too, and I'd spent just five minutes in the shower, so she could have the other fifteen minutes of hot water if she wished. I'd left the key card on the small, white plastic table, along with a quickly scribbled note. Then I'd sauntered off out, from what was beginning to feel more like a private hospital ward than a hotel, into the early morning sunshine. Of which, sadly, there wasn't any. However, the storm had obviously blown over, the wind had dropped, the sky was reasonably clear, and it was looking, weather-wise, like a considerably more promising day. I climbed up into the cab of the Foden, and ever mindful of her batteries, turned the key to start her before switching anything electrical on. She fired up first click of the key, and I let her run for a few minutes until the temperature gauge read '*warm*', or normal. All the gauges still appeared to be working fine, including fuel, oil pressure, battery charge, etc, and I was presuming that the electrical fault had been caused somehow by the extreme downpour of rain during the stormy latter part of yesterday's journey. So I was keeping my fingers crossed that, because the rain had finally ceased later on that previous evening, maybe everything had dried out overnight, and the problem had resolved itself. I switched on the wipers. *Nothing! Of course it hadn't fixed itself! What was I expecting exactly, a magical lorry?!!? Fairies alighting from the ether at the stroke of midnight?!!?* I suppose the best I could hope for was that I hadn't simply bought myself a lorry load of gremlins, or a bag of nails, as they say in the trade! I checked the lights, just to be sure, and again, nothing. So there we go, now I was sure! Proper daylight had arrived by now, so I took a better look up under the dash, and around the rest of the inside of the cab too, and again checked all the fuses, but everything seemed just fine to me, I couldn't figure out where the fault was. So I'd just have to wait for the callback from the RAC. I switched the engine off, jumped back down from the cab, then called Helen by phone to ask her to come let me back in to the hospital ward, *er, sorry, hotel!* However, there was no answer. Oh well, I guessed she'd be in the shower then.

I wandered around the back of the F1 to the Chevron truck-stop café, and noticed a little sign in the window announcing '*petit déjeuner de €2.50*'. Hmm, '*breakfast*', I thought, and strolled inside.

"Bonjour Monsieur," I greeted the chap behind the counter cheerfully. "How much is a full English? Désolé, excusez-moi, combien est un Anglais complet?"

"C'est quatre euros soixante-quinze monsieur, plus le café," he replied.

"Okay," I said, "seulement un café au lait, juste pour l'instant, s'il vous plaît."

I sat down at a table and texted Helen to let her know where I was. A couple of minutes later a waiter appeared from the kitchen and brought my coffee over to me. I sugared and stirred it absentmindedly, whilst deep in thought about what this current episode might be about to cost me, and whilst waiting anxiously for 9am to arrive, and the duly expected callback from the RAC's UK headquarters. 9am arrived, and more or less at the same time, so did Helen, but no phone call.

"Morning babe," I said, again cheerfully, "tea or coffee?"

"Morning. Tea please," she replied.

I ordered her a pot of tea and we sat there chatting for a while. She didn't have any complaints just yet about the F1. She just said she'd found it '*kinda cute*'. And with that her tea arrived, but still no phone call. We carried on chatting, whilst watching the clock on the wall tick ever closer to 9.30am, which I knew was when it'd be me making the call to them, as opposed to the other way around. However, at precisely 9.25am my ringtone went off. I grabbed the phone and hit '*answer*' immediately.

"Good morning Mr Reason," a deep, intelligent-sounding gentleman's voice said, "we understand your predicament, we have all your details, and we've been in contact with one of our international network of breakdown companies, who happen to be based just a few kilometres from your present location. One of their team is currently on a call-out not too far from you, which they hope to complete relatively quickly, and they've informed us that they should be able to get to you within approximately one hour. We do hope they manage to resolve your problem quickly and efficiently. If no one arrives by midday your time, or if you have any further questions, please don't hesitate to call us back. Good day to you sir."

I said '*thank you very much*' to him, hung up, strolled up to the counter, and ordered two full English breakfasts, and an extra large pot of tea for two.

As I sat back down I said to Helen,

"Breakfast's on its way, straight after which we get the truck fixed, then we'll be off on our way towards Paris, no more problems."

She looked up at me, smiled sweetly, and didn't say a word. Breakfast arrived, and although it comprised of some odd flavoured sausages, hash browns, scrambled eggs, fried mushrooms and toast, I'd've called it more of a full French than a full English. However, after I'd scraped every single one of Helen's mushrooms off her plate on to mine, on account of her being quite seriously allergic to them, it turned out after all to be really quite tasty, and neither of us left one single morsel. We sat there together, drinking our tea and just chatting generally, whilst watching carefully out of the windows and waiting for some kind of breakdown lorry to show up. Luckily, from where we were sat, there was a window in the far back corner of the café through which I could just about see the old Foden, parked up across the far side of the F1's car park to the rear of us. And sure enough, a few minutes after 11am, a scruffy old red Citroen van, with a single revolving yellow light in the centre of its dented roof, pulled up alongside her, and two people got out. I hurriedly exited the café and jogged around to the car park to meet them.

One of them was a wizened old man, early sixty's, long grey beard, flat cap, and wearing very dirty old mechanic's overalls. The other was a young lad, maybe nineteen-ish, clean shaven, and wearing very *clean* mechanic's overalls, which appeared to be at least two sizes too big for him. '*Ah, the owner and his apprentice*' I thought, or at least *hoped* to myself.

"Bonjour mesieurs," I said, "RAC?"

"Oui, oui," the old man countered, "RAC break-a-down de Angleterre, what is problem?"

Good stuff, seems the old chap spoke a little bit of broken English. A bit like my little bit of broken French I suppose. We should get on fine together! I hopped up into the cab, started the engine, left the door open, and demonstrated to him that when I switched the wipers on they didn't work. Lights, *no lights!* Horn, *no horn!* I switched every switch and pulled every lever, just so that he was clear that none of the electrics were operational. Then I turned the engine off.

"Jump down," he said, "is very simples."

He then crawled in under the dash, removed the fuse box cover, and said, "Is just fusers."

"No, no, no," I exclaimed, "I already checked all the fuses, twice, they're all fine."

"Is must big fuser be," he said.

"Oh," I said, "okay, where is big fuser be?"

"Box next," he replied.

He removed the cover, then said,

"No, is good also."

"Yeah," I muttered, "I checked that one too. *Me no dafty-foolio-types!*"

"Oh *merde*!" he replied, "I go see further."

And with that, he crawled so far in under the dash that just his feet were left sticking out of the door. He shouted loudly to his young oppo, who immediately stubbed out his Gauloise, peeled himself off the bonnet of the Citroen, and answered,

"Oui patron."

I didn't get any of the rest of what was said between them, it was all in a rather strange, colloquial French dialect, but I'm pretty sure it went along the lines of '*pass me this, pass me that, pass me the other. No, not that other, you blithering idiot, the other other!!!*' After about ten minutes the old man squirmed back out from under the dash, leaving an array of tools scattered across the floor, whilst holding in one hand a small rectangular box, about the size of a one litre carton of orange juice, which had a short length of four core cable sticking out of each end, and what appeared to be a series of magnetic coils linked together inside.

"Regulator," he announced, "*c'est kuput!*"

"*Oh MERDE!*" I exclaimed loudly. "How is happen? What can do?"

"Rains, much rains, through front cabin-grille, has wetted, is kaputted. But, maybe, I think I fix. I try, with solder-wire and cable-wire, I see my best job for you. Maybe one half hour, you wait please."

Well blow me, I never even knew there *was* a regulator, let alone where the heck to find it. And even if I had I certainly wouldn't have had a clue how to fix one. In fact, I probably wouldn't even recognise it as being damaged. Apparently it was *very* damaged! Let's pray to God he can repair it, because God alone knew where or when I could find a replacement, if at all even.

And *then what . . . ?* It didn't even bear thinking about. I rejoined Helen back in the café, ordered two more cafés au lait, and sat down with my fingers, toes, arms and legs all crossed. *its very tricky trying to drink coffee like that!* With that, just as I finished my coffee, the old mechanic walked into the café with a big beaming smile, and said,

"Me good electricity-man, me mend, looks all good. See?"

He showed me the array of coils inside the long plastic box, which appeared to have new strands of wire soldered on here, there and everywhere, and I exclaimed '*brilliant, well done, you're a star!*' back at him, even though, realistically, I had little understanding of what I was looking at. I offered to get him and his lad a coffee, which they accepted, but they gulped theirs down ten times quicker than Helen and I, stating they had to get back to it, fix the mended regulator back up under the dash, wire it back up exactly the way it had been unwired, and test it to see if it worked. I wished them good luck, then added that a lot, *an awful lot,* was counting on them.

I asked Helen to go grab all of our kit out of our room and bring the bags back to the caff with her, and just sit with them for the time being. It was getting on for twelve noon, which is when the key card was due to expire, and if we ended up having to stay another night, well then we'd just have to shove another twenty euros into the appropriate slots. However I didn't want to have to pay twenty euros just to go get our bags back out of the room, so it had to be done before noon. Helen took the key card and walked back towards the F1's entrance porch, whilst I followed the guys back over to the Foden, again with my fingers crossed behind my back. I watched intently as the old man once again squeezed his body gradually up underneath the dash, all bar his legs, and set to with the various tools he already had close at hand. Again he called for various items from his youngster, who eagerly fetched them from the back of the old Citroen van, one of which I noticed to be a large roll of black electrical insulation tape. And I also noticed, by the time he'd managed to extricate himself from the cramped, inverted space that he'd been slaving away in, and jumped down from the cab, that not only was he sweating profusely, but also that almost the whole roll of insulation tape had been used up.

"*Is finito!*" he said proudly, somehow mixing up his English with a little Italian. "We must try, see if is okay now for workings."

I climbed in and started the engine first, just to be safe with the batteries. Then I tightly closed my eyes and switched on the headlights.

"*Workings!*" the old man called.

I breathed a massive sigh of relief. And when I say massive, I mean *MASSIVE!* I tried the indicators.

"*Workings!*"

Brake lights.

"*Workings!*"

Windscreen wipers.

"*Workings!*"

Yes, I could see that! I tried the interior light, the warm air fan and the CD player, which was still plugged into the cigarette lighter socket. All good, all working. Finally, as I'd just remembered, the horn. I pressed down on the small dish in the centre of the steering wheel, and nothing, other than a slight popping sound, followed by a small puff of blue smoke from under the dash.

"*MERDE!*" I shouted angrily.

"Non," said the mechanic man, "seulement fuser."

He removed the fuse cover from under the dash, and pulled out a clearly blown fifteen amp fuse.

"Is ok, I have," he said, and told his youngster to go get one out the back of the old red Citroen. He replaced the fifteen amp horn fuse with a new one, pressed the horn again, and sure enough, same thing again. Pop, followed by puff.

"Is ok," he said, "no worry," and called something over to his young lad.

"Now we put thirty amp fuser, is will be all good."

He slotted in the thirty-amp fuse, pressed the horn pad, and '*BAARRRRRRPP!*' *Perfectamundo!*

He refitted the fuse box cover, grabbed his array of tools, and jumped down from the cab. I stepped up and in, and just ran through everything once again. Lights, side and head, dipped and full, brakes, indicators, wipers, interior light, fan, music, and this time I even switched on the twin revolving yellows on the roof. And whilst every available electrical item was switched to '*ON*', I kept my hand pressed down on the horn pad for a full five seconds. It worked. *Everything worked!* All of it, and all at the same time too. Maximum load draw, no more fault. *Hoorah!* After I switched the engine off and climbed back down I did a little jump for joy, and I got the impression that the old man was somewhat astonished when I gave him a great big hug. But he came back at me with a broad grin anyway, and said,

"Me good at electricity, you have problems no more. And when rains, still is no problems!" and he proudly held up the almost empty roll of insulation tape.

"*You my hero!*" I stated, entirely honestly.

I didn't attempt to ask him what he'd done with it however, and I probably wouldn't have understood his answer anyway, so I decided I'd just have to trust him on that one. I asked him if he wanted another coffee, and he looked across at his lad, but his lad simply held up a phone and gesticulated to the affect that they had to go attend another callout.

"Ok," I said, "how much do I have to pay you?" and offered up my credit card.

"Non, non," he replied, "you only come signing my papers."

I walked around with him to the driver's side of his old Citroen, the opposite side to mine of course, and he sat and filled in various details on an A4 triplicate worksheet pad, on which I could see, written in part English, part French, all of my own details had already been completed. I guess what was missing was just the '*parts* and *labour*' section, but he'd completed the remainder within a matter of seconds, and then said,

"Signing, s'il vous plaît."

I duly signed his paperwork then firmly shook hands with him, during which a twenty euro note was subtly exchanged between us.

He'd said '*Non, non, non,*' but I'd insisted, and motioned the point, in my very best sign language, that he should get him and his lad a couple of drinks after they'd finished their day's work.

He expressed his gratitude, they both hopped back into their little old red Citroen van, and headed off towards their next callout. I myself headed back towards the Chevron café to announce the good news to Helen, who'd been sat there waiting ever-patiently for me. Luckily she'd brought a decent-*ish* selection of paperbacks along with her.

"All sorted," I announced cheerily, and with a big sigh of relief I added, "We're all set to go."

"Thank God for that," Helen replied. "Can we go look for a slightly better standard of hotel for tonight please, my back's killing me from that horrible mattress in there!"

"Of course we can darling," I said, putting my arm around her and kissing her on the cheek. "I'll just go settle up the bill first, then we'll be off on our way."

As I strolled towards the counter to pay the attendant for the breakfasts and coffees, I passed the young waiter who'd served us earlier. He'd just ambled in through the front door carrying a basket of what appeared to be used white bed linen and damp white towels. *'Ah, now I get it,'* I thought to myself, *'same business, same staff, one and the same establishment! What a great way to keep your overheads down.'* I also noticed a few lorry drivers sitting in the café. They'd obviously stopped off for their lunch breaks, and seemed to be crowded around the nearest tables to the counter, all drinking coffees and smoking cigarettes. The air was thick with the combined smell of stale smoke and diesel, along with the constant clatter of French profanity.

I paid the bill at the counter, grabbed both of our overnight bags, which Helen had been patiently sat keeping an eye on, and stepped outside into the cool fresh air. Helen followed immediately behind with the two smaller bags; my kit-bag, with all the important stuff in, such as passports and money, etc, and her handbag, which I guess, to her, contained kit that was equally as important, such as lipstick and eyeliner, etc.

[I'm sorry, but to this day I just don't get women's handbags! It doesn't matter how small or how big they are, they're always completely full up; and then they can never find anything they're looking for whenever they need it! Hey ho, best that remains yet another one of life's unsolvable mysteries I suppose!]

Both of us, now with considerably renewed vigour, climbed up into the cab of the little Foden, which by now was hidden behind the half dozen or so French articulated monsters, lined up neatly side by side across the centre of the car park. We piled our bags on top of one another on the centre seat, and made ourselves comfortable. By this time it was getting on towards one o'clock, and I was feeling like we were running somewhat behind schedule. However, as we didn't actually have a schedule to run to, I put my mind at rest with the fact that it really didn't matter, and made do with a simple little silent prayer, thanking the RAC for their excellent services. I started the engine. According to the fuel gauge we still had just under half a tank of diesel left, but realistically I didn't want to drive too much further before stopping to refuel, and I figured it made sense, given the current time, to look for a hotel at the same time as the fuel stop. And indeed, hopefully one of a slightly better standard. I released the air brake, and we pulled out onto the road that led down to the T-junction, where we turned right, and trundled slowly along to the Péage toll booths that gave access back onto the A16 AutoRoute.

Helen wound her window down, reached down and pulled the little paper ticket from the automated machine. Big smiles all round, we were on our way again; heading south, following the little coloured-in cardboard sun that I'd stuck to the visible face of the sun-visor. Well there was certainly no other sun available for me to follow! But hey, at least it wasn't raining anymore. It was just cloudy, dull and grey; but regardless, in our own minds we had our own sunshine going on.

"Okay, Paris here we come!" I announced enthusiastically, as we bypassed Amiens via its virtually traffic-free ring road.

Not that we were going into Paris of course, that wouldn't even be possible.

CHAPTER TWELVE

"Why can't we drive through the centre of Paris itself?" Helen asked with a mild air of disappointment.

"Simply because of our height babe," I replied, pointing at the little cardboard sun stuck to the visor in front of me. "We just wouldn't fit under any of the low bridges that cross over the inner ring road at regular intervals. Which is a shame, I have to say, because it means we'll be missing all the sights. But the fact is hun, our load is 4.1 metres high, and I can only vouch for the minimum 5.5 metre bridge and electricity cable clearance heights, etc, on all the main arterial routes. Which means, I'm afraid, we have to skirt Paris via its outer ring road, which has two distinct disadvantages. One, although its a dual carriageway, its rather slow because of the number of lorries that are forced to use it. And two, because you won't get to see any of the spectacular sights of central Paris itself, so I'm afraid its going to be rather boring. But not for too long though, hopefully. We'll be leaving it well behind us before you know it."

"That's a real shame then," Helen sighed, "I *so* would have liked to have caught a passing glimpse of the Eiffel Tower, or even Notre Dame maybe."

"Well we can go and attempt a minor detour if you really insist chick," I muttered sarcastically, "but I can pretty much guarantee that somewhere along the way we're gonna get the Phoenix wedged pretty tightly inside one of those underpass tunnels, and possibly even the one that you may have seen on the news a few years back."

"Oh God, yeah, I'd forgotten about that awful day," Helen recalled, deep in thought. "Its okay babe, you just drive wherever you know's best. I'll sit back and follow. No matter if some of its boring, I'm sure the whole trip won't be."

"Some of it will be, for sure," I replied. "Some of it most definitely won't be!"

I'd visited Paris on several previous occasions, both for work and for sightseeing holidays, as well as simply passing through whilst heading further south. I was fully aware of both its inner and outer ring roads, and the advantages and disadvantages of each. But I also knew that overhead heights were only guaranteed to highways minimums around the outer ring, hence why all the commercial lorries constantly used it. This also served to keep the majority of the heavier traffic, such as ourselves, out of the city centre itself; all the better for tourism. So I guess we'd just been lucky that we hadn't encountered any low bridges on the short section of B-road that we'd taken through the village of Landrethun-le-Nord, where we'd encountered the '*joke*' traffic cops. I made a mental note anyway to take extra care when negotiating the back streets of Barcelona in due course.

We joined the west side outer ring road, knowing that the only sights to see would be mile upon mile of high rise tower blocks, all crammed way too close together, and forming the semi-slum areas of Paris's dense and dangerous unemployment, care in the community and migrant communities. It did at least, however, have two *positive* advantages. Firstly, the west side ring road was a significantly shorter distance for us than the east side, and barring any traffic snarl-ups should only take around an hour or so. And secondly, it was Sunday. Although I knew that articulated lorry drivers generally worked seven days a week, due to their extremely long distances of travel, coupled with relatively low rates of pay, I'd hoped that the traffic wouldn't prove to be too manic. And I was right too. Although this road only had two lanes it certainly wasn't anything like as bad as the M25 on a weekend, and we were making pretty good progress at a steady 40mph without having to slow down or speed up around other traffic. All was running well, and the little Foden's three litre, six-cylinder diesel engine sounded like she was singing sweet music to us. Or maybe that was just the sound of Joe Cocker's voice crooning away on the little stereo in the background. *Who knows?*

We'd accessed the west side outer ring road at Saint-Denis, just north of Paris, and our intention was to exit shortly before Orly Airport to the south, then head for the A10 AutoRoute which would take us on down south towards Orleans, on our way towards France's Massif Central. The highest point of the Massif Central is 6,280ft above sea level, some fifty percent higher in fact than Ben Nevis in Scotland, but I knew that the roads that would lead us up onto this huge plain, and back down again the other side, much further on towards the south of France, were relatively gently sloping, with very few having much in the way of steep gradients. *Apart from the one!!* Unlike the winding roads that took you twice as high up through the steep and rugged mountains of the Pyrenees just a few hundred miles further to the west. I figured we'd get ourselves well clear of the madness of Parisienne road users, and some distance before Orleans we'd stop for fuel and look for a hotel, this time hopefully well before it got dark. Two thirds of the way around the west side ring road, after leaving the depressing high rise apartment blocks some way behind, Helen spotted a signpost pointing off to the right.

'*Versailles – 3 Km*'.

"Ooh!" she exclaimed, excitedly. "Look Chris, shall we? Can we go visit the palace? Please? I've never been there before, and I've always wanted to. Just for an hour? *Please?*"

"I've always wanted to go visit the Palace of Versailles too my dear," I replied. "Its absolutely stunningly spectacular. My parents took me there once when I was a little kid. We didn't stop for long, but I always remembered how beautiful and how massive it is. Especially the gardens. We didn't go inside the palace then, we just looked at it from the outside, but I promised myself that one day I'd go back and take a look around the place properly."

"Well then, shall we go see?" she queried.

"I really don't think now's the right time for that sort of thing darling," I answered back in a tone of mild sadness. "You'd need at least a whole day to take it all in properly, and that would mean two hotel nights, right here, right now, and probably very expensive ones at that. And given the agenda that we've already got, to be honest I'd rather just press on. The sooner we get to Barcelona, the more comfortable I shall feel about everything. So if its okay with you my love, the short answer is *no!* Having said that, I promise, one day, when we've both got a little more free time on our hands, I'll take you there for a day, and then the next day we'll go climb the Eiffel Tower together. How does that sound?"

"Proper promise?" she questioned.

"Of course babe," I responded.

"Okay," she said, "you're on!"

'*Hmm*m . . .' I thought to myself, and ran the idea over in my mind, '*I wonder when or if we'll ever actually get around to doing that?*' Still, at least the thought was worth hanging on to, for the time being anyway.

It was getting on for 4pm, we were getting well on towards Orleans, the daylight was beginning to fade ever so slightly, and the fuel gauge was heading rapidly ever closer towards the '*empty*' mark. Time to stop for the night. Helen had nodded off to sleep anyway, so I'd figured I'd try and surprise her by pulling up alongside some bright lights outside the front entrance to some posh-*ish* hotel somewhere, allowing the bell-boy himself to wake her from her doze. '*Great idea,*' I thought to myself. I'd clearly forgotten to take one thing into account!

Although I knew Orleans to be a very attractive city, straddling the picturesque River Loire, I was somewhat reluctant to take our loaded truck into city centres for the night for fear of not finding anywhere suitable to park. It made far more sense to stop at smaller rural villages, but large enough to accommodate maybe a couple of hotels, a few shops and restaurants, and hopefully a fuel station. There'd always be a fuel station somewhere not too far away anyway, they were more than plentiful around the outskirts of all French towns and cities.

We pulled off the A10 at a junction signposted Saint-Jean-de-la-Ruelle, just north-west of Orleans, and immediately ran in to the Péage toll booths. '*Bugger!*' I thought, '*there goes the surprise illuminated hotel entrance idea out the bloody window! Oh well, no matter.*' I'd forgotten, just for one brief moment, that we'd been driving along an AutoRoute, so the toll attendant was therefore on Helen's side of the cab. I shook her arm gently as we pulled up alongside, and as she opened her eyes I softly asked her to hand the uniformed lady the little white ticket. She wound her window down and passed it across, and a second later the little illuminated sign flashed up the figures '€5.20'. Helen handed over the cash and we drove on slowly, heading towards the village, and keeping our eyes wide open for a half decent looking hotel. She was wide awake now, and pretty damned hungry too, just as I was. Other than a bar of Snickers and a can of Coke each, which I'd cleverly stashed in my '*all-things-important-and-useful*' kit-bag, we'd had nothing since our full English's back at the Chevron F1. We kept our eyes peeled.

As it turned out it wasn't in the slightest bit difficult. Just before we reached the traffic lights at the crossroads in the centre of the little village, on the right hand side of the road, set back just a little between two rows of terraced houses, was a pretty looking, traditional French double-fronted hotel. It had an illuminated sign that ran the whole length of the frontage, immediately above the fully glazed verandah that ran between the two entrances. It boldly displayed the name '*Hotel Regence De Saint Jean*'. I pulled the Foden onto the block-paved front driveway, only just slightly off the road itself, and switched off the side lights. It wasn't yet quite dark enough for headlamps. I pulled on the air brake and shut down the engine, then hopped down from the cab and walked towards one of the entrance doors. Oops, wrong one! Clearly one was just for the restaurant, the other was for the hotel itself. I'd then entered the correct one and walked up to reception.

"Bonsoir madame," I greeted the concierge, "avez vous une chambre pour une nuit s'il vous plaît?" I asked politely.

"Oui, oui, pas de problème," she replied, and figuring immediately that my French wasn't particularly up to much, proceeded to point to the little cardboard sign standing to one side on the counter.

"Ah, bon, bon, merci beaucoup. D'accord, deux personnes pour la moitié du tableau s'il vous plaît," I requested.

"Oui, bon, c'est soixante-quinze euros au total s'il vous plaît. A quelle heure voudriez vous votres petit déjeuners monsieur?"

"A sept heures s'il vous plaît, nous avons un début précoce. Avez vous le parking pour mon camion petit s'il vous plaît?"

"Oui, oui," she replied, "première a droit, et encore première a droit, et il est auteur du dos. Et aussí, depuis, vous utiliser l'entrée arriere."

"Merci bien madame," I replied, and after she'd processed my credit card I walked back out of the entrance, hopped up into the cab and started the engine. And this time, as time had marched on a little, I switched on the dipped headlights. I then proceeded to explain my short French conversation in simple English terms to Helen,

"Okay hun, we're all good. We have a room for the night, and the receptionist is really helpful. So, we turn right, then right again, find the car park around the back, park up the lorry, and use the rear entrance to the hotel. I've already paid in full, seventy-five euros for half board. That's bed, breakfast and evening meal. Not bad eh? Plus, their restaurant looks pretty smart to me, and I've ordered breakfast for 7am in the morning, on account of the fact that we really should get an early start and put a decent amount of miles behind us."

"Sounds pretty much like perfection to me," stated Helen happily, "I just hope the mattresses are a tad more comfy than last night's!"

I'd kind of lied just a tiny bit about the lorry being '*little*', or so it would've appeared. The car park around the back was literally that; a car park. There were six parking spaces down one side, in which were parked two cars, and six down the other, in which, thankfully, there were none. I'd backed the Foden into that side of the car park, and left it pointing back towards the rear lane, taking up all six parking spaces. But hey, it was safe and it was free. We grabbed our bags, I'd locked up the cab, and we'd walked in through the rear entrance and back up to reception. The concierge handed me the key to room number three, just up on the next floor, and informed us that dinner was served between 6pm and 9.30pm. Perfect, just enough time to change and freshen up, then pop down to the little bar for an aperitif before ordering an early dinner. Helen immediately jumped in the shower, no time limit on the hot water this time, and I'd laid down on the double bed, which appeared to be far more than just comfy. It was even better than our own one at home! I proceeded to study the RAC roadmap that I'd brought in with me in a little more detail. I'd then taken a quick wash and changed, and we'd both headed downstairs for dinner at a little after 6pm.

We sat in matching armchairs either side of a wonderful, roaring open log fire, and ordered a bottle of house red whilst perusing the menus. They were relatively simple, being as dinner was included in the half board cost. There was nothing extravagant available, but it all looked like good, wholesome hearty food, and I ordered the veal whilst Helen went for the chicken. The wine, which was obviously an extra, was delicious, the food itself was wonderful, and we both finished up with a small dish of Black Forest gâteau each, with fresh cream. At least it had *said* fresh; it was actually evaporated milk that had just come out of a tin, but it was delicious nonetheless.

We then retired to our comfy little chambre for an early night, on account of the fact that we were getting an early start in the morning, and I wanted to get as many miles behind us as possible. It was Monday the following day, and I was aiming for us to get a flight from Barcelona to Malaga, fingers crossed, on the following Friday. I set my alarm for 6am.

"Nite nite Christoff," Helen mumbled wearily after snuggling down.

"G'nite Mary-Ellen," I mumbled back, taking the mickey.

CHAPTER THIRTEEN

I was in the shower when I heard the alarm go off. Oh well, Helen would have to get it instead. After I'd dried and dressed Helen took her turn in the shower whilst I continued studying the roadmap. We were both sat down together for our petit déjeuners just before 6.30am.

"I'd like us to get well up into the high plains of the Massif Central today babe. I think we should aim for somewhere like Aumont-Aubrac or La Canourgue, somewhere like that, somewhere not too far north of Millau, because I know Millau, and I know its going to be, well, how can I put it, shall we just leave it at '*interesting*' for the time being!"

"Yes, I totally agree," responded Helen, without having a single clue what I was talking about. "Tell you what," she added, "how about I just keep following you?"

"Okay, good plan," I mocked, a little sarcastically. "So, its 185 miles from Bristol to Folkestone, and 260 miles from Calais to Orleans. That means, so far, we've done 445 miles on one tank of diesel, which if I'm right and it does hold 35 gallons, which I'm pretty sure it does, then that means we're averaging roughly twelve and a half miles to the gallon. And that's pretty much spot on what I'd reckoned she'd do, so I'm happy with that. More than happy in fact; three litre diesel, nine tons in total, twelve and a half miles per gallon, that's actually *brilliant!* Of course, we haven't actually hit any proper hills as yet, but even so . . ."

"Which reminds me, we need a fuel station."

"So, from here to a few miles north of Millau, that's gonna be some-where around three hundred miles, averaging somewhere in the region of 50mph, plus a short stop for lunch somewhere around halfway-ish, I'd say give it seven hours, so we should be looking for a hotel somewhere round about 3pm-ish, give or take. That's an awful lot of '*somewheres*'!" I said, rubbing the back of my head as if it was aching from the maths.

"Okay, I'll hold you to it!" Helen fired back at me.

We finished our breakfasts, then went back up to our room to pack our stuff. We carried our bags back downstairs and stopped at reception to check out. I handed over the key, paid for the previous night's bottle of red on my card, and asked the concierge directions to the nearest fuel station. She told me to come back around from the car park, but then proceed on up to the traffic lights at the village centre. Go straight ahead, and after half a kilometre, on the left, just before you leave the village, there's an Elf fuel station.

"You see," I said to Helen, "one in every village!"

She had no idea what I'd meant, as she didn't speak a single word of French, and so hadn't understood a thing the receptionist had said anyway.

I held up the Foden's keys, and simply said '*fuel!*'

"Au revoir," I said cheerfully to the friendly receptionist, as we walked down the corridor towards the rear exit carrying our bags.

"Bon voyage," she replied with a genuine smile.

As we reached the car park at the rear of the hotel I turned to Helen and said,

"First things first babe," and with that I pulled a small wad of loo roll from my pocket. Luckily, both the engine dipstick and the radiator cap were easily accessible on the Foden without the need for tilting the whole cab forward, which was necessary to access all other parts of the engine and gearbox, etc, etc. I wiped the dipstick on the loo roll, checked the level, and found it to be spot on the '*full*' mark. *Great!* She wasn't using any oil. I binned the loo roll then removed the radiator cap, which was accessed through a small hatch in the front grille. *Which, thankfully, wasn't taped up with black insulation tape!* Finger in, wet, *great, again!* No need for water either. Still, always best to check, and always best to check when the engine's cold.

We scrambled up into the cab, settled our bags on the middle seat, fired up the engine, and drove the half kilometre to the outskirts of the village, where, sure enough, we found the Elf fuel station. I pulled alongside a pump, hopped down from the cab, and removed the screw cap from the fuel tank, which was located just underneath the flatbed, and just behind the driver's side of the cab. I noted the fact that standard diesel was just 99.9

cents per litre, considerably cheaper than in the UK, especially given the excellent pound/euro exchange rate at the time, and proceeded to fill the tank to the brim. Pretty much spot on one hundred and fifty litres, at pretty much spot on one hundred and fifty euros! That worked out to thirty-three gallons. Blimey, she really was getting close to sucking in air, *must remember not to do that again!* Which, by the on-the-day exchange rate, worked out to fractionally over one hundred pounds. *Excellent!* Extremely happy with that! A hundred quid's worth of fuel to get from Bristol to Orleans! *Brilliant! Oh God, how I wished it were that cheap back in dear old Blighty!* Whilst I was filling the tank Helen had popped in to the fuel station shop to stock up on a few drinks and snacks to munch on along the way, and she came back out just as I was going in to pay for the fuel.

"*Ships in the night,*" I whispered meaninglessly to her as we passed in the doorway.

I paid for the fuel, hopped back up into the cab, and swung the Foden back out onto the road, back the same way we'd come, until we reached the Péage junction that we'd come through the previous evening. Helen took yet another little white ticket from the machine, and we rejoined the A10 AutoRoute heading south. Shortly before crossing the bridge over the beautiful River Loire, just outside of Orleans, the A10 veered sharply off to the west, and we continued straight on along what had now become the A71, although you wouldn't have known any difference. We crossed the Loire and settled back comfortably into our seats for the long, three hundred mile journey ahead.

I glanced at my watch, 8.15am. Perfect, exactly as planned. And blue skies for a change too, although it was still a little chilly; we kept the heater in the cab on '*warm*'. The Carpenters were playing on the CD player. Not exactly one of my favourites, but we'd previously decided to take it in turns to select whatever music we wanted to listen to, and this one was Helen's choice. What did please me, however, was the fact that the roads were relatively clear. Despite the fact that it was Monday morning there seemed to be very little traffic around, quite a surprising little pleasure to be fair, and I settled the old Foden into a steady 55mph along a relatively flat terrain.

I've never really been overly keen on northern France. Apart from the fact that quite a few of the beaches lying along the northern English Channel coast tend to be pretty spectacular. But once you drive a little further inland I've always found it to be pretty dull and uninteresting. Maybe that's just me. Maybe I've never really explored Picardie, Normandie or Ile-de-France properly, but that's always been the impression I've got. However, its always appeared to me, regardless of the time of year, that the further south you go, the prettier the countryside becomes. Of course its entirely possible that this has something to do with the weather, or its equally possible that its simply a reflection of my state of mind on whatever particular day that happened to be. Either way, as we drove on, the further south we went, the nicer the weather became, the prettier the countryside appeared to look, and the happier I became. And what's more we'd already passed by Vierzon, and as we steadily approached Bourges I had Gary Moore playing on the stereo, so now I was perfectly content.

Helen had nodded off. She tended to do that a lot whenever playing the part of passenger. Cool, maybe I'd just keep my own choice of music on for a bit. Bourges came and went, then Montluçon, then Riom, all of which we bypassed via their ring roads, and now we were circling around the outskirts of the city of Clermont-Ferrand, where far more traffic appeared to have joined us along this busy section of dual carriageway. The A71 continued on around the city towards its eastern side, and as we branched off to the south, now taking the A75 towards Issoire, once again the volume of traffic became a lot lighter. We were now gradually, but noticeably, heading steadily higher and higher, up into the huge plains of the Massif Central, although the little old Foden had hardly even noticed any of the gentle inclines as yet. On a couple of occasions she'd slowed to just over 50mph, but then she'd made it back up to almost 60mph on the flatter sections of road, so we were still running pretty much perfectly according to schedule. Or at least the very loose schedule that I'd had in mind for that particular day.

Sadly however, that steady little status quo was not set to remain for too much longer. Peering ahead through the clear blue skies, dotted here and there with little, fluffy, white cumulus clouds, I could clearly make out in the far-off distance what appeared to be; *hills!* They weren't exactly mountains as such, they were more like series upon series of beautiful, rolling green fields, stretching as far as the eye could see. But slowly and steadily they were very clearly increasing in altitude. I already knew that we weren't going to encounter any seriously mountainous roads as such, *at least, not just yet,* so I just kept my fingers crossed that we'd come across nothing any steeper than a one in ten, as anything much greater than that, I felt pretty sure, would put the little Foden quite seriously to the test. As it turned out it was just about to happen. We watched Issoire fly past us at 55mph over both sides of a long, steel, elevated flyover, somewhere down in the pretty green wooded valley below, and after another few miles, as the uphill gradient steadily increased, we passed a road sign that clearly read '*15% – 10 Km*'. I blinked twice as we passed it, and muttered '*oh merde!*' to myself. This was going to be by far the steepest hill we'd yet encountered, much steeper than Bristol to Tormarton on the M4, and what's more it went on for ten kilometres. Ten kilometres! Six and a quarter bloody miles! '*Come on baby! Come on, you can do it! Give it your best shot, we'll be fine, you'll see!*' its an uncanny feeling in a way, when you find yourself talking to an inanimate object, and patting it gently on the dash as if to offer some kind of sympathetic encouragement. Three litre straight six diesel, nine tons fully loaded, fifteen percent gradient for ten kilometres, let's see how she copes with this one then! Luckily for us, as I'd already noticed, just as we'd passed the little sign, there was the start of a crawler lane. By now however, the volume of traffic using the road, particularly in the direction that we were heading, had significantly increased, and Sod's Law, just our luck, a lot of them were very large lorries. Oh well, I guess we'd just have to slot in line with the rest of them.

It didn't quite work out like that! After two kilometres we were down to 40mph, and I could tell that the poor little Foden was going to struggle somewhat with this. Another two kilometres, and the needle was hovering over 35mph, and after six kilometres we were down to 30mph. '*Come on! Just four to go!*' By now there was a long queue of articulated lorries following behind us. Every now and then one would gradually creep by, followed by a queue of a dozen or so cars and vans, but more worryingly most of them were just sticking behind us, and we were still slowing. Seven kilometres, 25mph, and after almost eight the needle was hovering over the 20mph mark, and I had to shift down into third gear. '*Come on baby, only two K's left, you can do it.*' With that, as I checked the passenger side door mirror, I noticed more and more lorries desperately trying to pull out inbetween the faster travelling cars and vans in an attempt to overtake us, and somehow I could tell that frustration and impatience was building in their minds. '*Not exactly a great recipe for road safety!*' I thought to myself. I switched on the twin revolving yellow flashing lights on the cab's roof, just as Helen awoke and asked why we were driving so slowly. I simply pointed at the road, she glanced in her door mirror, and immediately recognised the situation for what it was.

"I do hope all those lorry drivers manage to keep their patience about them," she said.

I just gritted my teeth and stared straight ahead, although I'd already got the impression that the yellow flashing lights on the roof had slightly diffused the situation. You couldn't actually see the lights themselves from directly behind us, as they were shielded from view by the bulk of the Phoenix, but because they were extremely bright their reflection was bouncing off every available shiny surface, including the bows and windows of the boat, and to all those vehicles that had actually managed to overtake us they became entirely blatantly obvious. Which, I'd felt in a way, gave us some kind of excuse for our ridiculously slow speed. One kilometre left, and we were down to 18mph, and as we topped out over the brow at the very end of the long summit, still using third gear, the needle on the speedometer had very nearly touched 15mph. *But not quite!* Then, suddenly, far quicker than I'd anticipated, we'd begun to speed up. Fourth gear, 45mph, yellow lights off, and now somewhat more of a gap between us and the lorry immediately behind. Twenty yards now, instead of the twenty inches it had seemed just a few minutes before. The crawler lane came to an end, and very shortly afterwards I spotted one of the most welcoming signs that I'd seen for a long time; '*Aire de Pique-nique – 1 Km,*' with a little picture of a couple sat opposite each other at a peaceful garden table. *Excellent!* I indicated, slowed down as we ran into the slip road, and stopped as far over into the picnic area as possible. I pulled on the air brake and breathed a massive sigh of relief. Helen could visibly see that I was stressed, and didn't utter a word. Whereas I myself chose to lean with my back against the driver's door, looking straight through the passenger door's window, and started counting the lorries passing the picnic area, one by one, nose to tail. All of which had been queued up tightly behind our worryingly slow little load for God knows how far, maybe even the whole ten kilometres. *Ten, twenty, thirty*, I lost count and gave up after I got past *forty!* I jumped down from the cab and took in a long, deep breath of wonderfully chilly, clean mountain air. Then I slapped the little Foden playfully across her tail lights, and whispered gently, '*good girl!*'

"Well that was fun!" I uttered, sarcastically. "*Not!*"

If only I knew, there was worse to come! Not that particular day, but I more or less knew what to expect in Millau, and that wasn't too far away now. But for the time being however, I was just going to savour the peace and tranquility of this beautiful bit of French countryside, with its lush, green, rolling hills, and row upon row of tall poplar trees, stretching for as far as the eye could see. Helen climbed down from the cab, carrier bag in hand and asked,

"Fancy some munchies babe? I'm starting to feel like its lunchtime already."

A few other lorry drivers had pulled into the picnic area too, I'd guessed for their lunch breaks, but most of the drivers were still sat in their cabs, on account of it being pretty damned chilly. After all, we were three thousand feet above sea level by now, but the skies were still blue, and the sun was still shining. There was also very little wind, so we sat opposite each other at the little wooden picnic table, strategically positioned on the neatly mowed grass, simply obeying what we'd been instructed to do by the welcoming little road sign half a mile back. We zipped our ski jackets up tightly, and munched away on Mars bars, crisps and Coke.

"Its 1.30pm babe," I said, depositing all the empties in a nearby bin, "we should hit the road."

As was normally the way with the majority of foreign rest areas, public conveniences were provided on site, and were generally very well looked after too; cleaned, tidied and restocked on a regular basis. This particular picnic stop was no exception, and so after briefly taking advantage of the services provided, we'd both climbed back into the cab, and reset the music. Helen's choice this time, *bloody Whitney!* I'd turned the heater up just a little, and we'd got going on our way ever southwards.

Thankfully the roads appeared to have levelled out now as we began driving steadily across the high plains of the Massif Central, and we were able to stick to a relatively steady 55mph. Within a few more miles we came across a row of Péage toll booths. Helen handed over the required amount of cash, and from then onwards, for the most part, the roads appeared to have become single carriageway, with no longer any central barrier or hard shoulder. The only two-lane sections were where crawler lanes had been added to some of the uphill gradients, and whilst these didn't prove particularly steep, we certainly weren't in any position to overtake anything, and simply slotted in line with the other lorries, whilst cars and other light vehicles whizzed past us whilst they had the opportunity. Each time we reached the next town however, instead of circling around it via a ring road, because we were no longer running '*Péage*' we had to drive through their centres, and in the centre of each town there was always a crossroads and a set of traffic lights, which slowed our journey considerably. However, each time we exited yet another town, the traffic seemed to have thinned a little more, and progress across the open plains became steadily easier and easier. Saint-Flour, Loubaresse, Les Monts-Verts. *The Green Mountains, how very appropriate!* Aumont-Aubrac, they all seemed to blur into one, despite having to stop for the lights in the centre of almost every single one. Marvejols; we stopped again just before the centre, but this time I glanced quickly at my watch, and as it had turned a little after 3pm, I looked across at Helen and announced,

"Okay, 'tis '*stop time*' now me thinks, let's keep our eyes peeled for a hotel somewhere".

We didn't appear to be having much luck, there was very little in the centre of town, it seemed to be more industrial than anything, or at least the part of town that we were skirting through did. Still, we weren't exactly there for the sight-seeing, all we wanted was a bed for the night, so as we drove on at an annoyingly slow pace, we thoroughly scanned the beginnings of every side street and turning that we passed. *Nothing!* We drove on out of the southern end of town, and just as I was about to pick up speed again, there we saw it! Through the trees lining the verge on the opposite side of the road, standing alone, surrounded solely by a large, empty green field, was what appeared to be an ordinary, detached private residence. However, there was a big old wooden signboard fixed into the ground right next to the entrance to the drive that simply read '*HOTEL*'. It was immediately obvious that the little Foden wouldn't fit through the gates to the driveway, which was filled up anyway by the three cars that already occupied it, however the little lane just the other side of the row of trees, off which the driveway to the house ran, appeared to be wide enough to park up without obstructing anything, and at the first opportunity that arose I swung the truck back around the way we'd come and pulled into the little lane behind the trees. I parked up in a slight pull-in area, just shy of the drive entrance, switched off the engine, told Helen to wait where she was, and hopped down from the cab. Ironically, just as my feet hit the road, a small overhead light came on, faintly illuminating the face of the wooden hotel signboard. Dusk would soon be approaching, and I took the switching on of the signboard light to mean that they must have vacancies. If they didn't we'd simply carry on to the next town and keep looking, however I strolled up the drive purposefully, and knocked hard on the big old brass knocker fastened to the front of the white painted wooden front door. After half a minute passed a wrinkled old lady, who looked to be well in to her hundreds, answered the door, and I asked her politely if she had a room available for the night.

"Oui, oui," she replied, "s'il vous plaît, entré, entré, nous avons beaucoups de chambres."

I explained that I'd just go fetch my wife first, and whilst walking back towards the lorry I thought to myself *'Yeah, I'm not surprised you've got plenty of rooms available my love, you're a tad hidden out of the way over here!'*

Helen passed me down the bags, then slid across the seats and climbed down from the driver's side. She couldn't exit the passenger door, as I'd parked the old Foden right close in to the bushes, as tight to the side of the lane as I could possibly manage. After I'd locked up and crossed the lane, I looked back from halfway up the driveway and got the impression, in the rapidly approaching half light, that a tall tree was actually growing through the roof of the Phoenix. *Good job she had a heavy duty rubbing strake!!*

"Merci beaucoup madame," I said to the old lady, "ici c'est ma femme, Helen, et je m'appelle Christophe."

"Bonsoir Helen, et bienvenue a notre petite maison."

She made us feel very welcome indeed, although the little house was clearly nowhere near as *'little'* as she implied. As we followed her up the stairs towards our room, it also became obvious that she was probably nowhere near as old as she initially looked. Either that or she was extremely spritely for her age. She showed us into a beautifully made up room, with a double bed, en suite, and a large picture window that overlooked the vast expanse of green fields out back. As she held Helen's hand whilst passing her the room key, she explained to me that she had two other pairs of guests staying that night, foreign travellers just like ourselves, but that she herself lived alone, and therefore the only service that she offered was bed and breakfast. For this she charged the princely sum of twenty euros per person, which I immediately thought to be a bargain, and she explained that there was a nice little restaurant back towards the centre of town just a five minute walk away. I hadn't noticed any such restaurant myself on our way here, but she pointed roughly opposite the house, then told us to cross the main road and walk half a kilometre up the side street. She left us to it, and we proceeded to wash, change and freshen up, ready for a walk into town in search of dinner.

After resting for a bit and taking our time to get ready, we took a leisurely stroll along the little side street towards the centre of town. It turned out it wasn't just a highly industrialised place after all, it was a beautiful, *oldie worldie*, traditional French town, with a wide archway running directly underneath the centre of its ancient cathedral, just to one side of the cobbled square in the town centre, which itself was illuminated all the way around with black-painted ornamental street lights. Had I remembered to bring my little camera along with me it would have been nice to have taken a couple of photos. Never mind, eh, maybe another time. *Or another place!* There were several little café-bars dotted around the square, most of them completely empty, but one that looked like it might have a half decent menu, so we entered and took a table close to the front window overlooking the square. A great place for people watching, had there actually been any people around to watch. Dinner was simple, cheap but pleasant, as was the single bottle of red wine that we downed between us. Helen followed hers up with a café au lait, whereas I ordered myself a small Stella Artois.

"Forty miles to go until we hit Millau," I stated nonchalantly.

"What's so special about Millau?" Helen came back with.

"They haven't built the bridge yet!" I said in a simple matter-of-fact tone.

"What does that mean exactly?" she asked.

"Well, basically, it means I've allowed a whole day, just in case, to drive all the way down to the bottom of the Tarn Gorge, then through the pretty little town of Millau itself, then all the way back up again, and then onwards from the other side, forever southwards."

"Just in case of what?" she asked.

"Who knows? Let's just see how it goes eh. its a beautiful town, is Millau. I've been there a few times. I camped there once with my parents and my two brothers when we were very young. It straddles the gorgeous River Tarn, most of which I've canoed on two separate occasions; once with the Scouts and once with Taunton Canoe Club. And not too many years ago, before Tori and Alex were born, I travelled down this way one summer, camping with Rachel, and we stopped over near Millau so that we could go visit the caves up in the Tarn Gorge, where they make Roquefort cheese. That was an interesting day. Roquefort's the most exquisite and most expensive cheese you'll ever come across; its not made anywhere else in the world, and I absolutely love it. Once we get down into Millau, down in the very depths of the beautiful Tarn Valley, if I can find somewhere safe to stop, maybe we'll find a little coffee shop somewhere and go buy some."

"*Yuck,*" said Helen, "*you're welcome to it!* The only time I ever eat Roquefort is when its made into a very mild sauce, then poured over a fat, juicy, delicious sirloin steak."

"Mmm, the stronger the better for me!" I replied.

We finished our drinks, paid for dinner, ambled slowly back to our hotel, and took to our bed for yet another early night. I had a nervous kind of feeling that tomorrow wasn't going to be the easiest of days on the road. If only they'd completed that damned bridge the year before we arrived here, instead of a couple years after! Hey ho, it was what it was, as I kept telling myself.

CHAPTER
FOURTEEN

*E*ggs! We were given lots of eggs for breakfast. And I mean lots! *Beaucoup d'oeufs!* All the old lady had asked was whether we liked our petit déjeuner fried, poached, boiled or scrambled, and we'd both asked for poached, s'il vous plaît. And out they came; four on each plate, with a rack of warm toast and a large pot of tea. The other two couples, also sat in the breakfast room close by to us, kept looking over, as if to try and spot if we'd been served up the same as them, which clearly we had. I'd already figured that one couple were Dutch, the other German, and that we all had entirely different agendas. However, quite clearly we'd all been served up with the same large plate of eggs each. My best guess was that the old lady, who realistically was probably only in her mid-seventies, kept chickens. And by the looks of it far too many of them. I have to admit however, they were pretty damned tasty eggs, and after finishing the lot and polishing off the tea and toast, we got up from the table to go up and fetch our bags.

"Plus d'oeufs?" the old lady asked, almost as if willing us on to say '*oh, yes please.*'

"Non, merci, c'est tout pour nous. Seulement l'addition s'il vous plaît."

Four each had been plenty thanks. Could we please just pay the bill. Helen went up for the bags, struggling back down with all four in the one jaunt, whilst I settled up the tab, which, despite the rather odd breakfast, I still felt was a bargain. We said '*merci et au revoir*', crossed the little lane and unlocked the driver's cab door. Helen climbed in first and slid across, I passed up the bags then climbed in myself and started the engine. I pulled the little Foden gently out of the bushes, allowing the Phoenix to part company with the tall poplar tree that she'd been snuggled up alongside all night long, and drove slowly to the end of the little lane, whereupon we rejoined the main road. We turned left, and resumed our journey southwards along the single carriageway A75. We were already well out of town, and within a minute or so we were flying along again at a steady 55mph. By now it had just turned 8.30am, and again the sun was shining, although it was still very low. There seemed to be far more white, fluffy clouds scattered around the sky that morning, and it was certainly very chilly, but it was my turn to choose the music, so I selected some Chris Rea, leaned back comfortably against my seat and relaxed. My thoughts turned immediately to the roads in and out of Millau, and how the little old Foden, with her overweight load aboard, might, *or might not,* cope with them. Forty clicks to go, and then I guessed we'd just have to find out the hard way. It didn't bode particularly well though, the fact that we were both cooped up in this tiny little cab together, having just consumed eight eggs between the pair of us, whilst contemplating the winding lanes of the Tarn Valley through Millau, or whatever I could remember of them. My nervousness suddenly became considerably worse when Chris Rea's *'Road to Hell'* started playing.

As we drove on, we had both passenger's and driver's door windows half open on account of the eggs we'd consumed earlier. La Canourgue flew past, virtually unnoticed, followed shortly afterwards by Severac-le-Chateau. Very shortly after that the A75 changed from an old, single carriageway road into a relatively new dual carriageway, the relevance of which, for some reason or another, escaped me entirely at that particular moment in time. The other traffic, that we were both following as well as being overtaken by, was really quite average, neither busy nor quiet, just very normal. In fact everything around us seemed to be pretty normal. Until, suddenly, peering way ahead of us into the distance, I spotted something that appeared far from normal. *WTF? 'Is that some kind of apparition I see before me?'* The closer we got, the stranger it appeared, until it gradually began to dawn on me exactly what it was. *But WOW!!* What an amazingly spectacular vision. I'd never seen anything quite like it before, and the chances were I never would again. And to be fair, I never have, that's just how spectacular this vision before us was. *It was simply awesome!* Nowhere near what could even remotely be described as '*normal'*!

We were fast approaching the deep, steep-sided gorge that the River Tarn had long since carved, some two thousand feet below our current position, right through the middle of the Massif Central. Whilst at our current altitude we were surrounded, all around us, by bright blue skies, with a few scattered, small, fluffy white clouds. The Tarn Gorge however, at the very bottom of which lay the pretty little town of Millau, was full to overflowing with dense, greyish-white fog, which appeared to be spilling out over the top of the cliffs just like dry ice rolling across the floor of a theatre stage. The gorge clifftops were around two miles apart, and as we drove ever slower towards them we found ourselves staring, somewhat dumbfounded, right across the top of two miles of boiling white soup. But that wasn't the most amazing part. Far from it! What looked eerily spectacular were the seven tall tower cranes, strategically positioned across the whole two mile expanse of thick, rolling fog; and each one, or so it seemed, reaching desperately for the blue sky above. Seven massive black construction cranes, all in a perfectly straight line, simply poised atop the huge expanse of fluffy grey-white cloud. To me they seriously resembled seven black candles, evenly spaced across the top of a white iced birthday cake, but each one with a single, straight, long black arm near its pointed top, outstretched towards the little, fluffy white clouds. It immediately became obvious that the solid concrete columns that each one of these tower cranes was sat upon were hidden deep within the broiling mass of fog itself, and just the cranes themselves seemed to be hovering there, enjoying the blue skies and sunshine like magic fairies, risen high above the tall trees of their densely wooded forest. Oh, *how I wish*, still to this very day, that either I or Helen had grabbed my little camera there and then. However, despite being far too mesmerised by that spectacular vision right in front of our very eyes to even think about it at the time, that amazing image will remain in my mind for the rest of my life. Little did I know at the time, but those two thousand feet tall concrete columns were the beginnings of the construction of the now world famous Millau bridge, a two mile long award-winning project that has now become the tallest road bridge in the world. It takes just five minutes to drive across it; but it hadn't been built yet, *Goddammit!* It was about to take us five hours instead, just to cover the same distance, and we had to do it the hard way; two thousand feet downwards, and then hopefully, somehow, back up again. And what was worse, or so it appeared, *the whole valley ahead was thick with fog!*

All of a sudden the dual carriageway appeared to come to an end. There were tall, solid steel barriers right across the road, and big red and white chevrons directing all traffic off to the left. This was the start of the old D809, the steep, windy little road that took us down into Millau. After a mile or two we came across a prominent road sign that clearly read '*Avertissement, Colline Abrupte!*' *Warning, steep hill! No shit Sherlock!* A minute later there was another sign, '*20% – 12 Km*'. Not a problem; I had no issues whatsoever with driving *down* steep hills, I'd simply let the gears do the work for me. It was driving *up* them that bothered me! I couldn't for the life of me remember what the road out of Millau, heading south, back up onto the high flat plains, was like. All I knew was that it was bound to be pretty bloody steep, but just how steep I really had no idea. And with that we disappeared into a thick blanket of fog. I switched all the lights on. The old Foden didn't have any red rear fog lights, but I switched on the yellow flashing roof lights, and most eerily they seemed to make the whole area of fog around us flash yellow too. It was as if we were driving along surrounded by a massive yellow flashing aura. Still, at least no one would miss us. Both despite and because of the fog we stood out pretty much like a sore thumb. *Situation normal there then!* I engaged third gear, kept my foot off the throttle, and we coasted along, down and down, around and around, one hairpin bend after another, at a steady 25mph, simply keeping a safe distance between ourselves and the articulated lorry immediately ahead of us, whose brake lights were permanently on, and only just visible through the thick fog. I barely touched the Foden's brakes, other than the odd occasion when the traffic ahead of us slowed to under 20mph, which happened maybe half a dozen times along the seven and a half mile length of that hill. Then, just as suddenly as we'd become shrouded by it, the fog cleared, and we began to notice buildings, instead of trees, along either side of the road. It had taken around half an hour to negotiate that hill down to where we'd emerged from the fog, and after a further ten minutes of far more level terrain, still following the same lorry at around 25mph, we noticed a large black and white sign announcing '*Bienvenue a Millau*'.

Just a hundred yards or so after that the traffic ground to a halt, and we sat there, stationary, for what seemed like an eternity. I'd even switched the engine off, and just as I was considering popping into one of the little shops that now lined the busy little street that we were pulled up in, just to see if I could partake of un petit morcel de fromage Roquefort, we started moving again. Roadworks, it had turned out. Single file traffic only across the ancient little stone bridge that spans the Tarn right in the centre of Millau. We'd stopped again, this time somewhat closer to the traffic lights, and sat waiting, again with the engine off, whilst a long stream of traffic came towards us from the opposite direction. I didn't dare leave the cab though, and shortly after that it was our turn again to go, so I fired her up and put my foot down. We crossed the Tarn, then began looking for somewhere to stop, but without success. At least, without success anywhere near the town itself. However, after a few more miles of relatively flat terrain I spotted a long lay-by on our side of the road, and pulled into it for a short break.

"Never mind babe," I said, disappointment noticeable in my tone, "we'll find you some Roquefort somewhere along the way, don't you worry."

"I'm not worried in the slightest," Helen replied, "its you that wants some, not me. I'm more worried about this next hill we have to drive up. Anyway, here, have some chocolate instead," she said, tossing a Kit-Kat across to me.

"Thanks," I returned, "and don't worry about that either, this old girl will cope with it just fine."

That's when I noticed the next road sign, just before the first sharp bend up ahead in the distance. It said '25% – 5Km'. 'Bugger!' I thought, 'twenty-five percent, that's one in four, that's like bloody Porlock Hill in Devon, the steepest hill in England, and I certainly wouldn't be attempting to take that one on, at least not with this horrendous load onboard!' What's more, Porlock Hill is less than two miles long, this one's more than three! Oh well, 'shit or bust' I guess, as the saying goes. I jumped down from the cab and wandered around the truck, absentmindedly kicking tyres as I went, whilst finishing a small plastic bottle of Ribena. Then I looked upwards towards the sky, and realised that I couldn't actually see very far at all. In fact I couldn't even see the tops of the trees that surrounded us, they were all sticking up into the thick fog that seemed to be lingering some twenty feet above my head, just waiting to swallow us up as we drove on into it. 'Great,' I thought, 'one in four for three miles in thick fog, just what we bloody well need! Oh well, it is what it is, let's crack on and get stuck in.' I unstrapped the ladder from the flatbed, rested it against the boat's starboard rubbing strake, and climbed up into the Phoenix. I took the emergency spare yellow revolving light out of its box, and fastened it securely to the stern transom of the boat, the very furthest point back from the lorry's cab. I then grabbed the separate extension lead, the one I'd bought in Halfords specifically for this purpose, plugged the light's trailing lead into that, then plugged that into the Phoenix's own cigarette lighter, which was just to one side of the dash in the boat's central wheelhouse. I then reached down underneath the port-side aft cabin seating and switched on the battery isolation switch. The silver reflector inside the yellow light began to revolve around the bulb, and there we had it! An emergency rear flashing yellow light that was almost as bright as those on the roof of the cab. its just that I couldn't control it from the cab; I'd have to climb back up into the boat to switch it off again. But hey, it was the best I could do, I could do no more with the equipment we had, and anyway, it looked pretty damned impressive to me! So that was it, *blue sky, here we come!* I climbed back down, re-strapped the ladder to the flatbed, hopped back into the cab, started the engine, then switched all remaining available lights to '*ON*'. I'm pretty sure we'd looked more like a busy fairground ride than a road vehicle by then.

Due to the roadworks back in town there appeared to be long intervals between the streams of traffic heading the same way that we were going, and I waited for one of these long gaps before indicating and pulling out. I was going to do my damnedest to build up as much speed as possible before hitting the steepest part of the hill. We rounded the first sharp bend at just over 30mph, and immediately got swallowed up by the fog. It wouldn't be long at all before the first set of vehicles caught up with us after being released from the roadworks across the bridge. Let's hope it would be a slow moving lorry as opposed to a fast moving car. And thank God for that emergency yellow light at the back too! More gradual incline, 35mph, 38mph; *and then it started!* We couldn't see the road ahead properly because of the thick fog, but what little we could see, and the sheer steepness of it, looked mighty scary! Even after the first corner we were down to 20mph in third gear, another corner, 15mph, and just a few seconds later we were down to 10mph in second gear, and still three miles to go. In the passenger side door mirror I suddenly caught the blazing headlights of a large lorry. Luckily for us, *and for him,* he was travelling relatively slowly too, but he very obviously had to brake quite sharply as he came up behind us. Oh well, there it was, they'd all just have to wait, slow down, calm down, and follow us at a snails pace up this long, windy road, up through the clouds and up, hopefully, fingers crossed *yet again* into the clear blue skies above. Somewhat worryingly however, the hill appeared to have got even steeper, and we'd slowed to just over 5mph as I'd shifted into first gear. And still about two miles to go! This was becoming somewhat tedious, as well as rather worrying with regard to the queue of traffic behind us. And not just the length of it, which was clearly going to steadily increase as we went, but also the attitudes and potential impatience of the French drivers. I just hoped to God that nobody lost their patience and tried to overtake, because there was sporadic traffic heading in the opposite direction, coming towards us, and even on the straight sections of road it wasn't possible to see more than forty yards ahead. I was keeping a really good ear on the engine revs, and the fact was, even at just 5mph, they sounded pretty good to me, and I'd gradually become increasingly more confident that at least we weren't going to stall. But the gradient just kept on going, on and on and on, hairpin after hairpin, for what seemed like hours and hours. It wasn't quite that bad, but we had been crawling along, ever upwards, at only 5mph, for just over half an hour. Somewhat ironically I'd been humming away to this tune that had been playing on the CD player, '*All the leaves are brown, and the sky is grey. Barcelona dreamin', on a winter's day.*' I began to feel that '*The Road to Hell*', which had been playing earlier, was probably far more appropriate, although realistically I was actually hoping for some kind of '*Stairway to Heaven.*' Or at least, s'il vous plaît, for this damned fog to clear. *It didn't!* But the gradient gradually lessened, and slowly but surely we began to pick up speed. Second gear, third, and then back up to 30mph in forth. '*That's better,*' I thought to myself, although the fog was still very dense, so I wasn't prepared to go any faster for the time being. A mile or so further on however, and with God only knows how many vehicles tagging along behind us, the fog suddenly cleared, and we burst out once again into clear blue skies. And better still, after another mile or two, having now picked up to an even better speed, we spotted yet another road sign saying '*Aire de Pique-nique – 1 Km*', along with the now familiar couple sat motionless at the peaceful-looking picnic table.

"Ah, perfect timing," I said to Helen, relief more than obvious in my voice. "Fancy stopping for a coffee?"

"*Oh God, yes!*" she replied. "*And a wee, I'm bloody desperate!*"

"No worries," I said, "I'll race you to the toilet block."

Which I didn't! I pulled slowly into the picnic site, parked up, and after switching everything off I glanced down at the engine temperature gauge. Still bang on the '*normal*' mark. Well that was a big relief, *I can tell you!* The next thing I did was unstrapped the ladder, climbed up into the boat, unplugged the yellow revolving light, and threw the battery isolation switch back over to '*OFF*'. Following which I jumped down, re-strapped the ladder, locked up, and *then* ran for the toilet block. It turned out that there wasn't an actual toilet block as such, and we weren't actually, as such, in your average picnic area. We'd pulled into a full-on service area, with a fuel station, restaurant, motel, and a massive open car park area, which now appeared to be steadily filling up with hundreds and hundreds of forty-ton lorries. '*Well blow me,*' I thought to myself, '*I wonder where the bloody hell that lot have come from all of a sudden? Hmm, best we keep our heads down and get the hell out of here asap!*' I walked into the fuel station shop, used the facilities, then caught up with Helen just as she was buying some more drinks at the counter. We were already beginning to get dirty looks from some of the other drivers who'd stopped off as well, so I gently elbowed Helen and motioned to her that we should get a move on. Suddenly however, whilst still standing in front of the counter, out of the corner of my eye I noticed something. Something that I'd been dreaming about for the previous couple of days. Something soft, moist, blue-veined, strong smelling and *deeply delicious.*

"Hang on just one sec babe," I said, turning to one side and opening the upright door to a large, glass-fronted chiller unit. I reached inside, grabbed three medium sized packets, and threw them on the counter next to Helen's drinks, "Would you mind paying for those for me too please?"

"I'll gladly pay for them," she replied, "just so long as you don't expect me to eat any of them."

"No way," I retorted sternly, "*they're all mine!* Mmm, Roquefort, my favourite!"

Helen paid for the snacks and we shuffled off silently, out of the door, quickly back to the truck, climbed back in and fired up the engine. The coffee would have to wait I'm afraid, I'd felt extremely uncomfortable back there. But there again, I suppose it had taken all those poor old sods a little over an hour to do what normally, probably, would have taken them around ten to fifteen minutes. *Such is life!* I steadily swung the truck back around the car park, headed out of the exit, and we set off again on our way, once again with blue skies and fluffy white clouds, chilly, fresh, clean mountain air, and for the first time in at least a year or more, the sight of the first snows of winter lying in some of the areas alongside the verges that were shaded by the hedgerows. I turned the heater up just a notch more. After another ten miles or so, just after we'd driven through La Cavalene, the D809 rejoined the A75, and we picked our speed back up to a steady 55mph again. It was 1.30pm, or thereabouts, and we'd been on the road now for a little over five hours.

"One day," I said to Helen, "once its finished and open, we're going to drive across that new Millau bridge, I promise you. That'll cut at least four hours and four gallons of fuel off the journey, and I bet it'll look absolutely spectacular in the summer sunshine. Maybe next time we'll even make the time to stop and take some pictures. Oh, and by the way, sorry about the lack of coffee back there, but to be honest, I just wanted to get the hell out of the place. Still, at least I managed to find some cheese, so all good for me."

"*Cheese Grommit?*" she mocked in return. "Yep, well done to you. As for the coffee, I don't mind too much, providing we can find a hotel somewhere relatively soon, and not just keep driving on and on and on, searching for one for miles and miles to come!"

"No worries babe," I said, "we'll stop at the next available opportunity."

We drove on steadily, and every now and again, without deliberately trying to do so, I noticed our speed gradually start to pick up. I kept backing off on the throttle, however it had now become obvious that we'd very gradually begun to descend, slowly but surely, from the high, level plains of the Massif Central, down towards the lower and more fertile lands of southern France, as we headed ever closer towards the Mediterranean Sea. Another thirty minutes and thirty miles went by and we came across a massive overhead road sign, signalling Montpellier off to the left, AutoRoute de Péage in one kilometre. We passed the turn off, carrying straight on along the A75, still heading very gradually downhill and forever southwards. Another road sign, '*Béziers – 44 Km*'. We'd be needing to stop for fuel somewhere near Béziers, that will have been yet another four hundred miles since our last fuel stop, and I didn't want to run the tank quite so low this time. I also now wanted to find a hotel as soon as possible, the stress of those hills down through Millau and back up again had really taken it out of me. Another road sign, '*Clermont-l'Herault – 5 Km*'.

"Hotel coming up shortly babe," I smiled across at Helen

Some two kilometres before we reached *Clermont-thingummy-jig* however, just as we rounded a sharp bend going *marginally* too fast for comfort, we saw a big sign planted firmly in the middle of a long green field, clearly stating '*MOTEL*,' and pointing off next right. I safely managed to negotiate the remainder of the bend, slowed considerably, and pulled off at the next slip road up to an overpass roundabout. Following the signs, we turned left, and after a quarter of a mile along the little B-road, turned left again into a large, expansive, Tarmac car park, at the top end of which lay a very modern looking single storey motel. We knew for sure by now that it was definitely a *motel*, as there was another big sign immediately above the entrance door proclaiming the fact, '*MOTEL*'. We parked up in the middle of the flat, half-empty, Tarmac car park, switched everything off, jumped down with our overnight bags, and walked through the entrance up to the reception desk.

"Good evening sir, madam, how may I help you?" the young receptionist asked in almost perfect English. Great, that made things a little easier! For both of us as a matter of fact, as we were both clearly tired and stressed by now, even though it wasn't overly late by then.

"Just a room for the one night please," I answered. "Hopefully dinner somewhere a little later this evening, and maybe a continental breakfast in the morning if that's okay? Definitely no eggs though, if you don't mind."

"Very good sir, that'll be a total of one hundred and twelve euros please. That includes a free bottle of house wine with your dinner, desert, coffee and mints to follow, and as much fruit juice, tea and coffee as you wish for the duration of your stay. The dining room's just through that doorway, dinner is served from 7pm until 10pm, breakfast from 6am until 10am, and latest checkout is by twelve noon. Is there anything else I can help you with?"

'*Well, how extremely polite,*' I thought to myself, as I handed her my credit card, which she duly processed.

"No thank you," I replied, "just the room key please, I think we're going to go take a bit of a nap for a short while."

She handed us a key card, and we wandered off, bags in hand, along a pleasantly decorated and well lit corridor, until we reached room number nine. Key in slot, bags dumped immediately on floor, we collapsed, sprawled across the bed, with our arms thrown around each other, and immediately nodded off, still dressed in our coats and shoes. We didn't doze like that for too long though, maybe twenty minutes or so, as we weren't overly comfy in that position. So we took it in turns to take a nice, long, hot shower, then dressed in more casual attire, chilled out and read for a bit, then wandered back along to the restaurant to take a seat for dinner. We were clearly a little early, the kitchen wasn't quite ready for us yet, but the wine certainly was, and by the time we were handed our menus I'd just *had* to order a second bottle. You know, just to make sure that the first one was as good as I'd thought it had been, and that I wasn't mistaken. And *I wasn't!* The second was just as tasty as the first. We enjoyed dinner together, and I spent most of the time telling Helen that we could probably reach Barcelona late tomorrow if we pushed it a little, and all the possible things we could get up to once we arrived there. Apart from all the important things that we had to get organised first, we might even find the time for a tiny bit of sightseeing too. *Hmm, chance would be a fine bloody thing!* As we clung to those won-derful thoughts though, we finished our deserts, then headed back to our room and collapsed into bed, pretty exhausted from what had been a con-siderably stressful, but nonetheless highly successful day's driving.

"G'nite Helen," I said lovingly.

"G'nite John-Boy," she fired back sarcastically.

I gradually drifted off into a deep and comfortable slumber, dream-ing sweet dreams of Barcelona, and the beautiful, blue Mediterranean Sea beyond, whilst wondering what delights might be held in store for us once we reached the '*Magical City*' sometime later on the following afternoon.

CHAPTER FIFTEEN

I was rudely awoken, far too early the following morning, by the dreadful sound of some female's voice singing, totally out of tune, and way too loud for my liking. '*That's weird,*' I thought to myself in my semi-conscious state, '*that sounds remarkably like Helen's voice, what's up, what's going on?*' I shook myself awake, peeled one eye half open, and clocked the fact through the tiny gap between the curtains that daylight had already arrived.

"*Happy birthday to you, happy birthday to you, happy birthday dear Christoff, happy birthday to you!*"

"*Oh my God!*" I exclaimed, opening both eyes wide and sitting bolt upright in bed. "*Its my birthday, isn't it! Isn't it? I forgot!* No idea how I forgot babe, but I forgot! *WTF?* What time is it?"

"Its eight o'clock," Helen replied, "and don't worry, *I didn't forget,* you must've know I *wouldn't!* And neither would any of your kids either; they never have, and they never will, even if *you* might! Anyway, I thought I'd let you have a bit of a lie-in today, its not like we're in a tearing hurry or anything, so I switched the alarm clock off. So, here you go, these are all for you . . ."

With that she placed a handful of sealed birthday cards in my lap, and sat back with a big, beaming smile across her pretty little face.

"Oh, thank you darling. I love you ever so much. You do know that, don't you? I can't believe I forgot! What day is it? How old am I?"

"Open your cards and see if they give you some kind of a clue," she simply said.

"*17 – 18 – 19 – 20 – 21 – Jeez, is it bloody Wednesday already?*"

"It certainly is my love, Wednesday the 21st of December, your birthday; now open your cards."

"*I will, I will,*" I replied enthusiastically.

'*Happy 90th Birthday*', the first one boldly pronounced, with a picture of a beautiful, ancient, four-masted tall-ship on the front. Inside was neatly written '*Hippy burpday you crazy old codger ⊠ Safe travels. All my love always, Shellypoos X X X*' Hmm, just what I'd expect really from my dafty twenty-two-year-old smart-ass of a daughter. '*Thanks Michelle,*' I thought to myself, '*you're too kind!*'

Tori and Alex's cards were both far more polite, and far more straight-forward, but after all, they were only eleven and nine years old respectively, bless. Most thoughtfully, however, both too had pictures of boats on the front. Tori's showed a pretty little sailing yacht, whereas Alex's portrayed the most luxurious superyacht imaginable. Tori had drawn lots of hearts inside her card, and coloured them all in with a red felt pen. Alex had simply written the five words I'd been saying to him repeatedly ever since he was much younger, '*This time next year Rodney . . .*'

By now I was sufficiently awake to remember that I'd just turned forty-five years old, not that that held any particular significance for me, although I made myself a mental note to text Michelle at some point, thank her for her lovely card, and inform her that I'd cut it precisely in half! Helen handed me her card, which I quickly opened, only to find on the front of it a wonderful image of a big, bright red London bus, along with the simple message '*Happy Birthday*' in bright, bold, silver metallic letters.

"Sorry babe," she whispered gently, "I couldn't find a card with the picture of an old car transporter on the front of it, so I thought this might do as the next best thing."

'*Strange or what?*' I thought to myself. I then understood perfectly when I opened it and read what she'd written inside, '⊠ *We're all going on a WINTER holiday, no more working for a week or two. Fun and laughter on our WINTER holiday, no more worries for me or you, for a week or two ⊠*' On the other side it simply read '*Happy Birthday Christoff, With Love, Always and Forever X X X X X*' I leaned across to her, put my arms around her, kissed her gently on the lips, then whispered softly in her ear,

"*I love you princess!*"

I then sat myself upright, and boldly uttered those five words that every girl wants to hear first thing in the morning,

"*Let's go get some breakfast!*"

We both showered, dressed, wandered along to the dining area, and took a table closest to the long window that overlooked the car park. Most of the other vehicles that were parked there the previous evening had already left, so the lovely old Foden with the pretty Phoenix loaded aboard stood out proudly, in perfect plain sight from where we were sat, right in the centre

of the huge expanse of Tarmac. There was a self-serve, buffet-style continental breakfast bar, so after setting my birthday cards out neatly around
the centre of the table we both went up and helped ourselves to orange
juices, tea, toast and marmalade, and half a dozen warm croissants. Halfway
through breakfast I looked across at Helen and said,

"As soon as we're done with brekkie babe we need to go grab our bags,
check out and get going. We've still got a little over two hundred miles to
go, and we need to make a fuel stop along the way, preferably somewhere
near to Béziers. Mind you, by the looks of it, although I reckon its a little
chilly, the weather seems to be holding up pretty well. So, *Happy Birthday
to me!* ⊠ *Barcelona here we come!*"

After a second pot of tea, three orange juices each, and the last of the
croissants, we packed our bags, birthday cards carefully laid at the bottom
of mine, approached the reception desk, handed the key card over, and
paid cash for the additional bottle of wine that we'd had the previous evening. I politely said '*merci pour votre hospitalité, et au revoir*' to the young
receptionist, and even Helen managed a slightly awkward '*merci, au revoir.*'
To which the receptionist replied, again in almost perfect English, '*thank
you, goodbye, and have a safe journey.*' As we stepped out into the chilly but
clear and bright morning air, I looked at my watch and saw that it had
just turned 10am. We both climbed into the cab, bags thrown up into the
middle seat, and made ourselves comfy.

"Steady trip today babe," I said, reassuringly. "Mostly downhill at first,
but nothing too steep, and then pretty much flat for the rest of the way.
By 3pm-ish this afternoon we should be checking into a hotel somewhere
near the centre of Barcelona. Or more likely a *hostel*, 'cos they're far more
prevalent in most Spanish cities."

"Coolio," she replied with a smile, "*I'm lovin' it*, let's go!"

I turned the key in the ignition, and the starter motor whirred over. And
over! And over and over. And it kept on whirring over, but she wouldn't fire
up. '*Shit!*' I thought, '*now what?*' I took the key out, pushed it back in and
tried again. *Whirr, whirr, whirr, nothing!*

"*BOLLOCKS!*" I exclaimed angrily, "*Houston, we have a problem!*"

"What is it?" Helen asked.

"I've no idea hun, but there's no point in you sitting out here whilst I try
and figure it out, you're just gonna get really cold without the heater running. Remember they said inside we could have unlimited tea and coffee,

etc? Go grab yaself something whilst its still available, and take a seat some-where, I'll give you a shout just as soon as I've fixed it."

Helen climbed down from the cab, took her handbag with her and strolled back towards the motel entrance. I tried the ignition once more. *Whirr, whirr, and still nothing!* The fuel gauge showed a little over half, and all the ignition lights were working as they should. The twin heavy duty twelve volt batteries sounded absolutely fine, for the time being at least, although I knew I needed to protect them really carefully. I certainly couldn't afford to run them flat, otherwise we'd be in even more trouble, so I needed to start exploring potential avenues of fault, rather than just keep turning her over and hoping for the best. I scratched my head. It must be a fuel issue, surely? She's a simple, basic, six-cylinder diesel; fuel flows from the tank, through a filter, into a pump, where its forced under pressure into each of the six injectors. Nothing more complex than that. *Okay Chris, check the fuel tank.* I jumped down from the cab, zipped up my ski jacket, and knocked the side of the fuel tank. Yep, sounds about half full to me. *Okay, check the filter.* A copper pipe ran from just above the bottom of the tank along the underside of the flatbed, fastened along the outside of the chassis. After about eighteen inches there was a small in-line glass dish, filled with what appeared to be clean diesel. I unscrewed it, removed the wire gauze filter, and diesel started pouring from both ends of the copper pipe, splashing all over the Tarmac. No problem there then. There was no dirt or water in the glass dish, the gauze filter was perfectly clean, and so I quickly screwed the glass dish back into place so as not to waste any more fuel, or create too much spillage over the car park, whilst taking care not to misalign the O-ring seal.

'Dammit!' I thought, '*I'm gonna have to tilt the cab forward so that I can access the engine.*' I reached up into the cab and grabbed the three bags, set them on the ground, then proceeded to clear everything from the dash. CD player, roadmap, a couple of half full bottles of drink, two paperbacks, and various assorted rubbish. I packed it all into the bags, picked them up and walked back into the motel entrance with them. Whilst passing the reception desk I mentioned quite abruptly that I had a problem, and whilst I'd done my best to keep my voice down and calm, I knew straight away that the receptionist had sensed just how annoyed I was. I dumped the bags down next to Helen, who was sat at the same table we'd had breakfast at, and asked her if she was okay.

"I'm fine, thanks," she replied, pointing to yet another large pot of tea on the table in front of her. "Any idea what the problem is?"

"Nope, not come across it yet I'm afraid," I replied. "I need to hinge the cab forward so I can get at the engine, so I'll have to leave these bags here with you for the time being. Your books are just inside the front pocket of yours if you need them, which I expect you will, chances are this could take me a while!"

"Okay, thanks," she said, "I hope you fix the problem soon."

"Gonna give it my best shot," I replied positively, but then added, "although I'm not exactly a qualified diesel fitter, as well you know, but hey, all I can do is try."

"Good luck," she called as I walked back passed reception and out into the car park.

'Broken down again,' I muttered to myself, 'I don't FUCKING believe it!' I slid the sprung catch lever around the back of the cab to one side, then lifted the back of the cab up with one hand, which tilted all the way forwards until it stopped on its central retaining strap. It was a simple, easy process, with the whole of the cab itself being counterbalanced over its pivot point, making it appear to be virtually weightless. So now, instead of the back of the cab being perfectly upright, it was sitting at roughly a forty-five degree angle from its original position, and the whole of the engine, transmission, and all other associated mechanical components had become not only visible, but also, thankfully, easily accessible. 'Pretty clever dynamics for such an old girl,' I seem to remember thinking at the time. The trouble was, I really had no idea what I was looking for, but I looked anyway, and looked hard. The fuel pump appeared to be fine, everything was clean and dry up to that point; I didn't notice any leaks anywhere. Until I looked a little harder! Injectors one to five all looked good, but just below injector number six there appeared to be a tiny little drop of diesel, just a smudge, appearing down the side of the engine block. Luckily the fuel pump and injectors were on the driver's side of the engine, which meant that with the cab tipped forward I could now reach the ignition key and turn the engine over, whilst watching to see what was going on with the mechanics on my side of the truck at the same time. I did so, and whilst holding the key, with the starter turning the engine over and over, I could see a tiny, sporadic little jet of fuel briefly squirting out of the side of injector number six, roughly once every second, and plonking itself firmly and directly onto the Tarmac below. And as I turned the ignition off that's when I noticed the tell-tale rainbow effect of a very small, but steadily growing, splash of fuel oil spreading across the dry Tarmac, directly underneath where the cab had been sat before it was tilted forward. *'Hmmm . . .' I thought to myself!* Two things immediately sprang to mind. Two things that, far from being anywhere near an expert on the subject, I was perfectly well aware of. Firstly, if an injector was blowing out fuel, then it would also be sucking in air, meaning that cylinder number six was never going to fire up properly. And secondly, a six-cylinder diesel engine should fire up perfectly well on only five cylinders anyway. So even though this problem needed fixing there must be *another* problem somewhere as well. *Great! Just bloody great!* Oh well, the least I could do was to try and seal up the leaking injector, that would do for starters. Maybe it had just worked itself loose somehow, maybe it just needed tightening up. I unstrapped the ladder from the truck's flatbed, leant it firmly up against the starboard rubbing strake of the Phoenix, and climbed up into the boat to fetch my toolbox. I'd placed it somewhere easily accessible, just in case, and just as well too. I grabbed it with two hands and heaved it up over the gunwale. On reaching the ground again I set it down, opened it up and started searching through my collection of old spanners. Having located one that perfectly fitted the injector collar, I proceeded to crack it open, and pretty much as expected, it loosened far too easily. *'That must've been why it was blowing fuel out,'* I thought to myself. Now, I'd seen this done on diesel engines several times before. In order to expel any air from the system you have to pump fuel through the pipe whilst tightening it. So, with spanner in the left hand and ignition key in the right, I turned the engine over, and whilst steadily tightening the collar with the spanner, I gradually stemmed the flow of diesel from the injector, until the collar was tight and the leak was sealed. I turned off the ignition, gave the collar one final tweak with the spanner, just to torque it fully down, checked the remaining five injector collars to make sure they were all still tight, which they were, and threw the spanner back into the tool box. I then tried the ignition again. *Whirr, whirr,* nothing. *Whirr, whirr, treble-bloody-whirr,* still nothing! Although at least injector number six wasn't still squirting tiny jets of fuel all over the ground anymore. I'd managed to fix one thing at least; but where was the fault? What the heck was going on here? I spent another ten minutes searching for a possible fault, but again, I really didn't know what I was looking for. So I gave up. *'There's only one solution Chris,'* I said to myself, *'call the bloody RAC out again!'* I left the ladder where it was, hauled my toolbox up onto the flatbed, and headed off back towards the motel entrance in search of Helen and my phone. I started humming a little tune to myself along the way, '*Happy FUCKING birthday to me, happy FUCKING birthday to me, happy FUCKING birthday dear FUCK-WIT, happy FUCKING birthday to me! NOT!!!*'

Helen was sat on a brown leather Chesterfield sofa at the far end of reception when I walked in, our bags stacked neatly beside her, reading one of her girlie novels. Apparently the breakfast room had all been cleared away in preparation for that evening's dinner settings, and as they didn't serve lunches I was becoming evermore grateful that we'd gorged ourselves at breakfast time.

Helen looked up from her book, "Any luck?" she asked inquisitively.

"Yes and no," I replied, "although sadly, not enough '*yes*' and far too much '*no*'. Can you pass me my phone out of my kit-bag please, I'm afraid I'm gonna have to call the damned RAC out again!"

"Oh great!" she threw back at me. "So I guess we're going to be stuck here for some time then?"

"Sorry princess, but its looking that way, yeah. I'll let you know what they say as soon as they give me some kind of answer."

With that she handed me my phone, and I strolled back outside into the chilly, clear morning air, well away from the ambient background music that was playing softly throughout the motel. I looked at my watch and noted that it was 11.30am. '*Let's hope they can get an engineer over to us fairly quickly,*' I thought. '*Its going to be well dark now by the time we reach Barcelona.*' I'm not entirely sure why, but for some reason I was quite surprised when I discovered that all I had to press on my phone was '*redial*'! Anyway, a very helpful lady in an office in Bradley Stoke near Bristol took all my details, just like the previous time, and told me someone would call me back within the hour. I wandered back inside and plonked myself down on the Chesterfield, whereupon Helen just looked at me quizzically.

"They're going to call back," I said grumpily, and grabbed a trashy old paperback novel of my own from out of my kit-bag. Surprisingly though, I hadn't even got as far as page two when my phone rang.

"Hello Mr Reason," a different female voice said, "we've managed to get through to our nearest regional automotive franchise to your current location, and the good news is that they'll definitely be able to get someone out to you today. There is a caveat to that promise however. In view of the problem with your vehicle as you've described it, they've decided to despatch a heavy goods tow truck, just in case they can't effect the necessary repairs there and then on-site, and the nearest depot that has such a vehicle available, along with suitably qualified staff and equipment aboard, is located in Montpellier. The vehicle and its engineers will be available for despatch relatively soon, however, their approximate ETA at your location is going to be somewhere in the region of 16.00hrs local time. We do appreciate that this will cause you some considerable waiting time, however, under the circumstances, I'm afraid this is by far the quickest and most efficient service that we are able to organise for you. I do trust that you find this service acceptable, and that our franchised engineers manage to get you all fixed up and safely on your way again. Mr Reason, should you have any further queries or problems, please don't hesitate to call us back on this same number. Thank you for choosing RAC and good day to you sir."

'*Hmmm . . .*' *I thought to myself yet again!*

"So, listen up babe," I said, trying my best to make light of the situation. "Best case scenario is this; breakdown truck arrives at four o'clock, and let's say the engineers manage to get the Foden all fixed up and working by five o'clock. Do we then want to be driving through the night and searching for a hotel, along with somewhere to park, either in or close to Barcelona, in the dark, in the very early hours of the morning? Or should we just stay here for another night and set off early tomorrow morning? Or worse case scenario is this; they can't fix it here at all, so we get towed to their depot in Montpellier, and although that's only about forty miles out of our way, it means the problem with the truck is far more serious. So I guess we'll just have to cross that bridge how, when and if we come to it, and take it from there. Fingers crossed they'll be able to fix her here though, they know diesel engines a thousand times better than I do. Anyway, that's the score I'm afraid, nowt I can do about it either way. And I'm not looking for an answer from you just yet, I just thought I'd run that by you as a little bit of food for thought."

"Oh," said Helen thoughtfully, and then a few moments later, "Food for thought's one thing; *how about food for tummy?*"

"Surely you can't be hungry just yet babe, not after all that breakfast that we just scoffed down?"

"No, I'm not," she replied, "but I certainly will be come five o'clock, if we can't at least get some kind of snack for lunch. And I'm not just talking about the half a Kit-Kat that you chucked in the top of my bag either."

"Okay," I said a few minutes later, having given a little more thought to the situation, "here's what we'll do. If we get towed, we get towed, there's nothing I can do about that. But don't worry, we'll work things out from Montpellier onwards, just as soon as we get fixed up and running again. And if we get fixed up here, which, by the sound of it, isn't gonna happen until at least five o'clock, well then we'll check in here for another night, and we'll get to have dinner again at seven. In the meantime, either way, I'll go see if I can find us some kind of lunchtime snacks from somewhere."

"Also in the meantime," Helen added, "whilst you're doing that, and whilst the ladder's still up against the side of the boat, any chance you could fetch our suitcases down so that I can do a swap-over of the clothes in our overnight bags? You know, *clean-for-dirty,* and all that kind of stuff. I need to, and you *certainly* need to. What you're wearing right now is *filthy,* and you've only got worn stuff left to change into in here, after five days and four nights on the road!"

"That's very thoughtful of you hun," I said, "what a *damned* good idea, well done."

I dragged both suitcases out of the Phoenix and back down the ladder, one at a time, then carried them both into the motel reception. I found a spot well out of view, over in a corner behind some stacked up furniture, and set them down carefully so that Helen could get stuck into her clothes sorting out routine. I then went off in search of some kind of snacks that we could buy from somewhere for our lunch. It turned out, as chance would have it, that I didn't have to search very far at all. I approached the girl at reception to ask the question, whereupon she immediately stated,

"Monsieur Reason, I do believe your vehicle outside has broken down?"

"Oui madame," I replied, "I'm waiting for a breakdown company to come and help me with it. They have told me that they might be able to get here for around four o'clock, and I'm hoping that they might be able to fix the problem whilst its still here. But my wife, Helen, she is going to be hungry by then, so I was hoping you might be able to tell me where I can go, somewhere very near to here, to buy some snacks for our lunch?"

"Don't you be worrying now Mr Reason sir, I will ask one of the staff to make you up some nice sandwiches of ham and cheese from the kitchen. I'm sure that won't be any problem, and you can have some tea or coffee or whatever you might like to go with them. I will work out some kind of price for you later, whilst you are eating, but it won't be costing you very too much. I can be assuring you of this."

"Well," I said, genuinely surprised, "that really is very, very kind of you, *thank you very much."*

I walked back over to where Helen was sat cross-legged on the floor in between the two suitcases, clothes of all types strewn everywhere, all around her. Although, to be fair, I knew her well enough to know that she understood exactly what she was doing with it all, and just how quickly and efficiently she'd have it all done too. I informed her of exactly what we'd been promised for lunch, and she beamed a big smile back at me and stated,

"Aren't *ALL* birthdays supposed to be *interesting*, in one way or another?"

I just stood there, dumbfounded. I had no answer whatsoever for that one.

After Helen had finished the clothing swap-over, replenished our over-night bags with sufficient clean kit for a few more days, and shoved the dirty laundry bag back into one of the suitcases, I carried them both back outside, humped them one at a time back up the ladder, and placed them securely back inside the Phoenix. I left the ladder in-situ, just in case the engineers needed to use any of the tools from my toolbox, which was still sat on the flatbed. Their tools would most likely all be metric, whereas the spanner I'd used to to tighten the injector collar with was a very old Whitworth type. Good job I'd always kept all my old British-made tools really. Whitworth and UNF components ceased to be manufactured many years back, but one still came across them from time to time, and metric-sized tools simply weren't suited to the good old fashioned styles of British mechanical engineering. I rejoined Helen in reception, pulled a crib board out of my kit-bag, and we played cards together for a while. At around 1.30pm, a young lad wearing a striped apron, whom I could only assume was one of the junior kitchen staff, appeared from behind us carrying a tray of food. He set it down on a broad coffee table that stood in front of the Chesterfield and said,

"Voila madame et monsieur, c'est pour vous. Rouleaux de fromage et jambon, et beaucoup de café au lait. S'il vous plaît, profiteer a votre guise."

"Ah, tres bon, merci beaucoup mon amie," I replied politely.

Well that was a pleasant surprise indeed. A whole fresh French stick, cut into four, split open and stuffed full with slice upon slice of delicate ham and tasty cheese. They'd even buttered the inside of the bread first, which was highly unusual for the French, although they were well aware of the fact that they were, unusually, catering for a misfortunate, stranded English couple. One of whom, or so it would appear, had a birthday, and therefore, quite clearly, deserved his bread to be *buttered!* Along with the cheese and ham rolls was a huge stainless steel flask filled to the brim with strong, fresh, piping hot coffee, a large jug of fresh milk, a bowl of sugar, cups, saucers and teaspoons.

"How very thoughtful of them," I said to Helen, "particularly given that they don't ordinarily serve lunches. What I fail to understand, however, is why they've given me *three* rolls, whereas they've only given you the *one?* Strikes me as a little odd that does, but there again, I suppose it is *MY* birthday, after all!"

"*You cheeky muppet!*" she replied, tucking in to her first roll whilst I poured the coffees.

"These are delicious," I remarked, "I wonder how much they're gonna sting us for this little lot then? Not that it matters in the slightest, however much it costs, its most welcome indeed."

After we'd finished our lunch we sat together on the comfy Chesterfield and read our books. Periodically Helen would squeeze my hand, and without even the slightest hint of sarcasm, wish me a happy birthday. And even more periodically, I would look up from my book, peer out through the large picture window, only to notice that no breakdown vehicle had arrived as yet. Three o'clock came and went, as did four o'clock. Around fifteen minutes later though, a huge yellow breakdown lorry, with a massive crane mounted right at the back, its chain and grab hook firmly secured to the oversized rear crash bar, pulled into the car park, parked up alongside the little Foden, dwarfing both it and the Phoenix entirely, and switched on its multi array of yellow flashing lights mounted atop the extended roof of its passenger cab, just for a few seconds, just to let us know they'd arrived. *As if anyone could bloody well miss it!* It was certainly the largest breakdown truck I'd ever seen, and I'm quite sure it would've been more than capable of dragging a fully loaded forty-tonner halfway around the world if necessary. I put my book down, asked Helen to just stay put with the bags, and walked out into the car park. I was greeted by two very capable-looking engineers, both dressed in matching, clean, very smart orange overalls. I introduced myself, said '*thank you for arriving so promptly*', or words to that effect, and shook hands with both of them. It immediately became apparent that neither of them spoke much in the way of English, and that I was therefore going to have to try and explain the problem, along with what I'd already done by way of trying to fix it, by using my very best sign language, and basically just pointing at things. *If only someone, somewhere, could invent something called 'Google Translate'! If only, if only! Maybe one day, somewhere in the dim and distant future!*

Where shall I start? I indicated to them just to be patient and bear with me whilst I try to explain. I knocked the side of the fuel tank to show that it was half full, then turned the ignition over and over to show that it wouldn't start. I then partially unscrewed the fuel filter bowl, to show them that it was clean and clear, and the water separator only had diesel in it, then tightened it back up, sticking my thumbs up so as to indicate that wasn't the issue. Next I grabbed the five-eighths of an inch Whitworth spanner from my toolbox, pointed to the small puddle of diesel on the Tarmac under the front of the engine, and demonstrated the fact that number six injector collar had somehow worked itself loose, and that I'd bled it through and torqued it back up. I then stood back, scratched my head and held my hands out, as if to say *over to you, guys.* Suddenly, a large yellow hydraulic door automatically opened upwards halfway along the nearest side of their vehicle to the Foden, revealing a range of tools that would make even a professional mobile *Snap-On* dealer jealous, and with that the more senior of the two smartly dressed mechanics asked me if he could borrow my old Whitworth spanner. I gladly handed it over to him, and stood back a little to watch them go to work. *Monsieur Whitworth*, as I'd then begun to refer to him, cracked open injector number six again, and held his finger over the end of the copper fuel pipe whilst his mate turned the ignition key for a few seconds. He then shook his head, saying *ce n'est pas bon, ce n'est pas bon,* and then the two-way conversation between the pair of them began in earnest, with me understanding virtually nothing of what they were saying. I simply resigned myself to the fact that I was entirely in their hands, but I continued to watch their every move very closely, because I wanted to know for myself exactly what the problem was. Monsieur Whitworth called me over to look at number six injector, and indicated the fact that the olive was slightly misshapen, and wasn't making a perfect seal within the collar, which could well result in air being sucked into the cylinder even if fuel *wasn't* squirting out. Clearly I'd missed this little gem. He pulled some Emery cloth from a drawer in their tool kit, looked ominously at his watch, wrapped it around the olive, and begun sanding. In the meantime his mate pulled out a wooden slatted board with four small rotating wheels attached, one at each corner, lay across it on his back, and slid his whole body, along with a large, bright torch, underneath the Foden's chassis. Half a minute later he slid himself back out, grabbed a whole bunch of stuff from their tool kit, including a full roll of duct tape, and slid back underneath again. After another minute or so he slid himself back out, jumped up, held up a small, filthy, black glass bowl, and with a broad smile across his face, proudly announced,

"*Voila filtre numero deux!*"

'*Well knock me down with a fucking budgie's feather!*' I thought to myself, '*how the hell would I have known there were TWO sodding fuel filters?*' He showed it to me very closely, and judging by the state of it even Paul and his team of mechanics back in Keynsham couldn't have known it was there either, it clearly hadn't been cleaned out for *years*. Somewhat sympathetically the mechanic got me to look down underneath the flatbed, and pointed out exactly where the second in-line filter was located, and to be honest I wasn't entirely surprised that no one, including me, had spotted it. The fuel line itself ran around in a loop and back through a bulkhead in the chassis, the underside of which was partially panelled in, and this was where the second filter was fastened, to the inside of that section of chassis, pretty much hidden from view by the panelling. *How bloody ridiculous!* The fuel line then continued to run on forwards again towards the fuel pump. This, apparently, to my very best understanding of colloquial French, meant that the pipe running from the tank to the fuel pump was almost three metres long, and therefore, inevitably, it would need to be fitted with more than one in-line filter. '*Mon Dieu! But of course! Inevitably!*' Furthermore, not only was the zinc gauze inside the filter horribly clogged up with thousands of miles worth of gunge, the O-ring seal was also badly perished, meaning that air was being sucked into the system from here too. The mechanic walked across to his vehicle, pulled open another small drawer, and *luckily for me,* located precisely the correct size replacement O-ring. He then walked over to Monsieur Whitworth, who was still busily sanding away around the injector olive with the Emery cloth, and once again they engaged in deep, meaningful French conversation together. I leant against the Foden's flatbed, trying to glean what they were talking about, but I never understood a single word. Another four or five minutes went by, then Monsieur Whitworth looked up and said '*Okay, bon!*' He then attempted, in his very best *Frenglish,* to explain to me exactly why they now needed me to help, and precisely what it was they wanted me to do,

"Quand je dis, s'il vous plaît, tournez la clé de contact, et maintenez-la tournée."

"Oui monsieur," I replied, only just managing to leave off the word '*Whitworth*', "je comprend."

Monsieur Whitworth went back to work with my old spanner and an oily rag, whilst his mate slid himself back underneath the Foden with the freshly cleaned off zinc gauze, and a nice, clear glass bulb, fitted with a new O-ring seal. They talked amongst themselves for a minute or so, and then Monsieur Whitworth announced,

"Monsieur Reason, *maintenant* s'il vous plaît."

I stood on the Tarmac, one hand inside the cab of the Foden, the other hand held behind my back with my fingers crossed, and turned the ignition key. *Whirr, whirr, whirr,* nothing. But I kept her turning over and over, non-stop, just as instructed, and after about another seven or eight whirrs, without so much as a cough or a splutter, she suddenly sprang back to life.

"*HOORAY!"* I shouted at the top of my voice! I let go of the key, and their she sat, purring away, just like new, entirely giving me the impression that nothing whatsoever had been wrong in the first place. That illusion quickly disappeared when the two mechanics pulled back from their work positions and turned to face me. Both of their faces, necks and collars were splattered and soaked with diesel. The three of as stared at one another with seriously glum expressions for just a brief moment, and then, simultaneously, all three of us burst out laughing. *Oh, the joys of bleeding air locks out of diesel fuel systems!* They both grabbed clean towels from a side locker within their awesome mobile tool chest, and whilst they were wiping the majority of the fuel and grime from their arms and faces, I secretly smiled inwardly to myself, smug with the fact that the only tool they'd really needed to use was an old, British, open-ended Whitworth spanner.

"C'est tout bon maintenant." Monsieur Whitworth confirmed, as the little Foden sat there, still purring away like a happy little kitten.

"*Oui, merci, merci, merci,"* I replied gratefully. "Est ce qué un problème très simples?"

"Non, non, non," he replied back, "parce qué nous avons besoin trois personnes pour la réparation. Sans pour autant trois personnes, ce n'est pas possible!"

Well, at least that was good to know! *It wasn't just me being dim!* The problem wasn't simple at all, it was a combination of three separate issues, which, come the end, needed all three of us to successfully get it done and fixed, and without the three of us working together, wouldn't even have been possible. Or, at least, something along those lines. I didn't care anymore, I was just eternally grateful that we'd managed to get the old bus up and running again. Once they'd decided their hands were clean enough I thanked them graciously for there efforts, shook hands with both of them, and offered them twenty euros each in cash as a minuscule token of my massive appreciation. To my surprise they both politely declined my little tip, and simply asked me to sign their paperwork in order that they could get on their way back to Montpellier. I did so, and they packed away their hundreds of thousands of euros-worth of Snap-On tool kit, climbed back up into their giant, bright yellow monster truck, and disappeared off out of the car park. I threw my little old Whitworth spanner back into my £5.99 Halfords tool box, climbed the ladder and plonked it back on the aft floor of the Phoenix, then slid back down window-cleaner style. I lashed the ladder back onto the flatbed, and as I hinged the cab back upright, securing it back into place with its spring-lever, the broad smile that had appeared across my face grew ever wider. I left the engine running for just a minute or so longer, revelling in that sweet sound of six beautiful little cylinders all humming in unison, then switched her off and locked the cabin doors. And as I strolled purposefully back towards the motel reception, I begun humming this little tune to myself again, albeit far more happily this time, 'Happy fucking birthday to me, happy fucking birthday to me . . . .'

It was getting on towards six o'clock by this time, and dark outside too, as well as mightily cold. I hadn't noticed the cold whilst we were working on the Foden, but my guess was that it was by now somewhere around the zero degrees mark. I walked across to Helen, who had nodded off on the Chesterfield, open paperback still in hand, and gently shook her arm until she awoke.

"Hi honey, I've got good news and bad news," I said, as soon as I felt she was sufficiently coherent to comprehend. "The good news is, *there isn't any bad news*. But the bad news is, *there isn't any good news*."

"*Don't be so bloody ridiculous,*" she scowled, "what's going on? What's happening with the lorry?"

"Okay," I replied, a little more sensibly this time, "the good news is, the lorry's all fixed, up and running and good to go. But the bad news is, we're not good to go ourselves! its six o'clock, nigh on, its cold and dark, and I vote we stay here for another night, and hit Barca during the middle of the day tomorrow. What d'ya reckon princess?"

"Well," she said, "I reckon they've got rump steak on tonight's menu, the food here's not half bad, the people seem very nice, and the wine's just as tasty as anywhere else. So, as we're already here, what better place for a slap up birthday meal? Yeah, let's stay, I'm sure we'll still get to Malaga in time anyway. *Won't we?*"

"Hmm, pushing it a little, me thinks, but hey, we're best off avoiding night drives wherever possible anyway, and if everything goes swimmingly well from now on, well I reckon we should just about be okay. *Close,* mind you*, but hopefully okay*. So yeah, we'll stay for another night. Fancy a drink?"

"D'you know what, I actually really do," she retorted. "A gin and tonic would be absolutely bloody marvellous right now!"

I wandered back up to reception and explained that we'd decided to stay for a further night, to which the receptionist replied that she'd figured as much anyway, but was super pleased for us that we'd managed to get our transport back up and running. She'd even had exactly the same room made up and set aside for us, and once again handed me the key card to room number nine. I asked her nicely if she could possibly knock together a nice double G&T, and maybe find me a couple bottles of Stella, but she said she was very sorry, it wasn't possible to open up the bar until seven o'clock, as the manager kept hold of the key and he wouldn't be in until then. What she could manage, however, was to try and nobble a nice bottle of red from the wine rack in the kitchen, and seeing as how she knew it was my birthday, and what a stressful day it had been for the both of us and all that, she'd do her very best to get her hands on a decent bottle of Châteauneuf-du-Pape. I said merci beaucoup, wandered back over to the Chesterfield, and plonked myself down next to Helen. Suddenly, lo and behold, less than a minute later, the same young lad that had brought us out the coffee and rolls at lunchtime appeared once again from behind us, this time carrying a silver tray with a pair of empty wine glasses, and *what do you know it, an opened bottle of 1984 vintage Ch*âteauneuf-du-Pape!

"Voila Monsieur Reason," he announced, "bon anniversaire, celui-ci est sur la maison."

"*Wow*," I replied, "*merci BEAU beaucoup!*" I then turned to Helen and whispered,

"On the house, *my arse!* I bet they add that to the cost of the lunch, which they haven't even told us about yet. Still, the sentiment's very much appreciated, and it is a *very* decent quality red. *Shall we?*"

"*Be rude not to,*" Helen responded.

She immediately poured two very full glasses, which, I have to say, didn't really get savoured the way they justifiably should have been. In fact, to be honest, they hardly even touch the sides, but what the heck, I felt sure there were plenty more bottles of the same vintage where that one came from! We gradually finished the luscious bottle of red between us, then carried our bags back to room number nine. I showered and changed; at least I now had a new wardrobe, or *hold-all* rather, of clothing to choose from. We then settled at a table in the dining hall together, ready to order dinner.

"Apologies for the lack of G&T earlier babe," I said. "Would you like one now, now that the bar's open?"

"D'you know what?" she replied with a grin, "I don't really, not now, but I do fancy another bottle of that *Château*-what's-its-name, that was absolutely delicious."

And so the night went on. Two very rare, juicy rump steaks, two more bottles of delicious Châteauneuf-du-Pape, and far too much cheerful singing of '*happy birthdays*' later, and we were both just the tiniest bit the worse for wear. Come ten o'clock, following a couple of additional bottles of Stella each, and much more tomfoolery, we gave up on our puddings and headed back off to our room. Not long after, lying there worn and weary from a stressfully long day doing virtually nothing, Helen put her arms around me, kissed me one last time, and said again,

"Didn't I once tell you that *ALL* birthdays are always supposed to be '*interesting*'?"

"Well that one was certainly *different*," I replied, "although I'd really rather *never* have another one like it. Let's hope for a better day tomorrow eh? Nite nite princess. Love you to bits."

"Nite nite to you too, you crazy old codger," she answered back. "Happy birthday. Love you to the moon and back."

CHAPTER SIXTEEN

I'd set an alarm for an early start the following morning. The 21st of December 2002 may well have been a birthday to remember, but sadly for all the wrong reasons. It was horribly messy, extremely non-productive, and now we were running behind schedule again. As we sat once again at the exact same table by the window, munching our way through another identical continental breakfast, we discussed between ourselves the pros and cons of the previous day. Yes, it could easily have happened somewhere far worse than in a motel car park; yes, I was now even more confident about the mechanics of the dear old Foden; and yes, we'd ended up having a great evening meal, and turned the remainder of the night into a right proper good old laugh. But no, I didn't ever want a repeat of it, not even close thank you very much, and if we were going to get to see Mandy in Malaga on the day that we'd promised her we would, then we'd left ourselves pretty much zero room for any further error.

"Which means, my love," I began, with an air of authority and determination, "that we need to get ourselves gone from here, back on the road, and just hope to God that nothing else goes wrong along the way."

"Agreed," replied Helen, pouring herself yet another cup of tea, in some kind of vain attempt to rid herself of what appeared to be a half decent hangover. "I'll be ready whenever you are."

I left the table and headed over to reception to settle the bill. Once again the same, polite, English-speaking lady was sat behind the counter, and she greeted me with a broad smile.

"Good morning Monsieur Reason," she began, "I trust you had a pleasant evening, followed by a good night's sleep, and also that you have a successful onward journey today, following yesterday's repairs to your vehicle. I have spoken earlier with our manager, who has confirmed some figures for me, and subsequently I have now prepared your bill for you, which I trust you will find acceptable."

She slid a copy of a printed off sheet of A4 paper across the counter towards me, which essentially read as follows,

Motel half board standard room €112

2 x special preparation lunches €20

2 x vins Châteauneuf-du-Pape €32

4 x Stella Artois €10

TOTAL €174

Merci pour votre coutume

"*Wow,*" I said, "*that's a real bargain, merci beaucoup indeed!*"

I handed over my credit card, which she duly processed and handed back to me. True to their word, one of the marvellous bottles of plonk rouge had indeed been provided on the house, and most gratefully received too.

I strolled back to the room, grabbed up the three bags, two of which now contained their replenished clean clothing supplies, and walked purposefully back to reception, where I handed over the key card. Helen had finished her final cup of tea, somewhat groggily scooped up her handbag, and met me by the front door. Several '*merci, et au revoirs*' all round later, and we strolled out into the chilly morning air, crossed the car park and climbed up into the cab of the Foden. Bags and bodies nicely settled, I pushed the key into the ignition, shut my eyes and said a little prayer to myself, then turned the key. She fired immediately, first turn, and I muttered '*thank God*' to myself under my breath. I checked my watch, almost 8.30am, and then commented on the fact that, whilst it appeared to be a little foggy, I was pretty sure it was only early morning mist. The sun, or what little of it there was at that time in the morning, and at that time of year, was definitely trying its best to make an appearance, and hopefully it'd clear away fairly quickly. I switched on the Foden's headlights anyway, released the air brake, and we headed off out of the car park back towards the A75. Once back on the main road, heading more or less due south, whilst carefully following the little yellow cardboard cut-out sun still stuck to the cab's sun visor, just above the top of the windscreen, it was clear that we were still heading very steadily downhill. Down, down, down, from the elevated heights of the Massif Central plateau towards the sparkling blue sea of the Mediterranean, as it gently lapped the sandy shores of the French Riviera. After half a dozen miles or so we suddenly emerged from the underside of the hill fog into bright sunlight, with clear blue skies ahead for as far as we could see, and I switched off the little Foden's headlights.

"Okay, all good babe, next stop Béziers for more fuel, then onwards towards the Spanish border," I declared cheerfully to Helen.

No reply. I waited until we'd rounded yet another relatively sharp corner, then looked across at the passenger seat, upon which my dearly beloved wife had fallen fast asleep, and was beginning, just very faintly, to snore. '*Bless her, with her little vin rouge hangover, best I leave her be for a bit,*' I'd figured. I carefully slipped an old Dire Straits CD into the little stereo, which I'd placed back on my side of the dash, along with the road map, which I'd really hardly even used. '*These mist covered mountains, are a homeland for me...*' Not anymore they're bloody well not, *España here we come!* We steadily left the hills and the corners further and further behind us, and as the roads began to straighten out ahead of us across the lower, broad plains of the region of Languedoc, we picked our speed back up to a respectable and steady 55mph. Just as I was beginning to wonder to myself whether they could get that spectacular Millau bridge finished in time for our return journey, *knowing full well that they still had at least another couple of years to go with it,* we came across a large, overhead sign that read '*Béziers – 8 Km*', and my thoughts turned to finding a fuel station somewhere. Luckily it was easy. We didn't even need to go anywhere near the centre of busy old Béziers Town. After following the A75 ring road halfway around the outskirts we came across a fully equipped service area, and pulled off the main road into yet another Elf fuel station. I pulled the little Foden up alongside a commercial diesel pump, and just as I was about to jump down from the cab, Helen awoke from her early morning slumber and asked me where we were.

"At a fuel station on the outskirts of Béziers," I replied. "Its not even half nine yet babe, we've still got 180 miles to go before we hit Barcelona, I just figured here was a good place to top up. You can go back to sleep if you like, we're not gonna get there 'til at least one-ish."

"No, I feel fine now thanks, that little doze has done the trick. I could sure do with a drink of water though, can you grab a couple of bottles for me please whilst you're in there?"

"Of course I will hun. I'll stock the kit-bag back up with a few extra munchies too, everything's gonna be way cheaper around here than it will be in downtown Barcelona. *Especially diesel!*"

I hopped down from the cab, and purely as a matter of habit walked once around the truck, kicking each of the tyres as I went. All hard, all good; and I already knew the oil and water levels were fine, I'd checked both of them the previous evening whilst the agency mechanics were still working on the fuel system. I took the cap off the fuel tank and poured in a little under a hundred litres of diesel. For a little under a hundred euros. That worked out to a little under sixty-five quid. *Oh, how times have changed nowadays!!!* At the counter in the little shop I grabbed four medium-sized bottles of spring water, several bars of chocolate, a few small bags of crisps, and a large bag of Haribo. As I paid on my card the guy at the till bagged all the snacks up for me, and I climbed back into the truck, started her up and headed off out, back onto the A75 main road. I passed the carrier bag across to Helen, and after downing almost a whole bottle of water in one go, she tore open the bag of Haribo and sat it in the centre of the dash, next to the CD player, for both of us to share.

"Thanks honey," I said, "can you pick out all the fried eggs for me please?"

"*Absolutely not!*" she replied, sticking the first of the fried eggs in her own mouth with a big grin.

"Plus," she continued, "its my turn to choose the music."

The Dire Straits album had finished, and she slotted it back into the CD storage bag and pulled out a collection of Rod Stewart's greatest hits. I was actually quite a fan of dear old Rod, so I let it ride without comment, and hummed away quietly to myself as we wiled away the miles. Shortly after Béziers the A75 terminated by joining the wider and considerably busier A9, this being the coast road that ran around the western reaches of the French Riviera, from Montpellier on down to the Spanish border. Unlike the majority of the A75, the A9 was now a dual carriageway, and as we were still heading slightly downhill, as we got steadily closer to the coast, I found myself once again having to lift off the throttle every time our speed crept over the 60mph mark. And whilst we were making great time, with excellent fuel efficiency too, I had no intention whatsoever of overstepping the limits that I had initially set both myself and our somewhat overloaded vehicle. By a little after 11am however, we found ourselves skirting around the outskirts of Perpignan, still thankfully using a relatively clear Péage-free dual carriageway, and some twenty minutes after that we reached the border with Spain. Now, whilst I was fully aware of the fact that there were no longer any physical borders between any of the countries within the European Union's mainland, we had quite clearly just driven past several large electronic road signs flashing up in bold orange letters '*DETENER A FRONTERA*' (Halt At Border) However, another half a mile further on, and all became clear. Several more flashing signs denoting '*PEAJE DE AUTOPISTA*' clearly confirmed the simple fact that, from here onwards, we would have to pay to use the Spanish motorway system. Hey ho, it couldn't be much more expensive than the French AutoRoutes! *Could it?* And it wasn't like we had all that far left to go anyway, maybe around ninety miles or so. Helen wound her window down and pulled yet another ticket from the automated machine, and we continued on our way, steadily picking up speed along what was now a far better standard triple-laned carriageway, namely the E15. Half an hour later the traffic grew heavier as we skirted around Girona, and then lighter again as we left that city far behind us. Almost another hour went by, and as the traffic grew steadily heavier again we approached yet another large overhead sign, clearly displaying Barcelona off to the right at the next junction. This was followed by more flashing, illuminated signs announcing *'PEAJE – LENTO'. (Toll – Slow)* We took the slip road off the E15, which took us up and over to the left, across a long flyover, and then steadily downhill towards the Peaje toll booths just a few miles further on ahead. We stopped at a pay-cash booth, and again Helen wound down her window and inserted the little card. A small illuminated screen flashed up the amount to pay. It read *'€18.70'.*

"*Eighteen bloody euros! That's daylight bloody robbery!*" I exclaimed, handing Helen over a twenty euro note. "*Bloody Spanish government!*"

She pushed the note into the machine, which subsequently spat €1.30 in coins back into the little semi-circular change dish. Helen scooped them up, shoved them into her purse and announced,

"Yep, agreed, looks like I get to keep the change though!" and laughed out loud.

We carried on steadily, following the signs for the *'Centrum'*, or city centre. I had half a plan in mind, so I knew exactly where I was heading for, but whether this plan was going to work in my favour or not I had absolutely no idea. Shortly after the Peaje the three lanes became two, and industrial estates seemed to spring up by their hundreds, everywhere we looked, all around us. A few miles further on and the industrialised sprawls gave way to sub-urbanisation, the twin lanes became single, and as we marvelled at the enormity of row upon row of high-rise tower blocks, stretching out to either side of us for as far as the eye could see, the traffic thinned out even more. And as we continued on very steadily for mile after mile, the apparent abject poverty gradually but noticeably transformed itself, through sobriety and sensibility, into overwhelming wealth and success. Flats became semis, semis became houses, houses became mansions, and ultimately mansions became palaces. This was far from being my first visit to Barcelona, but this stunningly beautiful city never failed to impress me, and to captivate my imagination possibly more so than any other city that I'd spent more than a day or two exploring. I'd always assumed that the artist and architect, Antoni Gaudi, most likely had much to do with planting those wonderful images of this ever increasingly impressive place firmly and indelibly in my mind. And to be honest, had the opportunity ever presented itself to me, which it never had, and realistically was never, ever likely to, then I would more than likely have chosen to spend the remainder of my days there. I absolutely loved the place. Even if finding somewhere to safely park up a nine ton load was likely to prove, how shall I put it, *somewhat taxing?*

As we headed further towards the city centre the streets gradually got narrower, the buildings became steadily taller, and seemingly much closer together. Surprisingly however, and rather suddenly too, I seemed to notice there was very little traffic around. In fact, given that it was a weekday, very little indeed. And then I glanced at my watch. *'Ah, that would explain it!'* I figured to myself. It was 1.15pm, *Spanish siesta time.* Traditionally, people living in hot climates, particularly the northern Mediterranean, and particularly Spain itself, took a *'siesta'*, or rest break, during the hottest part of the day. And in Spain, that meant strictly from 1pm until 4pm. Everyone downed tools, the kids came out of school, and families headed off, either home or to café-bars for their lunch, followed generally by a brief nap, before resuming their work duties after the most intense heat of the day had passed. Yes, one 'til four was siesta time, and to me, at that specific moment in time, it meant only one thing; *absolutely nowhere available to park! Ha, we'll see about that!*

So, perseverance was the order of the day, and as we hadn't yet quite reached my intended destination yet we pressed on. As the streets were becoming increasingly tighter our speed had slowed to a crawl, and on the odd occasion I even had to stop and get out, just to make doubly sure that we could squeeze through the gaps without knocking over row upon row of badly parked mopeds and scooters. Several times I pictured the thought of the domino effect of mass metallic clattering, and at one point I even gave it some serious consideration. Luckily for the owners, *and for me too, I'm sure,* we just managed to squeeze through. I felt sure there must have been a far simpler route towards the city centre, but I was still navigating purely by my own sense of direction, and following that little yellow cardboard sun immediately above my forehead, constantly reminding me that our load was 4.1 metres high! None of which, I have to say, had ever let me down previously, at least not in a serious way. Plus, so far, we'd not encountered one single bridge, let alone a low one. So we pushed on, through ever narrowing streets, until suddenly the whole city seemed to burst wide open into a massive expanse of blue skies and parkland. There were beautiful tall trees all around in every direction, and cobbled walkways criss-crossing the open lawns, at the centre of many of which were a series of ornate fountains, gushing forth with stream upon stream of clear, sparkling water.

And there, immediately opposite this extremely welcoming, vastly open space, lay my intended destination, Sant Railway Station. I'd specifically picked on this spot to aim for, partly because I knew it was well signposted along the way, but mainly because of the huge quantity of parking areas around the station, which were mostly made available for buses, coaches and taxis, as well as drop-off and pick-up zones for the general public. So I knew that we'd at least be able to stop somewhere safely without causing any kind of obstruction. I drove around and into the coach park area, where only about half of the spaces were occupied, with hundreds of people milling around everywhere, mostly either climbing aboard or alighting from the various coaches. The remaining spaces were empty, with no people milling around them whatsoever, and I backed the Foden into the one that was farthest away from all the commotion, pulled on the air brake, switched off the engine, and exhaled another huge sigh of relief. We may not have been parked up entirely legally, but I defied anyone to come up and ask us to move along. Unless fifteen coaches were to turn up simultaneously of course! I wasn't intending for us to stay there for very long anyway, I had another cunning little *Chrissy-plan* up my sleeve, and I just needed to take a short walk to try and see if I could pull it off.

I told Helen to sit put for the time being, and if anyone was to come along and demand the Foden be moved, just point directly out of the passenger window, the opposite direction to the train station, and say in a very firm, loud voice '*POLICIA, POLICIA*'. She'd've been pointing directly towards the central police station, indicating that that's where I'd gone, and most likely for some kind of emergency. She didn't seem too happy about the idea, and I wasn't entirely convinced she'd be able to pull off a little white lie such as that anyway, but I told her not to stress about it, I'd only be gone for five or ten minutes. *'If push comes to shove, just play the dumb English tourist act. Works every time!'* Then I grabbed my phone, jumped down from the cab, and jogged off across the lawns towards the enormous main front entrance to Sant Station. I had absolutely no idea how or why this particular memory had lodged itself somewhere deep within my mind, but the last time I found myself wandering around central Barcelona, probably some five or six years previously, for some strange reason I'd just happened to notice, parked up all over the roof of the huge, tall, single storey building that was Sant Railway Station, was a huge array of assorted commercial vehicles. And it wasn't like they were all from one specific company, or of one particular type even, there was an enormous variety, and plenty of them too. From small, Transit-sized panel vans, to class three seven and a half tonners, one or two Pantechnicons, and even an empty full-sized car transporter. I knew there were both underground and multi-storey car parks dotted all across Barcelona, just as there are in London, but my guess was simply that the roof of Sant Station was used as a public *commercial* vehicle park. And for some reason, maybe just because architecturally, if anyone bothered looking up in that direction, it appeared so outrageously incongruous with its surroundings, maybe that's why that image had always stuck with me. Who knows, although it was a very handy memory to have. I just prayed that I was right, because if not, Plan B was likely to cost me way more than I had been bargaining on. Not that I had a specific Plan B in mind at that exact moment in time!

The main front entrance to Sant Station was over a hundred metres wide, and resembled more of an airport than a train station. Out front were three wide traffic lanes; drop-off, pick-up, and assorted taxi chaos. There were literally hundreds of people milling around, coming and going, walking and running, along with all those who simply stood still in the middle of any available space just to pose for or take photographs. Slightly beyond the general traffic's entry and exit lanes, at each end of the station, tucked just around each corner of the massively expansive building, were two wide concrete ramps that spiralled their way up onto the roof, both of which were guarded by simple electronic lift barriers, accompanied by an intercom system, and clearly marked with huge white arrows painted on the ground at the start of each ramp. The arrow painted on the concrete on the ramp to the far left-hand end of the building pointed upwards, and on the ramp at the opposite end it pointed downwards. I weaved my way through the hoards of travellers and tourists to the far left-hand access ramp, walked up to the intercom and pressed the push button.

"Hola?" I said loudly into the microphone screen.

"Sí?" came back an immediate, deep, gruff response.

"Hola señor," I continued, "mi camion con barca son neuve toneladas, estábien estácionar aquí en él techo por favor?"

"Sí, sí, tirar hacia la barrera y te dejare entrar. Cuántos dias te quedaras?" he asked.

"Sólo por una noche por favor," I replied.

"Okay, bien," he continued, "pagaras con tarjeta en la salida."

"Muchos gracias señor," I finished up with.

No problem sir, one night's parking, pay by card on exit, simples!

I fought my way back through the crowds and jogged back across the lawns to our little lorry, where Helen was comfortably sat reading yet another trashy girlie novel. I climbed back into the driving seat.

"Any hassles from anyone?" I asked.

"Nope, not seen a soul since we parked up," she answered, "other than a small group of Chinese students who stopped to take photos of us. Did you get something sorted okay?"

"I did indeed," I replied with a grin. "I had a hunch, and I reckon its paid off, let's go see shall we?"

I started the Foden's engine, released the brake, and as I slowly pulled away from the empty section of coach park towards the front of the station, I turned to Helen and said,

"What d'you suppose these young Chinese tourists do with all those photos that they keep snapping everywhere? They must have billions and billions of them, surely they can't find the time to sit down and go through them all?"

"Probably not," she replied, "I expect they just print off the odd interesting one now and again. Like, for example, an old five-ton boat sat on the back of an old, English three-ton lorry, parked up right where you'd expect to see a tidy, modern Spanish coach, in a park in the centre of Barcelona. Quite interesting, wouldn't you say?"

"I guess so," I continued. " '*Look, Ma and Pa, we went to Barcelona, and here's a picture of Gaudi's wonderful Sagrada Familia, and here's another one of Chris and Helen's famous overloaded lorry!*' Maybe slightly interesting, but not quite as interesting as what's about to happen next. *Watch this babe!*"

With that I pulled carefully into the clearest lane in front of the station, the one that was full of hoards of people, rather than the foul-up lane full of pick-up and drop-off vehicles, or the chaos lane full of argumentative taxi drivers, and made our way, at just one mile per hour, towards the far end of the building. On reaching the start of the spiral concrete ramp, the red and white striped barrier immediately raised itself, and we drove on up, around in a full 360 degree circle, and onto the massively expansive flat roof of the station. Many of the wide, long parking spaces were already occupied by an assortment of various commercial vehicles, but there were plenty of empty spaces available. I backed the old Foden up tight to the crash barrier that ran around the perimeter of the building's roof, protecting the structure of the four foot high wall immediately behind it. This left the stern of the Phoenix very slightly overhanging the wall itself, but it was screened from view below by the branches of the long row of evergreen trees, which lined both sides of the wide esplanades that flanked either side of the whole length of the station itself. I could also see that the whole of the roof area was covered, and hopefully monitored too, by CCTV cameras, mounted on steel masts at regular intervals around the roof's perimeter, which gave me some considerable reassurance as to our load's overnight security. I pulled on the air brake and switched off the engine.

"*Wow*," said Helen, "that *was* pretty spectacular, I wasn't expecting that in the slightest!"

"Just another one of my cunning little *Chrissy-plans*," I replied smugly. "Welcome to Barcelona darling, shall we go look for a hotel somewhere?"

CHAPTER
SEVENTEEN

We gathered up our bags between us, making sure that nothing was left visible on the dash, or anywhere else in the cab for that matter, and hopped down onto the solid, flat concrete roof. I locked up, and we proceeded to walk back around the spiral concrete ramp, sticking carefully to the slightly elevated walkway section to one side, back down to the street level below. Despite the huge throng of tourists milling around everywhere I knew we wouldn't have any problems finding accommodation for the night somewhere close by, and we headed off across the expanse of lawns in front of us and up into the first narrow side street that we came across. It was getting on towards three o'clock in the afternoon, and still Spanish siesta time, hence there was still very little traffic around. Almost immediately I spotted a sign, sticking outwards high above the pavement, that read '*HOSTEL*' in large black letters on a white Perspex background. We walked in through the entrance, and rang the bell that was sat on the end of the minuscule little counter. Halfway along the corridor a rather large elderly lady, dressed in a traditional black Spanish cotton dress and headscarf, appeared from behind a doorway and politely informed us that they were fully booked for the night. However, if we turned right as we exited, continued to the next junction and turned left, immediately on our left hand side we'd find another hostel that, she was pretty sure, would have availability.

We did exactly as she suggested and continued on along the narrow little street, turning left at the next junction as instructed. Whereupon, what we discovered was not, as we'd expected, yet another pokey little cheap hostel, the type of which Barcelona was all too famous for, but was, in actual fact, what appeared to be a fairly reasonable looking hotel. A small subtle sign fixed to the outside wall said Hotel Santa Maria. We walked up the steps into the bright and airy reception, and up to a counter that was at least manned. The uniformed gentleman behind the counter said yes, they had several vacancies, and pointed to a tariff card sitting in a neat little frame attached to the wall. I leaned over and studied it, and was pleasantly surprised to note that a standard twin room was just twenty-eight euros for the night. Evidently they didn't have any eating facilities available, not even for breakfast, but that wouldn't prove to be an issue, there were café-bars and restaurants every which way you looked in Barcelona. I requested a twin room for just the one night, then produced my credit card. The concierge took my payment via his machine, handed us a key to a room on the third floor, and pointed us in the direction of the elevator. He then explained that there was a small café virtually next door, it served an excellent breakfast, and was open on weekdays from 6am onwards. I said '*muchos gracias señor*', and we picked up our bags and bundled ourselves tightly together into the tiny little lift. I'd forgotten, until I located the floor buttons and pushed number three, that they don't always have a floor zero on the continent. The ground floor when abroad is often referred to as floor one, and therefore, to reach floor three you only have to go up two floors. Trust me, when you get used to it, its far simpler than our strange old English system! As are so many other things abroad, such as driving on the right for example, although that doesn't necessarily apply when driving a right-hand drive vehicle!

Room 33 on the third floor was pleasant enough; twin comfy beds, a large mirrored dresser, en-suite with shower, sink, toilet and bidet, and a pair of tall but narrow windows overlooking the busy little street below, which was bustling with people but still very little in the way of traffic. We threw our bags on the beds and pulled out some more suitable attire with which to go off in search of somewhere to eat a little later on that evening. After chilling for a bit, then freshening up and changing, I looked across the room towards my wonderfully patient wife, who was sat at the dresser applying a fresh laminate of makeup, and said somewhat apologetically,

"You do realise Helen, we were supposed to arrive here yesterday. That was my hope, and its what I'd always had roughly in mind all the way here. Because if we had, we'd've been able to spend most of today sightseeing. And believe me, there's no better place to spend the day sightseeing than Barcelona; its an amazing city, and I've always wanted to show you around here, there's just *so* much to see. But hey, sadly it wasn't to be, it didn't quite work out that way, and I'm really sorry for that."

"No matter sweetie," she replied sympathetically. "What's far more important is that we just get this job done. We get the Phoenix safely over to Fornells, and then get ourselves safely back home again. That's all that really matters. We can go visit places like the Palace of Versailles and the Sagrada Familia another time, and loads more places too, which would be just great. You know I'll enjoy doing all that kind of stuff with you. But for now, don't worry about Barcelona, we'll just come back another day. Anyway, I'm happy enough with the fact that we're flying to Malaga tomorrow to spend Christmas with Mandy, that's enough for me, I don't need to do any more than that."

"Well, yeah, I s'pose," I answered back. "Plus, at least we're here now, and not still stuck halfway up a French mountain out in the middle of nowhere, so I guess we've got that to be grateful for."

"Yes, and to thank the RAC for too," she reminded me. "Anyway, I don't suppose you happened to find out anything more specific about those flights from Barcelona to Malaga by any chance?"

"I found out what I could babe," I replied, "but I couldn't book anything in advance because I couldn't guarantee when we'd be likely to arrive here. Anyway, it shouldn't be a problem, I spoke to the Iberia office at the airport and they told me that their internal flights are really simple, just like their national rail network is too. There are two regular flights per day on weekdays, one at 0700hrs CET and one at 1745hrs CET. That's seven in the morning and quarter to six in the evening, Monday to Friday. And we can book and pay at Iberia's office in the airport, providing we check in at least one hour in advance."

"Okay, coolio," she replied. "So we're flying there tomorrow, that's Friday the 23rd, and flying back here on Boxing Day, which is next Monday the 26th, is that what we're aiming for?"

"Yep, and *if* that all works out okay, that'll be just perfect, because that's exactly how I left it with our Mand," I finished up with. Or at least I *thought* I'd finished up with!

"What d'you mean '*if*'?" Helen questioned.

"Don't worry princess," I said, brimming with confidence, "everything'll work out just fine, you'll see. Anyway, I've gotten us this far okay, haven't I?"

"Yeah, just about, by the skin of our teeth!" she replied, and smiled a huge, freshly painted, bright red lipstick smile at me in the mirror.

"Okay," I said, changing the subject. "Tonight's dinner; I have a cunning little plan, are you pretty much ready to go?"

"Oh dear, not another one?" she sighed, somewhat wearily.

However, she was indeed ready, and we grabbed our coats, took the cramped little elevator down to reception on floor number one, and stepped outside onto the narrow pavement. It was almost six o'clock, siesta time was over, and it would've seemed far darker in reality had it not been for the overstated array of glaringly bright street lamps, coupled with the head-lights of countless stationery vehicles, sat there with their engines idling, waiting for the traffic lights at the end of the narrow little one-way street to turn from red to green. We zipped up our jackets against the chilly evening breeze, I grabbed Helen's hand, and we strolled back around the narrow streets towards Sant Railway Station. As we approached the front entrance I squinted up through the branches of the trees, and reassuringly just about made out the white canoe-shaped stern of the Phoenix, still protruding frac-tionally over the parapet wall surrounding the roof. We wandered inside, spotted a large, bold sign displaying '*Metro – Sants Estácio*', and took the escalator down one level. After locating the automatic payment machines, I paid just €1.50 each for two tickets, which would take us just one stop further along the '*green line*', heading in a south-easterly direction towards the sea. We hopped aboard the metro train, and hopped off again at the next stop, Plaça Catalunya, and as there was no escalator, climbed the stairs back up to street level. And just as we strolled out of the station entrance together, initially hand in hand, I threw both my arms forwards towards the spectacular sight that immediately presented itself to us, and joyfully announced to Helen,

"There you go my love, one of the many wonders of Barcelona! *Officially the world's most interesting street, let me introduce you to Las Ramblas!*"

Helen just stood there in stunned silence for a few moments, taking in the enormous variety of sights and sounds that we were suddenly sur-rounded by. Then she threw her arms around me and gave me a great big long hug.

"That is one *seriously* amazing sight!" she exclaimed excitedly. "I won-dered where on earth you were taking me then, I've never been here before. *This place is just crazy!* It looks more like a circus than a main road. All these different street artists, they're just *so good*. And the animals too. Look at all the birds everywhere. Can I hold the monkey and get my photo taken? *Please?"*

"Of course you can darling," I replied, "if you really fancy paying ten euros just to get your ear bitten! Come on, let's just walk for a bit, there's loads more to see. its three-quarters of a mile long, this street is, takes you right down to a 200 foot tall statue to Christopher Columbus in the middle of a large square, just before you cross the road to reach Port Vell and the cruise ship terminal. The square is normally full of market stalls selling cheap tacky crap to the tourists, so I don't think we'll bother walking that far down, but somewhere along the way we're bound to find a half decent restaurant."

"That'd be just great," she replied, "I'm starving! And I can't think of anywhere more interesting to sit and eat, and watch everything going on around us. Look at that silver-painted guy over there, standing on a box, making out like he's a statue of Julius Caesar. He hasn't moved a single muscle for ages. He must be absolutely freezing on a night like this!"

"Yeah, go chuck a couple euros in his hat babe, poor bloke. He's far more deserving than monkey man back there."

As Helen bent forward to drop a few odd coins in the street artist's little hat sat on the pavement just in front of him, dear old Julius leaned down from his soapbox and placed his hand firmly on her shoulder. She jumped out of her skin and screamed loudly as she spun around, only to find that she was surrounded by a hoard of other tourists, all cackling their heads off at Julius's cheeky little antics. I think she felt quite embarrassed, but at least Julius gave her a nice big smile, and bowed his head towards her, as if to say thank you for the donation, before resuming his statue-like pose atop the soapbox.

"Come along chickadee," I said sympathetically, "there's a nice looking restaurant just over here, and it looks pretty warm and cosy inside. I really don't fancy sitting outside a street café in this temperature, but you'll still be able to look out the window and see what's going on. And what's more, you'll be pleased to hear, they've got paella on the menu."

"*YAY!*" Helen shouted back enthusiastically, "*My first paella of the hols so far!* Just what I've been looking forward to. I adore Spanish paella, its my favourite."

We entered the restaurant, took a seat at the one and only vacant window table, called the waiter over, and ordered immediately,

"Buenas noches señor. Sangria litro por favor, y dos copas. Uno paella de mariscos, unas chuletas con pimiento verde asado, y patatas fritas, uno gaseosa de naranja, et uno caña, gracias."

(That's a litre jug of sangria with two glasses, one seafood paella, lamb chops with a roasted green pepper and chips, a fizzy orange and a small beer. Just what the doctor ordered I do believe!)

The meals were absolutely delicious, and we rounded the evening off with zillionaire's cheesecakes and ice cream, followed by the customary complimentary Limoncellos. *Yuk!* Plus, I suppose all along I'd been expecting an outrageous bill at the end of the evening anyway. After all, Las Ramblas isn't just the most interesting street in the world, its also probably one of the most expensive. When I asked for '*la cuenta*' therefore, I guess I was really quite surprised when it was handed across to me at '*only €86.50*'. Hey ho, it *was* just a one-off. *Special day, special treat,* as they say in Barcelona. Or at least, *I do!* I paid on my card, said '*muchos gracias*' to the waiter, and we took our leave, ambling slowly back up Las Ramblas towards the Metro station at Plaça Catalunya. After buying two more €1.50 '*green line*' tickets we took the Metro back to Sants Estácio, took the escalator up to street level, and wandered off through the chilly night air, back up the narrow little side streets to our hotel. We chatted to each other incessantly along the way, mainly about how the following day was likely to pan out. I'd said that there was no way we were going to attempt to catch the early flight to Malaga, that simply wasn't practical, given the logistics of what we had ahead of us. So we'd aim for the evening flight. But because of it being Friday the 23rd of December and all that, it was inevitably going to be stupidly busy everywhere, so we'd have to get ourselves going pretty early in the morning, find somewhere suitable to park the truck up at the airport, secure our tickets, and just spend the rest of the day milling around the duty-free shops waiting for our departure slot. As we prepared ourselves for bed that night, safely back in our cosy little room on the third floor, Helen asked me what time it might be best to set the alarm for, and I suggested maybe 6am, the same time that the little café next door opened for breakfast. She argued that 7am was a far more sensible time, so we compromised on 6.30am, settled ourselves down on our crisp, white, comfy pillows, and kissed one another goodnight.

CHAPTER EIGHTEEN

'*What's that bloody jangling noise clanging away in my ear right now?*' I thought, and dragged myself groggily out of my deep and comfortable slumber. '*Oh yeah, I guess it must be morning already then!*'

"Morning honey," said Helen cheerfully, "sleep well?"

After opening my eyes and sitting up with a yawn, I answered, "No idea sweetie, I was fast asleep! So yeah, I guess I must've done, thanks. What time is it?"

"Half past six on the dot, exactly as agreed," she replied, and then continued rather excitedly, "and guess what? *We're going on holibobs!!* Come on, get yaself up and dressed, let's go get some brekkie."

We showered and dressed, packed our bags up, then left them sat on the bed whilst we trundled off along the corridor to the tiny little lift, which, *eventually*, took us down to reception. As we passed by I mentioned that we were just popping along to the café for a brief while, we'd be back shortly for our bags, and the concierge raised one hand from behind his newspaper in acknowledgement. We stepped out onto the narrow little pavement, turned to our left, and headed off towards the little café just a few doors up. The air was chilly, and it looked as though a bit of a wind had got up too, but at least it was dry; we hoped it would stay that way, at least for the next few days. The little side street was very busy with traffic, as well as pedestrians, and as we entered the tiny little backstreet café, initially we couldn't find a single vacant table, the place was packed full and buzzing with atmosphere. Just as we were about to walk out again, two smartly dressed businessmen, who'd been sitting at a table nearest the front window, got up to leave, and we grabbed their seats immediately and plonked ourselves down. Straight away a young waitress came over, wiped the table over with a damp cloth, and asked us what we would like,

"Buenos dias señorita," I began, trying my very best to remember my extremely limited knowledge of the Spanish language, "huevos fritos con beicon, brindis con mantequilla y mermelada, y café con leche por favor. Dos iguales, gracias."

"Okay," the young waitress replied in perfect English. "Bacon and eggs, toast with butter and marmalade, and coffee. Two of the same."

She grinned and continued, "Is there anything else I can get you, sir, madam?"

I laughed and said, "Oh, and a small bottle of water each please. Where are you from exactly?"

"I'm originally from Madrid," she replied, "but I went to university in England. In a place called Bristol, I don't suppose you know it?"

"No, not really," I lied back to her with a wink and a smile. "I went there once," I continued, "sailed up the Avon Gorge and right into the city centre on a scruffy old ex-navy ship, but we only stayed for the one night, so I can't really say I know the place."

"Its a beautiful city," she continued, "I spent three wonderful years there, living in Clifton. I only moved to Barcelona a year ago, but I really miss Bristol, I had a great time there, and that's where all my friends still live, back in Clifton. I'm hoping to go back and see them all soon, just for a holiday, but right now I have to work here, all over Christmas. And New Year too. its *SO* expensive over here, this is the only way I can afford to pay my rent. And I share with three others too!"

"Oh," I said, "well good luck here in Barca, and I hope you get back to see your friends in England very soon. Could we have some sal y pimienta, y vinagre balsámico por favor?"

"Sí señor, of course," she replied and hurried off back towards the kitchen.

"*Chris!!*" Helen hissed at me scornfully. "That was a bit rude wasn't it? You cut her off really abruptly then! She sounds like ever such a nice girl, and really interesting too!"

"Yeah, I know," I replied, half apologetically. "And to be honest, I probably could have sat and chatted to her all day. But we don't have all day babe! I've got a lot going on in my head at the moment, and all I want right now is to get ourselves done and gone. So, no offence intended all round, but we've got a plane to catch, remember, and we don't even have any tickets for it yet!"

"Okay hun, you're forgiven," she said, a little more relaxed. "Let's just hope today goes entirely according to plan then. *Unlike a couple of other days I can think of over the past week!*"

'Hmmm . . .' I thought to myself, '*that'll be the "Make-It-All-Up-As-You-Go-Along" plan then!*' Hey ho, here we go, fingers and toes all crossed, *yet again!*

The nice friendly young waitress brought our breakfasts over to our table, balsamic vinegar included, and as we got stuck into them we'd both agreed that they were pretty damned delicious. For some reason, I've no idea why, but I've always much preferred Spanish bacon to English. Who knows, maybe its simply down to the way they cook it; but their coffee always seems to taste far better than English coffee too. We finished up and asked for la cuenta por favor, whereupon, most unusually for me, I made a little bit of a show in front of Helen about leaving a half decent tip for the young girl. The bill came to €15.20, and as we stood up and pulled our jackets back on ready to leave, I placed a €20 note inside the bill folder, called out '*muchos gracias señorita*' across the room to her, and cheerfully waved '*adios*' as we left. We then retrieved our bags from our hotel room, and checked out at reception simply by handing the room key back. We then strolled back around the narrow little streets until reaching the wide open expanse of Plaça de Sants, then walked purposefully across the lawns towards the wide front entrance to Barcelona's main railway station. We headed across to the left-hand corner of the building, skirted around the end of the red and white vehicle control barrier at the bottom of the massive, heavy duty spiralled concrete ramp, and took the footway back up to the roof, where we found the little Foden still parked up, and thankfully, seemingly untouched. We climbed aboard, settled our bags and ourselves, and I started her up. There were clearly visible signs pointing towards the salida, or exit, but I couldn't see anything anywhere in the way of a pay station; so we just drove, very slowly, keeping a careful lookout, towards the '*DOWN*' ramp. Nothing transpired along the way, and so we took to the ramp, steadily spiralling downwards, whilst assuming that we'd have to enter a card somewhere into a pay slot when we reached the control barrier at the bottom. However, upon reaching the barrier at the bottom of the ramp, to our amazement we found it to be already raised, and our exit ahead was entirely clear. Although, to say that it was *entirely* clear was not altogether true. There were even more people and taxis, and drop-offs and pick-ups and tourists, milling around taking photos of one another, than there had been the day before. However, slowly but steadily, we managed to safely edge our way through them all, eventually making off down the esplanade that ran along the southern side of the station, and led us towards the main westerly road out of Barcelona, heading in the direction of the AutoPista that leads towards Barcelona's *él* Prat airport.

"*Well, wha'da'ya know?*" I said joyfully to Helen. "Free parking for the night, right in Barcelona's city centre, who would've guessed it?"

"I'm not entirely sure it should've been free," she replied, "maybe security were just off shift or something? Or maybe they'd just forgotten to lower the barrier after the previous vehicle left?"

"Or maybe it was simply a genuine Christmas concession, who knows? After all, today is the very last working day before the dreaded X-word. Anyway, all I know is we got lucky. Let's go see if we can get lucky with parking at the airport too, you never know, we might even be able to wangle the next one *FOC* as well."

"Wishful thinking I reckon," was Helen's response, "although you're the expert, I'm sure you know best."

I returned her gaze, and began to mimic Manuel from Faulty Towers: "*H'i know nuuthing, h'i from Barthelona!* Anyway babe, that's pretty much the truth of it, you know I'm just making this all up as we go along, don't ya?"

"Yeah, but I know you," she smiled confidently, "you're making it all up *intelligently.*"

"Hmm, we'll see, eh!" I said, and began to concentrate more on which lane I was supposed to be driving in.

We followed the B10 along past Port Vell, and as Helen stared across in awe at the huge array of luxury cruise ships, all moored up within a ten minute walk from the bottom end of Las Ramblas, we joined the C31, the Autovia de Castelldefels, which took us, thankfully toll-free, just the fifteen minute drive to Aeropuerto él Prat de Llobregat's Terminal Numero Uno. After driving straight past all the signs pointing towards '*arrivals*', '*departures*' and '*car rentals*', etc, we continued along the outer ring road for several more hundred yards, after which we came across a large sign pointing off to the left reading '*ESTÁCIONAMIENTO COMERCIAL*'. '*Hmmm...*' I thought, '*I'm sure I saw a similar sign somewhere near Sant Station! Doesn't say anything about it being free though! Oh well!*' We turned in and drove up to the first vehicle control barrier, which immediately raised itself, allowing us to continue onwards to a second barrier, adjacent to which was a small security office, much like a Portakabin, with a sign above the single glazed window clearly stating *'SEGURIDAD'*. I thought it best to go have a proper one-on-one conversation with security, and so I applied the brake, switched off the engine, grabbed my passport from my kit-bag, jumped down from the cab and walked around the front of the truck to the small window, which had by then been slid open by whomever was inside. I addressed the uniformed security guard with a polite *'buenos dias señor'*, showed him my passport, and explained to him, once again in my very best Spanglish, that my wife and I were flying down to Malaga for a few days, and would it be okay for us to leave our lorry here for a short while, *por favor?* I'd looked around the lorry park on our way in, and noticed two things about it. Firstly, it was absolutely massive, a whole kilometre long at least I would guess; but it wasn't particularly wide, so hopefully not too far to walk to the rear entrance of *'departures'*, which we could clearly see a short distance across the Tarmac just beyond the security office. And secondly, it was virtually empty, and I didn't really know whether that was a good thing or a bad thing. Either way, it didn't seem to make any difference to the security guy, all he wanted to know was how many nights we wanted to park up for. *'Tres noches por favor'*, I had said to him, explaining that we would be flying back sometime on the coming Monday the 26th. He said that was no problem, tapped some digits into the keyboard of his computer, and a small machine to one side of it printed out yet another little white ticket. As he handed it over to me, he informed me that, upon our return, I needed to insert it into the pay machine just inside the terminal building, and pay by credit card before exiting, whereupon we'd be issued with a further ticket which would allow us to exit the lorry park. Bien, all understood señor. He then proceeded to suggest that we pull up somewhere halfway between his office and the entrance to departures, because we'd have to walk back to his little office once parked. The commercial parking rules demanded that, once we'd left our vehicle for the specified duration, we were required to leave our door and ignition keys behind the desk at security, as well as any alarm details if appropriate, just in case. Not that our little old Foden had any such modern-type gadgets aboard anyway. *'But just in case of what exactly?'* I questioned, although I didn't actually get an answer to that one. Or at least, if I did, I certainly didn't understand what it was. Never mind, *'rules is rules'!* I then informed Señor Security Guard that, *'just in case'* we have any issues with purchasing tickets, we'll be leaving everything here for the time being, and once we've secured our tickets, we'll be back to sort out our kit, lock up as best we see fit, and *then* we'll hand over the keys. '*Este bien señor?*' GOOD! I jumped back into the cab, fired up the engine, and after the security barrier had been raised, swung the truck around behind the security office, and pulled it up neatly into a space clearly numbered '*155*'. I switched off, threw my passport back into my kit-bag, which I slung over my shoulder, and jumped down onto the Tarmac. Helen grabbed her handbag and climbed down too, then I locked the cab up and off we wandered, across the virtually empty lorry park, and in through the double fully glazed doors that opened automatically directly into the rear section of departures. And luckily for the both of us, immediately adjacent to the twin entrances to the servicios *(toilets). Hoorah!*

Following which we took a few moments to get our bearings, and to adjust to the hustle and bustle of the crowds, but after a minute or so of gazing around the vast open expanse of Terminal One, we very soon spotted exactly what we were looking for. In actual fact, it wasn't as if it was difficult to spot, you couldn't really miss it to be fair. At one end of the terminal building was a long rank of car rental offices, probably a dozen or so in total, most of which had customers queueing at their various service counters. Adjacent to the car rental offices was sited a Starbucks coffee lounge, with a long queue of customers waiting to reach the single checkout till, and a large comfortably arranged seating area, most of which was already fully occupied. And right opposite the coffee lounge was a long brightly illuminated counter with four computer terminal positions directly behind it, each of which was fully manned by busy and efficient looking staff, all of whom were smartly dressed in matching pale blue uniforms. And fixed right in the centre of the high white painted wall above, running the full length of the row of counter positions, was a bold illuminated sign which clearly read IBERIA AIRWAYS. In addition to the bright long sign, fixed centrally immediately above it was a large digital clock, the bright yellow LED numbers of which clearly displayed 09.20 against their matt black background. Three of the counter positions were occupied with other customers, but one was vacant, and as we stepped up towards the attractive young lady behind the counter, who appeared to be wearing the identical uniform to that of the company's cabin crew, including the smart little hat with the Iberia logo embroidered on the front, I turned to Helen and said,

"This shouldn't be too difficult babe. We have to check in a minimum of one hour before flight time, or so I was informed, but as it stands, we're actually more than eight hours before, so I know it means we've got some waiting around to do, but hey, better early than late eh? So hopefully we'll be somewhere near the front of the ticket queue, fingers crossed."

"And toes!" Helen responded.

The first thing I noticed, standing to one side on top of the counter, was a little framed notice declaring, *'Here We Speak English'*, in six different languages, English, French, German, Portuguese, Dutch and Italian. *'Hmmm...'* I thought to myself, somewhat amusingly, *'I wonder if that means that none of them speak Spanish?'* Or maybe it was just somewhat stupidly! Whatever! Still, touch wood, at least I wouldn't have to keep struggling to make myself understood. I placed one hand firmly on the wooden counter top and addressed the young service agent,

"Good morning miss. Please can I purchase two economy tickets for this evening's 17.45 flight to Malaga, returning back here to Barcelona next Monday the 26th on the 15.45 afternoon flight, muchos gracias."

"I'm very sorry sir," the agent replied politely, "this evenings 17.45 flight is already fully booked."

"Oh MIERDA!" I turned to Helen and shouted in Spanish. *"Now what are we bloody well gonna do? I'm not bloody well driving down there, its more than six hundred sodding miles!"*

"Its okay sir, its okay! Hopefully there is no need for you to worry yourself. It is because of the English holiday period that this flight was fully booked some time ago, so Iberia Airways have laid on a second flight for this evening. The departure time of this extra flight will be one hour later, at 18.45 hours, arrival time in Malaga will be 20.00 hours. I hope you might find this acceptable sir, as we do still have just a few tickets available, but I think they will all be sold very soon."

"Phew!! Well done Iberia!" I breathed a big sigh of relief and calmed down a little. "We'll take two of those right now please, consider that a definite booking. What about the return flight for the Monday?"

"Again sir, I am very sorry, but the 15.45 flight from Malaga to Barcelona on that day is also completely sold out; and that's the only scheduled flight there is for that day, I'm afraid the morning flight had to be cancelled. However, there is a morning flight for the following day, 09.00 hours Tuesday the 27th, arriving in Barcelona at 10.15 hours, and again sir, we still have a few tickets remaining."

"Excellent, we'll take two of those as well please. *Sold to the young English couple over here with the very large boat on the very small lorry!"*

"I beg your pardon sir?" the confused young agent asked.

"Never mind," I replied, *"just ask the Phoenix.* Anyway, so that's two returns to Malaga, how much will that be por favor?"

The smart young agent tapped away at the keys on her computer's keyboard, and after half a minute or so, she looked up and said,

"Okay, I confirm now for you sir. So, that's two economy tickets, Barcelona to Malaga today at 18.45 hours, returning Malaga to Barcelona 09.00 hours Tuesday the 27th, that'll be a total of €1448.00 please. How would you like to pay?"

"Shit the bed!!" I exclaimed rudely, turned to Helen and said, *"D'you have any idea exactly how much that is in real money babe?!!?"*

"I do," she replied. "By today's rate that works out to £964.00, which, to be honest, given the time of year and how busy everything is, I don't think is all that bad. *PLUS, its available!!* So please hun, just get your card out and hand it across to the nice lady, *quickly,* before they've all sold out!"

I did exactly as I was told, immediately, *for once,* and the pretty young agent behind the counter processed it, looked very briefly at our names in our passports for proof of ID, then handed them back along with my card. She then pressed another series of keys on her keyboard, and a moment later there was a *whirr, whirr, click* from a small box next to her computer, and she handed across four neatly folded flight tickets. She then said,

"Thank you for your custom sir, madam. Please check in at counter number 36 at least one hour before your flight, pass through security, then keep an eye on the screens for your departure gate number. Have a good flight, and good day to you both. Siguiente cliente por favor."

"Chances are," Helen started, as soon as we stepped away from the Iberia flight desk, "that if we'd flown direct from Bristol to Malaga for Christmas, and then back again on Boxing Day, I expect it would've cost roughly about the same amount anyway, if not more. And if we hadn't picked on Malaga, then the chances are we would've flown somewhere else, probably at even *double* the cost. So all in all I reckon we're doing pretty good so far. *Plus, YAY, we've got our tickets, Malaga here we come!* Oh, and another thing," she continued, "I promise, as soon as we get back home to Bristol, once I've been paid at the end of this month, I'll go halves with you on the cost of the flights. Sound fair?"

"That sounds more than fair sweetheart, thank you very much," I said genuinely, wrapped my arms around her and kissed her lovingly on the forehead. "Best I give our Mandy a call then, and confirm our flight times to her, I'm sure she'll be just as excited as we are, we've not seen her in almost a year."

"Yeah, and don't I bloody well remember it!" Helen stated mockingly. "Last New Year's Eve in fact, the three of us together in the Railway Tavern in Fishponds, and how drunk were you exactly?"

"*ME??*" I exclaimed in protest. "Come on babe, it wasn't like it was *only* me, now was it? It was all three of us! And if I remember rightly, you were the first one up on the dance floor, Mandy was the very last one *off* it, and halfway through the evening I landed with a painful *thump* on the floor after attempting to dance on the tables with Trevor."

"Yeah, but at least you managed to keep all your clothes on all night though," she giggled, "unlike our Trev! Then Mandy stayed over at ours, and the three of us woke up together in the lounge later the next day with the biggest hangovers we'd ever had in our lives. *Bloody Tequila Slammers!* Great party though, or at least I think it was, *from what little I can remember!*"

"Yeah, it was indeed babe, and if I remember rightly too," I continued, "Mandy was supposed to fly back to Malaga the day after that, but somehow she managed to miss her flight. Luckily she'd only stayed over at ours for the one night, so it wasn't like it was our fault or anything, but I seem to remember feeling rather shocked when I bumped into her in the Shakespeare Tavern a couple of days later, and she was *still* having a right old moan about some taxi company or another having not turned up after she'd already pre-booked them."

"Hmm, possibly six and half a dozen, and all that malarkey maybe?" Helen sniggered. "Anyway, talking of missing flights, you need to call Mandy and tie all these details up nice and firmly with her, and double-check she's okay with it all. And I need to repack our overnight bags yet again. We need to get some of our smart clothes out; if we're having Christmas dinner with friends we should make the effort to look our best for the day. So if you wouldn't mind, can you grab the suitcases down out of the boat again please?"

"No problem hun," I replied, "that was always my intention anyway."

We'd wandered back across the rear commercial lorry park whilst we'd been chatting, and as we'd approached our little Foden transporter I'd noticed that a lot more vehicles had driven in. Whilst it was probably still around three quarters empty, it was clear that during the course of the day, and maybe even more so after work hours had finished later that evening, the lorry park would steadily be filling up. Not that I was bothered in any way, it was absolutely *huge!* I unstrapped the ladder from underneath the Phoenix's trailer and propped it securely against the boat's starboard rubbing strake. I then climbed up, and one at a time I lifted our suitcases out of the Phoenix's wheelhouse, carried them back down the ladder, and laid them neatly, side by side, on the rear sloping section of the flatbed. I then unlocked the cab, grabbed our overnight bags, and sat them down either side of the two suitcases. It was still quite windy, but it was dry, it was reasonably warm, and every now and again, the sun peeked out from behind another large white cloud; so I'd figured Helen wouldn't have any problem doing an outdoors clothes swap over, and I left her to it whilst I wandered around the truck, kicking the tyres one by one as I went. I pulled my phone out of my pocket and dialled Mandy's mobile number. She answered it almost immediately. She was really pleased to hear from me, and even more pleased when I told her that we'd got to Barcelona okay. And when I told her that we'd managed to sort out our flights to Malaga okay, she screamed down the phone with delight, shouting *'YIPPEE, YIPPEE!'* at the top of her voice. I had to tell her to calm down and listen, because the flight times were important. *'You know all about flight times, don't you my love!'* I seem to remember throwing at her somewhat sarcastically. Anyway, all being well we'd be waiting for her at the *'pick-up'* area, immediately outside the *'arrivals'* entrance at Malaga airport, at around eight thirty that evening; and if it was still okay with her, could she please drop us back to *'departures'* for seven o'clock on the following Tuesday morning. After shrieking excitedly down the phone yet again, something to do with the fact that we'd be staying over for four nights, instead of the three that I'd initially suggested, she said that would be absolutely perfect, and she'd look forward to picking us up later on that same evening. I said *'looking forward to it very much too me old mucker, see you very soon',* and hung up. I strolled back around to the rear of the truck, where Helen informed me that she'd successfully finished the clothing swap, and could I close the lids of the suitcases please, and put them back up in the boat.

I asked her if she'd remembered to pack the box of crackers that she'd bought specially from John Lewis's, to which she'd replied *'yes, of course I did, along with your crazy Hawaiian Christmas shirt and matching tie!'* I said *'well done chick, good stuff',* closed down the suitcase lids, and carried them one by one back up the ladder. I placed them tidily against the locked cabin door in the wheelhouse, made sure that everything else was neatly in place, and then securely fastened the tonneau cover back down, double-checking that it was properly fixed all the way around. I then slid back down the ladder, and strapped it down securely on top of the flatbed underneath the trailer. I then checked the cab, made sure that everything we needed had been packed, and nothing of any importance was left on view, then locked her up. I told Helen to wait by the Foden with the two overnight hold-alls, slung my kit-bag over my shoulder, and ambled the short distance back across the Tarmac to the security office. I tapped on the glass window, and Señor Security Guy inside slid it to one side and said '*Sí, que?*' I handed over the Foden's door and ignition keys, keeping the remaining keys safely in my pocket. I wrote down the make and registration number, with '*sin alarma*' in brackets, as well as my name and my mobile phone number, on the small paper tag that he handed me. He then tied the tag to the keys with the length of string that was attached to it, and hung them up on one of more than a thousand numbered hooks, fixed into a board that was attached to the rear wall, above a row of desks that ran the whole length of the Portakabin-style security office. My keys had quite clearly been hung up on hook number 155, the number of the parking space that we were occupying, and I wondered at that moment in time just exactly how much in the way of '*security*' that provided you for your money. Not that I had any idea how much the parking was likely to cost, although I was sure I could've found out easily enough if I'd've bothered to read the information printed on the sign fastened to the front of the pay point machine just inside the rear entrance to the main terminal building. But I didn't bother! To be honest, I didn't really want to know. I had no choice but to park there anyway, so I figured I'd just swallow the cost, whatever would be would be, and I'd just find out when I shoved the little white card into the machine upon our return. I sauntered back to the Foden, walked all around it one more time, just to make doubly sure I was happy with the way I'd left every-thing, then Helen and I both hoisted up our overnight bags and trundled off back into Terminal One's departures lounge.

I'd taken hundreds of flights over the years, some good, some bad, and I suppose I'd even considered myself to be a '*frequent flyer*' by then. It still never ceased to bother me though when every time I approached an air-port somewhere, I'd look up and see that massive sign saying '*TERMINAL!*' Always a worry!! *Hey ho!* We weaved our way steadily through the crowds until we found a small, reasonably quiet seating area, only about half of which was occupied, and each grabbed ourselves a comfy armchair to sit in. I looked over my shoulder at the wall clock directly above the Iberia Airways desk, and noted it clearly saying 11.44. I turned to Helen and smiled, then relaxed completely, safe in the knowledge that everything was totally sorted, and the next few days would be pretty much out of my hands. I didn't need to concentrate on much from now on, at least until we arrived back here again, so I could simply relax, enjoy some good times with great company, and simply watch the world go by, soaking up whatever it had to throw at us. I closed my eyes and started to picture the Phoenix, sat there, bobbing about in the sunshine, whilst tied up securely to her new little mooring, just off Ses Salines in Fornells Bay. It was a wonderful image. Until, suddenly, the *world* threw something at me. As I opened my eyes, I realised it wasn't the world at all, it was just Helen, and all she'd thrown at me was a rolled up pair of socks.

"*Wake up!*" she half shouted at me. "Those aren't my socks, they belong in your bag, not mine. Plus, I'm hot, I really can't be doing with wearing this jacket anymore, I need to take it off."

"I know you're hot babe" I responded, tongue in cheek, "*all* my mates keep telling me that!"

She just ignored me, then continued,

"I think we should go and check in right now. I know we could leave it for another six hours if we wanted to, but firstly, we'll most likely avoid the queues if we go now; and secondly, we could really do with dumping these bags off. It'd make it so much easier for us to carry our jackets around, which I know we need to keep with us. Plus, as per usual, my bag's way loads heavier than yours. Can we, please?"

"Yep, of course we can babe, that's a damned good idea," I replied. "Let's just double-check first that we haven't left anything inside them that we might need for the flight, then we'll go and check in and get shot of them 'til Malaga."

"I already double-checked all that hun," she said, "unless of course you want to chuck the CD player in your kit-bag so that you can listen to some more Daniel O'Donnell songs on the plane? I've got some earphones you can borrow?"

"No, that's okay darling," I replied, "I'd rather spend an hour in the dentist's chair than listen to that! Just leave it in your hold-all for now; although, glad though I am that you didn't leave it in the cab of the lorry, you should've just shoved it in one of the suitcases."

"There wasn't enough room!" she stated adamantly, "dirty, *diesel smelling* clothes seem to take up a lot more space than clean clothes do!"

"Hmm," I said, frowning a little, "once we get over to our apartment in Tamarindos, I'll see if I can rearrange everything completely differently, so that you no longer need to worry about the dirty laundry side of things."

"Good move," she said, "thank you."

We both picked up our overnight bags, and lugged them halfway around the terminal building until we came across check in counter number 36. There was no queue whatsoever, as expected, however, due to it being a scheduled flight, as opposed to a charter, thankfully, the counter was already manned. As a last minute thought, I grabbed one of my little packs of Roquefort cheese from the bottom of my hold-all, and chucked it in my kit-bag. That would do me just fine for the flight. We then placed our bags on the weighing conveyor, and handed our tickets and passports over to the pretty young uniformed girl who sat behind the counter, and who, oddly enough, looked remarkably like the same pretty young girl that we had just bought the tickets from earlier that morning. She looked at our faces, then looked at our passports, checked our tickets, which had our names printed on them, then asked us nicely if we were Mr and Mrs Reason? I felt a *really* sarcastic answer coming to mind, but before I could get it out, Helen just said *'yes we are, and yes we both packed our own bags, thank you'*. The young Iberia check-in agent took our bags on through, handed us back our passports, along with two new boarding passes, and politely reminded us that we still had more than six hours to wait until boarding. I didn't have a problem with that though, we'd just find a nice little café-bar somewhere, once we'd cleared through security. Clearing security hadn't proved entirely straightforward for me, but then it very rarely does. Helen had sailed straight through, no problem whatsoever, but although I'd declared all my relevant essentials; phone, belt, jacket, boots, watch, etc, and placed them all in the trays provided, they still insisted on turning my kit-bag inside out and carefully examining every single thing inside it. Including the contents of my wallet!

"*You can bloody well leave that one alone for starters . . . !*" I began, but then thought better of continuing down that route, buttoned it, and let them carry on with their job. Needless to say that all was eventually found to be satisfactory, *including,* surprisingly enough, the Roquefort cheese, and they neatly packed it all away for me, just as it had been, handed it back and said I was free to continue on my way. '*Gee, thanks a lot guys,*' I thought, but allowed the remainder of that thought to trail off somewhere into the ether. I caught up with Helen in Duty Free and said,

"We can't buy any of this stuff chick, we're not leaving the country, so our boarding passes won't authorise it."

"I know," she replied, "I'm just looking. There's no harm in looking."

"Yeah, I guess you're right," I answered back. "So, that being the case, I'm gonna wander over there and *just look* at the bar. *No harm in looking!*"

She laughed, said she'd catch up with me shortly, and could I please find a table and a menu somewhere close by, it was coming up towards lunchtime. So that's exactly what I did. And that's exactly where we stayed. Right up until our flight was called. We'd had a damned good nosh-up, *if a little expensive,* drunk our way through a whole bottle of costly red plonk, just to wash the paella down with of course, and followed it all up with a couple of pints of Estrella for me, and an extra large G&T for madam. By the time we heard *'Final call for flight number IA314 to Malaga'* over the tannoy system, if I remember correctly, Helen was beating me twelve games to nine at crib. We quickly grabbed up our carry on bags and jackets, and ended up having to leg it the last *fifty odd miles*, along travelator after travelator, down to gate number 48! We showed our boarding passes at the gate, and immediately walked straight through, out onto the Tarmac, and up the rear steps onto the small, fully packed jet liner. After jamming our jackets and bags into an overhead locker, minus the Roquefort which I'd kept safely in hand, we took up what appeared to be the last remaining pair of unoccupied seats, and fastened our seat belts.

"So, we arrive at the airport eight hours early and *still* manage to almost miss our flight? *WTF?"* said Helen, clearly still a little out of breath.

"Ahh, situation normal!" I responded calmly, peeling open the little pack of rather smelly cheese. "Anyway, I'd rather be last on than first on, I hate sitting on these damned things just waiting for everyone else to sort themselves out, especially when its one as small as this. And what's more, we'll be first off too, 'cos we're sat right at the back by the exit, so we get to spend the least amount of time possible aboard. 'Tis all good my dear."

"S'pose!" she answered grumpily.

The doors were closed and secured, the stewardess ran through a brief safety procedure, which hardly anyone appeared to take the slightest bit of notice of, then we pushed back and taxied out towards one of the main runways. Barcelona airport had two runways back in 2002, with its third still partially under construction, and we were flying on a twin-engined, medium-range Bombardier CRJ900, which had somewhat cramped seating for just eighty-nine passengers. We accelerated quickly along the runway, taking to the air just halfway down, and reached our cruising altitude of 28,000 feet after just five minutes. '*Quite an impressive little piece of kit*' I seem to remember thinking, '*if a little noisy!*' But then again, we *were* sat right at the very back, and that's exactly where both engines were mounted, slightly forward of each side of the tail fin, one right next to each ear! Still, we'd been given allocated seat numbers, it wasn't like we'd had any choice, so we simply sat back and relaxed. Helen continued reading her paperback, whilst I munched away ecstatically on my little pack of Roquefort, making it last for the whole one and a quarter hour duration of the flight. Which, in all honesty, seemed to flash by in the twinkling of an eye, and before we knew it, it was eight o'clock and we were gently touching down on the one and only runway at AeroPuerto de Malaga. By which time, Helen had *almost* finished her novel, and I'd *totally* done in my whole delicious packet of cheese. Still, at least there were two more where that one had come from!

CHAPTER NINETEEN

As there was no passport control for internal flights, the expected inevitable delay was solely at the baggage carousel, however, it wasn't too long before it sprang into life, and after a few minutes our two hold-alls both appeared. We each dragged one off the moving carousel and headed immediately for the '*arrivals*' exit. Once outside, we scanned the busy, bustling '*pick-up*' zone, only to find there was no sign of Mandy as yet. My watch said 8.25pm, we were five minutes earlier than I'd anticipated, so we dumped our bags down on the kerb and sat down on top of them. Less than a minute later we heard the loud '*beep beep*' of a car horn, along with a brief screeching of tyres, and a large, bright gold Mercedes pulled up right in front of us, dazzling us both with its headlights. Someone leapt out of the driver's door, and just as we heard this shrill voice scream '*YAY! You guys, so great to see you again, its just like WOW, this is gonna be Soooooo AMAZING!!*', we kind of guessed it was Mandy. We both scrambled to our feet, all three of us threw our arms around each other, and we jumped up and down together in a frenzied little huddle. Mandy then turned, reached into the car to open the boot, and we grabbed up our bags and threw them both inside. I slammed the boot shut and climbed into the back seat, whilst the two girls sat together in the front. Mandy reversed back a little, then slowly edged out into the steady stream of traffic that was coming and going immediately outside '*arrivals*'.

"Hey, you're absolutely bang on time guys, that's like *totally amazing!*" she began.

"Yeah, the flight was typically Spanish, as in precisely on time! Plus I'd estimated thirty minutes to disembark and collect our bags, so yeah, all good Mand; spot on time, and thanks for being here for us, you're a super-star!" I answered back.

"Actually," she continued, "I got here a bit earlier than you said, like about quarter past, but you're only allowed to stop for two minutes max at '*pick-up*', so I had to drive on around the block again when you weren't there. *Two lousy minutes mind, that's all they sodding give you!* Ha, ha, ha, actually, five times I drove around that block, then got you both on the fifth!"

"Its just so great to see you baby," Helen chipped in with, "it really is a *MASSIVE* relief getting here finally, you wouldn't believe it! *SO much crap* happened along the way, several times I honestly thought we weren't even gonna make it here at all, for real!"

"Well you're here now sweet, you can quit ya worryin' and stick ya feet up for a coupla days."

"So firstly," Mandy continued, "I'm just gonna say, the traffic's totally manic at this time of night in Malaga, especially on a Friday, so its gonna take us a while to get all the ways back through it. But, once we do, there's this really cosy little local's bar that I know, down in the square, walking distance from the house. What say we park the car up for the night and wander straight down there for a few little drinkies together. It'll be too late for dad to start socialising by the time we get back to the house anyway, and he'll have gone on up to bed by the time we get home from the bar, so I'll introduce both of you to him tomorrow morning over breakfast, I reckon that'd suit best, if it sounds okay with you's twos?"

"Sounds great all round I reckon," I answered enthusiastically, "especially the *bar* part! I can totally stop concentrating on *everything* for a few days now, so thanks a million for that Mand, what say we all go get drunk together, eh?"

"*NOT A HOPE IN HELL!!*" both Helen and Mandy yelled in unison!

"Ha, ha, ha, remember the last time we all did that?" Mandy quizzed.

"Indeed we do," Helen replied, "last New Year's Eve, my hangover lasted for several days after that, and I seem to remember you missed your flight back home?"

"I did indeed," Mandy quipped, "although I still blame those bloody B&D Taxis for not picking me up exactly when they'd said they would!"

"I still blame the Tequilas," I chipped in, "on top of the port and brandies, on top of the wine, on top of the ten pints of lager! Yeah, maybe you're both right, maybe we'll just stick to a couple of jugs of sangria for the time being?"

"*Good plan!*" they both announced, again in unison.

"Great minds . . ." I added.

Its roughly fourteen miles from Malaga airport to Mandy's dad's house, which was situated in a pretty little suburban backstreet, just half a mile or so back from the seafront. And as Mandy had rightly pointed out to us, the traffic certainly was manic, at the very least, if not considerably worse. The roads around the entire centre of town, including the long straight road along the seafront, were totally gridlocked, this being caused, at an intelligent guess, by the fact that it was *home from work* time on the final day before the Vacaciones Navidenas. *(Xmas Hols!)* Luckily for us Mandy knew her way up across the hills, then back down through the backstreets of Spain's sixth largest city, but it still took a little over an hour to reach our destination. By the time we'd parked up, I'd grabbed what I'd needed out of my kit-bag, namely my phone and my wallet, then chucked that bag in the boot along with the other bags, and Mandy had locked up and set the alarm, it was pretty much dead on ten o'clock.

"Don't be worrying about the time," Mandy ordered, "the bars around this part of town don't shut."

"Don't shut until when exactly?" I asked.

"They just don't shut!" she chortled, and off the three of us trotted, arm in arm, laughing and joking as we danced our way down towards the little square that she'd said she had in mind.

A couple of hops, skips and jumps later and the street ended abruptly at a series of cast iron bollards, beyond which was a pretty little square, with a single tall plane tree growing right at its centre, and well lit up all around its perimeter by a series of café-bars. There were illuminated Guinness signs all over the place, Harp Lager, John Smiths, Heineken, and so on. Not that I'd expected anything less, having passed through Malaga on more than one previous occasion, but I had hoped to see at least one Spanish drinks logo, such as Estrella for example, hung proudly in a corner somewhere. No such luck! Okay, well we'd just have to make our own luck then! Mandy dragged us across to the left, and the three of us danced happily through the open front doors of Murphy's Bar. There were tables and chairs placed outside each of the bars, neatly scattered around the square at regular intervals, but none of them were occupied, it was way too chilly at that time of night, so the three of us grabbed a table by the window in the corner, and as is the done thing in Spain, waited for the customary table service. By the time a waitress came over and asked us what we'd like to drink, Mandy had already introduced us to at least half a dozen of her friends, both male and female, all English, and all of whom seemed very pleasant. The waitress herself was Spanish, but Mandy introduced us to her too, and by the looks of it, they also seemed to be reasonably good friends. I knew that Mandy lived in Benalmadena, but that was only a half hour bus ride from Malaga, and although I also knew that Mandy didn't have a car of her own, I guessed she still got to visit her dad's quite regularly. Hence why she knew most of the people in Murphy's Bar. I asked the waitress, quite politely I thought, for a bucket of sangria and three straws, but Helen said *'don't be ridiculous, we'll have a jug and three glasses please!'* A few minutes later, a jug of delicious, freshly made sangria arrived at the table, and I poured out three large glass-fuls. *Oops! And there it was gone!*

"*Chlamydia! Autra litro de sangria por favor!*" I called across to the young waitress after catching her eye.

'WHACK! WHACK!' Both Helen and Mandy clouted me simultane-ously across the back of the head, Mandy staring at me evil eyed, whilst hissing sternly,

"*Her name's not 'Chlamydia' you idiot, its 'Camellia'! DON'T GET THAT WRONG AGAIN!!* And another thing; there's no need to try and speak Spanish around here, pretty much everyone that lives on this part of the Costa del Sol either *is* English, or *speaks* English. So please, *stop trying to make a fool of yaself!*"

"Okay princess, I'm sorry. Just my little joke, I'll get it right in future. So, must remember; *Waitress, Camellia. Costa del Crime, English. Got it!*"

'WHACK! WHACK!'

"Yeah, I know, I asked for that one!"

The second jug of sangria arrived, and Camellia set it down on the table with a smile. Thankfully, my little *not very funny* joke had gone straight over her head, or at least, so the three of us had hoped. Either way, the second jug didn't last particularly long either and on catching the young waitress's eye yet again, I waved over a third, which duly arrived with equal efficiency. Followed by a forth, and then a fifth! Following which,

"*Enough's already enough for enough of us already thank you please,*" mum-bled Helen. "*I'm thinks we're all just about ready for my bed now!*"

"I'm not entirely sure that's altogether a good idea my love," I said, frowning a little, "but I think I know roughly where you're coming from. What d'ya reckon Mand?"

"Yep, I's is dunnded in toos, 'tis back oop thik lane, ah reckons!"

"Come along then, ya pair o' lightweights, let's get the two of ya's back home and inta bed! Camellia, sólo la cuenta por favor, y aquí hay cincuenta euros, gracias para su hospitalidad, y buenas noches mi preciosa niña."

I left the fifty euros in cash, way more than I knew the bill would come to, sticking out from underneath the fifth empty jug that was still sat there on the table, hoisted Helen and Mandy to their feet with one arm each around my neck, bid Camellia a fond farewell, and staggered out of the doorway into the square. It had gone midnight by then, the wind had gathered in strength a little more, and it had become considerably more chilly than it had been for the stroll down there. All of which, thankfully for me, had a significant sobering effect on the two girls, and all of a sudden, thank goodness, they both found themselves able to walk. Not entirely in straight lines, but at least, to a great extent, unaided.

"What are you like, the pair of you? I dunno, one and a half jugs of sangria each and you're anyone's! Come on, let's get the pair of you safely home in one piece. Left foot, right foot, left foot, right foot, that's it girls, you're getting the hang of it!"

By the time we reached the house just a short while later, both girls had sobered up considerably, although all Mandy could manage to keep saying was, *'Shhh, don't wake dad, shhh, don't wake dad!'* Still, at least she'd managed to unlock the Mercedes successfully without setting the alarm off, and after we'd retrieved all our bags from the boot, she'd locked it up again just as efficiently, and escorted us through the front garden of the house and around the back, where she'd unlocked the back door and again repeated *'Shhh, don't wake dad!'*. We tiptoed in one by one, Mandy leading the way, and after closing and re-locking the back door she'd shown us both upstairs to our bedroom. I believe we'd managed the entire operation with adequate stealth and silence, right up until giving Mandy a huge hug, wishing her a good night's sleep, and informing her that it'd been a *very* long day for us, and we wouldn't be getting up particularly early in the morning. Whereupon, I think, that's where it all started to go wrong. Mandy said she just needed to show us where the bathroom was, before we settled into our cosy little room for the night, and as she turned to point along the corridor to the first door on the left, she slid over on the decorative little mat that adorned the bare, highly polished floorboards, and landed flat on her back with a huge '*THUD!*'

"Got it," I said, "first door on the left, thanks babe, nite nite, sleep well," and immediately closed the bedroom door.

Following which, I heard another door open noisily, and a deep voice bellowed out '*WHAT THE HELL'S GOING ON OUT THERE?*' The only discernible response I could vaguely make out to that was Mandy's weakened voice continually whispering '*Shhh, don't wake dad, shhh, don't wake dad!*' followed by the loud slamming of what sounded like the very same door. I waited half a minute, then very quietly opened the bedroom door again, just to make sure that Mandy was okay, but she'd obviously got herself up off the floor and made her way back to her own room. Cool, there was no huge pool of blood oozing its way slowly across the floorboards; in fact, not even a single dirty fingerprint on the newly painted magnolia walls, so I quietly closed the door again and began to get undressed . As I explained to Helen exactly where the bathroom was, and how to be extra-careful with the small sliding rug just outside the bedroom door, she reminded me that, thankfully, we'd packed some pyjamas for this particular trip, and we both gladly put them on. I checked I had everything with me, plugged my phone charger into a wall socket adapter, put my wallet back in my kit-bag, zipped it up and slid it under the bed, and by the time I'd climbed in and leaned across to kiss Helen goodnight, she was already completely away with the fairies. '*Nite nite my darling,*' went through my mind, just as my head hit the pillow, '*I do hope you had a most pleasant evening!*'

CHAPTER TWENTY

I suddenly opened my eyes and looked at my watch. 10.20am. Blimey, now that's what I *call* relaxed! I looked around the nicely decorated little bedroom and immediately noticed a couple of things missing. Firstly, Helen; secondly, an en-suite! Then it dawned on me, *'first door on the left, avoid the booby trapped rug!'* I climbed out of bed, wandered down the corridor, and to my delight, found the door to the bathroom left open. I could hear voices downstairs, so I had a quick wash, got myself dressed and wandered downstairs to join them. The voices were coming from the large kitchen diner, where I found everyone sat around a large, rustic, rectangular solid oak table, drinking tea and eating toast.

"Morning sleepy head", said Helen and Mandy, both in unison yet again!

"Good morning everyone," I replied politely. "Thank you very much for allowing me a bit of a lie-in, it was much needed and greatly appreciated. its been a strange old week, we appear to have gotten ourselves down here the hard way! But hey, at least we've made it. Anyway, I do hope we didn't disturb anyone when we came in last night? How's ya back Mand? Any bruises?"

"I'm fine thanks," Mandy replied with a broad grin. "Happens all the time! Anyway, Chris, say hello to my father, Brian and this is his lovely lady wife, Rita."

"Good morning Brian, good morning Rita, its a real pleasure to meet you both, and thank you both ever so much for inviting us to stay over for Christmas, it really does mean an awful lot to us."

"Its an absolute pleasure," Rita replied. "Mandy's told us *so* much about you, we've been looking forward to meeting you both for weeks, and now here we all are, the day's finally arrived."

"Arrived with a bit of a *crash* though, *didn't it!*" said Brian grumpily, looking daggers at Mandy.

He then turned to me, and with a big smile, firmly took hold of my outstretched hand and shook it vigorously. I matched his grip admirably, as he greeted me with,

"Its a genuine pleasure to meet you Christopher. Do sit, please. Rita, would you pour this young man a nice fresh cup of tea please. Mandy, you look like you need to go and lie down again for a bit. I do hope my daughter manages to guide you back home a little less worse for wear the next time you're all out together. She really can be the most dreadful influence on people sometimes!"

"I think you'll find it was my fault entirely sir. I was just so relieved to have finally got here, after what proved to be somewhat of a, how shall I say, *arduous* journey! I simply ordered one too many jugs of sangria. A little over enthusiastic on my part I think, but nothing more."

"It wasn't anyone's fault," Mandy countered grumpily. "Its that *sodding* mat on the landing, I *do* wish you'd chuck it out or something, its *horrid!*"

"Mandy, I've told you many a time," Rita replied calmly, "it was a wedding present from your dear Aunt Lily, sadly now deceased, as well you know, and that's precisely where it lives; its going nowhere, *end of story!*"

"Yes Rita! Okay Rita!" Mandy fired back in sarcastic acceptance.

With that, whilst Rita was pouring more teas all round, we all sat down around the table and had a little giggle to ourselves, after which I got stuck right into the toast and marmalade. When breakfast was done, Helen began helping Rita with the clearing away, Mandy retired to the lounge and sprawled herself comfortably across the enormous leather sofa, whilst Brian and I fell deeper and deeper into more sensible conversation. The morning wore on, and before I knew it Mandy wandered back into the kitchen, announced positively that it was now well into the afternoon, and asked if anyone fancied going out for a late lunch. I chirped up with an enthusiastic *'yes'*, Helen said *what a very good idea, I think I'll be joining you'*, Brian announced firmly that he'd be taking his regular afternoon nap as per usual, and Rita said that she had far too much to do in preparation for the following day's extravaganza, and that she'd be most obliged if we would please just leave her to it for the rest of the afternoon. *'Too many cooks and all that kinda stuff…'* The three of us climbed the stairs and went to our rooms to change into clothing better suited to the nice looking weather outside, then met back up in the kitchen afterwards. Helen asked Rita if there were any last minute things she'd like us to pick up for her whilst we were out, but she said *'no, she didn't think so'*, although she'd ring Mandy's phone if anything came to mind. Then Brian chipped in with *'any chance you could bring us back some fish 'n' chips for tea please?'*

"Yes, of course we will," I replied. "What time do you like to have tea?"

"Tea's at eight o'clock," Mandy said flatly. "Tea's *always* at eight o'clock!"

"Eight o'clock please," Brian requested, just as we were about to walk out via the back door.

"Will do, 8pm, 2xF&C's coming up!" Mandy shouted back.

As we walked back around the side of the house and through the front garden towards the road, I noticed, for the first time, just how large the house was. It wasn't like a mansion or anything, in fact, it blended in very subtly and very nicely with all the other large, detached houses, set back from the road by their front gardens, in what I would normally describe as middle-class, affluent suburbia. In actual fact, it was really very, very lovely; well appointed, well decorated and well kept. And at a rough guess, I'd say worth a bob or two as well. What I found a little odd though, was the fact that, despite its obvious air of affluence, if you just happened to be walking along this street from one end to the other, not knowing or caring where you were particularly, I doubt you'd even notice it was there at all. Anonymity, that's precisely what it boasted. *A gracious air of anonymity!* I knew Mandy's dad was retired, but I had no idea what he'd done for a living before he'd retired, all I knew was that he'd worked for a while in Bristol, and he'd moved over here shortly after separating from Mandy's mum. So I asked,

"I'm guessing your dad was pretty successful back in the days when he was working Mand, what profession was he in exactly?"

"He was a jeweller," she replied casually. "He had his own jewellery shop, mostly selling gold and watches and stuff like that. He's still got a decent selection of gold chains back at the house, locked away in the safe. I expect he'll get them out later and show them to you, he's very proud of his collection. He'll probably even try to sell you one; beware of that mind, he's a pretty damned good salesman."

"Great, so am I," I replied boastfully. "I'll look forward to it."

'Hmmm...I guess that explains the anonymity then!' I immediately thought to myself.

So, *how* beautiful exactly? Saturday the 24th of December, Christmas Eve, beautiful blue skies and sunshine. *Proper sunshine!* One or two of the shops along the street that's one block back from the main seafront road were still open. The first one I noticed was the pharmacy, mainly because of its prominent little green and white wall sign hanging over the pavement above the door. Opposite the pharmacy was an ironmongers, which was closed, but adjacent to that was a small, posh looking hotel, and immediately above the hotel's main entrance was a large projecting LED sign, the numbers on which flashed alternatively from time to temperature. The time read 14.20. *Correct,* I'd thought, seeing as I was wearing my watch. *However,* when the numbers changed over to temperature, they read 21. *Twenty-one degrees! Mainland Spain! At Christmas! T-shirt weather! YAY!!* So that's exactly what we were all wearing, shorts and T-shirts. I couldn't believe we'd even bothered packing any! Apparently though, unbeknown to me, Helen had called Mandy shortly before we'd left Bristol, specifically to ask her about the weather, and also, I guess, to chat about other girlie stuff. As in the all important finer details that us blokes always manage to gloss over when organising things. Anyway, I was very glad she had, and glad to be wearing some proper summer clothes for a change too. What a huge contrast to central France! It actually felt like we were on holiday for real, and I hadn't felt quite like that since the last time I'd taken the family over to Menorca. Next we passed a small mini mart which was still open, followed by a very English-looking fish and chip shop, which wasn't; after which Mandy brought me back down to earth with a bit of a bump,

"Don't count on this weather stopping around for too long mind," she said, "its *really, really* changeable at the moment. This time yesterday it was only half as warm as this, and cloudy for most of the day too, and its entirely possible it could be raining tomorrow, we never know what its gonna do this time of year."

"Who cares," I exclaimed, bright and cheerfully, "'*live for today*', that's my motto! Let's go play on the beach. Come on girls, I fancy an ice cream, wha'd'ya reckon?"

"Yay, let's do it!" Helen chirped up with equal enthusiasm.

"Hey Mand, I don't suppose you've any idea what time that little mini mart back there shuts, do you?" I asked.

"I do," she replied. "Same time as the fish and chip shop shuts. Why?"

"No matter," I said, "just a thought. Anyway, what time does the fish and chip shop shut?"

"Whatever time they run out of fish and chips!" she replied with a laugh.

We crossed the street, walked down a tree lined series of steps in between two buildings, crossed the main seafront road at a set of pedestrian lights, and strolled playfully, all three of us hand in hand, down the wooden slatted walkway onto the warm, yellow sandy beach. A quarter of a mile along to the right we could see Malaga's main port and ferry terminal, and when we looked to the left there was nothing but a beautiful expanse of golden sand, stretching out before us for almost as far as the eye could see. A hundred yards or so directly ahead, and looking wonderfully inviting, was the flat calm, shimmering, azure blue Mediterranean Sea. I needed to paddle! I pulled off my trainers and jogged across the warm sand until I reached the water, splashing through the tiniest of waves until I was right up to my shins! '*Hmm, not quite as warm as it looks*', I thought, '*but not too bad for this time of year. Certainly swimmable, almost! Not that I'm going to bother, but it'd be nice if the Med around Menorca is as warm as this too when we get there.*' Clearly neither of the girls were bothered about splashing in the sea, so I jogged back across the beach, retrieving my trainers along the way, and rejoined them just as they were wandering across the open terrace of a beachfront café-bar.

"The Milky Bars are on me!" I called out happily.

So we chose a table on the terrace, right next to the sandy beach, in the sunshine, facing the sea, and that's exactly where we stayed for the remainder of the afternoon. We ate ice creams and drank cafés con leche, and snacked on small tapas dishes of jamón y queso, and chatted about Bristol and England and France and Spain and Menorca, and the world in general, until the sun began to sink slowly towards the hills beyond the port, and it started to go off a little chilly.

"Okay girls," I announced with an air of authority, "'*tis sangria time again!* But there's a new rule for today. We make just the one jug last between the three of us until its time to go get the fish and chips."

"I'll go along with that!" said Helen, and Mandy agreed too. "I didn't know we were *all* going to have fish and chips for tea though, although I'm happy to go along with that idea too."

"This is Malaga," Mandy chortled, "you *have* to have fish and chips when you come to Malaga, its the *law!* Right, I know a nice little bar back up on Main Street, its another cosy little local's bar, and they do a really good sangria too. Shall we go?"

I asked the waiter for la cuenta, settled up with the smallest of tips, and we look our leave, walking back across the seafront road and up the little tree lined steps. We turned right, towards the fish and chip shop, then immediately right again and through the front entrance of a typical-looking town pub, which appeared to be somewhat busy. In actual fact it was heaving, but the girls managed to find a table hidden away in a corner somewhere near the back, whilst I fought my way towards the bar in search of some service. Upon reaching the front it dawned on me exactly why the place was so busy, and why the majority of the customers appeared to be speaking English; on the wall directly behind the service counter, in large, brightly lit neon lettering, it read LINEKER'S BAR. '*Hey ho, I suppose there has to be a first time for everything!*' I thought. I asked the young waiter behind the counter if he'd kindly knock up a nice jug of sangria and bring it across to the table over in the corner, along with three glasses, muchos gracias. What seemed like an age later he duly obliged, and set the jug down, along with the glasses and the bill. And what seemed like yet another age later I settled the bill, and felt considerably relieved to be leaving. Not that I have any issue with Lineker's Bars per se, its just that they're not really my cup of tea. Or should I say glass of sangria? Pint of Guinness more like, *me thinks!* Anyway, no matter, the sangria was delicious anyway, but it was getting on towards fish and chips time, so thankfully we'd left. Helen and Mandy headed for the fish and chip shop, I said I'll have the same please, and headed off into the little mini mart. I bought three of the largest boxes of chocolates I could lay my hands on, all totally different; three cards, some shiny gift wrap paper, and a small roll of sellotape. The lady behind the till put them all in an extra large carrier bag for me, and then I wandered back into the fish and chip shop. I would have waited for the girls outside, but it had gone off decidedly cold. Plus, we had two hundred miles to go, it was dark, and we were wearing *sunglasses! No, actually*, in all honesty, I was still only dressed in shorts and a T-shirt, we all were, and so I just waited inside.

"What's in the bag? Helen asked.

"Never you mind!" was my whispered reply.

"I'll tell you what's in mine if you tell me what's in yours." Mandy added.

"I know exactly what's in yours," I answered her back, "five portions of fish and chips. Come on let's get gone, your dad'll be wanting his tea any mo, as will I."

"Me too", they both responded, yet again in unison.

We walked, a little more briskly this time, back to the house, where Rita had already laid out five place settings on the solid oak dining table. The three of us popped upstairs to change into something more appropriate, and when we sat ourselves back down ready for tea, as it so happened, it had just turned eight o'clock precisely.

"Well done guys," said Brian, "absolutely perfect timing."

I had to admit, the fish and chips were pretty damned delicious. Not quite as good as a couple other places I could mention mind you. Brixham, Padstow and St Peter Port in Guernsey immediately spring to mind. However, they were pretty damned good nevertheless. After Helen and Mandy cleared the table and washed up, the remainder of the evening was spent curled up on the large array of leather sofas in the enormous lounge, the five of us chatting together, whilst Brian and I tried one or two little samples from his expensive collection of exotic brandies. A little later I asked Rita politely if there was anything she needed doing ready for the following day, and when she said '*no, everything was all just tickety-boo thanks*', I excused myself, leaving the other four halfway through an old Clint Eastwood movie, and headed on up to our bedroom to wrap up the chocolates and write the cards. Helen came on up half an hour later, just as I'd finished and packed everything back in the carrier, saying what a great movie that was, she'd not seen it before, then slipped into her pyjamas, kissed me goodnight and climbed into bed.

"What's in the bag then babe?" she asked again.

"Just a little something from Santa," I replied. "Nite nite princess, sweet dreams."

I changed into my pyjamas, then lay on the bed reading. When I was sure that Brian, Rita and Mandy had all followed on up to bed a short while later, I crept back downstairs and quietly placed the three carefully wrapped presents, each one with named cards attached, neatly underneath the tall, nicely decorated, imitation Christmas tree that adorned one corner of the lounge. I then crept back upstairs, and after carefully avoiding the booby trapped rug yet again, climbed into bed and drifted off into a deep, comfortable, dreamless sleep.

CHAPTER
TWENTY ONE

'*HO! HO! HOOOOO!!*' was the very next thing I heard. '*Bugger!*' I immediately thought, '*X-word minus zero!*' And then, still far more asleep than not, '*hang on a sec, there's no goddam chimney in this room?!*' I lay perfectly still and sneakily opened one eye. *Thank God! Or St Nicholas, or whoever!* It hadn't come from inside our room! And Helen was still fast asleep too, so that was good. But it was close by. *Very close by! And scary too*, especially when I was under the impression that we'd laid our hats in a *child-free* zone. With that, there was a sudden '*Rat-Tat-Tat*' on the door, followed by yet another, even louder '*HO! HO! HOOOOOOO!!*', which, this time, woke Helen up too. Then it dawned on me. '*Ah yes, of course, the child! Mandy!*'

"What's the time?" I shouted.

"*SANTA TIME!!*" Mandy shouted back from the landing.

"*Bah Humbug!*" I called back in return.

"Merry Christmas to you too!" she replied.

I peeked at my watch, and just hoped that it wasn't 4am in the morning or something stupid like that. I'd already had my fair share of that kind of thing over the years, I could do with having a few years off for a bit, at least until I'd got young grandchildren of my own, which wasn't likely to be happening in the *immediate* future, thank goodness. Mandy, however, hadn't had any kids of her own up until this point, so she hadn't been afforded the opportunity of enjoying that little sufferance as of yet. And what's more, she was only virtually the same age as Helen. *34! Thirty-bloody-four! I'll give you Ho, Ho, bloody Ho!*' went through my mind, but only for a brief moment, because my watch had just told me that it was almost a quarter to nine.

174

"*FELIZ NAVIDAD DARLING!*" I shouted back through the closed door. "We'll be down soon."

"You're a grumpy old sod sometimes!" Helen said scornfully, and with a modicum of sarcasm she added, "*Merry Christmas, oh happy husband of mine!*"

"*Bah Humbug!*" I replied, and climbed out of bed.

And so the day had begun. However, despite my general and fairly well known lack of enthusiasm for '*Xmas-without-kids*', by the time everyone was up, dressed and sat downstairs around the kitchen table, tea and toast in hand, one could sense the positive festive atmosphere that had by then taken a good hold of all of us. I'd managed to swap my grumpy head for a far more cheerful one, kissed Helen gently on the lips, and genuinely wished her a Happy Christmas. I'd given Mandy a big hug too, wished her the same, shook Brian's hand and kissed Rita's. After breakfast we'd all taken to the extra-comfy sofas in the lounge, apart from Mandy, who'd simply jumped up and down excitedly, exclaiming '*I'll be Santa, I'll be Santa!*'

"Oh," I said, jokingly, "best I go fetch you a glass of sherry and a mince pie then!"

"I think maybe that should wait until after dinner, don't you?" Brian replied with an air of authority.

And it did too! Mandy and her folks had all exchanged pressies with each other, there were cards all around for everyone, including Helen and I, and much surprise and delight when they'd all got around to opening the rather delicious chocolates that I'd bought the previous day. Helen handed me a card she'd brought along with her, which was very beautifully written, and we placed all of our cards upon the mantelpiece above the gas Wonderfire in the hearth. It wasn't switched on, because the house was already plenty warm enough, thanks to some wonderful oil-fired central-heating. Brian then switched on the telly and informed us politely that we were all duty bound to sit and watch the annual Queen's speech. Apparently, or so he had said, at least half of Malaga would be watching it, as everyone he knew, which was basically everyone, had UK Sky TV satellites installed; albeit, to the best of my understanding, with chipped boxes! After the Queen had said her piece, both Helen and Mandy went off to the kitchen to help Rita with finalising the preparations for dinner, whilst Brian and I sat together in the lounge discussing some of the finer points of our chosen professions. Eventually, after Mandy called through that dinner would be served up shortly, I disappeared off upstairs and pulled the box of six John Lewis

Luxury Xmas Crackers from the bottom of Helen's hold-all, and carefully positioned one to each side of the five place settings that had been lovingly arranged around the huge old table. The sixth one I'd already placed carefully back in my own hold-all, as I had another cunning little plan up my sleeve for that one, hopefully in just a few days time.

Rita had certainly excelled herself in the kitchen, she'd done herself and the rest of us proud! A Christmas dinner fit for a king indeed! Rita took her seat at the table, whilst Helen and Mandy took turns in dishing up. Prawn cocktails for starters, during which we all pulled our crackers and donned the customary colourful paper hats. Inevitably these were followed by a completely useless lightweight metal toy, plus the obligatory corny joke, '*Why can't owls breed in the rain? Because its too wet to woo!*' '*I accidentally swallowed a handful of Scrabble tiles earlier. My next bowel movement could spell disaster!*' '*What do a midget and a dwarf have in common? Very little!*' And so on. The next serving was simply divine; roast turkey with stuffing, pigs in blankets, roast potatoes and parsnips done to perfection, mashed carrot and swede, plus, of course, loads and loads of *delicious* Brussels sprouts! Topped off, it has to be said, with the most wonderful gravy, and a large dollop of cranberry sauce. As opposed to the homemade bread sauce, which I left well alone in the centre of the table! Brian had bought in a whole case of a rather fine Rioja Spanish red wine, and by the time the traditional Christmas pudding, again homemade, with brandy butter and cream, had all gone, and the table had been cleared in readiness for the exotic spread of cheeses about to follow, I'd totally lost count of how many bottles of plonk we'd managed to get through between the five of us. All I knew was that it was also, *yep, you guessed it, absolutely delicious!* As were the cheeses when they arrived. And as were the brandy floater coffees when they arrived too!

"I think I'm gonna have to use the sofa for a bit," I announced, after at least two helpings of just about everything, "I'm not sure this chair is going to hold my weight for too much longer!"

Helen and Mandy cleared the rest of the table away, and we all retired to the lounge to watch the essential Christmas early evening movie together, leaving the washing up 'til later. *Much later,* as it turned out; because I'd volunteered to do it all myself, but I ended up falling asleep on Helen's lap instead, not long after the start of its A Wonderful Life. I never was the world's greatest James Stewart fan! Still, I awoke eventually, and got stuck into the washing up as best I could manage on my still somewhat wobbly old legs. Thankfully, Helen dried and Mandy put away, which, as

I accurately and most helpfully pointed out, was precisely the correct way around to do it, on account of Helen not having the faintest idea where anything was kept. I was clever like that sometimes! The washing up seemed to have taken forever, but now that the kitchen was back to being all nice and sparkly clean again, we yet again assumed our semi-horizontal poses back in the lounge. The telly had been turned off, and Brian was standing, empty handed, next to the rather ornate drinks cabinet.

"Anyone care for a brandy?" he asked cheerfully.

"I wouldn't mind a small glass of sherry please Brian," Rita asked. "How about you two girls, I'm sure you'd both much prefer sherry to brandy wouldn't you?"

"That's a wonderful idea," said Helen, "I'd love one please."

"Spiffing!" agreed Mandy.

"Thank you Brian, a large brandy would be absolutely marvellous please," I finished up with.

Once we were all sat down comfortably, full glasses in hand, Brian turned to me and said,

"I couldn't help but notice Chris, is that a Saint Christopher that you're wearing around your neck, underneath that there crazy Hawaiian shirt?"

"Indeed it is Brian," I answered, easily lifting it out from underneath my shirt, as I'd not bothered with donning the tie, "I've worn it for years, never taken it off. its my lucky travel talisman, and so far, touch wood, up 'til now its been very good to me. Why d'you ask?"

"Well," he replied slowly, "its just that . . . well, its a lovely charm and all that, but its just that . . . well, how shall I say this, the *chain* looks just a little on the *thin* side, wouldn't you say?"

"Oh, *now* I get it!" I said, laughing loudly. "Go on then, why don't ya, ply us with loads of alcohol, then see how much expensive jewellery you can manage to sell us? Ha, ha, ha! Okay Brian, go on then, give it ya best shot! Let's take a good peek at ya collection of gold then! Mandy's already told us its pretty special, so I'm *definitely* interested in looking. And yeah, you're absolutely right, this one came from Elizabeth Duke at Argos, and much as I love the charm, I've always been quite worried that this flimsy little gold chain might break one day. So yes please, I'd love to take a look."

Brian said '*okay, great*', then disappeared off upstairs. He came back down a few moments later carrying a series of what appeared to be rather heavy wooden trays, smartly clad in lush green baize cloth. Two of them he set down on the coffee table, the third he placed on my lap.

"*Wow!*" I exclaimed. "*Nice chains!* Nothing like that tacky bright gold stuff that you get to see on those plastic spools down the Sunday markets, eh? These are proper smart! And expensive too by the looks of them!"

"Most cheap gold, *especially* from market traders, and *especially* here in Malaga, tends to be nine carat. These are mostly eighteen carat, which isn't quite as '*shiny*', but its far classier than nine carat, and obviously a lot more valuable too. I do have a couple of really solid twenty-two carat chains, but they tend to run into the thousands. They're also *very* heavy, and not overly strong either, whereas eighteen carat is generally considered affordable, as well as being far more durable. What d'you reckon?"

I picked each one up in turn and ran them through my fingers. They were all a delight to hold, unlike the flimsy little thing that I'd been wearing for the last few years. Some were far too heavy though, and I'd guessed far too expensive as well, but further down towards the thinner end of the scale I found one that felt and looked just perfect. It was twice the thickness of the one I'd worn up until then, but it looked like it was probably worth at least ten times as much. I liked it. I liked it a lot.

"Go on then *Mister Goldsmith,* hit me with the bad news," I said, a little sarcastically, "how much would something like this set me back exactly?"

"Well, my boy, this could well be your lucky day," he replied, with a slightly exaggerated Eastend accent. "*Ordinarily,* back home in dear old Blighty, I'd be retailing that particular one for three hundred pounds."

My heart sank a little, but I kept listening intently anyway, just in case . . .

"To you though, young Christopher, just because its Christmas, *fifty quid!*"

"*SOLD!*" shouted Helen. "I'll take it please Brian. Happy Christmas babe! I've had no idea whatsoever what to buy you as a present; plus, you've been so preoccupied with organising this trip, I've not even found the opportunity to ask you what you wanted or anything. I was just hoping you might come across something along the way, and now it looks like maybe you have? So, if you really like it, and you really want it, I'll buy it for you right now, hows that?"

I tried it on. It fitted perfectly. Then I tried it on properly, with the Saint Christopher charm attached to it, and the old chain put down to one side, and it fitted even more perfectly. After worrying for years about my cheap little chain breaking, this one felt like it had been made especially for me.

"I absolutely love it hun," I said, "and I'd love it even more if you bought it for me as a present."

"Consider it yours," Helen said, and lightly shook Brian's hand. "Happy Christmas honey."

"Thank you darling," I said, shuffled across to Helen, and gave her a big, sloppy, Christmassy-type kiss smack on the lips.

"*YUK!*" said Mandy.

"I'm never, *EVER,* going to take it off," I said. "This one stays with me now, around my neck, always and forever. And if Saint Christopher doesn't look after me properly throughout my travels, the way he always has, and the way I hope he always will, well then I'd appreciate it very much if, as and when the time should arrive, you'll do me the honour of burying him along with me, chain 'n' all."

[That was said a little tongue in cheek at the time, some sixteen years ago now, however, despite several genuinely close shaves with death since then, I'm still wearing that very same talisman to this day. Other than for medical reasons, I have never, ever taken it off, and I stand by the fact, here and now, that my lucky Saint Christopher charm has proved, at least up until today, to be far luckier than anyone could ever imagine. If you should happen to believe in that sort of thing of course. I never did, but I do now, because SOMETHING, at least, has miraculously kept me from the clutches of the Grim Reaper on more than one occasion! So, maybe further episodes of A Momentary Lapse of Reason to follow? We'll see!]

"What's in the other two trays?" I whispered in Brian's ear as I shuffled back across the sofa, "I don't suppose you happen to have any decent, pretty, *affordable* ladies watches by any chance? Helen loves a bit of bling, and I haven't come up with a proper present for her myself yet either."

"Ha, ha, well, as it so happens . . ." Brian chuckled back at me.

He then picked up the bottom one of the two green baize drawers still lying on the coffee table, placed it delicately on Helen's lap, and said,

"And for you, my dear lady, I'm led to believe that maybe you'd like to choose yourself a new watch for Christmas?"

"See! What did I tell you?" said Mandy resignedly.

"*Ooohh, I love the look of that one!*" Helen said immediately, pointing to a sparkly little Guess watch right in the centre of the tray. "Can I try it on please?"

"Be my guest," said Brian.

Helen slipped it around her right wrist, stared at it admiringly for a moment, then showed it to me close up and asked me what I thought. It certainly was beautiful. It had a gold base, with an outer rim that was encrusted with tiny diamonds all around, and a gorgeous mother of pearl face with decorative gold hands that pointed towards ornate little Roman numerals. I knew my watches reasonably well, so I knew that Guess was a good make, and whilst I doubted the diamonds were actually real, I could tell straight away that the watch itself was genuine. If I'd been asked, I would've put a price of somewhere slightly short of two hundred quid on it.

"Go on then Brian, pray tell?" I asked with a slight sigh.

"As coincidence would have it my boy, to you again, just fifty quid," he replied.

"Sold, to the pretty young girl sat over here on the sofa," I happily announced, "the one wearing the beautiful Guess watch. Happy Christmas my darling."

Helen reached over and kissed me lightly on the cheek. "Thank you," she said quietly, "it looks like we've both ended up with something we both really wanted after all. I've always said *good things come to those who wait*, have I not?"

"I *GUESS* so!" I replied, cackling to myself at my simple little pun.

It was Mandy's turn to comment,

"So, looks to me like everyone's happy now then? Chris is happy 'cos Helen's bought him a new chain, Helen's happy 'cos Chris has bought her a new watch, dad's happy 'cos he's made two new sales this evening, Rita's nodded off to sleep 'cos she's seen this kind of thing happen *so* many times before, and *I'm* happy 'cos I've had one too many sherries. *Yippee!* Think I might just have meself another. Helen, care to join me?"

"Oh, *yes please,*" replied Helen.

"Another brandy Chris?" asked Brian.

"Oh, *yes please,*" replied Chris.

With that, Rita awoke, and asked sleepily if anybody fancied another mince pie. Everyone said *'yes please, just the one'*, and she pottered off to the kitchen. Brian switched the telly back on, and Helen and I sat happily on the sofa together, snuggled up with our arms around each other, slowly sipping our drinks. Rita came back in with five bowls, each containing a warm mince pie and some chilled fresh cream, and we all stayed up and enjoyed the late night movie together. Raiders of the Lost Ark starring Harrison Ford. I'd seen it a hundred times already, and I'd be perfectly happy to watch it another hundred times, its one of my all time favourites. Once the film ended, it was only Brian and I that were still awake. I thanked him, genuinely, from the bottom of my heart, on behalf of both Helen and myself, for a most wonderful day, and for his and Rita's perfect hospitality, and hoped that one day we might be able to repay the favour. He simply said, '*don't be so silly, any friend of my daughter's will always be a friend of mine*', and we shook hands once again. I gently woke Helen from her sherry-inspired dreamland, we both quietly said goodnight to Brian, and headed off upstairs to bed, leaving Mandy and Rita both curled up asleep together on their own huge, comfy sofa.

"That really was a very special day," said Helen wearily, as we reached the top of the stairs.

"It certainly was my love," I replied with a yawn. "*Feliz Navidad* sweetie, mind the rug!"

CHAPTER
TWENTY TWO

Back in England's green and pleasant land, the following day would have been Boxing Day. To the Spanish, however, Boxing Day doesn't exist, there's no such thing. They feast with their families on Christmas Eve *(Noche Buena)* on the 24th of December, and they celebrate Christmas Day *(Navidad)* on the 25th with yet more family feasting; but the traditional giving of presents, to children ONLY I might add, and that's only providing they've been GOOD all year long, happens on Three Kings Day *(Día De Los Tres Reyes),* which is on the 6th of January. Not dissimilar to our very British Twelfth Night in many ways; we *all* celebrate the twelve days of Christmas/Navidad in one way or another, its just that each nation's methods vary somewhat in accordance with their historically differing religious traditions. We follow the time-honoured Christian tradition in the UK, celebrating the birth of Jesus on the 25th of December, and ending our celebrations on the 6th of January by taking our trees and trimmings down. The majority of Spanish folk, however, follow a mixture of Catholic and Pagan traditions, ending their celebrations on the 6th of January by doing what us British traditionally do on the 25th of December, as in the giving of presents to the children.

[I say '*majority*', because I know there are certain regions of Spain where they *do* follow Christian traditions, and I know that *Papa Noel SOMETIMES* gives presents to *good* children on *Noche Buena,* the evening of the 24th, *however,* this book is *ABSOLUTELY NOT* meant to be some kind of religious historical *Wikipedia,* its simply about me trying to get the Phoenix to Fornells, and what happened along the way; and more importantly, what happened afterwards! So that's it folks, *religious history lesson over I'm afraid!]*

So anyway, when in Spain, do as the Spanish do, that's what I've always said. Not that we had done the day before! We'd spent a *very* English Christmas with a *very* English family in a somewhat *Anglo-Spanish* city. And it had been wonderful too. But this day, Monday the 26th of December, I'd already decided, was most definitely *NOT* going to be a traditional English Boxing Day! Nochevieja on the other hand, or *New Year's Eve,* the Spanish *do* tend to celebrate in exactly the same way as the dear old British, but that, as they say, can wait until another chapter.

I wandered downstairs to the kitchen diner to find Helen sat at the table chatting to Rita over tea and toast. I said buenos dias and joined them, buttered myself a slice of toast, and thanked Rita yet again for her exceptional hospitality the previous day. She said that we were more than welcome to stay any time, if we should ever happen to be travelling around the area again. Helen then informed me that Brian had driven Mandy back to Benalmadena so that she could check on her two ageing boxer dogs, both of which were being walked, fed and watered by a neighbour, and that they'd be back sometime during the afternoon. I looked across the kitchen at the clock over on the far wall. *Blimey! 10.40am already!* It *must've* been a good night! I asked Rita if any of the shops might be open, and she said *'some will be and some won't, they're a fickle old bunch here in Malaga!'* I suggested to Helen that we go take a walk together, down to the beach via some shops somewhere, as there was something I wanted to buy that I'd had in mind for some time, and maybe we'd get lucky. She agreed and disappeared back upstairs to change. The sun was shining again, I could clearly see that through the wide kitchen window that looked out over the expanse of lush green lawn that covered the majority of the rear garden. From the thick tall hedgerow that surrounded it though, albeit affording a perfect degree of all round privacy, I could also see that the wind had got up again, so I had no idea whether it was wam outside or chilly. I wandered out into the back garden, licked my right index finger symbolically, and stuck it up in the air. *'Yep, definitely T-shirt weather again!'* I'd decided. I'd already dressed in shorts and a T-shirt anyway, and as I stepped back into the kitchen Helen came back downstairs wearing a summer dress with a nice, warm open cardigan over the top. We'd both already laced up our trainers, and after saying cheerio to Rita, and we'd catch up with Mandy by phone at some point, we'd left once again via the back door, sauntered around the side of the house into the front garden, then stepped out into the street. Hand in hand we then set off downhill towards the little square, picking out various notable landmarks here and there as points of reference. Once again it was warm and sunny, and we were both extremely happy and content.

After crossing the little square we turned right onto the narrow road with the shops along it, whereupon I immediately noticed the large LED sign above the entrance to the posh hotel, the numbers of which were clearly displaying a temperature of nineteen degrees. *Lovely!* Instead of taking the steps down to the beachfront we continued straight on, heading in the general direction of the city centre, and steadily we came across more and more shops. As Rita had said, some were open, some were closed, and there didn't appear to be a whole lot of logic as to which were doing what, but there again it was supposed to be a holiday season. We wandered through square after square, up and down, around and around, until, after an hour or so, we were hopelessly lost! Which, to be honest, didn't matter in the slightest to me; because in order to head south, the direction in which the beach lay, all we needed to do was follow the sun. *Simples!* A short while later I was peering through the front window of an open bookstore when I suddenly spotted *exactly* what it was I'd had in mind for the last week or so. I entered the store and asked the young lad behind the counter if he wouldn't mind fetching it out of the window display for me, *por favor,* so that I could take a closer look. He duly obliged, and handed it over to me just as soon as he'd managed to extract himself from the window display again. It was a small wooden box, beautifully wrapped in embossed cream faux-leather, with two small silver clasps holding it closed. I laid it flat on the counter and open it so that Helen could see inside.

"Oh, that's absolutely perfect," she exclaimed. "Shall we? Shall we? I think we should!"

"I think we should too," I agreed. "In fact, I think we will. In fact, I *know* we will!"

So we did! We bought ourselves, right there and then, a wonderfully ornate, perfectly sized and ideally priced travel backgammon set. *Marvellous!* I handed a twenty euro note to the young lad, told him to keep the change, and wished him Feliz Navidad. I also told him not to bother wrapping it, gracias mi amigo!

"Aha!" I beamed, once we'd stepped back out into the street again. "Now we'll find out exactly who's the biggest smart-ass between the two of us. *Prepare to meet thy destiny, o' wench o' mine!"*

"Not a hope," Helen replied smugly, "I'm gonna walk all over you like I *always* do!"

184

"Ha, ha, we'll see about that," I countered, "one euro per point, as per usual?"

"You betcha," she answered. "And the loser of the first game pays for the sangria."

"*Deal!*" I confirmed, and we turned smartly on our heels and headed due south!

We reached the entrance to the ferry terminal first, at the far west end of the '*golden mile*', then ambled slowly, hand in hand, along the ornate paving that covered the wide seafront promenade. We stopped every now and again to marvel at some of the spectacular sand sculptures that had been lovingly hand-crafted along the top end of the beach by several extremely clever street artists. At each one that we stopped to look at we threw a couple of euros into the collection hat that had been placed on the sand just in front of them. Not the most lucrative way of earning a living, I'm sure, but they seemed to get by okay. After about half an hour we reached the same beach-front café-bar that we'd all been sat outside together on Christmas Eve, and we took our seats once again, in the glorious winter sunshine, at exactly the same table as before. A waiter came over and asked us what we'd like, and I ordered dos cafés con leche por favor. I leaned back in my chair, staring up at what I'd at first thought was a cloudless blue sky, whilst Helen set the counters up for our first game of backgammon. The higher up I looked, however, or more to the point the further back inland I looked, high up above the snow-capped mountains of the Sierra Nevada, the centre of which lay just fifty miles or so to the north of Malaga, the more cloud I noticed. They weren't storm clouds, or anything vaguely similar, that might've been likely to spoil the rest of our afternoon in some way. They were little white wisps of high altitude cirrus clouds, and ever so slightly worryingly, they appeared to be on the increase. Cirrus clouds meant wind, and generally lots of it. And whilst the Costa del Sol itself bathes in the shelter of the Sierra Nevada mountains, the Tramontana winds which hail from way further up north are forced rapidly upwards by these mountains, and then on over the top of them, forming those telltale white '*horse's tails*' of cirrus cloud, as they then head further on south towards North Africa. Basically, cirrus cloud equals strong high altitude winds. I shuddered at the thought and tried to shut my mind off to it, at least for the remainder of that particular day. It was our *day off*, and we were jolly well going to *enjoy* it! The coffees arrived, and Helen called '*roll to see who goes first*'. From then on, in between each move, I cast my eyes forwards towards the sea, instead of upwards towards the sky!

Fifteen minutes later Helen removed her last counter from her home quarter on the backgammon board, leaving me with nine counters still remaining in mine.

"Ha, ha, *told ya!*", she mocked. "Trashed again! That's nine euros you owe me. And a jug of sangria!"

I signalled the waiter over, ordered a jug, y dos copas por favor, and he took the empty coffee cups away with him. It was getting on for three o'clock by then, so I called Mandy to let her know where we were, and asked her if she want to meet up with us here a bit later for a bite to eat. She said that would be great, how did six o'clock sound? I said that would be perfect, we'd see her then, and hung up. When the waiter came back to the table with the jug of sangria and two glasses, I wondered to myself how on earth we were going to make the one jug last for the next three hours! Plus, we were both getting a little peckish already, so I ordered a small selection of little tapas dishes to be brought out; those plus the backgammon should slow the drinking down a little.

"Okay, roll again for starters," I said, "I'm gonna wipe the floor with ya this time!"

By the time Mandy wandered over to join us it had got dark outside, the wind had picked up a little more, and it had gone off decidedly chilly. We'd already moved from the terrace to the inside of the café-bar, and set up table close to one of the overhead gas-fired warm air ducts. I still only had a T-shirt on, although I felt fine sat in the warm breeze, and Helen had her cardigan wrapped tight around her shoulders, so she felt warm enough too. Mandy, however, walked in wearing jeans and a leather jacket, and after asking how our day had gone she said,

"Here, I thought you'd best have these to put on. Rita said you'd both gone out dressed like it was summer, but like I already said, it ain't *always* warm over here, *especially* after dark."

She handed Helen a large carrier bag containing two of Brian's warmest fleece lined tracksuit tops, and we both said thanks, agreeing that we'd most definitely be needing them for the walk home. For the time being though we were fine, and Mandy removed her leather jacket, pulled up a chair and joined us.

"What's the score then?" she asked.

"*Ha!*" I replied, "It depends how you look at it. On the one hand Helen's beating me by six games to five, but on the other hand she currently owes me twenty-two euros."

"I think we'd best leave it at that for now babe," Helen said, "I'll get me money back off ya next time we get the chance to play together. What d'ya fancy to drink our Mand?"

"Well, I see Chris is on the old Estrella's then! Did you not do any sangria yet? I quite fancy another jug of that if the truth be known."

"*No, no, no,*" I started, "we definitely di . . ."

"*YES, we did!*" Helen interrupted before I could finish. "But only the one. His lordship over there decided, for the *both* of us I might add, that one was enough for today. So he went on the lager after, and I opted to stick with the Fanta naranja."

"What I *meant* by that was, if you'd just let me *finish,*" I scolded her jokingly, "is that *one* would have to suffice until Mandy arrived."

"Yeah, yeah, yeah," she replied, "of *course* you did!"

I beckoned the waiter over, ordered a second jug of sangria, three glasses, and three dinner menus.

"We're still not gonna drink a whole jug *each* ya know, not like we did the other night, and *then some!* We've got an early flight to catch tomorrow, and the last thing I fancy is flying in *this* weather with a hangover."

"What weather?" Helen asked.

"Oh, nothing," I answered, "just cold, never mind. *PLUS,* neither do I fancy struggling to get the pair of you back up that bloody hill again, like I'd had to the other night. So just *one* more jug it is, okay? Come on guys, let's eat."

The waiter returned with the fresh jug of sangria and handed each of us a food menu. As it was our last night together we opted to share the speciality of the house, a *huge* dish of seafood paella for three, which the waiter placed carefully in the centre of the table, and I agreed to pay for. '*My treat, by way of a thank you*', I'd said, then agreed wholeheartedly that another bottle of Rioja couldn't do any harm either. We each helped ourselves to the delicious assortment of seafood spread out before us, and used the Rioja to drink a toast to '*great and solid friendships, here and now, always and forever*'. Not long after that, after all the sangria had disappeared, along with ninety-nine percent of the paella, and we'd refused postres and limoncellos, I'd brought our little party back down to earth with a simple straightforward reality,

"Our flight leaves at nine o'clock tomorrow Mand, so we need to check in *before* 8am. What time d'you think we should leave for the airport?"

"Well," she replied, after a brief pause for thought, "its a straight thirty minutes to the airport when there's no traffic around, and I doubt there'll be much around early tomorrow morning, but we'll need to allow a bit of leeway anyway, just to be on the safe side. So I reckon we wanna be leaving home around 7am? That sound okay with you guys?"

"Well you're driving us there chick," I replied with a grin, "so if that's okay with you, then its sure as hell okay with us too. Alarms for 6am it is then!"

We finished up the final dregs of the Rioja, I settled up la cuenta with my card, then Helen pulled the two fleece tops out of the carrier and handed one of them to me. We both pulled them on, Mandy pulled her jacket on too, and we stepped outside into the chilly evening air. And *chilly* it was too. All three of us zipped our tops up, then linked arms together, and with a hop, a skip and a cheery little jump we headed off across the road, up the tree lined steps, and back towards the house. It was almost ten o'clock as the three of us walked in through the back door, and both Brian and Rita were just about to head off upstairs to bed.

"We'll be joining you very shortly," I said.

"Oh dear, *I do hope not!*" exclaimed Rita. "There's *certainly* not enough room in our bed for *five!*"

I never did work out whether she was joking or serious, but either way it made all four of us guffaw with laughter. I then took Rita's hand, kissed it lightly, and thanked her once again for her outstanding hospitality. Brian's hand I then shook with a long firm grip, thanking him for inviting us to stay, singing praise for the two exquisite pieces of jewellery that he'd managed to sell us, both at a *bargain* price, and wishing that our worldly travels may bring us close together again at some point in the near future. Helen and I then bid both Brian and Rita a fond farewell as they headed off upstairs to bed.

"We should do the same," Helen said.

"I agree," I replied a little sadly.

We both took it in turns to give Mandy a great big lingering hug, and I kissed her gently on the cheek. We thanked her *enormously* for a most wonderful Christmas, and promised her faithfully that one day we'd return the favour.

"I'll hold you to it," she said. "Don't forget mind, alarms set for 6am!"

"As *if* we'd forget!" Helen said with a wicked smile, and a little too sarcastically for my liking.

"Its okay," I threw back at her, "I've got my *own* alarm clock!"

With that, we both turned and headed off up the stairs.

"Get some sleep princess," I called back down. "See you in the morning. Nite nite. *Mind the rug!*"

As I climbed into bed, for some odd reason, I had that nagging feeling at the back of my mind that I'd missed out on something during the day. Hey ho, I was sure it'd come to me in due course. I let it go, drifted off to sleep, and dreamt horrible dreams about wispy little cirrus clouds.

CHAPTER TWENTY THREE

Six-thirty the following morning, and Mandy, Helen and I were all sitting at the kitchen table, drinking tea and munching away on ever so slightly burnt pieces of toast. *Oops, my fault!* We'd been reminiscing over what a great Christmas we'd all had together, and how we'd have to try and catch up again a little sooner next time, rather than leaving it for almost a whole year. Mandy happened to remind me that Helen was still way ahead of me in the ongoing backgammon tournament, and I burst into a brief fit of laughter. Before I could finish the sentence '*Hah, we'll see about tha . . .*', however, Mandy had raised her fingers to her lips and whispered loudly, '*Shhh, DON'T WAKE DAD!*' So on that note, I suggested maybe we should get going for the airport, and promptly cleared the table. I left Helen to finish the washing up whilst I quietly took one final check around the house to make sure we'd definitely left nothing behind, then carried our already packed bags to the back door. We'd dressed specifically for travelling again. Jeans and boots, several thin layers, fleeces and ski jackets; and as I opened the back door and stepped outside I was jolly glad that we had, it was bloody *freezing!* Well, not quite, but it was still dark, and my guesstimate temperature-wise was somewhere around the six degrees mark. I know I wouldn't have been far out. We bundled our bags into the boot of the big beautiful old Merc, made ourselves comfy on its plush, albeit rather chilly leather seats, and waited for Mandy whilst she popped back into the house to grab something that she'd apparently almost forgotten. One minute later and Mandy slammed the boot shut, hopped into the driver's seat, and started the engine. And then we were off. *Adios Malaga, its been a pleasure, hasta luego un dia.*

We took the same route out through the backstreets of Malaga, and on up over the hills towards the airport, the same way that we'd come in. There was a certain amount of traffic around, but it wasn't exactly busy, and at 7.20am by my watch Mandy pulled the Mercedes into one of the very few available spaces in the departures drop-off zone, right next to a sign that clearly read PARANDO DOS MINUTOS MAXIMO. Mandy popped the boot lid open, and the three of us jumped out of the car and walked around to the back. It was time to say goodbye; *adios; ciao; y muchos, muchos gracias!* A warm heartfelt group hug was followed by kisses all round, then we hauled our bags out of the boot and set them down on the pavement. Mandy then pulled out a plastic carrier bag, obviously containing something that was meant for us, and with a big smile she announced,

"Rita packed this up and asked me to give it to you as a little going away gift. She said that, had you both been around during the day yesterday, she would've plated it up for you for lunch, but you both went off into town instead so it didn't happen. Anyway, you can have it now and take it away with you. its perfectly packaged, it'll keep just the way it is for quite a few days, especially in this cold weather; and when you *hopefully* arrive safely at your pretty little abode in Menorca you can stick it in the microwave and have it for lunch over there instead."

With that Mandy pulled out of the carrier bag one large, round, blue plastic Tupperware container, the lid of which was just clear enough to see through, even though it was all tightly wrapped up in clingfilm. I peered through the lid inquisitively, and could clearly see that the inside was split into four separate compartments. And then, all of a sudden, it dawned on me exactly what it was that I'd been missing out on the day before. *Dammit, I knew there was something!*

"*YEE-HA!! Looky here Helen, look what Rita's put together for us. I KNEW there was a good reason for sticking to a traditional English Boxing Day! How could I have forgotten?? Ha, ha, one of my favourite after-Christmas treats! BUBBLE AND SQUEAK!!!*"

"Not just any old bubble and squeak," Mandy chipped in, "that's one of Rita's specials that is. With *extra* Brussels sprouts in it too, I might add, put together the way only she knows how. In fact, we even get to call her Aunt Bessie sometimes!"

"And that's *exactly* the way it should be Mand, and *exactly* the way I love it too," I replied. "Please say a great big thank you to her from both of us, its really thoughtful of her."

"Look," said Helen, "isn't that just perfect? Two compartments full of bubble and squeak, and two full of delicious looking cold turkey. I'm not convinced this'll last all the way to Menorca mind you, I bet you we can find a microwave somewhere on the ferryboat."

"Zip it into the top of my hold-all babe, there's plenty of room. Then when we get back to the lorry I'll grab another of those little packs of Roquefort cheese out of my hold-all, and we can have a right old feast-up together, somewhere out on the beautiful briny old Med."

"Yuk!" said Helen, poking her tongue out. "I'll stick to the B&S if that's okay, you can keep the cheese all to yaself!"

The three of us all laughed together, then hugged one more time, and with our wonderful almost-forgotten lunch now safely stashed away, we grabbed up our bags, bid fond farewells one last time, and headed off into airport departures in search of the Iberia check-in desks.

Check-in was simple and straightforward. I showed the uniformed young attendant our boarding passes and passports, and she took our overnight bags straight through on the conveyor. Even security proved to be a doddle for once! No stops, no searches, no queries, and we wandered on through, pulled our ski jackets back on, retrieved our hand baggage, then plonked ourselves down on a row of comfy seats in a small coffee lounge, and waited for the departure gate to open. Eight o'clock, and by now it was fully light outside. I peered out through a huge row of tall windows that overlooked part of the runway, as well as an expansive area of concrete aprons and taxiways. The first thing I noticed was around a dozen relatively small twin-engined jet aircraft, all parked up in a neat row, each one of them brightly adorned in Iberia Airways livery. 89-seater CRJ900's, every one of them by the looks of it, the very same model that we'd arrived on. The second thing I noticed was that the sun was shining, and the sky, or at least most of it, was very, very blue. And the third thing I noticed was that those tiny little wisps of high altitude cirrus clouds had now become *gigantic* wisps. '*Hmmm...*' *I thought to myself!*

"Certainly looks like a beautiful day for flying," Helen said cheerfully.

"*Hmmm...*" I replied warily.

"Is there a problem?" she asked.

"No babe," I replied. "Just deep in thought, that's all. Nothing to worry about."

Eight-thirty, and our flight number came up on the screen, boarding at gate number nine. So off we trotted, bags in hand, and showed our boarding passes to the steward at the entrance to the gate. He glanced at them casually, and we joined the back of the queue that was already heading out of the door, across the apron, and up the steps into the little jetliner. We followed along in line, and within just a few minutes we were shoving our jackets and bags into the overhead lockers, and buckling ourselves into precisely the same seat numbers that we'd been allocated for the outbound flight. So, once again, one deafening engine per ear! Hey ho, that was the least of my worries just then. Once we were settled I suggested to Helen that it might be a good idea if she tried to get some shut-eye, on account of the fact that we'd most likely have a long day ahead of us once we arrived back in Barca. Then, as if to perfectly confirm the fact that I was telling little porky-pies, the head stewardess aboard, after rushing her way through a very quick safety briefing, announced the fact that unfortunately they would *not* be offering any kind of drinks or snacks service on this particular flight, and would everyone *please* keep their seatbelts tightly fastened for the entire duration. As indeed both her and her colleague would also be doing. '*Hmmm . . .*' I thought to myself yet again.

At precisely 9am, timed to perfection in true Spanish fashion as always, we pushed back, then trundled off down the taxiway towards the start of the runway. We swung around to a brief halt, then the twin General Electric turbofans revved immediately to full power, and we accelerated at a seemingly incredible rate down to our V2 lift-off point, gracefully taking to the air in a wonderfully steep climb. I've always *loved* that particular aspect of flying! As it turned out I certainly wasn't going to love any other aspect of that particular flight. In fact, to this very day, I still remember it as being probably one of the worst flights that I've ever had the misfortune of being on! I've had the displeasure of enduring many a bad flight in my time, both before and since 2002, for all sorts of different reasons *(one or two of them possibly even worthy of yet another episode of A Momentary Lapse of Reason!)*, but this one, I have to say, pretty much takes the biscuit. And it wasn't even dangerous or anything like that, it was just simply *HORRIBLE!* Ultimately I suppose, it comes down to the fact that aeroplanes are made for flying; *but people aren't! (The same principle can be applied to ships and sailing, but I'll save that little gem for the next chapter!)* Anyway, after just six or seven minutes we reached our designated cruising altitude of 25,000 feet, whereupon we immediately ran into what airline pilots generally refer to as *ECAT. Extreme clear air turbulence!* Yep, you've got it, those *damned* cirrus clouds! I did something at that precise moment that I've very rarely ever done before; I pulled my little gold Saint Christopher out from under my jumper, pressed it tight to my lips and gave it a good old kiss, carefully tucking it back into its rightful place immediately after.

Whereupon the whole plane started to shake quite violently. Up and down, side to side, *bumpety-bumpety-bump!* And continually too, on and on and on. And it didn't let up either, not for one single moment. More often than not ECAT lasts for just a few minutes, after which you get clear of it. Not this one though, *no siree!* Those strong northerly Tramontana winds were slamming into the north face of the Sierra Nevada mountains, rocketing skywards, and chucking us around like a dried leaf in a gale. How the hell the pilots managed to hold their concentration through one whole solid hour of those awful conditions, I have absolutely no idea, other than the fact that I fully accept they'd been adequately trained to do so. But I wasn't! Or rather, we weren't! No one was, including both stewardesses! So, ignoring the multitude of gasps and the occasional scream, all everyone onboard could do was just sit tight and hold on. And keep their eyes tightly closed too. Every time I opened my eyes everything before me had simply become a horrible out-of-focus blur, the shaking was that bad. The only thing that stopped me from comparing it with being shoved inside a tumble-dryer for a whole hour was simply the fact that we were all tightly wearing our seatbelts. If anyone had been stupid enough to have unbuckled theirs I'm pretty sure they would have ended up quite seriously injured. Luckily no one did! But it didn't let up, not even for a moment. On the odd occasion that I dared to open my eyes, everyone else that I looked at, including Helen, had theirs tightly shut too. *Although, to this day, Helen still swears that she spent the whole flight asleep! Amazing what a couple of Diazepam can get you through I suppose!* After one whole hour of what felt like trying to dance the extreme Jitterbug whilst riding one of those rickety old fairground Waltzers, and listening to assorted terrified screams instead of piped organ music, we began our rapid descent towards Barcelona, and thankfully, within less than a minute, the violent shaking suddenly stopped. People slowly began opening their eyes, and the previous interior silence, which had regularly been punctuated by the occasional scream, which easily stood out above the constant clattering of stores and kitchenware from the rear galley, turned rapidly into garbled Spanish chatter. Although I couldn't understand specifically what anyone was saying, the relief in all of their voices was certainly more than apparent. Helen, however, still appeared to be asleep, and so I left her be. A few minutes later, however, as we gently touched down on the Tarmac of one of Barcelona's main runways, she opened her eyes and said '*Oh, are we here already?*', or words to that effect. I wasn't really listening, even my ears had gone numb by then! When the plane had stopped moving altogether, we grabbed our bags and jackets out of the overhead lockers, and wobbled on rather unsteady legs towards the exit. Just as I grabbed tightly hold of the handrail that led down the steps towards terra firma, I turned to one of the stewardesses, and in perfectly plain English I politely stated,

"D'you know miss, in the whole of my life to date, I have never, *ever,* been more relieved to leave an aircraft than I am right now!"

She looked me straight in the eye, and to my surprise, also in perfectly plain English, she replied,

"I'm very sorry sir, but you have to appreciate that the in-flight weather conditions are entirely beyond our control, and we *must* fly at the altitude demanded of us by air traffic control, so on shorthaul flights I'm afraid there's simply no way of avoiding whatever conditions we might encounter. Although, I should add, conditions such as those just experienced, thankfully, tend to be *extremely* rare."

She then moved her head a little closer to mine, and whispered loudly towards my ear,

"If the truth be known however, and please don't tell anyone this sir, but I've never been quite so relieved to set back down on the ground again either!"

I smiled sweetly at her, then whispered back,

"Don't you worry miss, I promise I'll never tell a soul, your secret's entirely safe with me." *Oops!!*

Helen and I walked briskly across the short stretch of concrete apron together, and through the door into the arrivals lounge for internal flights. Whilst waiting for the luggage carousel to start up we'd both pulled our jackets on. It was quite clearly considerably cooler up in Barcelona than it was down in Malaga. Minutes later our bags arrived, and after exiting the baggage collection section and entering the main terminal building, I turned to Helen, puffed out a big sigh, and stated positively,

"Phew! I really need a drink right now!"

"Well," she said, "the sun ain't exactly over the yardarm yet my love, what exactly would you like this early in the day?"

"Vodka-Martini," I replied adamantly, "extra strong, *stirred not SHAKEN!!*"

"Had a bad flight did we?" she asked sarcastically.

"Remind me to steal some of those Diazepam off you at some point please babe. Come on, let's get the hell out of here. To be honest, the drink can wait, we'll have something decent together when we've checked in at the ferry terminal. Let's go hit the road. its not like we've got far to go, its only a few miles back towards town."

We shouldered all of our bags, and walked through the terminal building together until we reached the pay point machine, just inside the automatic glass doors that led out onto the lorry park. Bags down, and out of my wallet I pulled the small white ticket that we'd been given by security on entry. Credit card at the ready, I slotted the ticket into the machine, and shut my eyes so as not to see how much we owed. I heard a little whistle escape from Helen's lips, and guessed from that that it was going to prove quite costly, but as it was just a *little* whistle, hopefully not too much so. I opened one eye, just a little, and squinted at the small LED screen before me. €165.90. I thought it through for a moment, then accepted that even though we hadn't exactly found the same kind of bargain as we had on the roof of Sant Station, realistically, for a 'commercial vehicle' for nigh on five days, I'd reckoned it was really quite fair. I slotted in my credit card, there was a whirr and a buzz, and the little white ticket popped back out again. Now all we had to do was walk the fifty yards across the car park to where the Foden would be waiting, go collect the keys from security, fire her up, and off we jolly well go to the Trasmediterranea ferry terminal. We shouldered our bags again and walked out through the automatic doors. And right there in front of us, in the chilly morning light of this wonderful new day, what we could clearly see just fifty yards away, sitting directly underneath a clear blue sky, were three large numbers, white painted over black Tarmac, marking out space number 155. But no vehicle. *NO SODDING LORRY!* And no Phoenix either. Just . . . *nothing!* I cast my eyes around the massive car park, which once again was virtually empty, save for the odd van here and there, and a couple of large artics and a Pantech parked right down at the far end, about half a kilometre away from where we were stood. I immediately put my serious head on, and marched purposefully towards the security office. On reaching it I rapped my knuckles angrily against the sliding glass window, which, a few seconds later, slid to one side equally as angrily.

"*Si? Que?*" demanded the uniformed guard behind the hatch, a little too loudly for my liking.

"*Don't you fuc...*" I began back at him, but then, out of the corner of my eye I suddenly noticed, over his shoulder right across at the far end of the key hook board, the keys to the Foden, clearly tagged, and hanging on hook number 1186. And space number 1186, I immediately made an educated guess, would be located directly behind one of those huge trucks parked up right down at the far end of the car park. I calmed myself immediately, showed him my passport and parking ticket, gestured towards the Foden's keys hung on the board, and asked him to pass them across. He cross-referenced the details and then handed them over to me. I simply said gracias señor as he slid the little glass window back shut, and we marched off together towards the far end of the car park.

"I guess they must've been exceptionally busy here over Christmas then?" Helen suggested.

"Yeah," I answered back. "Although it looks virtually empty right now, I'd say its likely to be complete chaos here from time to time. That's obviously exactly why you have to leave your keys with security. I can just imagine this place jam-packed full, and then one flat battery on a forty-footer, or maybe a flat tyre even, and they could possibly end up with some kind of massive commercial vehicle jigsaw puzzle, just trying at least to get all the perishables back on the road as per their required schedules. A potential bloody nightmare sometimes, I'm sure."

"Well let's just hope they looked after her properly when they had to move her then," Helen said.

"Okay, here we go then babe, space number 1186 is just around the other side of this big white artic over here, let's go take a look-see shall we?"

Bags in hand, we both slowly and carefully peeked around the back end of the large white forty-foot trailer, and there, right in front of us, sat proudly in all her well-overloaded finery, was our wonderful little Foden, with the Phoenix perched majestically, *or should I say precariously*, aboard. Either way, I happily walked all the way around her, firmly kicking each tyre in turn as I went, and was extremely pleased to announce that everything appeared to be entirely in order, nothing had moved or come loose or any suchlike, '*and I strongly suggest my dear, on that basis, that we get ourselves the heck out of this place, and very firmly back on our way again!*' Helen was gladly, as well as enthusiastically, in total agreement with me, thank goodness. I unlocked the doors, we both climbed up into the cab, and piled our bags on top of one another in between us. I pushed the key into the ignition, waited a second or two for the glow plug light on the dash to go off, and she fired up first turn of the key. *Marvellous!* I then drove all the way around the small group of huge artics that we'd been hiding behind, and headed straight towards the exit. Helen reached down from her window and slotted the little ticket into the machine that was sat just in front of the barrier, whereupon, *thankfully,* the barrier raised itself, and before we knew it we were back on the main airport ring road, and heading back towards Port Vell in search of the Trasmed ferry terminal.

CHAPTER TWENTY FOUR

After just two or three minutes we joined the Ronda Litoral, the B10 main dual carriageway that takes you directly into the southern side of Barcelona City, and terminates more or less halfway between Port Vell and the bottom end of Las Ramblas. Finding the Trasmed ferry terminal turned out to be far easier than I'd expected too. It was well signposted off to the right, just after the huge container ship commercial docks, with its vast array of enormous automated cranes, and just before the cruise ship terminal, where the Independence Of The Seas was clearly visible in the distance from the junction that we pulled off at. We followed the road around, and on down towards the docks area, shortly after which it split into a series of clearly marked individual lanes. We pulled into lane number three, and parked up behind a long stationary row of assorted vehicles; cars, vans, and small trucks similar in size and weight to our own. Directly in front of us there was a large overhead sign which clearly read 'TRASMEDITERRANEA: Barcelona – Mahon – Palma – Barcelona'. I switched the engine off, turned to Helen and cheerfully stated,

"This'll be the one then, how simple was that exactly? All we gotta do now is hope they've got enough space for us on the next crossing. Although, to be honest, it doesn't exactly *look* particularly busy; and when I rang them from the UK just before we left they said there was no need to book at this time of year, just come join the back of the queue. Much the same as the sailings from Dover to Calais I guess, except that this one's a thirteen hour crossing, as opposed to a one hour one. Plus I knew it was going to be a night crossing anyway, hence why we're here now with plenty of time to spare. Wait here for a bit please babe, I'll pop into the office and see if I can grab us some return tickets, then we'll see what we can do about finding a spot of lunch somewhere."

"Okey dokey," Helen replied. "Try not to be too long though please, the warmth disappears out of this cab pretty damned quickly after the engine's switched off."

"Don't worry babe, if there's a long queue or anything like that I'll come back and get you."

I grabbed my wallet and both of our passports, jumped down out of the cab, and headed on over to the double doors that led into a long rank of two-storey office buildings running along one part of the quayside. Once inside I could see a long row of individual glass-fronted kiosks, each one manned by uniformed staff, and fixed to the cladding directly above each kiosk were small brightly illuminated signs declaring the various Trasmed destinations. Kiosk number three, as per lane number three, had a sign saying 'Barcelona – Palma-de-Mallorca *(via Mahon)*', which wasn't at all what we wanted; however, the kiosk right next to it, also labelled kiosk number three, portrayed a sign that simply read 'Barcelona – Mahon'. That'll be the one then! And yes, there *was* a queue, but it was only a queue of one. Or should I say four? Two adults, two children; four people, one booking. *'I think I'll just wait here in the queue whilst their booking gets processed, I'm sure it won't take long, and Helen's wearing her ski jacket anyway, she'll be fine.'* And I was right too. Five minutes later and I found myself asking the nice gentleman behind the counter if he '*habla'd any Ingles?*' '*Sólo un poco señor*', was his simple reply *('just a little sir')* Okay, let's see how well this goes then, shall we?

"Mi pequeño camion con bote y dos pasajeros a Mahon, por favor, luego él pequeño camion de vuelta y dos pasajeros pero sin bote por favor" I asked him politely in my very best-practiced piece of well-rehearsed Spanish.

"Can you complete this form please sir," he replied, in reasonably understandable English, and slid an A4 single sheet document underneath the glass screen towards me. I picked it up and stared at it, noticed that every single question was written in both English and French, as well as Spanish, and asked him for directions to the nearest restaurant. He produced a simple pocket-sized map of the whole of the Trasmed ferry terminal, marked an X in pencil over the office that I was currently in, then marked another X over the front of a building just inside the terminal entrance.

"Aquí está el café-bar del Capitan Cristobal Colon," he informed me most helpfully.

Excellent, Christopher Columbus's very own bar! And thankfully just a very short walk from where we'd stopped the truck too. Just what the doctor ordered. I was still desperately in need of a very stiff drink, after spending my second hour of the day strapped tightly inside a flying tumble-dryer! It had just passed twelve o'clock midday, and I knew that the overnight crossing was scheduled to sail at 1900hrs later that evening, so I asked the nice helpful gentleman behind the counter what time boarding was likely to begin, in order to ensure we got back to the truck well in advance of our queue disappearing off ahead of us. He informed me that boarding would commence at around 1700hrs, but I'd need to get issued with our tickets well before that, so probably best to get the completed *passage application document* back to him as soon as possible. I thanked him for his kind assistance, shoved the A4 document in my inside jacket pocket, and wandered back to the truck.

"Come on babe, jump down, there's a cosy little café-bar just around that corner back there. Can you throw my kit-bag down to me please, and bring your handbag along too, but the overnight bags can stay right where they are, they'll be fine. Oh, and by the way, zip your jacket up too, there's a strong chilly old wind blowing out here right now."

I locked up the Foden, and we walked back along the empty queue lanes and around the corner together, then in through the front entrance of the Café-Bar Capitan Cristobal Colon, which I must admit, I hadn't even noticed on the way in. It was quite a large caff, and probably only around half full with what appeared to be mostly Spanish folks, some of them families, some possibly tourists, and others quite clearly lorry drivers. *No matter what nationality lorry drivers may happen to be, and I don't mean this in any way offensively, but they really are a breed apart!* We took our seats at a table nearest to the counter, and a waitress approached immediately, asking what we would like to order. I asked her for dos cafés con leche por favor, uno taza vacia, uno Cognac mucho grande, y dos menus del dias, gracias. I then pulled out the ticket application form from my inside jacket pocket, and told Helen that we'd need to fill all our relevant information into it first, prior to paying for our tickets with whatever amount might then apply. I studied the form carefully for a bit, but it looked pretty straightforward, so I grabbed a pen out of my bag ready to begin. Whereupon the waitress plonked the tray of drinks down in front of us. Excellent! I poured one half of my milky coffee into the empty cup, and then half of the large Cognac into one coffee, and the other half into the other one. Helen had opted for the other alcohol-free coffee.

"*Listo! Perfecto!*" I announced proudly to Helen. "Two of the best coffees ever!"

"And well earned too my love; you've got us all the way here so far, and pretty much according to schedule too, so well done, you deserve a little treat. You go ahead and enjoy them," she responded.

"Purely medicinal I can assure you!" I quipped. "Now, let's get this form filled in so that I can go buy our tickets, after which we'll eat, and then we can get this little load of ours safely on its way to its final intended destination."

Estimated date of travel:- 27/12/2002. Lead passenger details; name, date of birth, home address, passport and telephone numbers:- Chris Reason. Additional passenger details; names and dates of birth:- Helen Reason. Vehicle make, model and colour; registration number, length, width, height:- Foden car-transporter with boat, red/white, 10.0m x 2.6m x 4.1m. Estimated total value of vehicle and contents:- £10,000 (€15,000). Cabin requirements (Nil/2-bed/4-bed/Qty):- 2-bed x 1. Special requirements:- *calm seas por favor!*

Estimated date of return:- 30/12/2002. Lead passenger:- Chris Reason. Additional passengers:- Helen Reason. Vehicle description:- Foden car-transporter (empty), red/white, 8.7m x 2.6m x 3.0m. Estimated value:- £4,000 (€6,000). Cabin requirements:- 2-bed x 1. Special requirements:- *as above.*

Essentially that was it. Simple form, straightforward list of details, let's go see what it costs then. I finished up the second of the delicious brandy-infused coffees, asked Helen to watch my bag and keep the table for us, and strolled out of the door back towards the Trasmed office. Along the way I noticed that the queue of vehicles, particularly in lane number three, had grown considerably, and this time, when I reached the check-in kiosk, there was a slightly longer queue than before. I waited patiently in line. Fifteen minutes later I was at the front, and I slid the completed document, along with both of our passports, under the glass screen to the same uniformed gentleman behind. He glanced at both passports, glanced at me, and immediately slid Helen's back under the screen. Evidently he only needed one for the lead passenger, and he duly photocopied mine and then slid that one back under too. He then carefully studied the form I'd completed, and fed each one of the details into his computer terminal. The screen click-click-whirred for a moment, in absolute silence strangely enough, following which the gentleman looked up at me and said *'Gracias señor, eso sera un total de seiscientos cuarenta y ocho euros por favor.'* Six hundred and forty eight euros; just over four hundred and thirty quid by the exchange rate of the day, and to be honest pretty much more or less what I was expecting. I'd done a certain amount of research on Trasmed ferry costs before we'd left Bristol, but I hadn't bothered trying to ascertain an accurate figure because there were far too many variables. Not least of which was the particular day on which you sailed, and evidently, much like the Brittany Ferry crossings, which particular ship you were lucky or *unlucky* enough to get allocated. Not all of them had cabins available, although those were generally used for the daytime crossings, and tended to be significantly faster and cheaper than the much larger ships that sailed overnight, the ones that were needed for all *commercial* freight. Anyway, I was entirely happy with the cost, and handed over my credit card; although by now, or so I was beginning to feel at the time, Señor MasterCard was becoming ever so slightly frayed around the edges! Having said that, there was still plenty of credit available on it, but somehow I was going to have to considerably restructure my repayment plan upon our return to dear old Blighty. *Hey ho, such is the life of the traveller!* Anyway, more clickety-click-whirrs, albeit this time audible ones, and a moment later the clerk passed through to me four neatly folded detailed boarding tickets, along with two key cards, both of which were clearly labelled Cabina 122. I pocketed all the tickets, said *'muchos gracias señor, y buenos dias'* to the very efficient cashier chap, and walked back out of the door. As I passed the Foden on my way back to Café Cristobal Colon I kicked the two tyres on the passenger side, then zipped my ski jacket up tight against the cold northerly wind, which all of a sudden seemed to be blowing much harder than it had been earlier.

On re-entering the café-bar I could see that Helen was poring intently over the menu, and I walked over to her and asked her what she was thinking.

"I've decided," she stated firmly. "I'd like the bacalao y papas frites por favor!"

"Ooh, get you!" I mocked. *"Learnt a tiny bit of Spanish have we?"*

"About the same amount as the French I learnt on the way here, *as in virtually nil!* Anyway, I cheated, everything on the menu's written in Spanish, French and English, so I know what everything is anyway."

"Well that's just fine with me too my love," I agreed, "I quite fancy cod and chips as well. So there we go, we'll get two of those on order then, and how about a nice big jug of sangria to go with 'em?"

"Yep, sounds ideal, go for it!"

The waitress came over to our table and I ordered the lunches. I then pulled the four Trasmed tickets out of my pocket and examined them closely.

The first one said 'Vehiculo Comercial Cargado', along with its registration number; Sr Christopher Reason, cabina 122, nombre del barco 'Juan J Sister', Barcelona – Mahon, 1900hrs, 27 de diciembre. The second one read virtually the same, the only difference being Sn Helen Reason instead of Sr Christopher. Number three stated 'Vehiculo Comercial Noncargado', plus reg, my name and then cabina y nombre del barco (ASI), Mahon – Palma – Barcelona, hora Fecha (ASI). And number four was exactly the same as number three, but again with Helen's name printed on it instead of mine.

So essentially our tickets were open-returns, with ASI translating to TBA, or '*to be advised*'. And we'd be sailing on the Juan J Sister, a 22,400-ton ship that carried just over eight hundred passengers, almost a hundred and fifty vehicles, and had a maximum speed of nineteen knots. And the weather forecast, apparently, was absolutely atrocious, with a '*very high*' sea state; although needless to say I didn't bother telling Helen about the last bit. Anyway, hopefully we'd be fast asleep for most of the crossing anyway, which, on average, subject to the weather conditions, generally took around thirteen hours, or so I'd been informed. As for the return crossing, or crossings as it were, well that was a different story altogether, but I'd keep my fingers crossed that at least, hopefully, the weather may have improved somewhat by then. The waitress brought over our lunches, along with a wonderfully mixed one litre jug of sangria, and set everything down on the table, along with cutlery, two glasses, and a small wire basket containing salt, pepper, olive oil and balsamic vinegar. There was also a small plate of bread and olives, as is usually the traditional Spanish freebie accompaniment. I must add here that cod and chips in Barcelona is by no means similar, in any way imaginable, to the fish and chips that we'd had in Malaga, or any other cod 'n' chips that you'd expect to get from your average English fish 'n' chip shop. This was whole fresh cod, straight out of the sea, pan-fried, skin-on, with all the bones still fully intact, and it was absolutely *delicious*. As indeed was the sangria! I checked my watch; just after two o'clock.

"Three hours to kill before boarding sweetie, cribbage or backgammon?"

"Backgammon!" Helen replied firmly. "I may be six-five ahead of you in games, but you're still twenty-two euros up on me in cash terms, and I'm gonna do my damnedest to turn that around before we sail."

"Good luck with that one then chick," I said with a chuckle, pulling the travel backgammon set out of my kit-bag. "*Camarera! Autra sangria litro por favor!*"

Six games later, and we'd won three each. So now Helen was up by nine games to eight, but she'd only managed to reduce her financial deficit to seventeen euros. And now there were *two* empty jugs of sangria sitting next to us, and the clock on the wall told me it was a little after four-thirty. I'd said I thought we'd best go sit in the truck and wait for the queue to start moving, which it probably would do fairly soon, and so I'd settled up la cuenta with the pretty young camarera, packed away the backgammon, shouldered my kit-bag, and headed towards the door. By the looks of it most other occupants of the large café-bar, which had filled almost to overflowing by now, were having similar thoughts to ours, and the poor young waitress, just as we left, appeared to be single-handedly trying to cope with the mass exodus. We'd zipped up our jackets before walking outside, as it was now dark as well as cold and windy, and we both walked briskly back to the Foden, unlocked the doors and climbed back in. I started the engine, and let it run for a bit with the heater turned right up, just to get a bit of warmth back into the cab. Five minutes after that I switched it back off, and a further ten minutes after that I switched it back on again, as the front of the queue had gradually begun to move, one by one, towards the huge gaping entrance at the rear of the Juan J Sister. A minute or two later and we started moving forward ourselves. Immediately before driving up one of the two massive steel ramps that led up onto the lower aft deck of the ship, a uniformed security guard stopped us and asked to see our tickets. I handed them down to him, he glanced very briefly at them, handed them back, and asked us to follow along behind the large red Spanish Pantechnicon which was now immediately in front of us, and thankfully, very slightly taller than us too. We followed the big old ten-wheeler up the starboard ramp and deep into the bowels of the ship's lower deck, whereupon, way too tight up to a bulkhead to be able to open the driver's side door more than an inch or two, we pulled up, applied the air brake, switched off the engine, and as instructed, left the truck in gear. As we then both jumped down via the passenger's side door, bags and all, I'd found it somewhat disconcerting to note that the crew were immediately clamping every vehicle tightly down to the steel deck-floor using the strategically positioned chain tensioners and wheel straps. '*Hmmm...*' I thought to myself, somewhat nervously, '*I reckon its gonna be a lot rougher out there tonight than I'd imagined!*' Thankfully Helen hadn't given it a single thought herself, and we grabbed up our bags and headed off up one of the stairwells in search of our cabin.

Cabin 122 was on the port side of deck three, immediately above the two vehicle decks, and thankfully, due to the rough seas that had been forecast for the trip, some way astern of amidships. It was an internal cabin, with no porthole, and as I switched the single bulkhead light on I immediately clocked the fact that it was absolutely the smallest room imaginable. Two narrow single beds, each attached to the side walls, with barely enough room to squeeze between them. That was good, those walls would come in very handy in a rough sea! Above each bed was a long wall mounted two door locker, much like an aircraft overhead locker, for stowing all of our baggage in. At the foot of one bed, tucked neatly behind the open door, was a small wall mounted wooden tabletop, with a single white plastic chair, and a wall mirror fixed above. And at the foot of the other bed was a tiny plastic wetroom, a shower cubicle combined with toilet and miniature sink, almost hidden from view by the white polyester shower curtain hung across its entrance. I found it somewhat fascinating just what you could squeeze into a 9ft by 5ft box! Still, I guess its all about '*bums on seats*', as the saying goes. Plus, in our favour I suppose, at least we couldn't get thrown out of bed during the night, the only place we could get thrown was on top of each other. *Oh, what joy!* We plonked our bags down on our beds and wandered back off outside with the intention of exploring the rest of the ship, whilst hopefully, somewhere along the way, discovering a self-serve microwave with which we could maybe heat up some of Rita's wonderful looking bubble and squeak, and have it a bit later on for our tea.

Other than stairwells, corridors and lobbies, deck three seemed to be comprised entirely of accommodation cabins, both internal and external. Up on deck four we found a large cafeteria towards the stern, which already appeared to be filling up with mostly Spanish truckers. Amidships to port there was a rank of jewellery, clothing, gift and souvenir-type shops, all of which were closed, and didn't look for one minute as if they were going to open. Opposite the shops, starboard amidships, was the purser's office, a manned information desk, and a long amusements arcade, the doors to which were also firmly closed and locked. And up for'ard, further on towards the bow, was the bar area, with its huge array of comfortable seating strategically placed around lipped wooden tables that were securely fastened to the floor. Directly in front of the seating area was a high panoramic window which stretched the full width of the ship, and looked out over what was now total darkness, and what also appeared to be the beginnings of light rain, spattering softly against the glass in the cold gusting wind. People, some with children, others without, were gradually beginning to occupy the assorted range of comfy chairs, however, the bar remained closed and shuttered, and as yet we hadn't come across any kind of self-serve microwave. So, on upwards to the open air deck five. To the stern of the ship lay a full-size games pitch, painted green and marked out with white lines for badminton. It was surrounded by a tall glazed screen, but was clearly out of use, and the net had been removed and stowed. For'ard of the games area was a huge white funnel, roughly the size of a small house, and immediately for'ard of that was a small blue painted swimming pool. It appeared to be quite deep, and was full up with clean clear water, but was covered over with tightly stretched safety netting. For'ard of the pool was an open sunbathing area, protected at the front by another tall glazed screen that partially wrapped itself around both sides at an inwardly sloping angle, then stopped just before the pool. All the sun loungers had been neatly stacked to both sides of the deck, protected by the sloping glazed screen, and securely lashed down so that they couldn't move. There were flights of stairs leading up to a sixth deck astern of the funnel, which appeared to be a simple open viewing area with a wooden-capped steel handrail around its entire perimeter, however the stairways had all been roped off, with access to this deck clearly forbidden. We returned back down to deck four, took up comfy seating positions in the lounge area, and waited patiently, along with the other eclectic mix of passengers, for the bar to open.

At a quarter to seven we felt a gentle deep sounding rumble reverberate around the ship as her twin Wartsila engines were fired up, and I left Helen sat in the lounge and wandered out on deck to watch as we exited the huge port of Barcelona. The shore crew cast off our warps, which were neatly wound onto motorised spools by the deck crew, and the bow and stern thrusters then gradually manoeuvred us away from the quay wall. It was precisely seven o'clock, perfect Spanish timing once again, just as I'd come to expect. As we sailed slowly out of the ferry terminal, and on into more open waters, I waved a temporary goodbye to the spectacular lights of that wonderful hillside city, and as we slowly picked up speed and began to leave the lights further behind I noticed just how strong that cold northerly wind had become, despite the fact that the sea appeared to be relatively calm. I knew, however, that we were still well within the protective lee of the Catalonian mountains, and that before very long the sea state was bound to change, inevitably very much for the worse. I strolled back inside where it was nice and toasty warm, unzipped my jacket and wandered casually into the stern cafeteria, which was half full of Spanish truckers. Being a sort of a temporary trucker myself, you'd be forgiven for thinking that I fitted in admirably with them. I didn't! In fact I felt quite uncomfortable and totally out of place. However, the café itself, which had by now opened up its shutters and was being well used, was one of those self-serve types, and there was an excellent range of both hot and cold foods on display. There was a large stack of warm white china plates at the start, for customers to help themselves to whatever they chose from the servery, and then queue to pay for it at the single cashier's position. After which you'd collect your cutlery and condiments, then take a seat at your chosen table. And right there, at the very end of the line, fixed firmly down on top of a wall mounted shelf, lo and behold, sat a self-serve microwave. I hurried back along the starboard corridor to the front bar, which was also now open and serving, and sat back down next to Helen in the comfy lounge chair.

"Are you feeling peckish at all yet babe?" I asked her quizzically.

"Not exactly starving," she replied, "but I wouldn't mind *something* for tea fairly soon. What are you thinking exactly?"

"Well, what I'm thinking *exactly,*" I continued, "is that very soon my dear, unfortunately, I'm afraid the sea conditions are going to deteriorate somewhat. And shortly after that, they're going to deteriorate even more. And not long after that, the chances are we probably won't even be able to stand up; its gonna get pretty bad out there! So, what say I cook you up something a little special *right now,* and then afterwards, as and when we feel the need, we'll retire to our cabin and attempt to sleep our way through it? How's that sounding with you?"

With that, as if by way of emphasising my point, the Juan J Sister pitched ever so slightly, and shuddered just a little as we gradually began to approach some of the ever growing offshore waves.

"I think that sounds like an extremely good idea!" Helen replied immediately.

I nodded, stood up, and headed back off down the corridor to the stairwell that would lead me down to the cabins on deck three. I was already having to keep a firm hold of the handrails in order to keep my balance, but I was loving the conditions as they were at the time. We were heading south-south-west, and so too, more or less, were the waves, and every now and again, as a large roller picked up the ship's stern, it felt just as if we were surfing. It was a great feeling; *for the time being!* I opened the door to our cabin with the little key card, unzipped my overnight bag and pulled out the round Tupperware container. I then stepped out of the cabin, and just as the ship rolled slightly to port I allowed the cabin door to slam itself shut. *Perfect timing!* I climbed the stairs again, making a point of holding the handrails, and walked a little unsteadily into the stern cafeteria. By now the Spanish lorry drivers were all sat at their tables eating their meals, and there was no one stood at the servery. I walked purposefully past the cashier's till position, opened the door of the microwave, slid the whole Tupperware container in, set the timer to ninety seconds, and pressed *'GO'.* I then grabbed some cutlery from the dispenser, along with a couple of serviettes, and searched around briefly on the off chance that I might find a sachet of cranberry sauce. Sadly there wasn't any, but no matter, salt and pepper would suffice. The microwave pinged, and I removed the plastic container and headed on back towards the for'ard lounge. I had to stop a couple times along the way and brace myself against the handrail as the ship ploughed into the crest of yet another breaking roller. Being a sailor myself I was still very much enjoying that particular motion, although I was rapidly coming to the conclusion that *'enjoying it'* wasn't the term that was likely to be lasting for too much longer. I removed the lid from the Tupperware container and placed it on the table in front of Helen, handed her a knife and fork, then plonked myself down in my own seat. *'Jeez, that's better!'* Sitting's easy during a rough sea; *standing isn't! Not to mention walking!*

"Wow, this tastes amazing!" Helen said, tucking in to Rita's wonderful bubble and squeak. "And its just the right temperature too, not too hot, just right. Who heated it up for us then hun?"

"Well, just as I'd hoped, there's a self-serve microwave in the truckers caff babe, so I just stuck it in and guessed at a minute and a half. Seems I got it right though, the turkey's absolutely spot on too. And Mandy was right about the bubble and squeak, it really is special. *Very special!* Must have something to do with the quantity of Brussels sprouts in it. Should make for an interesting night if nothing else!"

We both giggled at each other somewhat childishly, then I asked Helen what she'd like to drink.

"Ooh, I think I'll have a large red wine please," she answered.

I stood up, and slowly but surely staggered my way across to the bar. The sea was getting rougher, and we were no longer surfing along the top of large regular rollers, we'd begun to thud into the tops of huge breakers instead, with juddering regularity. I order a cerveza grande for myself, and a copa de vino tinto de la casa for Helen, then I held on tightly to the glass of house red, to stop it from sliding from one end of the bar to the other, whilst the waiter carefully poured me my large beer. I managed to make it back to our table without spilling anything, but only just, then sat back down and told Helen to hang on to everything tightly so as not to let it slide. So we sat, and we drank, and we ate, and we polished off every single morsel of turkey leftovers, along with Rita's absolutely marvellous bubble and squeak. The container was empty, our glasses were empty, we were comfortably full up, and the good ship Juan J Sister was rockin' and a'rollin' like a good 'un! Suddenly, as the ship slammed into yet another breaker, there was an almighty crash, and I looked back over towards the bar to see five or six previously full glasses of beer smashed all over the floor, and some poor young Spanish chap stood there, one hand tightly grasping the hand-rail along the front of the bar, the other clutching an empty drinks tray. *'Oops-a-daisy!'* Seems he'd not been quite as careful as I had, although, to be fair, the sea was getting rougher and rougher by the minute now.

"Time for bed?" asked Florence.

"Boing!!" said Zebedee.

"What?" said Helen.

"Nothing," said Chris.

'Its nine-thirty babe, so we're still only two and a half hours offshore, with *at least* ten and a half still to go, so my guess is that these conditions are gonna go from bad to worse during the night. And the best way of dealing with that is to lock ourselves in our cabin and sleep our way through it. Ships are built to deal with these kind of conditions; *people aren't I'm afraid!* What say we get going now?"

"I've no argument with that," Helen responded. "You lead, I'll follow."

"Okay," I said, "just make sure you keep a tight hold of the handrails all the way. Sitting in an armchair is one thing, walking in these conditions is a different ballgame altogether."

As we stood the ship slammed into yet another huge wave, sending jud-ders from bow to stern, and we immediately sat down again, albeit entirely by accident. We stood again, deciding to leave the empty Tupperware container on the floor, precisely where it had landed, and this time we made it across to the handrail in front of the bar without falling. The bar had shut, with its shutters securely pulled down, but the barman was still stood by the entrance with a mop and bucket, attempting to clear up some of the awful spillage that had happened a few minutes previously. Using the handrails to steady ourselves we made our way back along the corridor to the stairwell. Negotiating the stairs themselves proved particularly difficult. As the ship slammed, shook and pitched, our feet kept leaving the floor, and every now and again we found ourselves momentarily suspended in thin air, subsequently landing back on the next stair down with a bit of a thud. But we made it! Another couple of long corridor handrails later and we were back in our tiny little cabin without injury. We took our jackets off, then took it in turns to use the miniscule little en-suite. I poured some tap water into a small plastic beaker, and asked Helen if I could nick some of her Diazepam.

"How many would you like?" she asked.

"Four please," I answered flatly.

"You're only supposed to take two max," she exclaimed.

"Cool! In that case I'll take four! Please!"

Helen just shrugged her shoulders and put her handbag down on the bed. Just as she was about to pull out the little box of Valium pills the ship took an almighty lurch, and we were both thrown sideways across the room, landing on top of each other, but thankfully on one of the surprisingly soft beds. After picking ourselves up and examining our surroundings it appeared that the only casualty was the small plastic cup of water.

"Okay, let's try that again!" I said, ducking back into the shower room to refill it.

As I came out Helen handed me four little white pills, which I immediately downed. She then finished the remainder of the water by downing four herself, and after returning the beaker to its holder above the sink I crammed all four of our bags into the overhead lockers, slammed the locker doors hard down, ensuring they were most definitely firmly shut, then we each climbed into our small but comfortable little single beds, pulled the bedding well up under our chins, and tucked ourselves tightly in ready for the rollercoaster ride of a lifetime. I wedged my back firmly against the wall on one side, whilst gripping the tubular steel frame of the bed tightly with one hand on the other. It was a sufficiently comfortable position in which to sleep, so I closed my eyes, but the motion of the ship was literally like that of a rollercoaster, and so I opened them again.

"I guess you get to sleep in the wet patch then?" I asked Helen

"I'm fine," she replied, "most of it went on the floor anyway. I'm just hanging on here for dear life right now!"

"Ahh, we'll be fine," I said, "'tis nowt ta worry yaself about. She's a good old bird, this here Juan J, she'll look after us like a good 'un, you'll see. Anyways-up, when these here pills kick in, we'll be knowing absolutely nowt about it all 'til mornin', so you just chill yaself out now and get yaself some decent kip."

"Aye aye Cap'n Pugwash," Helen sniggered. "Nite nite."

"Nite nite Seaman Stains," I sniggered back.

I shut my eyes, and very shortly before drifting off into a relaxing Valium-induced slumber, the last thing I remember was hearing the ship's onboard tannoy system announcing, in what I vaguely remembered to be four different languages, *Use of all exits to external deck areas is now strictly forbidden! All foot passengers are now strictly confined to the forward lounge area only! All cabin passengers are strictly confined to their cabins until further notice! The bar itself will remain closed and shuttered for the remainder of the voyage! Thank you for your co-operation!*

And with that, kick in those wonderful Diazepam most certainly did!

CHAPTER
TWENTY FIVE

As an experienced sailor myself I'd become somewhat accustomed to long passages across a rough sea, albeit some rougher than others! *(Ooh, I feel yet another episode coming on!)* Whilst sailing my own boats, generally with limited availability to other experienced crew members, I'd got myself into the habit of working 4-on/4-off shift patterns, and encouraged my 3-man crew to alternate with me using the same pattern, *always* working together in pairs. That meant four hours at the wheel, followed by four hours of sleep, and so on. On some of my longer passages this clearly meant that the *sleep* aspect of the pattern became highly important, and as a result of my learned ability to function efficiently using this method, particularly as being both owner and skipper of these boats meant accepting full legal responsibility for the lives and welfare of all persons aboard, I had, over the years, as I'm sure most other sailors do, developed a rather uncanny ability to understand precisely what was happening aboard whilst remaining fully asleep. I'm obviously not talking in the way of minor details here, its more purely in relation to the safety of the ship itself, and the successful completion of our passage plan. So, for example, if I knew we were to sail a direct course at a constant speed for the next eleven hours, and I'd been sound asleep for just two hours, and then suddenly, for some reason unbeknown to me, our course were to change, or our engine revs were to drop, or indeed anything that may feel out of place were to occur, then I'd immediately awaken, and be straight up in the wheelhouse questioning my crew's watch as to what was going on. If, on the other hand, everything felt entirely as it should be, then I would simply remain sound asleep, fully recognising the importance of my sleep's limited timespan, but whilst still somehow remaining fully aware of the fact that our ship was continuing to make safe passage, absolutely as planned. To this day I still find this ability to be rather uncanny, although I have to say that it only ever manifests itself at sea; never in the air, and certainly never on dry land. This occasionally surprising talent of mine, somewhat inevitably I guess, also relates to the surrounding weather conditions during our passage as well. After all, safety at sea, or the lack of it, is all too often dominated by the weather itself. So if the weather is predictable, and in my considered opinion safe to sail in, *which clearly depends entirely upon your vessel, and the experience of your skipper and his or her crew,* then I shall always feel comfortable aboard, and confident in my sleep. If the weather were to deteriorate to the point where I considered it might potentially endangering the ship or its crew, then regardless of whether it was my own boat, or I may simply be just a passenger at the time, and indeed regardless of how many Diazepam I may have swallowed in order to help me sleep through exceptionally rough conditions, I would both immediately and automatically wake from my sleep, and dress accordingly. Were I to be acting skipper at the time, I would take control there and then, and most likely revert to Passage Plan B, which generally meant diverting to the nearest available port. However, as a simple passenger, upon being awoken by the uncanny instinct that something simply wasn't right, I'd simply find somewhere comfortable and sheltered to sit, most likely out on one of the upper open aft decks, and probably not too far away from one of the lifeboats either! Thankfully, tonight I was not only merely a simple paying passenger, but one in the hands of a skipper, his ship and his crew, all of which I felt entirely confident could be trusted with not only their ability to safely handle their vessel, but also their judgement in the ship's ability to handle the weather conditions in which they'd made the decision to sail in. Consequently I remained blissfully and comfortably asleep.

We'd probably been asleep for a couple of hours, so my guess was that it would've been somewhere around midnight when I felt a change in the wave patterns. We no longer appeared to be surfing the massive rollers of a following sea, occasionally breaching ever so slightly as we were picked up by the huge face of yet another giant monster, causing us to roll a little every time we did so, but not in an overly uncomfortable way; so far the skipper appeared to have the situation entirely under control. But my intuition told me that the wind had shifted direction, probably now coming from a little more towards the west, and the sea state was gradually becoming more and more confused. The huge rollers were still relentlessly travelling in a roughly southerly direction, although smaller but far angrier waves had now started traversing across them at an angle, occasionally breaking and sending creaks and shudders through the ship every time one slammed into our starboard side. The Juan J Sister took on more of a rolling motion; but it still appeared to be regular and controlled, and so basically, I just didn't bother waking up, even though I knew it was more than likely going to get still worse as the night wore on. I was enjoying my sleep, and in a strange, possibly even an *addictive* kind of way, I was enjoying the motion of the ship, whilst, and I'm guessing now, dreaming about '*A life on the ocean waves . . .*'

Another couple of hours passed, and during my enjoyable slumber in my safe, warm and comfortable little rollercoaster carriage, I had felt the confused sea state grow steadily angrier, and the ship gradually, albeit still predictably, take on more and more of a roll, whilst at the same time still slamming hard into the troughs of the huge rollers, whose wavelengths, thankfully, were slowly but surely increasing to significantly more than the five hundred feet length of our own vessel. I'm not entirely sure whether I *heard* or *felt* the lounge furniture on the deck above shifting around, but I was fairly sure that, had I been awake, I think it probably would have bothered me somewhat. But I kept my composure and stuck with my dream, whatever that may have been. Then suddenly, although its hardly as if I can say without warning, I was lifted entirely off my mattress, sheets, blankets and all, and dumped unceremoniously into the tiny little gap between our two beds, one leg on the floor, the rest of my sheet-entangled body wedged in just as tightly as our bags were in the overhead lockers. Needless to say I awoke immediately, however my own body's aerial movement was immediately accompanied by one almighty crashing sound, and I think it was more likely that than me that woke Helen up.

"What on earth's going on?" she asked in a sleepy and confused state of mind, whilst still lying comfortably in bed with her back pressed firmly against the wall behind her.

"Well," I replied calmly, carefully attempting to extricate myself from my *inter-bed* predicament, "we're not exactly *on* solid earth right now babe, we're currently on a rather fluid and considerably rough little sea. But hey, I'm fine, its fine, everything's all good, you just get yaself back off to sleep now, and I'm sure the next time you wake we'll be in far calmer waters."

"So what were all those crashing noises about then?" she asked rather worriedly. "Are you hurt? Is anything broken? What happened? And what's that dreadful smell?"

"Well, I guess we just ran into a particularly big wave, there's quite a few of them out there tonight, but nothing that could possibly trouble this good solid old ship, so nothing to worry your sleepy little head over. I'm pretty sure the crashing you heard was just some pieces of furniture moving around. I'll take a quick little look-see."

I managed to haul myself back up onto my bed, switched on my little wall mounted reading light, and sat up with my back propped firmly against the wall, holding on tightly to the metal bed frame. The ship lurched sideways again, quite violently, then pitched forwards into yet another trough after ploughing across the top of yet another huge roller. It wasn't enough to shift me from the position I'd braced myself into though, nor was it sufficient to move Helen at all, who luckily, unlike myself, had chosen the *correct* wall to properly brace herself against. It was enough, however, to send still more of the heavy lounge furniture on the deck above crashing noisily across the floor, and I wondered at that point what kind of state the rest of the ship must be in by now. '*Thank God they've chained all the vehicles securely down to the floor down on the car decks*' went through my mind at that particular moment in time. Despite bad weather forecasts, its not something that car ferry crews always bother to do, and often with disastrous consequences, but at least on this occasion they had. I'd watched them doing it, and paid particular attention when they'd secured the Foden down, the result of which I was entirely happy with. The furniture itself, obviously providing no one was sitting in it at the time, which I'd certainly hoped no one was, was actually of little consequence, and in the reality of the shipping world had to be replaced on a regular basis anyway. After shifting my position a little I cast my eyes around the room. All was in order, with the exception of two things. The white plastic chair that had been located underneath the tabletop dresser was no longer there, it was gone, nowhere to be seen; and the air in our cabin smelt distinctly as if someone had sprayed it with a whole bottleful of *Aux-de-Sprouts!* I wondered for a brief second who on earth that may have been!

"Okay chickadee," I said, trying my best to be my calm, collected and confident self as always, "that'll be where the crashing sounds came from then. Just be careful next time you step into the shower room, there'll be an upside-down white plastic chair in there somewhere. And trust me, if we had a window we could open right now, then I most certainly would, but sadly we don't."

"Mind you," I continued, trying to make light of it whilst attempting a little giggle, "it could well prove quite handy being able to have a sit-down shower in the morning. Either way, the chair can stay right where it is for now, there's no harm done, let's get ourselves back off to sleep now."

Helen relaxed, closed her eyes and very quickly drifted back into the land of nod. I clambered myself back into my little bed then tucked the overblanket firmly underneath both sides of the mattress, braced my back against the side wall, and clung tightly with one hand once again to the bed frame. Before switching off the little reading light I checked my watch; coming up towards 3am. Still another five hours to go, *at least!* The ship lurched to one side yet again, then slammed into another trough, but this time I was ready for it. The sea state had become still worse, and even through the insulated walls of our interior cabin I could hear the wind screaming through various bits of equipment, railings and rigging, etc, out on the decks. But although it was still horrendously rough outside it seemed to me that it had settled once again into at least some kind of predictable rhythm, and with that I felt confident enough yet again to close my eyes, in a further attempt to retrace the steps of my previous dream. The Diazepam was clearly still active within my system, and within a few minutes, still braced securely between the wall and the bed frame, I began to drift off into yet another of my '*heightened awareness*' forms of sleep. The very last thing I remember going through my mind were those immortal words of Thomas Fuller's that had been indelibly stamped deep within my psyche from a very early age. '*He that will not sail till all dangers are over must never put to sea.*'

The next time I awoke the sea had calmed significantly. I could tell straight away that we were still riding the crests of some decent sized southbound rollers, but the semi-confused state caused by the shift in wind direction seemed to have ceased, and things appeared considerably more comfortable now. I switched on the little reading light and peeked at my watch. It was 8.30am. We should have docked thirty minutes ago! *God, I love Diazepam!* I wonder where we are exactly? I quietly removed the plastic chair from the shower and slid it back where it belonged, then used the bathroom briefly, pulled on my jeans, jacket and boots, and left the cabin as quietly as possible so as not to wake Helen. Mind you, I have to say, if Helen had managed to sleep through the flight that we'd taken the day before, albeit Valium-induced, then I'm pretty sure she could manage to sleep through virtually anything, so there'd be little chance of me waking her anyway, at least not until she was good and ready. I climbed the stairs, walked the corridor to the for'ard bar lounge, and took a good look around. The skipper had clearly lifted the ship's lockdown curfew by now, as most of the foot passengers that had been confined to the for'ard lounge were now taking well needed breathers out on deck, but the lounge area itself was something else. *It was a total mess!* Not one piece of furniture remained upright, other than the tables, which were fixed securely to the floor; but tables aside, the whole room looked like a bomb had gone off in it. Thankfully, however, now that it had become daylight, and the seas had calmed sufficiently for me to at least be capable of walking in a straight line, without clinging tightly to one of the handrails, several members of the crew had begun righting the furniture in an attempt to put the lounge back into some kind of semblance of order. I had an overwhelming urge to go topsides, out on deck somewhere, in the hope that I might be able to take an educated guess as to our rough location. I walked around to a starboard side stairwell, climbed a further flight up, then stepped out onto an open deck area that connected the for'ard pool area with the aft games pitch. I took a firm grip on the chest high handrail and breathed in that wonderful salty Mediterranean air as deeply as I could possibly manage. It was still extremely windy, blowing straight into my face from a roughly north-westerly direction, but I was standing in a relatively sheltered position, and as it didn't feel overly cold I didn't find the need to zip my jacket up, which, all things considered, I found surprisingly pleasant. It was immediately clear as to why the seas had calmed, particularly from those violent, short reach, breaking westerly waves, as we were now sailing within the lee of the north-easterly shores of the island of Menorca, which was clearly visible some eight or nine miles off our starboard flank. The Juan J had slowed her speed considerably during the bad weather crossing, and as I'd assumed that the crew now had double duties in helping to clear up some of the internal devastation, I'd also guessed that she was no longer in any hurry to dock, and would most likely retain this relatively low speed until reaching the safety of the full protection of the deep water harbour of Mahon, almost down at the far southeast corner of the island. The swells that we were running were still massive, but their wavelengths were such that they had little effect on the stability of the Juan J. I did wonder, however, just how things would appear when these giant rollers hit slightly shallower waters, then crashed into the cliffs and beaches that littered Menorca's northern coastline. I was particularly interested in observing the effect of such dramatic seas on firstly the cliffs surrounding the northern entrance to Fornells Bay, and subsequently the effect of the residual waves across the inland waters of the bay itself. In the meantime though, as I'd reckoned we probably had less than a couple of hours to go before docking in Mahon, I thought I'd best go try to wake my dear wife from her deep, drug-induced slumber, and try to persuade her up onto the deck in order to witness entering the stunningly beautiful port of Mahon from the sea for the very first time in our lives. I set off back down the stairwells again in search of cabin number 122.

I found it easily, and using the key card I stepped inside quietly, expecting to find Helen still fast asleep in bed. She wasn't though, she was in the shower. *Happy days!* I pulled the little white curtain slightly to one side, stuck my head inside, getting my hair soaked in the process, and startled her half out of her wits when I said *'morning babe'*. I then informed her that we were going to be a couple of hours late docking, so there was no hurry for her to get finished; I'd meet her on the next deck up in the aft truckers caff whenever she was ready. Then, with just a small amount of struggle, I pulled our bags out of the overhead lockers and set them down on the beds. I rummaged through my own kit-bag until I found my little pocket camera, stuck it in my inside jacket pocket, then headed off out of the cabin and up the stairwell in search of some kind of breakfast. There was a steadily growing queue for the roped off café entrance, consisting of all manner of passengers, most of whom appeared somewhat ashen-faced, and it stretched halfway down the corridor almost to the information desk, which was by now both manned and busy. I stood next to some of the enquirers, whom I'd gathered were a mixture of Spanish and German, and tried my best to get an ear for what was going on. The gist of it amounted mainly to apologies for the mess that the ship was in, yes we were going to be late docking, yes all the vehicles were completely safe, there were no damages down on the car decks, however one or two people were still being treated by the ship's nurse in the first aid room, quite a few foot passengers were still vomiting outside on the more sheltered port-side decks, but the café should be opening for breakfast within the next ten minutes, once the crew and kitchen staff had finished clearing up the last of the devastation, and got the galley back into ship shape working order yet again. *'Please would all passengers be patient and remain calm!'* I took another flight of stairs up onto the starboard foredeck, stood in the shelter of the curved glazed screen for'ard of the swimming pool, and stared out across the rollers at Menorca's eastern coastline, whilst allowing the still strong, gusting wind to finish drying my hair. My watch read a little after 9am, and a big, bright yellow ball of sunshine was shining brightly low in the clear blue sky, directly off to the port side of the ship. Not up for long enough yet to warm the air, but it certainly wasn't anything like as chilly here as it had been back in Barcelona, and by the looks of it the day was promising to turn out very nice indeed. Even the wind was starting to settle a little, and I was beginning to get the impression that we'd now left the overnight storm well behind us. Hopefully it would soon dissipate entirely, and whilst I certainly wasn't expecting any glorious weather such as we'd just experienced down in Malaga, I kept my fingers crossed that the couple of days we were about to spend on our *'home island'* would at least remain dry and sunny. Right now though we were still surfing along on huge rollers that I estimated were well over half the height of our ship. The Juan J Sister had an overall structural airdraft of somewhere in the region of eighty feet, and I'd estimated our current wave height, from peak to trough, to be somewhere in the region of fifty feet. However, because our wavelength, as in the distance from peak to peak, was probably somewhere in the region of half a kilometre, the ride had now become smooth, comfortable and controlled. *But it was still good fun!* I turned to head back down to the aft café in the hope of joining Helen somewhere in the queue, then stopped and gazed in awe at the little swimming pool. Yesterday it had been full of clean, clear fresh water, covered over with a clean roped safety net. Today it was half full of filthy, frothing brown seawater, with clumps of seaweed entangled sporadically across the open rope mesh. I looked up towards the sky, and immediately spotted something significantly more frightening. The ship, as many often do, used a steel cable stretched from the top of the foremast to an anchor point atop the funnel assembly as a radio signal receiver. This cable would have been around eighty feet from the ship's waterline, and as I stood there aghast, I counted at least twenty fronds of wet, dripping, dark brown seaweed hanging from the entire length of the cable. I blinked three times, gulped hard, shook my head, and as I headed back towards the stairwell, for the second time in as many days, I pulled my little golden Saint Christopher out from underneath the neck of my shirt and gave it a great big smackaroony! *'Hmmm...'* I thought to myself. *'Some trips worse than others eh? Thank God we managed to sleep through most of that one!'*

As I reached the aft café the queue had changed position from the main entrance to the servery. Some people, mainly truckers, were already seated at tables tucking into their breakfasts, and all around appeared to be virtually back to normal. I'd guessed that the crew had probably worked extra hard, most likely throughout the night under exceptionally difficult circumstances, in order to keep as much of the ship as possible up and running and in a presentable fashion. I certainly had huge praise for the results of their efforts. I caught up with Helen near to the back of the queue, staring at a laminated picture menu attached to the wall. Spanish menus were often portrayed in pictures, it made for a far easier choice for those of us that forever struggled with the lingo.

"Hi honey, how was your night's sleep?" I asked, expecting the worst by way of an answer.

"I slept absolutely fine, thank you," she replied. "I seem to remember some kind of weird dream about flying chairs, but apart from that, no complaints, just as comfortable as ever. How about you?"

"Oddly enough," I said nonchalantly, "I think I had a fairly similar kind of dream. Hey ho, what are you thinking for breakfast hun?"

"Let's push the boat out shall we?" she said with a grin and a wink. "Get the day off to a good start eh? Full Spanglish for me I reckon; bacon, sausage, scrambled egg, hash brown, beans, toast and a big pot of tea."

"Good thinking Señora Reason," I agreed. "You go grab the cutlery and condiments and find us a table somewhere, I'll get two of those plated up and bring them over just as soon as they're ready. Mind your footing as you go though babe, this floor's still not quite as stable as it might appear in these huge swells."

It took two full trays to carry everything we'd wanted to the cashier's till position, and I paid her the twenty-odd euros in cash, then carried them one at a time across to the table that Helen was sitting at. She'd chosen one that was still available on the starboard side of the ship, and as I took my seat we both stared out of the windows across the bright, shiny blue rollers towards Menorca's beautifully green eastern coastline. There were nowhere near as many passengers in the café as there were passengers on the ship altogether, so my guess was that the majority of them didn't really feel much like eating that morning. Can't say as I blamed them, although our personal appetites, along with those of the majority of the other lorry drivers, seemed to be pretty much in tact as per normal. As we munched our way through our breakfasts, which could only be described as *average* at best, although entirely acceptable under the circumstances, Menorca's coastline grew steadily closer, and I watched intently as we sailed past what

I'd instantly recognised as the old watchtower high up on the hill above Cala Mesquida. I reckoned at our current speed it'd be about another twenty minutes before we'd hang a sharp right, then head into the safety of the bay of Mahon. Perfect timing to unhurriedly finish our breakfast, then wander up on deck together and marvel at the pretty little city of Mahon as we approached it from seaward in the bright morning sunshine. Which, after polishing off the last of the toast and downing the very last drop of tea, is precisely what we did. And as we stood together on the port side of the open, upper aft deck, in glorious sunshine underneath a beautiful, cloudless, bright blue sky, watching the timeless beauty of the ancient medieval and Moorish castles and towers that surround Mahon's harbour grow ever closer by the minute, I wrapped my arms tightly around my dear wife, pulled her close to me, wiped a little bit of egg off her chin with my sleeve, kissed her fully on the lips, and whispered softly in her ear,

"Honey, we're home!"

We clung together tightly for what must have been a whole minute, both of us, I seem to remember, with tears of joy rolling down our cheeks, Helen returning my kiss with an equal amount of passion. Together we stared across the bay with huge affection as we gradually drifted past one of our all time favourite restaurants, that of Dinkums on the pretty little waterfront promenade in Es Castell. I pulled my camera from my jacket pocket and shot off a dozen or so pictures of this beautiful city, that we'd had the pleasure of visiting *so, so* many times, but never seen before from this particular viewpoint. I made sure to get a perfect shot of Helen leaning against the handrail looking out over Es Castell's waterfront, somewhere that she'd known intimately from her childhood days, thanks very much so to her parents. I then handed the camera over to a young Spanish couple, and asked politely if one of them would mind taking a picture of the two of us together, arms around each other, which they most willingly did for us, snapping off a couple with differing architectural backgrounds. At that very moment in time we were essentially as happy as pigs in the proverbial; only to be brought back down to earth moments later by the ship's tannoy system noisily belting out, *'Todos los conductores y sus pasajeros regresaran inmediatamente a sus vehiculos . . . . Would all drivers and their passengers please return immediately to their vehicles.'* We kissed once more, just briefly, then headed off back down the stairwells towards our cabin in order to collect our baggage. Once packed and secured, we left our key cards on the table, hoisted them over our shoulders, and headed on down two more levels to the lower car deck. As we reached the passenger door of the Foden I'd felt by the juddering through the steel floors that the ship had already docked at the quayside, and half a dozen crew members were still busy unchaining the straps that had securely lashed each vehicle down to the decks, in order to stop them from shifting around during the violence of the seas throughout our overnight passage. Those retainers certainly appeared to have done their jobs admirably, as down below, as best we could make out, everything appeared to be entirely ship shape and *Bristol fashion!* I unlocked the passenger door of the truck, climbed up inside myself first, then pulled up the bags one at a time as Helen passed them to me, placing them once again on top of each other on the middle seat. Helen then followed me up, took her place in the passenger seat, and we sat and waited for the traffic ahead of us to begin to move. The twin steel ramps at the stern of the ship steadily lowered, and the larger vehicles, lorries and camper vans, etc, began exiting one by one. It was a slow laborious process, as each vehicle in turn had to turn around and drive back out the same way that they'd driven in, namely via the rear of the ship; however, the crew were clearly highly experienced in loading everyone in the correct manner. The lower deck had more than adequate beam within which to turn an articulated lorry around in comfortably, without the need for reversing, and several minutes later I fired up the little old Foden's engine, swung her around 180 degrees, and before we knew it we were off up the ramps and safely back, once again, onto terra firma. I checked my watch. 11.25am. It had just taken us sixteen hours to complete a thirteen hour crossing! Hey ho, such is the control that our weather exerts over us on occasion; *I've had worse!* So, onwards, *ever onwards!* Having just travelled from one part of Spain to another there was no Customs clearance to negotiate, and we simply drove around the quayside, out of the gates onto the main harbourside road, and headed off along the waterfront towards the northern outskirts of Mahon. *'WATCH OUT FORNELLS, HERE WE COME!!'*

CHAPTER TWENTY SIX

It was Wednesday the 28th, and at the back of my mind I had some kind of vision of spending New Year's Eve in Barcelona, so essentially time was currently on our side. I knew that the return sailing would take twenty-four hours, given a two hour stopover in Palma, Majorca, along the way, such was the route that our Trasmed tickets had been allocated for us. So I'd figured that we'd just drive to Tamarindos today and spend the rest of the day relaxing. We'd launch the Phoenix first thing tomorrow morning, then spend the rest of the day ensuring that she was comfortably secured to her new sinker mooring. Then we'd take the 10am sailing from Mahon on the 30th which would deliver us back to Barcelona in plenty of time to check into a hotel during the day on the 31st, allowing me adequate time to put my cunning little New Year's Eve Plan together. *Simples!* And indeed simples it was too. *Almost!* We drove out of the far northern reaches of Mahon Bay, and turned right onto the single carriageway road that took us the sixteen or so miles towards our home town of Fornells. Luckily the Repsol fuel station halfway there was open, and we stopped off to pick up a few basic provisions; bread, butter, milk, juice, biscuits, and some fresh fruit. They even kept eggs and vacuum-packed bacon in their little chiller, so we grabbed a couple packs of those too. Most other essentials, such as teabags, sugar and wine, etc, were already waiting for us in our apartment's tiny little kitchen.

The first thing I wanted to see when we arrived was just how spectacularly those massive rollers were crashing into the cliffs at either side of the narrow entrance to Fornells Bay, followed immediately afterwards by just how rough or calm we might find it where I'd laid the sinker mooring just off Ses Salines. As it so happened, Ses Salines, at the far southern end of Fornells Bay, was where our road would lead us to first, and so that's where we headed for first, opting to check out the sea conditions in the reverse order. I pulled off the main road and drove down the narrow little lane that took us right to the water's edge, pulling the truck up exactly where I'd parked the hatchback hire car a few months previous. The Foden blocked the entire width of the lane, but there wasn't a soul in sight, so we both hopped down from the cab and strolled hand in hand out onto the narrow strip of shingly beach. There, just over to our left, sat the old upturned wooden dingy, and right there, directly in front of us, some fifty yards offshore, was a round, tough-looking red plastic buoy, sat perfectly still, afloat on a totally flat calm shimmering sea. The wind was still gusting from time to time, sending shivering little ripples across the surface of the water in one direction and then another, but nothing so much as to even jostle the mooring buoy from its position, and I immediately felt both proud and comfortable with the fact that I'd chosen *'Lake Placid'* as the Phoenix's permanent mooring location. We strolled back to the truck, and before climbing back in I patted the Phoenix firmly on her pretty blue hull, and whispered *'not long now old girl, not long.'*

The best place to watch those massive rollers approaching the island from would be up by the lighthouse at Cap de Cavalleria, situated at the far end of a long promontory that constituted Menorca's most northerly point. It was several miles north-west of Fornells Town, and it meant driving along a rough, stoney old lane that hadn't yet been laid with Tarmac. But drive it we did, overloaded though we still were, and when we'd parked up and walked to the cliff edge the scene before us was simply spectacular. As I'd suspected, once those massive rollers reached shallower waters they'd become huge breakers, the likes of which I'd only ever seen before on the telly! They were smashing into the three hundred foot high cliff faces with such ferocity that we could actually feel the ground beneath our feet shudder with each and every impact. The wind all around us was whipping up huge masses of white foam, much like placing an electric fan next to a bubble bath, and the air itself was so full of moisture and spray it felt as if we were in some kind of saltwater shower at a spa facility. Except that it was cold. *And it was scary!* It was actually genuinely scary, I'd never witnessed anything quite like it before. It was just as if the sea was a real, live, angry monster out of some kind of X-rated horror movie, trying its damnedest to gobble up the whole island. And not only were we next on its prey list, we were getting absolutely soaked, even though we were three hundred feet above normal sea level. Today, however, the sea was clearly far from normal, and nowhere near level either, and we quickly climbed back into the cab, backed the truck around over some rough scrubland, and headed very slowly back down the track towards Fornells Town.

We pulled into the little car park right on the harbour front, jumped down and locked up. Not that there was any need to lock up I'm sure, there wasn't a soul in sight. But I wanted to go for a little walk. I wanted to see exactly what effect those massive rollers were having as they smashed into the cliffs either side of the narrow northern entrance to the bay itself, how far into the bay they continued, and how well the harbour wall protected our little fishing fleet from such atrocious northerly Tramontana winds. So we took to the footpath that ran alongside the beaches just north of Fornells harbour, and walked steadily towards the one hundred and fifty foot high cliffs at the entrance to the bay. The further north we walked the more the bay narrowed, and the more it narrowed the higher up the footpath took us. After about twenty minutes we reached a suitable vantage point, from which we were quite clearly able to see the state of play with the bay's entrance, as well as the whole of the bay itself, which stretched out before our eyes way off to the south. The breaking rollers were still massive, as they crashed into the cliffs either side of the entrance to the bay, gradually but steadily eroding them away over the millennia. But those tough old granite-like cliffs appeared to act very much like a funnel, a two-sided breakwater that had a significantly calming affect on the remaining width of each roller as they made their way through the entrance. The breaking rollers that were smashing into the cliffs up around Cap de Cavalleria were probably somewhere in the region of fifty feet in height. By the time they'd tracked a little further south, they'd lost a proportion of their energy as the water grew shallower, and as they crashed wildly against the cliffs at the entrance to the bay I'd estimated them to be somewhere in the region of thirty feet in height. Still cold, still highly dangerous, and in no way would I ever consider attempting to sail one of my own vessels through those kind of conditions. Leaving the bay by boat, virtually any boat, would have been entirely out of the question. However, the remainder of each roller that made its way through the bay's entrance, between the high cliffs on either side, made it through without breaking, and those far more settled rollers that ran in one after another with monotonous regularity, as well as predictably long wavelengths, by the time they'd entered the bay and begun fanning themselves out, were probably somewhere around ten feet from peak to trough. We walked back down along the little footpath, jogged past the pretty little sandy beach, then skipped up the steps that led onto the top of the harbour wall itself. I'd guess the top of the harbour wall would've been around twenty-five feet above sea level, and we walked right out to the very end of it, to where the twelve foot high steel mast, with its green-flashing starboard marker light, was blinking away at the entrance to the harbour, constantly, night and day. I peered over the edge of the wall, and as each wave continued to roll past us at regular intervals, having fanned themselves out significantly more as the bay widened still further, I estimated their height by then to be around three feet. I squinted through the bright, late December sunshine as I cast my eyes further south, and the more the bay widened out, the more the waves dissipated. From my viewpoint I could clearly see the foreshore of Lizard Island in the middle of the bay, and long before reaching this point the waves had disappeared altogether. The farthest couple of miles towards the southern end of the bay, all the way down to Ses Salines and the salt marshes just beyond, remained entirely flat calm, and despite the chilly inshore breeze, apparently totally tranquil. I breathed a huge sigh of relief, set my mind entirely at rest, and gave my wife another giant hug. Over a distance of some four and a half miles or so, the massive storm waves that we'd encountered on our overnight trip here had steadily gone from an angry fifty feet in height to a peaceful zero, and I now felt 100% confident that I'd made entirely the right choice in deciding on Ses Salines as the location to lay the Phoenix's new mooring.

"Come on honey," I said, taking Helen by the hand, "let's go check out our little home, just up over that there little hill. I know you've not been out here for some time now, but last time I was here all was well and good. Let's go take a look-see shall we?"

"Good move," Helen replied, "I could certainly do with sitting down for a while on something that isn't bloody *moving!*"

So, hand in hand we ambled back along the top of the harbour wall, took the steps back down to the bottom, and walked across the car park to the truck. We then drove the couple of miles or so around the lanes towards our pretty little apartment complex at Tamarindos. All day tomorrow would suffice for the launching of the Phoenix. The remainder of today would be spent warming up the little apartment, followed by a little desperately needed relaxation, after which we'd wander out locally in search of somewhere to have dinner. Not that there was going to be much in the way of choice, as I knew most establishments would be closed and boarded up at that time of year; but I felt confident we'd find something vaguely suitable fairly close by. I pulled the Foden into the empty little car park to the front of the pretty Tamarindos apartment complex, applied the air brake, and switched off the engine. *We'd made it! So far, all boxes ticked!* I leaned across the bags, pulled Helen a little closer towards me, and gave her another soft kiss on the lips. Then I checked the odometer on the dash, purely out of interest. The trip meter had registered 1,194 miles in total; not quite as far as I'd initially estimated, but then there was an additional 44 miles by train, and roughly 160 miles by ship. *Blimey, she HAD cut her speed back!* Plus a diversionary 1,200 miles or so by plane. Planes, trains, ships *and* automobiles eh? Well, all in all, despite some tough going and a couple of setbacks, I reckon that wasn't too bad an effort, all things considered. Especially over a 10-day period at one of the most difficult times of the year. I gave myself a little pat on the back.

"Well done honey," said Helen, "I *DO* love you. Despite some of the scary bits here and there, that trip was just awesome! And here we are, safely home, all in one piece!" She then gave me yet another little pat on the back. I *DO* like pats on the back!

"Come on," I said, "let's go warm the place up."

I jumped down out of the cab and walked around to Helen's side. She passed me down the bags then climbed down herself, and we walked along the path to the front door, then set the bags down on top of the old wooden pub garden table that was sat out front, something that had somehow managed to find its way there a couple of years previously, all the way from the Railway Tavern in Fishponds. *Hmmm...!* I unlocked the door, and we both stepped inside together. *Brrr, chilly!* Our little 2-bed apartment had no heating for the winter, neither did it have any air conditioning for the summer. As a general rule, whenever we were there normally we found it pretty much unnecessary, and not really worth investing in. However, every room had a ceiling-mounted electric fan, and more to the point, I'd stocked the place up with electric heaters during one previous winter visit, as I'd found out then just how cold the place could get, especially at night, and *especially* being right on the very edge of Menorca's northern coastline. But right now, even though it wasn't particularly warm outside either, the sun was still shining brightly, and I unlocked and threw open all the window shutters to let the light in. Next I turned all four gas burners up to *'HIGH'* on the cooker hob, and after throwing the main electricity trip fuse to the

'ON' position I took each of the three electric convector heaters out of the wardrobes, set one in the middle of each room, and turned them all up to 'HIGH' too. I also found a little two kilowatt fan heater in one of the cupboards, and I set that in the middle of the lounge with both bars fully on as well. Not that I'd leave that one running for too long, it'd eat up *far* too much electricity; and I'd turned the gas cooker off some twenty minutes later too, once the place had warmed up sufficiently. The three convector heaters, however, would most likely remain fully on for the entire length of our stay. *To hell with the electricity bill for them!* Helen brought the bag of food in that we'd bought in the fuel station, and set herself to work in the tiny little studio-style kitchen. I brought the remainder of the bags in and sat them down, one on each of the single beds in the kid's bedroom. All the beds were made up, but only with summer quilts on, so I reached into the top shelves of our own double wardrobe and pulled out two extra warm, king size overblankets, which I laid neatly one on top of the other over our extremely comfortable king sized mattress, that we'd spent a small fortune investing in a few years previously. The little apartment was warming up quite nicely now, and I opened one of the wooden patio doors that led out onto the minuscule little balcony. It overlooked the pretty communal gardens, with a fabulous view of the bay beyond.

"Ooh, can you keep that door shut please babe," Helen immediately scolded me with, "that cold draft's blowing right through me. And it looks like we've got another problem here too I think. As best I can tell it looks like the fridge-freezer isn't working. I think it might have given up the ghost."

I shut the little folding patio door immediately, she was definitely right about the draft, but at least I'd clocked the fact that, despite the overnight gales, all appeared to be tickety-boo out back. So what's with the fridge then? Best check the trip switch first, me thinks. I opened the little fuse cupboard yet again, but the kitchen utilities trip was fine, still in the 'ON' position. I opened the fridge door; no light. I moved it away from the wall and pulled the plug from its socket. There was no fuse to check, as Spanish 2-pin plugs weren't ever fitted with fuses. I checked that the kettle was working, which it was, then slid the fridge around and plugged it into the socket that the kettle had been plugged into. *Nothing!* No sound, no buzzing, no interior lights, nothing! I switched it off and switched it on again, still nothing! I kicked it hard, right up the compressor! *Still* nothing!

"Hmm," I said sadly to Helen, "I seem to recall there's a technical term for this particular problem."

"What's that honey?" she asked innocently.

"Its fooked!!" I replied.

I wound the cable around the condenser grid at the back, opened the solid wooden front door to the apartment, which Helen immediately closed behind me as soon as I was outside, and dragged the deceased fridge-freezer unit slowly and carefully out onto the pathway, across into the car park, then stood it upright not far from where the truck was parked. I'd deal with that little problem at a later date. I didn't really have the time or space in my head for crap like that at that particular moment in time. I walked back in and asked Helen if anything else appeared to have packed up, but she said no, everything else seemed to be working fine. I checked the electric hot water heater, and the red light was on, so I knew that was all good. I turned the TV on, which only received Spanish channels anyway, although we did have a fairly decent collection of DVD's, and that was working fine. Not that we ever watched the telly during the summer, we were always off out playing somewhere, usually with the kids, and generally in the sea beside a beautiful sandy beach. But at least we had one, and it still worked. As indeed, so it appeared, did everything else. So, just the fridge that was knackered eh? Oh well, it'd be cold enough overnight to leave the milk, etc, outside on the little balcony out back; and because our complex, as most very often are, was built on the side of a small hill, which led on down to the rocky shoreline, it meant that although our front door was at street level, our balcony at the rear was effectively at first floor level. Which essentially meant that it couldn't be got at by any of the multitude of wild/stray cats that constantly roamed the streets both day and night. So that's what I told Helen, and that's where all the stuff that would've gone in the fridge went, and it was all fine! *'And don't worry babe, I'll get a new fridge-freezer ordered, delivered and installed well before our next trip over here. You know how helpful our agent Jaqueline is, she'll take care of it for us, no problem.'*

I told Helen to sit and relax, so she removed her jacket and hung it up, then plonked herself down in a crumpled little heap on our comfy 3-seater sofa. I turned the little music system on, and selected a CD from the rack that was very familiar to both of us, one that we both really enjoyed listening to together, stuck it in and pressed play. Moments later the sounds of Candice Night singing *'Oh its good to be back home again!',* from good old Ritchie's latest album *'Fires at Midnight',* were wafting through the air waves, and if I had anything to do with it, hopefully wafting across the sea waves too. Helen looked up bleary-eyed at me, and a huge smile spread gradually from one side to the other of her pretty little face. I stuck the kettle back on and made both of us a nice strong cup of English breakfast tea, opened a packet of biscuits, set the tray down on the coffee table, plonked myself down on the sofa next to my wonderfully patient and tolerant wife, put my arm around her shoulders, and we cuddled up close together as we slowly sipped our piping hot tea, and munched our way through half a packet of custard creams. We were thoroughly loving the sounds of Blackmore's Night's Renaissance-style music, and we sat and listened to the whole album all the way through together. *Yet again!* And we simply sat there, did absolutely nothing, and just *relaxed*.

A couple of hours later our sunshine had left us all alone once again, and it was beginning to get dark outside. Halfway along the short road that runs around the hill from Playa de Fornells to Fornells Town, right next door to the community's management offices, which we'd passed on the way to the apartment, and which were now closed for the off-season, was a decent sized beach shop which was also closed. And next door to the beach shop was a decent sized restaurant, which again, was also closed. However, at the far end of the little alleyway that ran between the offices and the shop sat a small café-bar, which was run by the locals, for the locals, those very few members of the Playa de Fornells community that chose to live there all year round, with their larger 5-bed homes that not only had air conditioning and central heating, but also had *satellite TV!* And I knew, because I'd enquired on previous occasions, that Marco's Bar would not only be open that evening, but they would also be serving bar snacks. That would have to do for tonight, I'd had enough of driving for a bit, and I quite fancied meself a proper drink! So we pulled our jackets on, walked out into the chilly evening air, zipped them up and set off up the lane on foot. It was only a ten minute walk to Marco's, and sure enough they were open, but with no one present so far in the way of other customers. But it was toasty warm inside, so we removed our jackets and took initially to a couple of stools at the bar. A young lad, who spoke little in the way of English, appeared behind the bar and asked what we'd like to drink. I ordered a vodka and coke for Helen, mucho grande por favor, and a brandy and lemonade for myself, además mucho grande, gracias. The lad poured the drinks, and we sat and savoured them until Marco finally appeared. Who, as we knew from meeting him on several previous occasions, *did* speak relatively good English. He was certainly very pleased to see us, if somewhat surprised that we'd turned up at that particular time of year. I explained to him the reason why we were there, and briefly summarised our adventurous little trip that we'd had along the way. He seemed intrigued with all of it, and asked many questions about our journey, which we were both more than happy to chat to him about. Several more vodkas and brandies later, however, and we both suddenly felt the need to eat, and so we ordered from Marco's limited menu, then took seats at one of the very few laid up tables, whilst Marco disappeared off to the kitchen to prepare our dinner for us. Helen had opted for a simple dish of roast chicken with chips and vegetables, and I'd chosen the fish of the day, which, on that particular day, as per the majority of particular days, was swordfish, served also with chips and veg, as they seemed to be about the only choice of accompaniment available. After Marco had been gone for some time I asked his young lad if he would kindly bring us over a bottle of house red, which he duly uncorked and placed in front of us with a polite nod and a smile.

Shortly after that an elderly Spanish couple came in, and after Marco had served us up our food we were grateful to be left to ourselves for the remainder of the evening, whilst the other couple provided a suitable distraction in the form of utterly incomprehensible Spanish conversation with both Marco and his lad. The remainder of the evening, however, was not to last for very much longer. I desperately wanted to get an early night, and hopefully a well-settled night's sleep too, as I wanted to be up bright and early the following morning. It was going to be an extremely important day, the culmination of all of my efforts over the last few months, and I was still hoping to God that it was all going to go entirely according to plan. And whilst I felt reasonably confident that it would, I wanted to allow as many daylight hours as possible to achieve my goal. Our dinners were both delicious, although I have to admit the cheap bottle of house red left a little to be desired, but I paid Marco his thirty-two euro tab with a gracious smile, a handshake, and a muchos gracias mi amigo, then the pair of us pulled our jackets back on, bid both Marco and his young lad buenas noches, wandered back along the alley, and then headed off down the little road towards our, hopefully, nice and warm little apartment. It had become even colder outdoors, although I was feeling pretty warm inside, *especially* after consuming three very large brandies. Helen felt pretty much the same way too, and we both felt comfortably satisfied with the delicious meals we'd just eaten together. So, let's go see exactly how warm the apartment feels then shall we, after just walking out of somewhere proper toasty warm. I unlocked the front door, and we both walked in and immediately took off our jackets . . . *it was fine!* Albeit surprisingly so, but nevertheless our little home had warmed up adequately using just the convector heaters that we'd left on during our brief absence.

"Ah, that feels better," said Helen, "its all nicely warmed up in here now. D'you think we should turn the heaters down a little overnight?"

"Yeah," I answered, "I think I'll turn all three of them down from '*ten*' to '*five*', then see how the place feels when we wake in the morning. its just after ten o'clock now babe, I'm gonna hit the sack. Are you okay setting the alarm for six in the morning, I've got a bit of a workload on tomorrow."

"*I should coco,*" she replied positively, "6am sharp, you go jump in the shower, I'll get the bacon and eggs on the go."

"You're a darling," I said, "you really are."

I kissed her sweetly on the forehead, undressed, and climbed into our wonderfully comfortable, almost warm, king sized bed, then pulled the blankets tight up to my chin. Helen joined me a few minutes later, said nite nite, and we both drifted off happily into a long deep sleep. The last thought I remember running through my mind that night was something along the lines of *Lake Placid*. The only dream I vaguely remembered first thing the following morning had something to do with monster crocodiles! Thankfully that one faded within seconds, never to return.

CHAPTER
TWENTY SEVEN

Following the dreadful clanging of our early morning wake-up call the next day, by the time I'd finished in the bathroom Helen had a plate of bacon, eggs, fried bread and baked beans sat waiting for me on the breakfast bar, along with a steaming hot cup of freshly made tea.

"Morning gorgeous," I greeted her with, "I trust you slept as well as I did?"

"I've absolutely no idea," she replied jokingly, "I was sound asleep, all night long."

"Good for you sweetheart," I said, "I'm very glad to hear it. This looks delicious, thank you very much. And great to see the place is still nice and warm too. I assume you're also warm enough?"

"I am indeed hun, have been all night long. And no worries with the brekkie, just enjoy, I'll have mine whilst you're preparing the boat for launching."

I finished my delicious breakfast, then dressed in the same scruffy pair of jeans that I'd already been wearing for a few days, grabbed an old sweatshirt out of the wardrobe, and pulled that on over two even older T-shirts, then laced up my work boots over two pairs of socks. I was going to try my damnedest not to get wet whilst launching the boat, even though I'd be prepared for it, but I'd made other plans for later on that day, and *I weren't lookin' forward to the journey 'ome neiver!!* I told Helen I wouldn't be many minutes, and stepped outside into the chilly morning sunshine. Actually, to be fair, it wasn't altogether that chilly, even though the sun hadn't yet quite risen above the horizon. And anyway, I'd become pretty much immune to any kind of temperature over the years, having spent most of my adult life working outdoors in all weathers, and half of my earlier years as a canoeist, paddling the freezing white-waters of some of Britain's fastest rivers during the winter kayaking seasons. So yes, basically, I never went *anywhere* without a wetsuit. But hopefully I wouldn't be needing it for *'stage one'*. I unstrapped the ladder from the Foden's flatbed, stood it up against the side of the Phoenix, and climbed on up. One by one I removed our suitcases, took them back indoors and laid them side by side on our bed. I asked Helen to place all of our dirty laundry into black bin liners, to pack four day's-worth of clean clothes that we'd need for the journey home into our overnight hold-alls, and everything else that was clean, but that we wouldn't need for the journey, pack into either one or both of the suitcases. I then climbed the ladder again, then unlocked and let myself into the forecabin. The sleeping bags could come out, and I threw them over the side of the boat onto the ground. They could sit on top of one of the wardrobes indoors for the fore-seeable future. I then unplugged and removed the yellow flashing light unit, and everything else that related to the truck, rather than the boat, I carried back down the ladder and took indoors. I scratched my head a little over the 5-gallon can of spare diesel, as I hadn't actually given any prior thought to that, but decided eventually to leave it aboard, on the simple assumption that having spare fuel at sea was far more important than having spare fuel on dry land. I stashed the diesel fuel can in an under-seat locker in the forecabin. I also stashed the tool kit with it, along with the fire extinguisher and the spare coils of rope that I'd bought from Halfords, as I was pretty sure I'd have no use for any of that kind of stuff during the drive back to the UK. The heavy duty jack, the foot pump and the foreign road emergency kitbag I took back indoors with me. I then grabbed a set of waterproof over-clothes, the jacket and trousers that I'd always kept aboard, pulled them on over the top of my jeans and sweatshirt, slid down the ladder for, *hopefully*, one very last time, and strapped the ladder back to the flatbed just in case. So I was ready; or rather, *we* were ready!

"Come along Helen," I shouted across the little car park, "let's go get this baby's bottom wet again."

"On my way!" Helen called back, zipping up her jacket as she slammed the front door shut.

I didn't really need Helen to come with me, I knew, *or at least I hoped*, that I'd be doing this job all by myself. But I wanted her along with me for three reasons. Firstly, purely for moral support. Secondly; never, *EVER*, do anything even *remotely similar* to this without having someone stand close by you, even if the very least they can do to help you is by dial 112, *or 999 as it is in the UK,* if anything were, *God forbid,* to go horribly wrong. And thirdly, well, someone had to take some photos! So up we jumped into the cab, and off we drove, just a couple of miles into Fornells town. I swung the Foden around at the very top of the wide expanse of sloping concrete slipway, backed her ever so slightly down onto the slope, pulled on the airbrake, switched off the engine, and jumped down from the cab. Helen jumped down too, and I handed her my camera. I then told her to go sit on the wall over by the far side of the slipway, and no matter what she thought or witnessed, unless I shouted to her otherwise, *JUST STAY PUT! 'Oh yeah, and snap off a few pictures whenever you feel like it too.'* So, the first thing I needed out of the way was the ladder, along with its straps, all of which I set down at the top of the slipway apron. I then removed the remote control for the cable winch from its locked security box, and flicked one of the switches just to check that it was properly active. I then removed the tensioned ratchet straps that were lashing the Phoenix securely down to the flatbed, followed by the ratchet straps that secured the rusty old trailer down. This meant that the entire weight of both boat and trailer were now being held in position solely by the cable winch itself, along with its somewhat worryingly ancient assortment of internal components! I strolled down to the water's edge, which, thankfully, was dead-flat calm. It was also totally crystal clear, and for the first time ever I noticed precisely how that concrete ramp had been constructed. The slope of the slipway was roughly about twenty degrees, or one in five. *Nowhere near as steep as the hill that leads up and out of Millau!* And it continued on out into the clear cool sea for about fifteen feet, at which point the water was roughly about three feet deep. And then, *it simply ended!* And the water depth dropped off probably a further three or four feet at that point, and then steadily increased in depth further on out towards the bay. Well, I guess that's about all you could achieve with concrete structures in non-tidal waters then! *I hadn't actually thought about that!* Hey ho, it was what it was, I'd get round it somehow; and it wasn't exactly like I cared for the trailer much anyway. its just . . . well, its just that . . . well, once the wheels of the trailer reached the very end of the slipway, the point where it drops off into some six or seven feet of water, well the Phoenix wouldn't actually be afloat at that point, she'd still be sat high and dry on the bed of the trailer! Oh well, like I said, I had no use for the trailer anyway; at least not that particular year; although possibly in nine or ten months time I might, but we'd have to wait and see about that separate little plan, as and when the time arrived. Either way, whatever happened now, I'd always known from the way we'd loaded the Phoenix in Bristol Marina that there was only ever one way to take her out of the water, and that was by using a crane. Hence yet another reason for befriending my dear old buddy Pedro. But all of those ideas of mine could wait for the time being, at least until the following winter. Right now my considerations were solely for getting the Phoenix *in* to the water, not getting her *out!* I jumped up into the cab, started the engine, let off the air-brake, and allowed her to coast steadily down the slope until the back end of the flatbed was about three feet away from the water's edge. I then pulled on the brake, switched off the engine and left her in first gear. As I jumped down out of the cab I just caught a quick glimpse of Helen out of the very corner of my eye snapping off a couple of piccies with the camera. *'Good girl'* I thought to myself.

I walked around to the back end of the flatbed, unclipped the extension ramps, and slid them out from their secure slots located within the underside of the flatbed itself. I clipped them one at a time firmly into their positions level with the top face of the bed, then let their free ends splash down into the water. They were both around five feet long, and the very end of the Foden's sloping ramp was therefore now positioned some two feet out into the water. It was exactly what I'd planned all along, and certainly the best I could hope for, given the unexpected circumstances in regard to the premature end to the slipway itself. *Hey ho, here goes nothing then! Or everything! Or whatever!!!* I hit the *'DOWN'* button on the remote control, and the trailer, Phoenix and all, steadily advanced back down the flatbed. *'DOWN', 'stop', 'DOWN', 'stop', 'DOWN', 'stop',* and so on, one foot at a time. The trailer wheels rolled perfectly onto the extension ramps, and then right off the other end into about nine inches or so of water. I kept letting her back until the trailer wheels were almost submerged, at which point I was able to stand on the front bar of the trailer, reach up onto the foredeck of the Phoenix, and grab hold of the extra long mooring warp, one end of which I'd made fast to both for'ard deck cleats prior to the launch. So now I held a long mooring warp in one hand, and the cable winch remote in the other. And *now I was worried!* I knew I'd have to drop the trailer wheels right over the far end of the concrete slipway, but how far would I have to let the trailer go on before the Phoenix floated free? And just how easy would it prove to be in retrieving the empty trailer back over the lip of that solid mass of concrete again? *Oh well, only one way to find out I suppose!* I continued to let the trailer roll backwards until the wheels were poised right at the dropping point, half on, half off of the very end of the concrete, and the Phoenix was still sat very much high and dry. I'd guessed she needed another two feet of depth in which to float, and I'd also guessed that dropping the wheels over the end would've probably given her only another fifteen inches. *Not enough!* So I hit the *'DOWN'* button one more time, and then heard this almighty underwater crash as the wheels went over the edge, and the steel frame of the trailer smashed into the bottom end of the concrete ramp. *It wasn't enough! The Phoenix still needed more depth!* So I hit the *'DOWN'* button once more, wondering what on earth would happen next. But instead of the trailer rolling back any further, the front of it simply lifted up in the air. I kept the *'DOWN'* button pressed, and wanted to close my eyes, *but didn't!* And the more cable that ran out from the winch, the higher up in the air the ball hitch of the trailer rose. Three feet, four feet, four and a half, and then, all of a sudden . . . *KERRR-SPLOOOSH!!!* . . . the Phoenix slid herself backwards, perfectly, smoothly and effortlessly, right down the back end of the sloping trailer, and launched herself majestically straight into the sparkling, bright clear blue waters of Fornells Bay. *I guess we'd reached that perfect point of balance then; the 'tipping point'!* My instincts were torn in two directions at that moment. Secure the boat? Or secure the trailer? *I did both!* I immediately hit the *'UP'* button on the remote control, which brought the front of the trailer back down to earth again, whilst holding fast the mooring warp to make sure the Phoenix didn't drift too far out, but far enough out to make sure she wouldn't ground on anything. I kept my finger on the *'UP'* button until the wheels of the trailer were pulling tight against the back edge of the concrete ramp, but then the cable winch motor began to strain, and it wouldn't pull up any further. So I knew I'd run into some kind of problem with that, set the remote down on the flatbed, and left it all as it was for the time being. I then took the long mooring warp, hopped up over the wall that Helen was sitting on, ran down onto the first of the temporary mooring pontoons, and pulled the Phoenix gradually in towards me. Just before her bow struck the pontoon, I spun her around so that she was port-side-to, dropped her fenders down, and secured her properly, both fore and aft, to the pontoon's cleats. She'd be just fine where she was for however long I needed. Now, *how the hell do we get this bloody trailer back out of the water?*

I stepped off the pontoon and walked to the end of the wall that Helen was sitting on. I think she took a photo of me at that point, with the Phoenix in the water safely moored up right behind me, but I wasn't entirely sure, my concentration was elsewhere at the time. I peered through the water to see how the trailer was sitting exactly in relation to where the wheels were, and gave the situation some considerable thought.

"She'll come," I said aloud to Helen, after a few moments of deliberation. "Might be a bit of a strain, and I'm not gonna risk it with the winch cable either, but she'll come! I'll need you to go stand somewhere well clear though please babe, just in case anything goes wrong. Can you wander down onto the pontoons and stand by the Phoenix please? Oh, and feel free to snap off as many photos as you like."

Helen walked down onto the pontoon, well out of the way of my next move. I then took one of the ratchet straps, attached one hook to the ball hitch on the trailer, wrapped the webbing around the tow bar at the very back of the flatbed, attached the second hook to the ball hitch, then tightened the ratchet. I then did exactly the same thing with another ratchet strap, so that it was doubled up. Then I grabbed the remote and pressed *'DOWN'*, so as to leave a little slack on the cable, but left it attached just in case. Then I jumped up into the Foden, started the engine, and attempted to drive forwards. Initially she wouldn't move; and then I smelt the clutch burning! A few little wisps of blue smoke from the burning clutch blew out from under the cab in the breeze. I tried again, and the clutch burnt still further, to the point, apparently, that even Helen could smell it from where she was stood. Okay, third time lucky, and this time I was going to drop the clutch immediately. Only one of three things could possibly happen; either the trailer would come flying out, the engine would stall, or something inbetween would break. I revved the engine, dropped the clutch, there was an almighty underwater clattering sound, and the Foden shot forward, pulling the trailer up with it, dragging the two extension ramps noisily along behind, and carried on up to the flat upper section of the concrete ramp. *Without bursting either of the trailer's tyres! Phew!!* I pulled up immediately, switched off and jumped down. I then hit *'UP'* on the remote until the cable was taking what little strain now remained, which was virtually nothing, simply half a ton of soggy old trailer, then removed both of the ratchet straps and put them to one side. I then kept my finger on the *'UP'* button until the winch pulled the trailer right back up onto the flatbed, and stopped it in exactly the same position it had been previously. I disconnected the ramp extensions, and one at a time slid them back into their locating slots underneath the bed, locking them securely in position. I then took one of the ratchet straps and secured the trailer firmly down to the flatbed, then retrieved the little tyre that had been acting as a cushion between the Phoenix's bow and the HIAB, and fully launched it through the air into a nearby half full skip. So, *MISSION ACCOMPLISHED!* Well, almost!

Stage two next, and it shouldn't take too long, although time *was* still on our side; it was still only a little after 10am. And although it was still pretty chilly, the sun was shining brightly in a perfectly clear blue sky, and I was feeling exceptionally good about everything. Especially the fact that I'd come across an unexpected problem, and I'd successfully managed to get over it *without* the need to get myself wet. Stage three, however, inevitably *would* involve me getting wet, but hey, that was all a part of the plan anyway. I grabbed my phone out of the cab and dialled Pedro's number. He answered after half a dozen rings, immediately recognising my number as it flashed up on his screen,

"Hey, Mister Chris, how you do? You in Menorca? How I helping you?" he asked in his unmistakably cheerful broken English. It was good to hear his voice again, especially as I knew I'd be needing to use his services again many times in the future.

"Pedro, buenos dias, qué tal mi amigo? Sí, sí, I'm in Fornells right now, and I have a present for you."

"You are having present for me?" he asked inquisitively. "What is?"

"Its a trailer," I said, with a semi-feigned air of generosity. "Not a very good one for the road, but ideal for your yard. And its yours, you can have it for nothing. Where can I meet you with it?"

"I am working in old boat yard with big crane today," he replied. "You know where is?"

"Sí, si, señor, yo se dónde estáeso, I'll see you there in about half an hour or so."

I lashed the ladder to the flatbed, then coiled the remaining ratchet straps and placed them up in the cab. I walked over to where Helen was still standing on the visitor's pontoon and climbed aboard the Phoenix. From inside an under-seat locker I pulled out a two-piece neoprene wetsuit, a scruffy old pair of trainers, and an old beach towel, replacing them with the waterproof overclothes I'd been wearing up until then, which, as things had worked out, I hadn't actually needed anyway, then pocketed the keys and skipped back onto the pontoon.

"Ready babe?" I asked Helen.

"Where are we going?" she replied.

"To Pedro's shipyard in Mahon," I said. "I'm going to attempt to swap this old trailer for a genuine Spanish favour."

We both jumped up into the cab, fired the old Foden up, and left the Phoenix safely tied up to her temporary mooring, whilst taking the road from Fornells back towards Mahon. Some thirty minutes later I pulled our newly-lightened truck into Pedro's old shipyard, which was more or less opposite the scrapyard that I'd salvaged the sinker parts from, the other side of the road to the gin factory, and pulled up right next to the giant crane that Pedro was sitting in. He appeared to be in the process of returning a large commercial fishing vessel to the water from its chocks situated on the quayside, and so I backed the Foden safely away from the crane and waited patiently for him to complete the operation. Some ten minutes later he jumped down from the crane and jogged over towards us. I jumped down from the Foden too, and we met around the front, enthusiastically clutching each other's hands, and shaking them with firm, friendly grips. *Very firm!*

"Hola Mister Chris, how you are? What you have here for me?" Pedro asked excitedly.

"Hola Pedro mi amigo, I believe you've met my wife Helen once before?" I replied, throwing my hands up towards Helen's smiling face, beaming down on the pair of us from the passenger side window.

"Sí, sí, buenos dias Señora Helen," Pedro replied with a smile, "I am in pleasure for see you again."

Helen smiled back, and with her extremely limited Spanish vocabulary, simply said, "Hola Pedro."

"So," Pedro continued, "you have bring to me this *beautiful* lorry?"

"Sadly not," I answered, and then announced proudly, "However, this *beautiful* yard trailer sat on the back of it is all yours! You can keep it, for nothing, for free!"

"Oh, dearly, dearly me," he said with a bit of a frown. "I have many, many trailers for yards, you are asking me for to be adding this one for my collection?"

"That's really good of you Pedro, muchos gracias amigo, where exactly should I offload it?" I retorted, jumping the gun a little in an attempt to stay one step ahead of him.

"Well, I . . . I . . . I suppose is okay in this corner by over there . . ." he said, pointing across to the side of a slightly smaller single boom crane over in the corner of the yard.

"That's just *FAB* buddy, thanks a huge bunch for that. I know you'll make great use of it at some point. Tell ya what amigo, I'll let you keep this old aluminium ladder too, I'm sure you'll find a use for that as well at some point," I mouthed off to him cheerfully, in my very best incomprehensible Bristolian accent.

"Ladder?" he questioned. "Ladder *always* good. Gracias Mister Chris."

"Okay Pedro, is no problemo," I replied. "Now, I would like you to do me a favour in return please. I know the trailer isn't a very good trailer, but the favour isn't really a particularly big favour either. So, would you mind doing me a little favour, in return for my scruffy old trailer? Oh, and a half decent ladder too? Por favor, would you mind?

"What is favour?" Pedro asked.

"Okay," I responded, "so you know I have put my sinker mooring down in Ses Salines?"

"Sí, sí," said Pedro.

"Well now I have brought my boat, the Phoenix, all the way from England on this little lorry, and I have launched it into the water in Fornells, and I will be leaving it moored to the sinker in Ses Salines for the majority of next year. And I know you go to visit Fornells quite regularly to look after some of the fishing boats over there in the harbour. So every time you go to Fornells I would just like you to keep an eye on the Phoenix for me please. Maybe you could drive down into Ses Salines, just to take a quick look each time, so firstly the people that live there will know that you are keeping a watch over her, and secondly, if you see there is any problem with her at all, you can maybe call me, and I can come over to sort it out. Would you mind doing that for me Señor Pedro, por favor?"

"Is no problemo Mister Chris!" Pedro agreed willingly. "Every time I go Fornells, usually maybe one times in most week, I go to see your Phoenix to make sure she all good. If no good, I telephone you. *Bravissimo!* Tell me one thing now por favor. Is she having *seguro?* How you say, *insurance?*"

"Well," I began a little sheepishly, "she *does* have fully comprehensive insurance, yes. And I rang the insurance company and told them that I was taking her to Fornells in Menorca, and they told me that was no problem, all would be fine, she'd still be fully covered. But then they told me that there was one strict condition. She mustn't be left in the water during the winter months, November to April. She must be kept out of the water for that period, sat on the hard, chocked up on dry land, or firmly attached to a suitable trailer, if I should happen to have one available."

"But she is not!" Pedro said, frowning at me. "She is in the water now, and now it is being winter!"

"Well," I concluded, "I didn't really have very much of a choice. I needed to use this lorry to get her into the water, that's the only way I could manage to achieve that task on my own, and now I need to drive this lorry back to England and sell it. So what I'd figured I'd do is this. I'm just gonna take a chance on everything being okay weather-wise from now until next April, which I'm quite sure it will be, and then I'll use her with my family, hopefully many, many times during next summer, and then, when we get to next November, I'll ask you to come over to Fornells with your *mobile* crane, and we will find somewhere over there, on the outskirts of the harbour, where we can chock her up on the hard for *next* winter. And maybe, *just maybe,* you could drag this old trailer along with you? If its still usable by then? That would be simpler than chocking her, but I'll leave that choice entirely up to you. Anyway, either way, firstly, that allows me plenty of time to work out with the other boat owners where best to position her, and if I have to, sort out some decent wooden chocks for her. Secondly, given the storm that we've just experienced, I seem to have picked the safest place possible to moor her, down in Ses Salines, which is clearly very well protected. And thirdly, I just wanted to see her afloat right now, attached securely to her new little sinker mooring. I'm sure she'll be absolutely fine, but will you promise me, please, that you'll just keep any eye on her for me? *Pretty please?*"

"Mister Chris, you must understand that it is all of your own risk. But yes, I will watch for your Phoenix for you every time I am going for to visit in Fornells."

"Muchos, *muchos* gracias Señor Pedro, you are a *true* gentleman!"

With that we shook hands vigorously, then Pedro helped me winch the old yard trailer back off the Foden, and together we pushed it round by the side of the smaller of the two cranes, and left it sat there, hardly even visible amongst the long grass. I refixed the extension ramps, climbed back into the Foden, started her up, and both Helen and I waved cheerfully at Pedro as we drove towards the exit of the shipyard. The very last thing I noticed as we drove away was Pedro marching purposefully across his rough old yard with a long aluminium ladder tucked firmly underneath his arm.

CHAPTER TWENTY EIGHT

Before driving back to Fornells I made a brief diversion, up the steep little hill out of the port, deep into the backstreets of Mahon. I'd come up with what to me seemed like a particularly clever idea, and pulled the truck up nearby to a large professional ironmongery store that I just happened to know fairly well. I disappeared off inside, and came back out minutes later carrying a rather expensive high grade stainless steel padlock.

"What's that for?" asked Helen inquisitively.

"Just to be on the safe side babe," I replied. "Damned thing cost me almost fifty euros, but then it is stainless, and I just want to make doubly sure that no one attempts to move the Phoenix to a totally different location whilst we're not around. You never know, better to be safe than sorry and all that. Look, see what's written across the packet in bold red lettering? *ALTA SEGURIDAD!* That means *HIGH SECURITY!* Anyway, its the best they had available, and I'm sure it'll more than do the trick."

"If you say so hun," Helen replied, stifling a yawn.

It was almost midday, time to crack on with stage three of the operation! We drove back towards Fornells, but before reaching the town itself I pulled off down the little lane into Ses Salines, and parked up close to the beach. Firstly, where Helen could see the sinker through the windscreen of the cab, but secondly, this time, where we weren't causing an obstruction to other traffic, of which there didn't appear to be any around anyway. The next move was somewhat of a struggle in the front seats of the Foden's cramped little cab, but at least I managed it without *too* much swearing! I pulled off *all* my clothes, with the exception of my boxers, then pulled on my tightly fitting old wetsuit; full-length trousers followed by long-sleeved zip-up jacket. Then I jumped down from the cab onto the soft grassy road-side, and pulled on the tatty old pair of trainers too.

"Right," I said to Helen, my determination more than obvious in the tone of my voice, "you wait here babe, I should be back in somewhere under an hour. Feel free to go take a walk along the beach, or even through the village if you'd prefer, and keep that little camera to hand. I'll be back with the Phoenix before you know it, and hopefully you can snap off a couple of piccies once I get close enough. Back soon. Love you."

"Love you too babe," Helen replied. "And don't worry yaself about me, I'll be fine. I'm *always* fine when the sun's shining, no matter where I am."

And with that, I left the towel draped over the driver's seat, picked up the new padlock, which I'd already taken out of its packet, and added one of the keys to the collection of boat keys that were attached to a round floating cork. I gave Helen a quick peck on the cheek, and set off up the lane on foot towards the road that would take me back into Fornells Town. Keys and padlock in hand, I marched purposefully alongside the pristine azure-coloured water's edge, back towards the visitors pontoon that I could already see the Phoenix tied up to, some two miles or so ahead of me. The sun was still shining, there was little in the sky in the way of cloud, the wind had virtually ceased altogether, and I estimated the air temperature to be somewhere in the region of a balmy seventeen degrees. The water temperature, however, was a different matter altogether, hence the wetsuit! During the summer I'd be more than happy to simply swim out to the Phoenix wearing a regular cossie. This time of year, however? Nope, sorry, wetsuit only, or its not happening I'm afraid! Even if it was only going to be the briefest of dunks; if you've got it, *use it!* So I was, and as I contin-ued to walk towards the town, the neoprene chafing ever so slightly at my groin, I marvelled once again at just how beautiful this whole area was, and how much I was looking forward to bringing the family out here during the summer months, and taking them for boat trips around this beautiful, calm, safe little bay of ours. Drop the anchor for a spot of fishing, pull up onto a deserted little beach somewhere for a picnic lunch and a spot of sunbathing, exploring little coves that virtually couldn't be reached at all by land, or simply diving off the roof of the boat and swimming in the warm waters of one of the most beautiful places in the whole world. *Ahhh...* I stopped dreaming the minute I reached the outskirts of Fornells, and some thirty minutes after leaving Helen behind on Ses Salines beach I strolled down onto the visitor's pontoon and stepped aboard the Phoenix. *'Here we go then,'* I thought to myself, *'let's see how well this old girl behaves today shall we?'* I threw the battery isolator switch to *'ON'*, stuck the key in the ignition, gave it a twist, and her sweet little Ford diesel engine fired up first time. I patted her affectionately on her smart wooden dash, and whispered *'good girl'* into her black analogue rev counter. Then I cast off both for'ard and aft mooring warps, coiling them neatly down onto the decks, and pulled back aboard the two white plastic fenders that I'd hung out over the port side just before tying her off. *And then we were off and away!*

I reversed the Phoenix away from the pontoon, back around towards the slipway, and then slipped her into forward gear and slowly made my way out into the flat calm waters of Fornells Bay for the very first time. As we got a little further out into the bay I opened her up a little, then towards the middle of the bay, once the engine had warmed up to *'normal'*, I opened her right up, and at her maximum top speed of nine knots, leaving some considerable wake behind her stern, we cruised all the way around Lizard Island and back out into the middle of the bay again.

Everything was working absolutely perfectly, and there was nothing in the whole wide world I wanted more at that particular moment in time than to be right where I was, doing precisely what I was doing, and I felt very, VERY happy indeed!

I slowed her to her cruising speed of seven knots, not wishing to use up too much of the limited quantity of diesel she had aboard, took one more circuit around Lizard Island, then headed on down towards Ses Salines. My waypoint marker was the end of the old wooden jetty, which was clearly visible from some considerable distance away, although the English chap's large modern-looking yacht, which was generally moored there during the summer months, was clearly conspicuous by its absence. I motored past the end of the jetty, easily located my new bright red mooring buoy just a little beyond the other half dozen little fishing boats, all of which were safely attached to their own sinker moorings, throttled right back, and approached the buoy at dead-slow speed with the gears set to neutral. As I drifted up to within reaching point, I grabbed the steel ring on the top of the tough plastic buoy using the boat hook, then took the for'ard mooring warp through the ring and made it fast to one of the foredeck cleats. That would do for the time being. Now to safely stow away everything that wasn't needed, and fix up the long-term permanent mooring that I'd had in mind from day one. I switched the engine off, and left the key in the ignition for the time being. Anything of any value, such as my grab bag with all my navigation and emergency kit inside it, had been securely hidden away in a locked cupboard in the forecabin. I removed the aft mooring warp from its cleats, and stowed that in an under-seat locker in the forecabin too, along with both of the fenders. I'd already disconnected the anchor from its twenty metre length of tensile steel chain, and stashed that safely in a forward locker too. I then lay across the bow, reached down towards the buoy, and fastened the end link of the anchor chain to the steel ring on top of the buoy using the brand new stainless steel high security padlock. I let about a metre of chain hang loose over the front of the bow, just to allow the boat to move freely in the event that any waves might possibly lift her up and down, caused maybe, for example, by the potential wash from other vessels manoeuvring around the area. I then secured the run of steel chain around its geared winding mechanism, which was firmly bolted through the foredeck, locked it off tightly, and left the remaining seventeen metres or so sat at the bottom of the chain locker. I double checked that the anchor chain drive mechanism was securely clamped down and locked, then removed the for'ard mooring warp and stowed that in a forecabin locker too.

Just four things remaining on my checklist. I started the engine again, and pulled the gearshift into astern. The anchor chain tightened against the mooring buoy, which in turn pulled the heavy old underwater chain tight against the concrete blocks sitting in the mud some five feet down below. We weren't going anywhere, it was just like being tied to a solid concrete wall. I revved the engine a little more, took a visual bearing across the end of the jetty, and we still weren't going anywhere. I increased the revs in astern gear to maximum, sat with my eyes fixed firmly on my bearing, and *still* no movement. *Perfect!* I throttled back and switched her off. Next, I lifted up one of the aft deck interior floor panels, reached inside until I felt the stern gland greasing mechanism, and gave it a good firm twisting to make sure the gland was fully packed, and there was absolutely no possibility of any water leaking in around the end of the prop shaft. Then I isolated the battery, double checking that the automatic bilge pump, which bypassed the battery's isolation system, was switched to the 'ON' position. Not that it had ever activated itself anyway, the tonneau cover fitted far too well for that to happen. However, certainly better to have one than to not! And finally, I pulled the blue PVC tonneau cover out of its locker, and after securely locking up the forecabin, fastened each of the press studs all the way around the cabin roof, and back around the aft transom, tensioning it perfectly into position.

"*ALL DONE!*" I shouted across the water to Helen, who was happily sat on the shingly beach snapping off the odd photo every now and again. *'All sorted, secured, ship shape and Fornells fashion!'* And with that, key float in hand, I lowered myself gingerly over the side of the boat, and let myself slide down into the water until my feet touched the soft layer of mud on the bottom. I shivered and let out a little gasp as the cold seawater ran over the neckline of my wetsuit and flowed on down inside, feeling damned chilly and uncomfortable against my skin, although within just a few moments, due to the tightness of the layer of protective neoprene, the warmth of my body had warmed the thin layer of cold water up to my own body temperature, and I smiled to myself, pleased with the fact that I'd given sufficient thought to wearing one in the first place. I stumbled along the muddy bottom to the bow of the Phoenix, grabbed hold of the chain close to the padlock, and gave it a few of the most almighty yanks that I could manage, given the fact that I was standing neck-deep in cold seawater. Even so, everything appeared as solid as it was ever going to be. One final test. I pulled myself up using the front of the bow, and stood on the short loop of anchor chain that I'd left hanging over the bow. I kept my balance whilst putting all of my weight on it, and then attempted, somewhat clumsily, to jump up and down. It had the desired effect. *Nothing moved!* Everything was rock solid, and I was totally confident that the Phoenix would be safe and secure for however long I wanted to leave her there; come rain, shine, hell or high water. *Fingers and toes crossed, yet again!* I jumped back down into the water, and slowly, steadily, but *extremely* happily, waded back ashore. As quickly as I could then manage I stripped off my wetsuit, dried myself off with the scruffy old towel, and pulled all my dry old clothes back on that I'd been wearing earlier.

"*Happy now?*" Helen asked with a cheeky little grin.

"*EXTREMELY HAPPY!!*" I answered. "The successful culmination of almost a whole year's worth of concentrated efforts. Yes indeed babe, *you betcha life I'm happy!*"

I stood there at the edge of the little grass verge, my back leant against the cab of the Foden, my arm draped around my wife's shoulders, proudly and silently surveying the finished result of my efforts for a good few minutes. I beamed a huge smile towards the Phoenix, and in my mind's eye I could've sworn I caught her smiling back at me. She was simply a picture of perfection, looking more comfortable than she'd *ever* looked, afloat in her new home in the land of paradise. I allowed the moment of euphoria to linger for as long as possible, then turned to Helen and said,

"Come on babe, let's get ourselves going again. I've got another little *Chrissy-plan* up my sleeve for the journey home, and we have to leave early tomorrow, so we need to go pack some stuff up before we go out tonight."

"Ooh," said Helen with a look of surprise, "where are you taking me tonight then?"

"Its a surprise," I said, grinning like a Cheshire cat, "you'll just have to wait and see.

The two of us climbed up into the cab, I fired up the engine, and we drove off up the lane, out of Ses Salines, back around to Playa de Fornells, and on down to our cosy little apartment at the far end of El Communidad de Tamarindos. I pulled up in the little car park out front, and we both climbed down from the cab.

"Okay babe," I said, as we strolled along the path together, "show me exactly how you've managed to pack our bags would you please."

Helen led me on through into the kid's bedroom, and showed me exactly what she'd done, which was basically precisely what I'd asked her to do earlier.

"Those two black bags there on the floor," she began, "they're both full of dirty laundry that needs to be washed. Our hold-alls sitting on the beds are packed with clean, warm and tidy clothes, ready for the journey home. And in our bedroom, one of the suitcases contains all of our nice smart clothing that we wore at Mandy's for Christmas, that you said we wouldn't be needing, and the other suitcase is basically now empty."

"Coolio," I answered back. "Now, find both me and you a tidy enough set of togs to wear out somewhere half decent tonight, then lay them out neatly on the bed, whilst I go pack the truck up ready for the morning."

First I grabbed my dripping-wet wetsuit out of the cab and hung it on a hanger above the bath, so that it could safely be left to drip-dry in our absence. Next I packed all of the kit that we needed to keep with us, such us the jack, the foot pump, three ratchet straps, the bag of emergency roadside kit and the yellow flashing light, etc, into the empty suitcase, then carried it outside, along with the other suitcase, which was full of all our smart clothes and Hawaiian shirts, etc. I then heaved the broken old fridge-freezer up onto the flatbed, and set it down on its back, close to the crash rail, and right next to the cable winch. Next I lifted both suitcases up onto the flatbed, stood them up on their backs behind the fridge-freezer, and pushed the fridge-freezer back so that the suitcases were firmly sandwiched between it and the crash rail. Then I jumped down, wandered back into the master bedroom, and checked out the clothes that Helen had selected for us.

"Those'll do just nicely hun," I said, "and perfect for New Year's Eve in Barcelona too, so let's try not to spill too much gravy down the front of them tonight eh?"

"I *always* try not to!" she replied sternly.

"Yes, and *rarely* manage to succeed!" I retorted with a cheeky grin. "Come on sweetie, let's get dressed and go, I've got somewhere special in mind."

We both changed into our latest set of tidy togs, then I threw my scruffy old set that I'd just taken off, along with Helen's not-quite-so-scruffy old set, into another black bin-liner, knotted up all three black bags, and threw them up onto the back of the flatbed. I then lifted up the front door of the fridge, crammed all three bags of dirty laundry inside, then slammed the door firmly down shut and sat on it for a while, staring towards the sky as the sun began heading rapidly towards the horizon. I then took the two remaining ratchet straps and lashed the whole load securely in place, tight up against the crash rail so that it couldn't possibly move, no matter what.

"Intelligent thinking Captain Chris!" Helen called over to me from the front path.

"Ha," I replied, *"I'm not a pretty face ya know!"*

There was one last thing I needed before we set off into Fornells Town in search of an early dinner, and I popped back into the kid's bedroom and rummaged through the side pockets of my overnight bag. I found what I was looking for, and as it was beginning to get somewhat chilly outside again we both pulled on our jackets, then locked up and climbed back up into the dear old Foden. I fired up the engine, and we drove around the road through Playa de Fornells, back into Fornells Town, and pulled up yet again in the almost empty car park right on the harbourside. Before I told Helen exactly which restaurant I had in mind we took a brief stroll around the harbour, admiring for one last time, for these particular few days at least, the beauty, peace and tranquility of that perfect setting. As we strolled hand in hand back towards the slipway, Helen asked me once again where I was taking her, and I looked her in the eyes and simply pointed straight ahead.

"Ooh," she exclaimed excitedly, "we're not *actually* going to Es Pla are we?"

"We are indeed honey-bunch, one of your Fornells favourites. And the reason I've chosen it? Well, you won't be surprised to learn that I checked with one of the staff earlier today, whilst you were stood down on the pontoon next to the Phoenix snapping off photos, and yes, they *do* have lobster on the menu tonight, so you're in luck; in fact, we're both in luck. Mind you, we'll have to sit inside this evening, its way too chilly to sit out on the waterfront like we normally do."

"*Suits me sir!*" Helen acknowledged excitedly, whilst putting her arm around me and planting a huge kiss right in the middle of my cheek.

As we took up our table inside, which had already been pre-set for us, right next to the huge picture window that looked directly out across the sparkling waters of our beautiful bay, I picked up a white paper serviette and wiped half a ton of lipstick off my left cheek. A smartly dressed waiter appeared at our table almost immediately,

"Señor y Señora Reason," he said, welcoming us with a friendly air of familiarity, "buenas noches a los dos, cómo podemos servirles?"

"Buenas noches Manuel," I replied with equal familiarity. "As I'm sure you're already very well aware, both my dear lady wife Helen and myself would very much like to partake in some of your famous, fresh, locally caught lobster this evening, por favor. Accompanied, dare I ask, with just a few fresh prawns, some fine new potatoes, and a selection of your highly recommended vegetables of the day. And to accompany our delicious main course, por favor, uno *extra large* jug of your very finest champagne sangria. Muchos gracias mi amigo."

Surprisingly, given the time of year, there were two other couples sitting at tables in Es Pla, waiting for an early evening meal to arrive, which was good to see, as I didn't really expect to see anyone around in Fornells during our mid-winter visit whatsoever. Mahon yes, Mahon City was *always* busy, but generally, as my marine insurance company had not-so-subtly informed me, the majority of Fornells town itself, due to its location on the windier, and therefore chillier northern coast of Menorca, tended to shut up shop from roughly November through to April, as it wasn't a particularly popular tourist destination during the winter months, or at least, certainly not with the English contingent. So it was great to see that some places were still open. There were still people around, and quite clearly from their appearance, Christmassy-type tourists at that; albeit most likely Dutch or German. One of the reasons why the Restaurante Es Pla was a good old family favourite of ours was because, during the summer months, they set the tables out on the front sun terrace, right at the water's edge, and Tori and Alex in particular would always take up their own seats closest to the water, wait for a basket of soft bread rolls to arrive at the table, break them into little pieces, and spend ages feeding them to the huge shoal of harbour mullet that swarmed around the shallows, right at their very feet. *Happy days indeed!* Another reason was simply the fact that their food was absolutely adorable. Having initially each picked out our very own individual live lobsters from the huge salt-water glass tank, situated in the very centre of the restaurant, it wasn't too long before our wonderful meals were professionally served up before us, along with silver-service dining accoutrements, and a huge delicious-looking jug of golden, sparkling champagne sangria. I poured two large glasses of the strong, expensive golden nectar, and then, as a last minute little surprise, pulled the last one of the John Lewis Xmas crackers from my inside jacket pocket. I immediately handed one end of it to Helen, and with glasses in hand we sat there together looking out across the sparkling waters of the bay, which were now shining brightly under the reflection of a beautiful full moon, and drank a toast,

"*To the Phoenix, to the family, and to many, many more warm, sunny, happy times here together in Menorca!*" I announced with a firm air of pride and conviction.

"*Here, here!*" Helen heartily agreed.

We chinked our glasses together, downed a decent mouthful of delicious fruity bubbles each, and then, as if by way of making one final magical wish over our almost completed picture of perfection, we pulled our last little golden cracker together. '*Snap! 1ˢᵗ Eskimo; Where did your mother come from? 2ⁿᵈ Eskimo; Alaska. 1ˢᵗ Eskimo; Don't bother, I'll ask her myself!*' The little metal toy inside, ironically, in fact *very ironically*, was a little silver boat. It was actually identical to the little metal ship used in the luxury edition of Monopoly, and would even have doubled up as a spare. I decided to keep it as a lucky charm, and the next time we'd come out to visit our little home in the sun with the family, I promised myself that I'd stick it to the dashboard of the Phoenix with some superglue. I shoved it in my jacket pocket for the time being, and concentrated on getting stuck in to the gorgeous plate of fresh lobster that was sat in front of me. It truly was absolutely delicious, and Helen and I both sat there in complete silence and finished every single morsel, prawns, veg and all. Following which, over floater coffees, mine infused with Cognac, Helen's with Tia Maria, we chatted incessantly about how delicious the meal had been, how successfully the launching of the

Phoenix had worked out, what it was I'd had semi-planned for New Year's Eve in Barcelona, and the various options that were open to us for our long journey back to England's green, pleasant, *cold* and *wet* land. Finally, I summoned Manuel over, and settled la *rather expensive* cuenta in muchos cash euros, leaving him, as we invariably did, with a slightly more than generous tip. We then shook his hand in turn, and said muchos gracias señor as we bid him adios, politely requesting from him that the next time we visited, por favor, we'd like our table set up in the warm sunshine, right at the water's edge, as per usual. He promised faithfully that he'd definitely make sure that would be the case, and we both smiled, pulled our jackets back on, jumped back in the lorry, and drove the couple of miles back to Tamarindos. An early night off to bed was called for. I was pretty tired from a relatively exhausting day anyway, plus we had a ferry to catch the following morning, so an early start would be needed, *yet again!* As we undressed ready for bed, I turned all three electric convector heaters from '*five*' down to '*three*', as the little house was now plenty warm enough, and we climbed into bed, kissed one another goodnight, and within just a few minutes, our alarm set once again for 6am, we were both sound asleep.

"Morning gorgeous," I called from the kitchen, just as Helen hit the alarm to stop it from wailing in her ear. "Bacon and eggs get you off to a good start d'ya reckon?"

"Uhh, okay if I go have a shower first please?" was her sleepy, weak-voiced reply.

"Of course you can sweetie," I responded cheerfully. "I'll have it ready and waiting for you just as soon as you're dressed. Don't rush yaself, we've plenty of time."

Map of Fornells Bay, North Menorca

CHAPTER
TWENTY NINE

I'd woken and dressed a little before the alarm had gone off, and wandered out onto the front terrace, shutting the door behind me so as to keep the warmth in. It was still dark, but I could tell from the trillions of bright stars twinkling across the vast, clear expanse of blackness that there wasn't a single cloud to be seen anywhere. As I looked towards the east the sky gradually brightened ever so slightly into an eerie shade of deep turquoise, as if the sun were knocking to come in from somewhere deep down below. There was a perfect half moon sitting low in the south-western sky, and not a single breath of wind to be felt from any direction. It was still pretty chilly, so I didn't stay outside for too long, just long enough to soak up the total calmness of yet another perfect, peaceful Mediterranean morning. I'd had a good feeling about that day, a very good feeling indeed! After re-entering the apartment I took all the perishable food that we'd bought in the Repsol down out of the cupboards, grabbed the milk and the juice off the rear balcony, closed and locked the external balcony shutters, then closed the little wooden bi-fold doors and locked them too. I don't generally pride myself on being a particularly competent cook, in fact far from it if the truth be known, however, just as Helen walked fully dressed into the lounge, fresh make-up already applied, as if timed to absolute perfection I placed a perfectly cooked full English down on the little breakfast bar right in front of her.

"Wow, what more could a lady wish for?" she asked rhetorically.

"Tea maybe?" I replied.

I made the pair of us a nice hot cup of English breakfast tea, then stuck a CD into the little music system, turned the volume down, and took my place at the breakfast-bar in front of my own delicious looking brekkie. Ordinarily I'd've over-cooked the bacon, under-cooked the eggs, and burnt the fried bread. For some strange reason, that particular morning I'd got it all absolutely spot on. And as we tucked ourselves into our beautiful rashers of soft, tasty, Spanish smoked bacon, Phil Collins completed the irony for us, with his wonderful voice drifting across the airwaves, *'Its just another day, for you and me, in paradise.'* One of both mine and Helen's favourites. Helen did the washing up afterwards, then packed the crockery away, whilst I took the remainder of the unused perishables out to the communal bins at the end of the car park. Helen then finished packing our overnight bags, whilst I went around every room securely locking up each of the window shutters. I packed the three convector heaters back into our wardrobe, on the basis that the next time we visited, hopefully we'd need to be using the ceiling fans instead, and then, last of all, threw the main electricity trip switch into the *'OFF'* position. The sleeping bags could remain on top of our wardrobe for the time being, and my wetsuit, which was still dripping water into the bath every now and again, which was absolutely fine, that could stay exactly where it was too. We carried our bags out to the Foden, then I walked back along the little front path and securely locked the front door. We climbed up into the Foden's comfy little cab, sat all of our bags down on the middle seat, started the engine, then drove off out of the car park on our way back to the Mahon ferry terminal. *'Adios Tamarindos, hasta la proxima! Next time we come to stay I'm sure we'll be greeted by some of that beautifully warm sunshine that Menorca's justifiably famed for.'* A few miles down the road I turned left, and took the little lane down to Ses Salines. I pulled up onto the narrow grassy verge, hopped out of the cab, and ambled down across the pebbly top edge of the shingle beach. The picture before my eyes, to my own way of thinking there and then, was again one of sheer perfection. It was approaching 7.30am, and just beginning to get light. There still wasn't a single breath of wind in the air, and the bay itself was just like a sheet of glass. The Phoenix sat majestically at her new mooring, just exactly as I'd planned all those months ago, some fifty metres or so away from the water's edge. Her perfectly-still pretty little outline was reflected beautifully in the flat calm, shallow grey-blue water, and to me, at that very moment in time, I'd felt just like she'd laid her hat precisely where it was *always* meant to be. I'd finally achieved exactly what it was I'd set out to achieve from day one, and right then I'd felt extremely proud of myself. Helen walked up behind me and put her arm around my shoulders. I draped one arm over hers too, and we stood there in silence together for yet another full minute. There was no need for words at that particular moment in time. But the moment passed, as indeed, sadly, they always do, and I turned towards the Foden and said,

"Come on babe, we've got a ferry to catch!"

Helen kissed me on the cheek, whispered in my ear, *"well done honey, I'm extremely proud of you"*, then we strolled back across the beach, climbed back in the cab, and headed off up the lane towards the main road. Some thirty minutes or so later we pulled up at the back of a relatively short queue of assorted vehicles that were parked up all along the quayside, awaiting the boarding of our ship. The same ship that we'd sailed over on, the Juan J Sister, had just docked at 8am, precisely on schedule, which was very good news indeed, as hopefully that might indicate we'd have a far smoother crossing on the way back than we did on the way over. The weather for it certainly looked very promising, and as I rummaged through my kitbag in search of our two open return tickets, the steel ramps to the stern of the ship lowered themselves onto the quayside, and an assortment of vehicles, mainly commercial, gradually began exiting the vessel. The Juan J's never-ending schedule began generally, subject to weather conditions, with a nine hour cleaning, refuelling and restocking stop in her home port of Barcelona, followed by a thirteen hour voyage across to Mahon, where she stopped for two hours to offload then reload. Then it was a five hour sailing to Palma in Majorca, where she spent a three hour stopover, followed by a sixteen hour overnight sailing back to Barcelona. Oh, how things have changed for the better nowadays, with the advent of today's modern and much faster ships! She'd then sail her following schedule the opposite way around. Palma first, Mahon second, and so on, ad infinitum. So, it was Friday the 30th, we'd be sailing at 10am, in two hours time, and we had twenty-four hours aboard to look forward to. *Whoopee! NOT!* Hey ho, so long as it was a relatively calm crossing I was sure we'd find plenty to amuse ourselves with. After all, we had our backgammon set, at which Helen still owed me seventeen euros, we had a lovely little crib board, and we were happy to play both of those together until the cows came home. Not that you actually come across very many cows in the Med! Plus, Helen still had a couple of girlie books she'd not even started yet; and I'd only managed to get about a third of the way through the one and only fiction thriller that I'd brought along with me, one which, for my sins, I'd started reading some considerable months previous. Anyway, so we'd be arriving in Barcelona somewhere around ten o'clock the following morning, which would allow plenty of time, all being well, for yet another little *Chrissy-plan* that I'd got up my sleeve.

A short while before 9am the offloading finished, and some ten minutes later our queue of vehicles very gradually began to move forwards. A uniformed Trasmed officer was walking along the queue checking everyone's tickets. As he reached our empty little car-transporter, he obviously clocked it immediately as being English, stepped around the front, and approached the driver's side door, whereupon I handed him our pair of tickets.

"Buenos dias señor," he began after examining them, and then continued in almost perfect English, "Please present these at the pursor's office on deck three after boarding, and you will be allocated your cabin. Gracias, y buen viaje."

Not many minutes after that I swung the Foden around, and followed the queue of traffic down one of the steel ramps, and once again into the diesel smelling bowels of the Juan J's lower vehicle deck. I pulled up tightly into the position I was instructed to, applied the air brake, switched her off, and left her in first gear. This time both Helen and I had to jump down from the driver's side, as the passenger door was again too close to a bulkhead to open, however, after Helen had passed me down all of our bags and climbed down herself, I locked the driver's door, then double-checked that the ratchet straps holding the fridge-freezer and both suitcases in position at the front of the flatbed were still tightly secured, and that none of our remaining minuscule load could possibly shift around anywhere. It was all fine and good, and required nothing in the way of adjustment. The other thing I noticed was that the crew hadn't bothered chaining any of the vehicles securely down to the deck this time, as indeed they had for our previous crossing, which gave me still further hope that the good old Med had finally offloaded her recent bad-tempered attitude, and calmed herself down somewhat. We set off with our bags up the three flights of stairs towards the pursor's office. When we arrived it was shut, but a girl at the information desk next door told us that it would re-open immediately the ship left the quayside. Some fifteen minutes later we felt the floor begin to vibrate slightly as we listened to the deep rumbling of the ship's engines starting up, not long after which our bow and stern thrusters pushed us clear from the quayside, and a small, tough old pair of harbour authority tug-boats began to slowly spin us around, so that we were pointing back out towards the open sea again. Once we were clear of all obstructions the tugs cast off their heavy duty warps, the Juan J Sister's twin diesel engines revved up a little higher, and the purser stepped out of his office and up to the counter at precisely the same time as the ship began to move forward. The analogue clock fastened to the bulkhead directly above the centre of the information desk showed exactly ten o'clock. I handed our tickets over to the purser, who, after the briefest of examinations, produced two plastic key cards, and politely informed us that they were for cabin number eighty-nine, deck three, starboard side amidships. We carried our bags back down one flight of stairs, then bundled ourselves along the corridor until we reached cabin number 89. We were both pleased *and* surprised to find that this time we'd been given an outside cabin, and upon opening the door and stumbling inside with our baggage, we found a room that was identical in all respects to cabin number 122, but with one essential difference. *It had a window!* Not that it'd be overly important for the majority of the voyage, but given that the seas had now significantly calmed it would certainly be nice to wake up the following morning with some natural light and a half decent view. We dumped our bags down on the beds, then set off up towards topsides in order to wave one final goodbye to the pretty little city of Mahon from our unique location, aboard ship, inside its wonderful deep water harbour.

Within the hour, as Helen and I stood together looking over the starboard handrail of the Juan J's open top deck, the deck to which access had been denied during our previous sailing, we watched with fondness as the Illa de L'Aire just off Menorca's far south-eastern tip gradually faded into the distance behind us. The sun was still steadily rising into a bright blue, cloudless sky, and the air temperature had warmed noticeably. There was no sign of any of the huge rolling waves that had pushed us along on our rollercoaster ride down there, but then we'd be sailing a due south-westerly course for the next few hours anyway, well protected within the lee of the bulk of the Balearic Islands from whatever might remain of those vicious northerly Tramontana winds, if anything. We wouldn't find out for certain until after we'd left Palma, passed the Isla Dragonera at the very south-west tip of Majorca, and headed back on out into proper open seas. By which time it would be pitch-black anyway, and probably not too far off our bedtime. In the meantime, however, we were just pleasantly cruising along at an estimated twelve knots through virtually dead calm seas, still with very little wind, other than that brought about by our own motion, and so, with jackets zipped up to the chin, and arms linked tightly together, we just stood there for what seemed like an age and watched the world go by. The shores of Majorca's south-eastern coastline came into view well before finally losing sight of Menorca altogether, however, once we'd rounded the very southern tip of Majorca, coincidentally named the Cap de Ses Salines, somewhat ironically the wind began to pick up a little, the air developed a bit too much of a chill for our liking, and we headed back on down to deck four in search of some lunch. It was one o'clock, lunchtime for most, however there weren't exactly a great deal of passengers aboard, and so we helped ourselves to sandwiches, cakes and drinks from the self-serve cafeteria, with no queue whatsoever to worry about, paid at the checkout till and took a seat at one of the starboard side window tables, where we could continue to watch the pretty green coastline of southern Majorca gradually slide by. Two hours later and we'd be arriving in Palma, and for the three hours that we'd be stopped over in port I knew that neither the cafeteria nor the bar would be open, so dinner would have to wait until a little after 6pm. Let's hope that more people get off than get on whilst we're docked in Palma! At least that way we'd stand a good chance of being somewhere near the front of the queue. If indeed there was one! We finished our lunch, then went and sat in the comfy seats in the for'ard bar's lounge area, none of which, thankfully, appeared to be badly broken. Helen bought herself a small gin and tonic, but I didn't really fancy drinking just yet, I'd preferred to wait until dinner, so I just drank coffees. We played a few games of crib together until the Juan J slowed as she gradually began to enter the port of Palma de Mallorca. This was one that we'd both done before, albeit separately before we'd even met each other. Although, ironically, both of us holidaying at different times aboard the same cruise ship, the P&O Ventura. Just a tad more up-market than our present mode of transportation! Anyway, suffice to say that neither of us felt the need to walk out on deck to watch the sights slide by, as we entered Palma's commercial docks at the scruffier end of the cruise ship terminal, so we watched with little interest instead from the warmth and comfort of the lounge, whilst continuing yet another game of cards. Shortly before the ship docked, partly in order to avoid the comings and goings of various off- and on-boarding passengers, many of whom appeared to be Spanish truckers yet again, I decided we should retire to our cabin for a good old Spanish siesta. So that's precisely what we did. For the entire three hours that the Juan J Sister was laid up in Palma we lay on our beds, read for a bit, then steadily drifted off into a calm and peaceful sleep.

All of a sudden I heard this tremendous rumbling sound, followed by the most horrendous vibrations I'd ever experienced. *'Oh my God,'* I immediately thought to myself, *'the damned engines have blown themselves to pieces! There's flames everywhere, we're about to be engulfed by them! The plane's spiralling out of control! We're gonna crash, we're gonna crash! Where's my damned bloody parachute gone? Oh my God, oh my God...'* And then I opened my eyes! The ship's engines had just started up. What is it with daytime dreams, eh? How come they always seem to be so much more vivid than night time dreams? Hey ho, such is life I suppose! I dragged myself off my tiny little bunk, got undressed, and showered for the first time that day, hopping into the smallest shower I'd ever come across. Talk about *'room for only one!'* As I exited the shower, bath towel in hand, Helen was already sitting at the end of the bed, looking as if she was ready to get going already. I pulled my bag down from the overhead locker and swapped my scruffs for some attire that was somewhat more appropriate for dinner. Not that we'd be dining Michelin Star exactly! But it made me feel a little better anyway. Boots, watch, phone, wallet, backgammon...

"Fancy a little aperitif before dinner my darling?" I asked with a mock snobbish accent.

"I do believe it would be most rude not to sir," Helen replied, matching my mock snobbery with perfection.

We stepped out of our cabin and wandered up one flight of stairs, heading towards the bar. *'Oh dear!'* was my first thought. *'Oh dear, oh dear, oh dear!!'* was my second! It was immediately apparent that not only had far more people got on in Palma than had got off, but from the impression I was getting then, the whole ship was now jam-packed full to capacity. We'd already sailed, and as I peered over the top of literally hundreds of heads, and through the far starboard side windows, I clearly recognised Magaluf's magnificently illuminated seafront as we headed towards the lighthouse at the Cap de Cala Figuera. So, the bar was open, and the cafeteria was open too, and the queue for both stretched right out into the corridor, joining together at each end in front of the information desk.

"Quick babe, follow me," I said, tightly grabbing hold of Helen's hand.

By the looks of it most folks had headed straight for the bar without baggsying themselves a table beforehand, and I'd spotted the perfect one right next to a starboard side window at the forward end of the lounge. We took our seats, and I sat the backgammon set down on the laminated top of the fixed wooden table. The view out of the window, now that it had become almost completely dark, was quite breathtaking, and as we sailed around the 150 foot high Faro de Cala Figuera, the revolving light from which is permanently visible some twenty-five miles offshore, we altered our heading from south- to north-west, towards the Isla Dragonera, and the queue at the bar began to diminish a little. Not everyone had managed to find comfy chairs for themselves in the lounge, but most of those that hadn't had wandered off in different directions in search of other alternatives, and as the queue at the bar diminished still further I asked my dear wife what she fancied to drink.

"Well executed Chris," she said firstly, followed by, "I do believe I'll have myself a very large gin and tonic please, if you would be so kind."

"But of course madam," I answered, and as I wandered on over towards the bar I couldn't help but think to myself, *'I haven't executed anyone, have I? Who did I kill exactly?'*

After waiting not too many minutes at the bar, I ordered a large G&T for madam, and for myself an *extra large* Captain Morgan spiced rum, mixed half and half with ginger ale, and served in a tall glass over a large handful of ice, por favor. A habit I'd picked up somewhere in the Caribbean many years previously. I carried the drinks back to our table, only to find that Helen had already set the backgammon up.

"Oh dear,' I said, setting the drinks down on the table, "found the need to lose even *more* euros have we?"

Helen laughed: "Not a hope!" she said firmly.

After I'd won the first game the overall tally by then amounted to me being twenty-six euros up. After she'd won the second game she was back down to owing me just twenty-two euros, although that hadn't overly improved her humour due to the fact that it was her turn to visit the bar. One more aperitif and two more games later, and I was left just nine euros up. More importantly, however, we were just rounding the Isla Dragonera at Majorca's far south-western point, and as our trusty old steed began to hang a sharp right and start heading due north back towards Barcelona, what exactly were we likely to find in the way of sea state after leaving the protection of Majorca's lee shores? It was shortly after eight o'clock, and both of us were getting hungry, but how were we likely to fare at the dinner table if we were to find ourselves ploughing into still more of those giant Mediterranean rollers? Those that the vicious northerly Tramontana winds from a few days ago had been driving relentlessly towards the north coast of Algeria? As it turned out they seemed to have disappeared altogether! Once we hit truly open waters the sea state wasn't exactly what I'd describe as being dead flat calm, but it certainly *was* what I'd describe as being perfectly normal. So essentially, the Mediterranean weather had made our crossing over rather difficult, albeit successful, and now it was going to make our crossing back rather easy. *Hoorah, muchos gracias él clima Espagnol!* We finished up our drinks, packed up the backgammon, and wandered on down the corridor towards the self-serve cafeteria.

I'd begun to get the impression by then that rather a lot of Spanish families had either jollied their way across to Majorca in order to spend the X-word with relatives, and were now returning to the residential sanctuary of their motherland, or vice-versa, the Majorcans were jollying their way across to Barcelona to spend New Year's Eve, or maybe that and their Three King's Day too, with family and friends, yet to return back to their home island in the near future. Either way, the self-serve cafeteria, which had more resembled a trucker's transport caff during the voyage out, was now full to the brim with the clatter and chatter of hundreds of parents with noisy young children in tow, and pretty much devoid of lorry drivers altogether. There were many comings and goings at the food servery counter, but despite that we failed to spot a single vacant table anywhere, and simply stood there together, just inside the entrance, waiting for some dear group to get up and leave. Whilst leaning my back against the partition wall something dug sharply into my shoulder, and as I moved slightly to one side I spotted a small bright red fire glass box. Smashing the glass [*In case of emergency ONLY! Penalty for improper use probably somewhere in the region of €10,000,000!]* would activate the automatic tannoy system, which in turn would request all passengers please report *immediately* to their muster stations. *'Hmmm…' I thought to myself???* And with that, thankfully, yes indeed, a couple with a pair of noisy teenage lads sitting near to the centre of the dining hall did, luckily for us, begin to get up to leave. Straight away we were both across and on to that table faster than a cork out of a champagne bottle! In fact, as I seem to recall, I believe I actually sat myself down at the table before either of the young lads had even begun to get themselves up. But hey, other folks had begun queueing behind us by then, awaiting other tables to become vacant, and I wasn't about to miss out on an opportunity. *No sirree!* So sit we both did, *immediately!* I told Helen to spread a few things out across the four-seater table, such as her bag and the backgammon set, in order to make it appear to be fully occupied, which she duly did, following which I wandered on up to the servery in order to browse through whatever special delights were on offer on that night's menu. There was still a queue for the tables, but thankfully, at that moment in time, no queue at the servery itself, and so I wandered along the food counter at leisure, casting my eyes over each and every dish. I then returned to our table in order to report my findings to my wife.

"Well, dear wife," I began, "it would appear we have a choice between breaded plaice, tuna steaks, roast chicken, veal, or something that vaguely resembles a beef bourguignon. And then there's a fresh mixed salad, assorted boiled vegetables, or some rather delicious looking French fries, all sat waiting there to accompany whatever madam should decide she wishes to partake of."

I remained standing, I'd become somewhat ravenous by then!

"Hmm, let me think now...," Helen said, staring into space whilst I patiently tapped my fingers along the edge of the table.

"I think I'll go for a nice healthy tuna salad please waiter. And a fizzy orange too please, if at all possible," she finally replied, after what seemed like half an age.

I walked back between the crowded tables towards the servery. *'Waiter?!!?'* Oh well, I suppose I was in a sense. I slid two trays along the chrome counter rails, plated up Helen's tuna salad, plated myself up a fat juicy leg of roast chicken, some peas, green beans and cauliflower-cheese, and a giant portion of fries, then slid them further along to the drinks section. I selected a half decent looking bottle of Rioja, poured Helen a small Fanta naranja and myself a small Amstel from the dispenser, then carefully carried each tray separately to the pay till. Just under thirty euros in total. Not too bad I thought, considering we were there effectively as a captive audience. I carefully carried each tray individually over to our table, then made a third trip through the madding throng to collect cutlery, condiments, a large jug of water, and a free basket of assorted breads. I even managed to find a half full dish of individually wrapped portions of butter, something generally unheard of throughout Spain, and helped myself to a handful of those too. I returned to the table, set everything neatly out, then placed the three empty trays on top of one of the vacant seats beside our own. I poured the two of us a full glass of Rioja each, which, as it turned out, was absolutely delicious, and we both dived into our respective meals with enthusiastic eagerness.

By the time we'd finished eating later that evening it was getting on towards ten o'clock, and the huge caff's dining area was still full to capacity, mostly with Spanish parents who nearly all, for some odd reason, appeared to have precisely the same number of young children accompanying them, as in two per couple. As my mind began to wander, speculating as to whether the Spanish central government would prove sufficiently intelligent so as to introduce such a law, Helen suggested we retire once again to the far more comfortable and peaceful lounge area towards the front of the ship, and challenged me to one final game of backgammon, whilst we sat and enjoyed a nightcap each. I agreed immediately. Providing we could find ourselves a pair of comfy chairs somewhere in the lounge, it would be a great pleasure to walk away from the clatter of the noisy dining hall, with its bright fluorescent lights, Linoleum flooring and sterile white tin suspended ceiling tiles. Much as we'd both enjoyed our food, as well as the lovely bottle of Rioja, it was now time to put our feet up, so to speak. On our way back towards the bar neither of us could help but notice that we were both perfectly capable of walking in straight lines, without the need to cling to the handrails for balance. The Juan J Sister was gently rising and falling as she plodded along gracefully through the darkness over what little remained of the Med's previous monsterous theme park *unattraction,* and I was beginning to get the impression that the further north we headed the calmer the seas were becoming. We found a pair of comfy chairs quite easily, and whilst Helen set up the backgammon I wandered across to the virtually clear bar and ordered a couple of drinks. G&T for m'lady, port and brandy for m'self! As I set them down on our table, this time without fear of them sliding around, Helen rolled her first die. I followed suit, and as so often seemed to be typical of my luck, Helen started the game with a six and a four. It wasn't long before I caught up however, and I ended up winning that first one, albeit with her having just the one counter remaining.

"Ten euros princess, that's where we're at!" I announced smugly. "You gonna cough up, or d'you wanna go for yet another?"

"Just one more," she replied. "Gimme a chance to even it up whilst I finish off this *enormous* G&T!"

As it turned out she more than evened it up on that last game of the night; *she thrashed me!* As she removed her last counter from the board I still had *three* in my first quarter, as well as the *twelve* in my home base.

"Ha, ha!" she exclaimed with genuine delight. "Got ya back at last! Twelve plus six equals eighteen, minus ten; *you owe me eight euros Mr Reason!*"

"Hmm," I retorted grumpily, "you might win the game, but you won't win the fight outside! Anyway, 'tis another day tomorrow, we'll see what comes of it then eh?"

"Beat ya! Beat ya!" she smirked back at me.

"Come on sweetie, let's go get ourselves a decent night's sleep." I said, changing the subject. "At least that'll be a first for us aboard the good ship Juan."

"Good move," she agreed. "I'll follow you, I'm damned if I can remember how to find our cabin."

Actually, it wasn't that far, and it wasn't in the slightest bit difficult to find either, and after shoving all of our kit back into our cabin's twin overhead lockers, we kissed each other goodnight, and climbed into our respective tiny but comfy little single beds. Our cabin window was fitted with blackout curtains, but we both chose to leave them open. We were due to dock in Barcelona at 10am in the morning, and the sun was due to rise some two hours before that, and as we had a starboard-side cabin our little window faced towards the east. And when daylight deemed to awaken the pair of us the following morning, as we generally both chose that in preference to an alarm clock, if we should *happen* to wake to a cloudless sky then we might just both enjoy the pleasure of watching the sun creep steadily up over the horizon. I peered out through our little window into the dark gloom beyond, and watched as the mesmerising white foamy wash of our bow wave rushed passed us immediately down below. Less than a minute later I was sound asleep.

CHAPTER THIRTY

I was certainly right about being woken up by the daybreak. I was also right about the sea state steadily becoming calmer, as indeed by now it was virtually dead flat. Unfortunately I was entirely wrong about the cloudless sky! Simply wishful thinking on my part I'd presumed. It was actually cloudy and dull, and the sun was nowhere to be seen, but at least it didn't look much like rain. I checked my watch. Almost eight-thirty. I couldn't see land through the cabin window, but to be fair, if we were still an hour and a half out of Barcelona, then we were simply on the wrong side of the ship for that. I climbed out of bed and took a shower, knowing full well that the sound would wake Helen, which indeed it did. As I dressed I smiled down at her and said,

"Morning babe, I trust you slept well? Calm seas surround us, whilst Barcelona beckons not too far off in the distance. Shall I go see if I can grab us something for breakfast whilst you get yaself ready, we'll have to be out of here within the hour?"

"Morning hun," replied young sleepyhead. "Coffee and a couple of croissants would be nice please, if its an option."

I pulled on my boots, stepped out of the cabin, and headed upstairs to the cafeteria. Once again, every single table appeared to be occupied, although the queue for the servery itself wasn't overly long. I stood in line, and upon reaching the front I grabbed a tray and began covering it in various items that were on offer. When I finally reached the pay till I was loaded up with a decent pair of mini-continental breakfasts, consisting of croissants, butter and jams, cappuccinos, fruit juices, and two bowls of delicious looking, freshly chopped chunks of grapefruit. After paying in cash, and then adding the cutlery, along with half a dozen sachets of sugar, I was still unable to spot a vacant table anywhere, and so headed back off down to our cabin, keeping a firm grip on the tray whilst carefully negotiating the stairs. On reaching cabin number 89 I kicked the bottom of the door gently with my foot three times, and after a brief pause it opened inwards with a sudden rush of air. As I was just about to step over the threshold I noticed a middle-aged, half dressed Spanish gentleman stood there, holding the door wide open with one hand, a wet shave razor in the other hand, his face half covered in white shaving foam, and his mouth wide open, his jaw dropped in surprise.

"Vaya, lo siento muchos señor, creo qué tengo él numero de cabina equivocado!" I squawked.

'Shit! Wrong sodding cabin number!!' I beat a hasty retreat, and as the door slammed shut I could clearly read the bronze numbers *'87'* firmly screwed to the face of the door. I gently kicked the base of the next door along three times with my boot, and it immediately opened to the sight of Helen's pretty, smiling, welcoming face. *'Phew!'* I walked in and placed the tray down on the bed. Helen had already showered and dressed, and managed to extract our bags from the overhead lockers, and as we sat there munching our way through our rather delicious little brekkies I watched through the window as the leading light at the very far offshore end of Barcelona's outer harbour wall gradually slid past, less than a hundred metres away from our starboard side. We'd finally re-entered the commercial port of Barcelona, and at around two knots the Juan J Sister was now gently drifting past the moored-up gaggle of assorted cruise ships towards the Trasmediterranea ferry terminal at the far end of the docks. Suddenly, as if magically timed to perfection, the moment we both finished the very last remaining mouthfuls of our tasty breakfasts, we once again heard the same announcement over the ship's tannoy system, *'Would all drivers and their passengers please return immediately to their vehicles.'* We pulled on our jackets, grabbed up all of our bags, and leaving the messy, sticky breakfast tray still sat on the end of the bed, threw our key cards on top of the dressing table and headed back off down two flights of stairs in search of the Foden.

It turned out she was rather easy to find, her big black HIAB crane and bright yellow cab-roof lights sticking out in the dim lower-deck lighting a bit like a sore thumb. I couldn't help but feeling at that moment however, that in some sad kind of way, she just looked a little lost and forlorn without her best buddy the Phoenix still loaded aboard. It seemed a bit like as if losing her load was tantamount to losing her purpose in life, that's how I felt at that particular moment, the minute I laid eyes on her down in the very bottom of the Juan J's darkened lower vehicle deck. Which, when I thought about it with a little more clarity, was simply preposterous. *Of course* she had a damned purpose in life, she had to get Helen and I safely back to Bristol in one piece! And what's more, with no stupidly heavy load to carry on her back, she should be able to make the return journey in double-quick time! We'd both climbed up into the cab with our bags, neither of us even noticing the fact that the Juan J Sister had docked at her mooring until her engines began to shut down, and the twin steel ramps at her stern began to lower themselves. As I sat there pondering over what sort of top speed I was likely to get out of our old bus whilst heading back up north towards Calais, daylight poured into the ship's lower decks, and before we could say boo to a goose we'd got our engine up and running, and had begun to very steadily follow the stream of traffic heading gradually up onto the quayside. Once again there were no Customs to negotiate, and after driving up one of the long steel ramps and along the quayside towards the exit, we waved a very brief goodbye to Trasmed's trusty old Juan J Sister, and set our sights once again for the centre of Barcelona, with cunning little *Chrissy-plan* number one hundred and twenty something or other fixed firmly in mind.

"So, Captain Pugwash," Helen began by asking, just after we'd hung a sharp right onto the Ronda Litoral that would take us directly back into the city centre, "what surprise delights do you have in store for us on this exciting Spanish New Year's Eve exactly?"

"Well, Seaman Stains," I began by answering, "it goes like this you see!"

'Should I tell her? Or should I not? Surprise? Or let her look forward to something she knows is going to happen with eager anticipation and excitement? Which one do I opt for? Hmm, I think I'll run with the explanation, especially given that she's already asked me outright.'

"Some good friends that I know through work spent New Year's Eve over here in Barca a few years ago, and they told me that they'd put on the most amazing firework display down by the harbour, near to the front end of the cruise ship terminal. So what I thought we'd do exactly is this. We'll go stick this little truck back up on the roof of the station, then we'll go see if we can check in to the same hotel we stayed in last time we were here; the one just up around the back streets, if there's any room at the inn so to speak. And then what we'll do a bit later is we'll catch the metro from Sants down to Drassanes, then its a short walk from there across the park to Port Vell Marina. All along the front of which runs a long timber-boarded promenade, littered with a huge assortment of every type of restaurant imaginable, and from one of which, come midnight, we'll have an absolutely perfect view of the fireworks. How's that little plan grabbin' ya monkey-sponges chickadee?"

"Sounds like a good'un to me babe. How long have you kept that little surprise up ya sleeve for then?" Helen replied.

"Ooh, I'd say probably somewhere in the region of precisely a year maybe? Anyway, there was never any point in me promising to do it if there wasn't even a remote possibility of it even happening. But hey, here we are, so what the heck, let's make it happen. After all, *what could possibly go wrong?*"

As we drove around the roads through the southern parts of the city, marvelling as always at its awesome architecture, we laughed and chatted and giggled, and generally took the mickey out of both ourselves and each other, right up to the point where we approached, for the second time in just over a week, the spiral concrete ramp that leads up onto the far south-east corner of Sant railway station. Once again the whole area seemed to be teeming with tourists; there were pedestrians, taxis, cars, mopeds and buses tearing around in all directions, horns blaring and voices shouting. Once again we carefully picked our way through the crowds whilst slowly approaching the lowered entrance barrier, at which we needed to stop. I jumped down from the cab, walked around to Helen's side and pressed the intercom button. A gentleman's voice came through the little speaker box:

"Sí señor, cuántas noches te gustaria quedarte?"

"Sólo una por favor," I responded confidently.

"No problemo señor, de nada, y feliz ano nuevo para ti."

"Gracias mi amigo, y feliz ano nuevo para ti también."

The barrier raised itself immediately, and I jumped back in the cab and drove the little Foden back up onto the roof once again. This time there were far more vehicles parked up there than previously; vans, trucks, tractor-cabs, etc, but we were still able to find a suitable space quite easily, and I backed the Foden yet again up to the crash rail just in front of the low perimeter wall. The tree lined Boulevard was once again directly below us, but this time our little truck carried nothing worthy of being hidden by the branches of those wonderful old evergreens, so we took little notice whilst carefully offloading our baggage. I locked up, took a one-off inspection walk around the truck, habitually kicking tyres as I went, and seemingly happy with my findings we shouldered our bags, walked back down around the spiral ramp, and headed off across the lawns in search of the same hotel that we'd stayed in previously, the Santa Maria. Less than ten minutes later we walked up the steps into the reception, and the very same uniformed concierge behind the reception counter, who quite obviously recognised us from our previous stay, once again said he had rooms available on the third floor, twenty-eight euros per night, and after running my credit card through his PDQ he handed me the key to room 36. I thanked him kindly, and as we already knew exactly where the lift was we walked across the lobby, pressed the button for floor three, and when the door slid open, wedged ourselves and our bags tightly inside. Two floors further up and the doors opened automatically, but we couldn't move, we were absolutely wedged firmly in place with our bags trapped in between the two of us. The lift door closed itself again, however I just managed to reach the '*door-open*' button with my left thumb, just before it disappeared back down to floor number one again, and the door opened once more. I tried to keep my thumb on the '*door-open*' button for as long as possible, but then, all of a sudden, as my arm slid down by my side, Helen pushed hard against the back wall, and we both burst out of the lift together, landing in a heap on the floor on top of our crumpled baggage. The lift door closed, the lift itself disappeared back off downstairs, and Helen and I both lay there in fits of laughter for a good half a minute or so. It was only when another elderly couple walked along the corridor towards the lift that we picked ourselves up, dusted ourselves off, grabbed our bags, and headed off down the corridor in search of room 36, still childishly giggling away to ourselves. Once inside our cosy little room, which actually appeared enormous compared to our previous night's accommodation, we dumped our bags down on the floor then sprawled out on the bed, feeling somewhat satisfied that we'd had a particularly constructive day so far. I lifted my arm and peeked at my watch, which read just gone twelve-thirty midday. All in all, not bad going. I was very happy with exactly where we were at, even happier, *much, much happier,* with everything we'd managed to achieve to date, and very much looking forward to an enjoyable evening watching the Año Nuevo firework display with my beautiful wife down by the harbourside.

The next time I opened my eyes and peeked at my watch it had just gone three-thirty mid-afternoon. *Where the heck had those three hours gone exactly?* Hey ho, no matter! Helen was sat at the top of the bed, propped up against the headboard, reading one of her paperbacks. I pulled my own paperback out of my kit-bag and turned to a marked page, determined to get a little further through it.

"Well hello sleepyhead," Helen said, peering down at me. "What sort of time were you thinking about going out this evening?"

"Actually," I replied, looking up from the beginning of chapter three, "I wasn't thinking at all, I was sleeping. However, now that you come to mention it, I reckon we should leave here at around seven, with the intention of finding a table in a restaurant somewhere around eight. That sound okay to you?"

"Yep, that's cool," she agreed. "Should just about give me time to finish this book before I start to get ready."

"Okey dokey," I concluded, "that's a plan then. I'll see if I can manage to reach chapter four by the time you're done!"

A little before 6pm Helen turned the final page of her paperback, then plonked it down on top of the dresser with a satisfying thud, and disappeared off into the en-suite bathroom. I continued reading my own until she was almost ready to go out, then folded a page over halfway through chapter fifteen, and stuck it back in my kit-bag. I changed quickly into a slightly smarter set of clothes, opting for a brightly patterned shirt over two clean T-shirts, a clean pair of black corduroy trousers, and then pulled on my usual grubby old pair of walking boots. Helen had changed into a long flowing flowery dress, and wrapped a very Spanish-looking shawl around her neck and shoulders to hide the tell-tale outline of the T-shirt that she also wore underneath. She slipped the same pair of trainers on that she'd worn since leaving Malaga. All in all it would suffice for the both of us. We had a certain amount of walking to do, and it wasn't exactly warm outside. In fact, to be honest, it had actually got pretty damned chilly after getting dark, and on reaching the narrow brightly lit street outside the front of the hotel we both zipped our ski jackets right up under our chins. Suffice to say that on this occasion, without carrying our cumbersome hold-alls along with us, we'd successfully managed to negotiate the cramped little elevator together without incident. We set off down the street, crossed the park, then took the escalator one floor down to the metro's southbound platform at Estácio de Sants. A train pulled alongside some five minutes later, and after another ten minutes or so we were stepping off onto the platform at Estácio Drassannes. We took the steps up to street level, whereupon we found ourselves once again faced with acres of beautiful green lawns stretched out before us, criss-crossed with pretty cobbled walkways, and surrounded by tall, majestic evergreen trees. Beyond the park the waters of Port Vell glistened in the background, illuminated with the reflections of both its surrounding shops and restaurants, as well as the deck-lights that adorned the impressive array of multi-million-pound superyachts moored within the marina. We strolled gently across the park, arm in arm, heading towards the boardwalk. Once there, wandering slowly along beneath the ornate wrought-iron overhead streetlamps, we passed all manner of restaurants, all of which were open, with many appearing to be occupied, although not exactly overly busy as yet. Having said that, by Spanish standards, the night was yet young, and although there were already plenty of people milling about the boardwalk, we knew that as the evening wore on it would steadily become ever busier, inevitably finishing up at midnight with a crescendo of celebration, and cheering, dancing and singing, plus . . . their wonderful firework display.

As we wandered slowly along, stopping every now and then to briefly scan an assortment of menus, we passed, amongst others, a Chinese, an Italian, a Thai, a Lebanese, an Indian, and even a Burger King. Eventually, after putting much thought into it, we settled for . . . you guessed it, *a Spanish!* But not just any old Spanish. We deliberately picked on a traditional Spanish steakhouse that advertised delicious-looking Argentinian rib eyes. We entered, and took a table immediately inside the huge picture window overlooking the western end of Port Vell Marina, with the cruise ship terminal clearly visible in the background. I counted at least eight fully-illuminated cruise ships docked at their berths, although I have to say that, in the absence of a pair of binoculars, I couldn't put a name to a single one of them. However, I felt we'd settled, and this very location would indeed suffice for the remainder of the night. When the waiter approached I ordered un litro de sangria por favor, dos copas, uno caña, y uno Fanta naranja, gracias. Helen and I studied our menus whilst waiting on the drinks, although to be fair we both already knew what we wanted anyway. So as soon as the drinks arrived I ordered immediately. Rib eye for myself, por favor, *rare,* and rib eye for my wife also, por favor, *medium rare,* muchos gracias. The picture menu, which was printed in every conceivable language imaginable, clearly stated that all Argentinian steaks came with chips, vegetables of the day, and a choice of sauces on the side. Helen ordered a peppercorn sauce, I ordered a bearnaise. I passed Helen her fizzy orange, then sipped on my own small chilled beer whilst pouring two large glasses of their very delicious looking sangria. As more and more people steadily began to wander along the boardwalk, some every now and then taking to a table inside our own restaurant, I'd begun to get the impression that a further round of drinks would inevitably be required in the not too distant future; plus I was pretty sure there was every possibility that it wouldn't end there either! But the night was still yet young, and so initially we'd just relax and take things easy.

Our steaks came . . . And went! As did the whole bottle of accompanying Rioja. Boy was that lot ever *simply divine!!* If I could remember the name of the damned restaurant I'd fully recommend it to absolutely *anyone!* Well, not just anyone, obviously! I don't think it would be particularly suited to our vegetarian fraternity! But as far as dining out goes, that little lot came pretty damned close to the top of the list! I ordered a second jug of sangria, along with another small beer, and we sat and studied the dessert menus together. The waiter delivered the drinks; I ordered a Crème Catalana, and Helen opted for the sticky toffee pudding. And once that whole lot had been shovelled down as well, the two of us just sat there, staring into one another's eyes, fully stuffed to the brim, or as they say on those posh telly chef shows, *100% gastronomically satisfied!* My watch told me it was 11.15pm, my stomach told me, or rather it begged me, that it wanted no more food, but my head told me it was most definitely wanting yet another drink. *Greedy little bugger!* I asked Helen what she fancied, whilst we wound down the minutes towards the magical hour, and she politely requested a *small* G&T. I summoned the waiter, who cleared and wiped down our table for us, then ordered Helen's *small* G&T, a *large* spiced rum with ginger ale for myself, *plus,* specifically for the witching hour, a nice big bottle of chilled Spanish Cava with two champagne flutes, por favor. The waiter came back a couple of minutes later with the drinks, followed immediately by a second waiter who delivered an ornate silver ice-bucket to the centre of the table, then firmly wedged a half decent looking unopened bottle of bubbly in amongst the ice, carefully placing two tall, empty champagne glasses down beside it. I said gracias to the pair of them, then savoured a large cool mouthful of my iced rum and ginger, whilst, for the first time since we'd entered the establishment, observing our immediate surroundings so as to try and ascertain who, or at least what nationality, our accompanying guests might prove to be. At the table immediately behind us, again with a perfect view across the harbour through the huge picture window, sat two well-dressed couples who were very clearly *very* English, my best guess being that they'd escaped from one of the smaller non-all-inclusive cruise ships. The window table to our other side was surrounded by a very noisy, very young, and very obviously French party of students. And at the other nearby tables, as best I could make out through the ever increasing din, sat mainly Spanish folk, some of them families with young children, others who appeared to be, much as the French youngsters clearly were, parties of students. The noise grew ever louder as the night wore on.

Shortly before midnight virtually everyone grabbed their drinks and bundled themselves off through the double entrance doors, and out onto the wide boardwalk outside. I grabbed the bottle of cava by its neck, Helen snatched up the pair of champagne glasses, and we followed them all outside. I very much got the impression that everyone was either far too drunk, or far too excited, to even notice the cold, but Helen and I had both slipped our jackets on anyway, just in case. After all, we had absolutely no idea how long the firework display was likely to go on for. A minute or so later, as the hands on my watch almost simultaneously pointed themselves directly towards the number twelve, a noisy cacophony of every language imaginable began shouting the inevitable countdown, 10 . . . 9 . . . 8 . . . 7 . . . 6 . . . 5 . . . 4 . . . 3 . . . 2 . . . 1 . . . *BANG!* I popped the cork from the bottle of cava, aiming its trajectory perfectly over everyone's heads and far off into the harbour somewhere below, and as the bubbles spilled forth from the mouth of the bottle I managed to direct *most* of them straight into the two glasses that Helen, both greedily and excitedly, held out in front of me. As the bubbles were still pouring, this massive incomprehensible cheer went up from the enormous crowd gathered by the waterfront, and as we chinked our glasses together we both joined in at the top of our voices, in our very own *comprehensible* language, '*HAPPY NEW YEAR!!!*' One or two of the bubbles had somehow found their way up my nose, and a few more were dribbling their way down Helen's chin, and I leaned over to her, kissed her full on the lips, and whispered to her loudly,

"Happy New Year my darling, here's to a wonderfully successful 2003, and many more happy family holidays together in sunny Menorca."

"Here, here," Helen responded, following it up with, "And here's to *us,* and here's to the Phoenix too, may she bring us all the pleasures we wish for this coming summer, and for evermore."

"Here, here!" I concluded, and we chinked glasses yet again, then necked the remaining bubbles from both.

I topped us both up, each glass full to overflowing, and we pushed our way through the noisy, cosmopolitan throng of revellers until reaching the railings close to the water's edge. We both leaned on top of the varnished wooden capping rail, and patiently waited for the loud *KA-BOOM* from the first barrage of aerial fireworks. And we waited . . . and we waited . . . and we waited . . . and . . . *nothing!* A great big fat *NOTHING!* Oh dear, what a disappointment! As the revellers continued to dance and sing and shout, we hugged each other, shrugged our shoulders in glum acceptance, wandered back into the restaurant with what little remained of the cava, removed our jackets and sat back down. I drained the remainder of the bottle equally into both of our glasses, then turned to the nearest of the English folk sat at the table adjacent to ours.

"Excuse me sir," I asked politely. "I hope you don't mind me interrupting you for a second, but I'd been given to understand that they held a spectacular fireworks display down here by the port every New Year's Eve. its looking rather like I may have been fed some duff information somewhere along the line. Would you happen by chance to know anything about it at all?"

"Indeed I do young man," the gentleman replied. "Three years ago there was an amazing New Year's Eve fireworks display put together out across the water very close to here. It was organised and paid for by a consortium of cruise ship companies as an integral part of their spectacular one-off millennium celebrations. It really was awesome, we all watched it from here together, as we tend to visit Barcelona rather a lot these days. But it certainly doesn't happen every year I'm afraid, it was just a millennium special, so I'm sorry for your disappointment."

"Oh, its no problem really sir, its not as if we came here especially for it or anything," I answered him back cheerfully in an attempt to conceal my disappointment. "We've just got off the Trasmed ferry from Menorca, heading back to Bristol via Calais, so we're stopped here for the night anyway, and I was just going by what I'd heard. I guess my friends must've been here that same year too. Shame we missed it ourselves I guess. Never mind. Anyway, thank you very much for letting us know."

"My pleasure," he finished with. "Enjoy the rest of your stay, Happy New Year, and have a safe journey home."

"Thank you sir," I countered, "and the very same to the four of you, and a Happy New Year to you all too."

I turned back towards Helen, and changing the subject altogether, suggested that we ought at least to text a Happy New Year's message to all of our friends and family, to which she agreed and said she should do the very same. We pulled our phones out, typed in *'Happy New Year to one and all from a rather chilly Barcelona xxx',* then ran through our contacts list, selecting all those we wished to send it to. Finally, after ticking off twenty or so names, mostly family, I hit *'SEND'*. Immediately my screen lit up with the words *'NETWORK NOT AVAILABLE'*. Oh well, I guess the whole of Europe were probably all texting at the same time. Hey ho, the message would go eventually, they'd all get it in due course. I called the waiter over and asked for la cuenta por favor, and a minute later he set it down on the table in front of me, neatly folded inside a gilt-edged leather wallet. I opened it and stared, somewhat incredulously, at the long paper bill. *'WTF?'* went through my mind initially, but then I gave it considerably more thought and came to the conclusion that, because of *where* we were, and because of *when* we were there, and especially because of *what* we'd had, taking *all* of that into consideration, then I suppose €214, including their ten percent service charge, wasn't altogether *too* bad. *€214!!! Just over a hundred and forty bloody quid!* Oh well, what the heck, it was a special night anyway; the food was absolutely delicious, we'd both had far too much to drink to care that much about it anyway, and to hell with it, fireworks or no fireworks, we were both just enjoying simply being in Barcelona anyway. I stuck my credit card inside the little leather wallet and handed it back to the waiter. We pulled our jackets back on, bid our neighbours farewell, and after retrieving my duly processed credit card, took our final leave from their gastronomically delightful establishment.

Upon returning once again to the chilly outdoors, we both immediately realised that we'd had ever so slightly more to drink than we had initially intended on consuming. As in, basically, we were both pretty much *drunk!* We held each other up as we began to cross the road heading back towards the park, but then I spotted something familiar at the edge of the road, and immediately had one of those *lightbulb* moments. It was a taxi rank! And sat there idling away at the very front of said taxi rank was...yep, you've guessed it, a *taxi!* I opened the black and yellow taxi's back door, and we both fell inside with a thud, landing in a giggling mess across the back seat on top of one another.

"Buenas noches señor, *hic!* Hotel Santa Maria cerca el, *hic!* Estácio de Sants por favor, *hic!*"

Bloody hiccups! I bloody *hate* hiccups! The taxi took off at speed, and whizzed us halfway across the city in what seemed like less than half a split second, although I must admit, as he pulled up to the kerb immediately outside the entrance to our hotel, I was somewhat surprised to find Helen shaking me roughly by the arm in an attempt to wake me up. However, wake up I did, and paid the taxi driver the twenty euros cash he asked me for, *double* his regular charge because of NYE! I opened the rear door, and the two of us stumbled out as carefully as we could manage, making our very best attempts not to land on the pavement in yet another crumpled heap. The taxi drove off, and we tripped up the front steps and crashed noisily through the front doors into reception, inducing some rather filthy looks from the miserable old concierge behind the counter. '*Hola señor, feliz nuevo ano!*' I managed to slur loudly at him as we staggered past and over towards the lift. '*Still,*' I'd figured to myself, '*I suppose we couldn't ALL have fun on New Year's Eve, now could we? Some of us would HAVE to keep on working, surely? JUST NOT US! Ha, ha! Ha, ha, ha, ha, ha!!!*' We crammed ourselves together into the tiny little lift, which slowly plodded its way up to the third floor, whereupon, once again, we fell out noisily together, then scuttled off down the corridor to our room. Once inside we dumped our jackets on the floor, kicked off our boots, managed to remove probably about half of the remainder of our clothes, gave each other a great big sloppy kiss, and literally fell into bed. I was about to recount what a brilliant fun night we'd spent together, in all its glorious detail, when it suddenly dawned on me that Helen was already very lightly snoring. So with that I gave up on the idea, closed my eyes and joined her.

CHAPTER
THIRTY ONE

I've always felt that the best way to avoid a hangover is to sleep your way through it; to allow yourself to wake up perfectly naturally without the use of any artificial aids, such as an alarm clock, or the wife screaming *'Oi! Wake up! You're already late for work!'* right in your face. Following which one should then drink a minimum of one full pint of water *before* taking a long, hot, leisurely shower, then dress casually, and relax over a peaceful breakfast of boiled eggs, tea and toast. Not too much, not too little. I finished the remainder of my pleasant little dream, opened my eyes, and squinted blearily at my watch. *'Bugger! its 11.40am! We're supposed to vacate our room by noon! What day is it? Oh yeah, its okay, its only New Year's Day; plus its a Sunday, I don't think anyone's gonna be overly bothered either way. I'll let it ride anyway, what the heck!'* I left Helen fast asleep and took my long, hot, leisurely shower. The rehydration would have to wait; I certainly wasn't going to drink that sort of quantity from a foreign tap, and sadly we hadn't given any thought to buying a couple of bottles and leaving them in our room before setting off out. As soon as I stepped out of the bathroom Helen breezed passed me with the briefest of *'morning!'*'s and dashed on in. *Oh, cool, at least she's still alive!* As I methodically got dressed into my usual travelling clothes, I began thinking to myself: *'Okay, that's good, clear head, and despite the lack of drinking water as yet, no hangover! Hooray! So, maybe the little café next door is open, maybe its not. Either way we're bound to find some bottled water somewhere on our way back towards the truck. I know for starters that everything in Sant Station will all be open, that one's a given for sure. But I don't wanna be hanging around here for too long, we really do need to put some decent miles between us and dear old Barca before the day's out.'*

"Morning beautiful," I said as Helen stepped out of the bathroom, "how's the head today?"

"All the better for a good night's sleep, followed by a decent hot shower," she replied. "Mind you, I could probably kill for a bottle of water right now. What are the chances?"

"If the little caff's shut babe, which it most likely will be, then we'll grab some bottles to take with us from a kiosk in the station, everything's bound to be open over there. We'll grab a few munchies too, if poss, but I don't wanna stick around here for too much longer, I'd rather be looking for a hotel at least somewhere near Béziers before it starts getting dark. Good to see neither of us have much in the way of hangovers though, despite a great night out."

"Yep, it sure was a great night, even if the fireworks *didn't* happen," she agreed. "And anyway, I'm feeling just fine and raring to go. Amazing what a decent lie-in can do! So come on, let's do it!"

"Okey dokes. Well its a hundred and eighty motorway miles to Béziers, which is where we'll have to make a fuel stop anyway, so I'm guessing that'll take around three hours. Which means, realistically, the sooner we leave the better. So we may end up having to forego a leisurely brekkie for the pleasures of food-to-go whilst driving. If that's okay with you babe?"

"Its all fine," Helen replied soothingly. "We just gotta do what we gotta do. Come on, let's go."

We finished packing our bags, then shuffled off down the narrow corridor, organising ourselves a little more intelligently this time into the *room-for-only-one* elevator. I politely said '*muchos gracias señor*' as I set the room key down on the reception counter, but the concierge simply muttered '*adios*' grumpily, without even looking up from his computer screen. '*Oh well, I guess some folks just gotta work New Year's Day too!*' I was right about the little café next door. Closed! So we walked down the narrow street together, which was pretty much deserted, then crossed over the park, which was bathed in glorious sunshine, albeit there was a proper chill in the air, and walked through the front entrance of Estácio Sants, which, as per usual, was bustling with both tourists and commuters alike. At the far opposite end of the enormous building I spotted a very welcoming and highly recognisable large yellow illuminated '*M*' sign.

"Hey hun," I announced positively, "I've got an idea. Follow me."

Ten minutes later we walked back out of McDonald's with a carryout bag containing two plain cheeseburgers, two medium portions of fries, two small cokes, and four bottles of water. We both immediately gulped down one whole bottle of water each, I tossed the empties into a nearby recycling bin, and we set off back towards the spiral ramp that leads up onto the roof. Once we located our pretty little red and white mode of homeward-bound transportation, I unlocked the doors, and Helen climbed up into the passenger seat. I passed the hold-alls up to her, followed by my kit-bag, then her handbag, and lastly the carry bag full of food, from which I'd already stuffed one of the paper serviettes inside my jacket pocket. I pulled down the front grille flap, removed the radiator cap, and stuck my finger in to check the water level. Full to the brim! Next I removed the dipstick from just behind the cab, wiped it clean on the serviette, then dipped the oil reservoir to check the level. Spot on the *'full'* mark! Finally, my never-ending habit, I walked all around the truck giving each and every tyre in turn a good solid clump with my right boot. All good, all firm and solid! I jumped up into the cab, and when she started immediately upon my very first flick of the key, I turned and looked at Helen, then sang out to her cheerfully,

"I'm lovin' it!"

With which, as if bang on cue, she handed me my wonderfully warm Maccy-D's cheeseburger. I took a huge mouthful, and whilst savouring it I peeled the brightly coloured little yellow cardboard sun from the sun-visor, and stuck it in the side pocket of my hold-all. *We certainly wouldn't be needing that anymore!* Firstly, we were no longer anywhere near 4.1 metres high, and secondly, we'd be heading north from now on, leaving sunny Spain way behind us. We drove off across the roof, at the end of which I spun the wheel one-handed, something which I now found relatively easy with no heavy load aboard, and descended the spiralled exit ramp to the bottom, whereupon I found the barrier to be down. I pulled on the air-brake, hopped out, walked around to the intercom, and pressed the buzzer. A rather tinny Spanish voice immediately came back at me,

"Seran veintidos euros señor, por favor puede introducir su tarjeta de credito en la maquína."

I pulled out my credit card, shoved it into the little automated machine, tapped in twenty-two euros and hit enter. A couple of moments later the barrier raised itself, and I removed my card, jumped back up into the cab, and off we drove, fighting our way somewhat more easily this time through the less busy streets of central Barcelona, then off up into the northern suburbs and beyond. Both of us kept our eyes peeled for any kind of recognisable road sign, something that might point us at least roughly back towards the way we'd originally come from, although at first this didn't prove to be overly straightforward, due mainly to the complexity of their one-way systems. Eventually however, whilst I continued picking at the bag of ever-cooling French fries sat on the edge of the fully loaded seat right next to me, Helen motioned towards a large blue overhead sign that read *'Girona via Autopista de Peaje'*, with an arrow pointing, thankfully, in precisely the direction in which we were already heading.

"That'll be the one then chick," I acknowledged confidently. "Wave bye bye to the wonderful city of Barcelona, not long to go now before it'll be *adios España and bonjour La France,* then before you know it you'll be saying *hello* once again to England's green, pleasant and probably rather cold, wet and dreary land."

"Well its not as if I'm in any kind of tearing hurry to get back to work or anything," Helen chirped up with, "and for the *most* part I've enjoyed our little *'mini adventure'* together, so far . . ."

"*And?*" I asked patiently.

"Oh, nothing really," she replied. "Its just that, well . . . , how long d'you think its likely to be before we get back home?"

"Don't you worry your pretty little head about that my sweetheart," I replied, possibly a little over-condescendingly. "I've got another cunning little *Chrissy-plan* up my sleeve, I'll talk to you about it in a little more detail when we stop somewhere for the night."

With that I pulled up at the start of yet another expensive Spanish Peaje, and Helen reached down out of her window and pulled the little white paper ticket from its slot. It was shortly after two o'clock, probably an hour and a half to the French border, then another hour and a half to Béziers. So it was going to be dark by the time we arrived. Okay, so let's see what this little old bus'll do exactly.

"Hang on to yer hats folks," I shouted loudly once we'd got going again, *"we're really gonna go for it now, big stylie!"*

And with that, I slammed the *pedal to the metal,* and the speedometer steadily crept up towards the 40mph mark. And then 50 . . . and then 60 . . . and then, after reaching the brow of a slight incline and heading on downwards over the other side of the hill, we hit 70mph, and even topped out at around seventy-five as we neared the bottom of the slope. And that wasn't even a steep one! *Yay, this was gonna be a damned FUN ride home!!!*

[Okay folks, its at this point in the story where one relevant factor becomes abundantly clear. That being, basically, the difference between the drive down

there, and the drive back again. The drive down, due mainly to the slight over-loading of the dear old Foden, I would describe essentially as 'SOMEWHAT TRAUMATIC!' The drive back home, however, as unconducive to the sto-ryline as it may seem, I have no alternative but to describe as 'VIRTUALLY UNEVENTFUL!' And so for that reason alone, I've chosen (you may be pleased to learn!) to write very little about it. Plus, the simple fact of the matter being, as the majority of it simply flew past in the blink of an eye, there's very little I can remember about it anyway. Until, that is . . .]

Some ninety-odd miles later we pulled up at the last of the Spanish Peajes, and once again Helen slotted a twenty euro note into the automatic machine, receiving just €1.30 in change. A mile or so later we crossed the French border, and just as we touched the 70mph mark on yet another downhill stretch of Péage-free dual carriageway, I turned to Helen and asked her to look through the bag of CD's, and see if she could find *Speed King* by Deep Purple. I was right in the mood for it by then! After sarcasti-cally suggesting that maybe I'd prefer something a little less brash, such as *I'm In Love With My Lorry* by Queen, I settled for the next best thing she could come up with, an old classic by The Grateful Dead called *Truckin' (Yep! What a long strange trip its been! Damn right!!)* Following which, after yet another ninety-odd Péage-free miles, as we pulled into the very same Elf service station on the outskirts of Béziers that we'd used on the way down, I was only too glad to jump down from the cab and leave Helen to whatever music it was she'd swapped over to, as by that time it had become her choice. I believe she'd referred to it as something called *West Life,* or something along those lines anyway; I'd never heard of 'em meself! I filled the tank to the brim with diesel, yet another hundred euros or there-abouts, paid on my card, and whilst wandering around the Foden in the dark absentmindedly kicking tyres, I just happened to notice, on the side of the little grassy hill behind the fuel station's typically transport-style caff, a long, brightly illuminated, single storey Novotel. *Perfect!* It was shortly after five o'clock, and we were both beginning to get peckish once again. I drove the Foden around the narrow lane to the front car park of the hotel, parked up, we both jumped down with all of our bags, wandered into the reception and checked in for the night. There was very little in the way of facilities in the hotel itself, but the café-bar next to the Elf station hadn't looked too bad, so an hour or so later we wandered back down the lane and grabbed a vacant table amongst a moderate ensemble of French truckers. I actually felt as if I blended in quite well, although I'm not entirely sure Helen did!

Either way, we ignored our assorted foreign company and simply ordered off the menu, and over dinner I began chatting to Helen about my next little *Chrissy-plan*, or more to the point, our available options for the journey back to Calais.

"Okay sweet cheeks," I began, after pouring the both of us a second glass of red, "as things stand right now we've basically got two options available to us for the drive home from here, so I'll just run them both past you, and you can tell me which one you prefer. Although, to be honest, I can probably guess what your answer's gonna be anyway."

"Okey dokey," she replied with a smile "I'm all ears."

"Good. So, option one is we go back the same way we came," I continued. "That will entail negotiating Millau once again, not that that'll prove an issue without the Phoenix onboard, but the simple fact is, as I'm sure you're well aware, its a relatively slow old road for much of the trip, and although its the *shortest* route back it'll inevitably involve *two* more hotel stopovers somewhere along the way."

"Okay, I don't have a problem with any of that," Helen retorted. "What's the other option then?"

"Right. Option two," I began positively, "is that we take the main motorway route further over to the east, which is a slightly longer but much faster route, and all being well we'll only need *one* more hotel stopover along the way, probably somewhere near Reims."

"Ah, I see," said Helen, looking a little puzzled. "So, there's a slow road down here and a fast road back eh? So why exactly did we not take the fast road down here in the first place?"

"That's a very fair question indeed babe, I was kind of expecting that one," I replied. "It might help me to answer it by saying that, given everything that happened on the way down, I'm sure as hell glad that we came the way we did. Anyway, let me explain why."

A waiter approached our table and cleared away our empties, after which we ordered desert, and a second bottle of red, which, as it turned out, was extremely tasty, as well as proving to be relatively inexpensive.

"Okay," I continued. "The road that runs all the way down the eastern side of France, otherwise known as the '*Route du Soleil*', or the Road to the Sun, is firstly a very fast three-lane motorway. And although its relatively flat for the majority of its length, its not a road that I'd feel overly comfortable driving an overloaded lorry along, stuck in the slow lane at just

50mph. Trust me, I've driven it by car, and regardless of the speed limits, 100mph generally seems to be pretty much the norm."

"Right, I get that," Helen began to query, "but surely there must be other heavy good vehicles that use it too?"

"Some do," I replied, "but most try to avoid it because of another of its disadvantages, and that's the fact that its an AutoRoute de Péage *all the way*, and for some reason, best known only to the French government, the toll costs are really quite ridiculously high. Especially compared to what we've been used to so far."

"Okay, that's two semi-good reasons so far," she acknowledged, "now give me a third!"

"Yes, well the third my love is by far the most important," I continued, "and the main reason I chose not to take this route right from the start. And to be honest, thank God I did!"

"Meaning what exactly?" she queried again.

"Breakdowns!" I said bluntly. "Although the motorway has a hard shoulder, you're simply not allowed to stay on it, the traffic cops won't allow it. So, if you break down, and you have no choice but to stop, with the whole length of motorway being covered by CCTV cameras, they simply despatch a tow truck immediately, to tow you *off* the motorway at the next available junction, then they leave you parked up safely in the nearest available lay-by, more often than not in the middle of nowhere. And *then,* they charge you for it! And believe me, those charges are *not* cheap. I'd take a guess at somewhere around €500 to remove our fully-loaded obstruction to a safe location, which is precisely where we'd have to sit until the RAC arrived; and you know now just how long that can take over here! So, the simple moral to this particular story my dear, is that if you think there might be any remote possibility whatsoever of breaking down, stay the hell off the Route du Soleil!"

"Right, well I guess that really *does* make perfect sense then," Helen agreed, "especially given what *did* happen to our little old bus on the way down. So, how confident do you feel about her now then? Confident enough to risk the Route du What's-it-Called? D'you think she's going to behave all the way back?"

"I *know* she will chickadee, without a doubt. After all the work that's now been done to her, followed by relieving herself of her considerably tiresome burden, I can already tell from the couple hundred miles we've done so far she's acting like an unbridled horse who simply wants to gallop off, rein-free, way ahead of the pack. So guess what, *we're gonna let her!*"

"Okay honey, well you know I've always totally trusted your instincts anyway," Helen replied submissively. "So does that mean the decision's made then? Or are you still asking me for my opinion?"

"I'm more than happy to still ask babe," I replied. "Your opinion counts just as much as mine."

"Well in that case," she said decisively, "I vote we take the fast route, even if it does prove more costly because of the tolls."

"Okey dokey," I concluded, "so that's the way we'll go then. And for what its worth my love, I totally agree with you."

I leaned across and gave her a quick peck on the cheek. Shortly afterwards we settled up the bill, then headed off back to our little room up at the Novotel. An early night was called for once again, we had some 550 miles to do the next day if we were going to make it to Reims for the night, which I'd estimated would probably take somewhere in the region of nine hours or so. I set my alarm for 6am once again, kissed my delightfully tolerant wife goodnight, then lay my head down on my comfy little down-filled pillow.

CHAPTER
THIRTY TWO

The following morning, immediately after deux oeufs pochés sur pain grillé et deux cafés au lait in the little truck-stop caff, we grabbed a bagful of assorted munchies and drinks from the fuel station shop, and hit the road once again. It had just turned 7am on the Monday morning, and already the roads were extremely busy, particularly with far more commercial traffic than I'd expected. Still, we had some 550 miles to go to our next planned stop in Reims, so in an attempt to get there at a reasonable time of day I wanted to wind our speed up to as high as possible. Conversely, however, in an attempt to be as economical as possible with our fuel, I wanted to keep my right foot as high up off the floor as I could manage, whenever that proved to be practical. After the first few ups and downs I gradually settled into a rhythm, compromising generally of 60mph uphill and 70 mph downhill. That average of sixty-five should get us to Reims in roughly eight and a half hours. Allow half an hour for a brief lunch stop somewhere along the way, and I'd reckoned on looking for our next hotel around about 4pm. I stuck an easy-listening compilation CD into the little music player, and we cracked on up the A7 AutoRoute de Péage towards Lyon. A few hours later Helen turned to me and said,

"Hey babe, d'you realise, that big blue lorry up in front, the one with *LECLERC* written all down the side of it, he's overtaken us five times so far going uphill, and we've overtaken him five times so far going down. Don't you find that a bit odd?"

"Nah, not at all chick," I replied, "he'll be fitted with a limiter, which is obviously set to sixty-five, and he's probably just sat a brick on top the accelerator so he can put his feet up and relax. You know what that means, don't ya babe?"

"Nope!" Helen replied. "No idea whatsoever. Pray tell?"

"Give a big shout out to LECLERC," I replied with a grin. *"Serious truckin' (no G!)"*

"Idiot!" she said, only *mildly* amused. "My turn to choose the sounds."

At roughly 11am we bypassed Lyon, probably the most beautiful and interesting city in the whole of France, and after paying €46 at the end of the A7 Péage Helen grabbed another ticket from the machine at the beginning of the A6, and we continued to head northwards, still comfortably averaging around 65mph, in the direction of Dijon. At one o'clock, somewhere around the outskirts of Dijon, I pulled the Foden off the AutoRoute and into an Aire de Pique-nique, which had a fuel station that we didn't need, and a café-bar with toilets which we most definitely *did* need. After using the *toilettes* we both ordered a café au lait and a croissant each, and sat at a table for a brief respite from the ever increasing quantity of cars that were whizzing past us at over a hundred miles per hour. I must admit, I certainly hadn't noticed any radar speed-traps up until then; not that they were of any concern to us anyway. Thirty minutes later we were back on the road again, now heading towards Reims. 60mph uphill, 70mph down, it was becoming a little monotonous. Still, the thoughts of our success, as well as the dreams of how we'd be spending much of our future, not to mention the music itself, were all we needed to help keep our spirits up. I said *'not to mention the music'* specifically because of what Helen had selected to play. *So I won't!* Shortly after four o'clock we pulled up at the Péage on the outskirts of Reims, where the A6 terminated, and Helen pushed *three* twenty euro notes into the machine, one after another. *Change,* I hear you ask? *Nil! Zero!* Hey ho! After less than a mile we came across yet another signposted Aire de Pique-nique, this one having pictorial images of its available services included, one of which was a picture of a bed. I swung the Foden onto the slip road, keeping my fingers firmly crossed that we'd not discover yet another grotty little F1. We were in luck, it turned out to be yet another Novotel, which was absolutely fine. We pulled up in front of the hotel, and I cast my eye over the truck's gauges on the dash one last time before switching off. Temp, *normal!* Oil Pressure, *normal!* Battery Charge, *normal!* Fuel, *empty!* Oh well, there was a Repsol fuel station and a cafeteria on-site too, that could all wait until the morning. I switched her off, we stepped down with our bags, and checked into the Novotel for the night. Later that evening, over dinner in the dull but adequate café-diner, I reminded Helen that, all being well, this would prove to be the very last night of our holiday, and with a bit of good fortune we'd be back home in Bristol by the following night. If my memory serves me correctly, I'm fairly sure, for some reason that currently escapes me, we packed ourselves off to bed extra specially early that night!

Oddly enough, the following morning, we followed precisely the same routine as we had at the previous Novotel. A 6am start, followed by two poached eggs on toast and a coffee each in the little café, and then a munchies restocking trip to the fuel station shop. The only difference this time being that we needed fuel as well. I pulled the Foden up next to a commercial pump and poured in a little over thirty gallons. *Damn, that was cutting it fine again!* Still, by my approximate estimation, off the top of my head, I'd reckoned that had worked out to somewhere in the region of seventeen miles per gallon. *Yay, 17mpg, well happy with that!*

We hit the road again, starting this time with a ticket-pull at the first Auto-Péage at the beginning of the A26. Judging by the weather, we were very clearly now driving along the *Route FROM The Sun,* as opposed to the *Route TO The Sun!* Helen stuck her own choice of music on, and then promptly nodded back off to sleep, so the minute I got the opportunity I swapped her CD over for one of my own choice. Nothing too heavy or loud though, there was no need for me to rouse her from her little snooze. For some strange reason, Elton John's *Madman Across The Water* seemed to fit the bill perfectly at the time. Some three hours later, shortly before ten o'clock, we hit the Auto-Péage just outside Calais at the end of the A26, this time Helen slotting in *two* twenty euro notes, and once again getting absolutely *zilch* in the way of change.

"There's the comparison then babe," I concluded to my freshly awoken wife. "€55 for the drive down, €146 for the drive back. Still, no matter, let's go buy a train ticket shall we?"

"Good plan skipper," Helen agreed. "Maybe we'll make up for the toll costs by saving on the Chunnel. Surely its gotta be cheaper without the Phoenix on the back?"

"Hmmm," I grunted with little confidence, "let's go see what they say then."

Ten minutes later we pulled up at the French-controlled commercial vehicle toll booth entrance to the Channel Tunnel, and joined the back of a very long queue of stationary lorries. Every minute or so we restarted the engine, moved forward one vehicle length, and then stopped again. Eventually, after about half an hour, we reached the pay booth at the front of the queue, where apparently an automatic scanner read the total length of our vehicle at 870 centimeters, or so I was told. Still, at least I knew it worked correctly, and called across through the passenger window,

"Oui monsieur, c'est correct, alors combien cela nous coûtera-t-il alors s'il vous plaît?"

"Ce sera juste €338 monsieur s'il vous plaît."

"Hmmm," I grunted again at Helen. "Some bloody saving that is, *just as I suspected!*"

"Why?" she asked, as I handed her my credit card to pass across to the guy in the little glazed cabin. "How much did it come to? What did we save exactly?"

"*Twenty-five bloody quid!*" I said bluntly. "£250 here, £225 back! Still, it is what it is I suppose, no point in grumping over it, let's go get on the next available train shall we?"

"Good idea," she replied, handing me back my card. "At this rate, with a little bit of luck, we should be back home before dark."

Sadly, however, that *little bit of luck* was just about to run out! After ten minutes or so following the queue of lorries crawling ever-steadily towards the top end of the ramp that led down to the rear carriage of the awaiting commercial shuttle train, we ran into the English Border Control Customs Brigade, and got *randomly* picked on! Two uniformed officers stood in front of our vehicle, signalled at us to pull into the side entrance of a secured search area, then switch off the engine and step down from the vehicle.

"Good morning sir, madam," a uniformed Customs Officer with three gold bands on the cuff of his smartly-pressed black jacket began, "and where would your journey be taking you today may I ask?"

Two other young male uniformed Customs Officers, accompanied by two slightly older female officers, one of whom had securely shut and *locked* the door we'd just driven in through, began walking around the little Foden, looking her up and down with more than obvious suspicion. There were five of them in total, only one of whom, the one who appeared to be the most senior of the team, had been prepared to acknowledge either of us personally. '*Guilty until proven innocent eh? How bloody rude!*' I thought. Especially given that they were so-say '*compatriots*'! Bright overhead lighting snapped on high above us, and I began to feel as if you could cut the atmosphere with a knife. '*Dammit! I feel an argument coming on already!*' I looked the chief officer directly in the eyes, kept my voice perfectly calm, and answered his question with as much honesty, sincerity and politeness as I could muster,

"Home!" was my simple reply. I don't think it helped the situation in any way.

"Listen," I continued, "if your colleagues are going to continue prowling around creating this awful air of suspicion, trying their best to give us the impression that we're *already* nothing but a pair of criminals, which I can assure you we're most definitely not, then I'm afraid you're not making this situation conducive to getting much in the way of cooperation from either of us. Now, can I suggest, please, that you ask each and every one of them to adopt a far more acceptable air of civility? Unless you'd prefer me to file a written report to your superiors at a later date that is!"

The chief took each of his subordinates to one side and had a quiet word individually in each of their ears. *Jeez, I hoped I hadn't overstepped the mark!* There's no way I'd attempt to speak to *French* officials in that kind of manner. *Oh wait, maybe I already had once!* Oh well, civility costs nothing, as they say, so fingers crossed again! A moment or two later, each of the other four officers politely acknowledged the both of us, one of the young male officers commenting on what a *'lovely old piece of kit'* the Foden was, and within seconds the atmosphere eased a little.

"Thank you guys, and good morning to every one of you too,' I said loudly, ignoring the echo in the enormous prefabricated corrugated tin shack.

I turned around very slowly and deliberately on my heels, throwing a brief look at each and every one of them straight in the eye, before once again addressing their commander in chief.

"Thank you sir," I began. "Civility costs nothing, as I'm sure you're well aware. So on that basis, I shall now provide you with a civil answer to your question. In fact, I'll go several steps further than that, I'll give you a very brief run down on the full scenario."

"That would be most appreciated," he replied with a noticeable lack of interest.

"Okay," I continued, "firstly I just want you to know that this is *not* a commercial vehicle, and we're *not* engaged in any form of paid employment. Nor have we been transporting anything whatsoever for hire or reward. This is simply a private venture, which was effectively supposed to be nothing more than an interesting festive holiday for the two of us, albeit with a positive plan for the future thrown into the equation."

The chief rolled his eyes *almost* imperceptibly, and sighed,

"Go on," he muttered with ever growing impatience.

"So, I had this boat in Bristol which I wanted to take over to Menorca. So I bought this here truck, loaded it up, drove down to Barcelona, and got on the ferry. So now the boat's in the water in Menorca, the truck's back here in your little shed, and we're on our way back home to Bristol. *Simples!* Can we go now please?"

"Pass down your hand luggage please sir," he said with a distinct air of authority, "we'll have to take a quick look through that first I'm afraid."

I pulled all of our bags down from the cab, and set them down on one of the series of makeshift trestle-tables that had been set up along the back wall of the shack. The two female Customs Officers immediately started rummaging through them with over-exaggerated eagerness, pulling items of clothing out and scattering them across the tables.

"There's nothing breakable in either of those hold-alls," I willingly confirmed to them, given that neither of them had even bothered asking, "and its unlikely you'll find anything in there that suits you, none of its your kind of style. Apart from maybe one of my ... *oh never mind!*"

"What's in the fridge-freezer exactly sir?" the commander in chief asked. "Would you mind opening it up for us please?"

"Really??" I said, beginning to get just a tad impatient. "Its full of black bin liners, which are all full of *dirty laundry! That's all!* Do you not have one of those commercial radar scanners this side of the sodding channel?"

"No sir, I'm afraid we don't," he replied. "Open the box please!"

'I'd rather take the sodding money!' I muttered to myself, as I walked accompanied along the flatbed and began slackening off the ratchet straps.

After casting the straps to one side I threw open both of the white insulated doors, and one of the chief's minions peered inside. One by one he removed the black bags, and passed them down to his colleague, who set them down on another section of table. By now the Doris's were carefully repacking the hold-alls, whilst looking excitedly at the next items in the queue, namely my kit-bag and Helen's handbag. At the same time the two young uniformed lads begun undoing the black bags one by one, and scattering dirty laundry all across the tables. Honestly, there were dirty knickers and smelly socks flying in all directions."

293

"*Oi!!*" I shouted angrily at the pair of them. "Show a little respect for fuck's sake!"

"*Language!*" the chief chastised me with sternly.

"*I'll give you fucking language in a minute!*" I muttered back at him. "And you two, yes you ladies over there, before you *don't* bother asking, yes there *are* breakables in the next two bags, so *search them carefully, PLEASE!!*"

One of them pulled a packet of cheese out of my kit-bag.

"What's this?" she asked with faked innocence.

"What does it say on the packet?" I asked back at her.

She stared at it, thought for a second, and then answered "Roquefort."

"*Well its fucking Roquefort then, isn't it!*" I shouted sarcastically, and added under my breath "*Fucking moron!*"

Even Helen was beginning to get her arse out of gear a little. Actually, to be fair, probably more than just a little. One of the Doris's scattered the contents of Helen's handbag across the table, and Helen began hurling her own form of abuse at her, which, to her credit, was always considerably more polite than my own. Their behaviour, however, was beginning to wear a little thin with me by now.

"Tell me chief," I asked the boss, looking him straight in the eye once again, "what is it exactly you're looking for? Maybe I can be of some assistance if I know where it is you guys are coming from?"

"Drugs!" was his simple one-word answer.

"Okay," I continued. "Well, firstly, I can assure you 100% that you are wasting both your's and our time, as well as countless English taxpayer's pounds, because we are *not,* I repeat, *NOT,* carrying, consuming, smuggling or unwittingly concealing any form of drugs whatsoever. We simply don't do drugs, end of. And secondly, if you don't start conducting your activities in a more polite and respectful manner, then I shall have no option other than to call the police, and have your movements both monitored and supervised. So please, *start acting professionally!*" (FFS!)

With that, whilst one of the young muppets began trying to cram all of our dirty laundry back into the black bags that he'd clumsily torn open, the other one lay down on the ground and rolled underneath the truck in order to make a closer inspection of the underside of the flatbed, and the intricate components of the chassis.

"You may as well chuck him a sleeping-bag," I said to his boss with increasing sarcasm, "he's not gonna find anything, so he could well be under there searching for *weeks!*"

I leaned down under the truck's flatbed, and called across to the youngster lying on the floor with a torch in his hand, shining it upwards into the gubbins of the chassis,

"If you fail to find any illegal immigrants burning their asses to pieces on that red-hot exhaust you're about to brush your curly locks against, which you *won't*, because I would've noticed them myself, *I've got eyes in the back of my sodding head,* then would you mind *awfully* just checking that the sight glass on fuel filter number two is still clean and clear for me. *PLEASE!!!*"

No response! *There's a surprise!* The chief asked me what was in the suitcases.

"Get one of your skivvies to open them up and check," I replied stubbornly. "There's tools and road kit in one of them, and clothes in the other. Oh yeah, and *NO BLOODY DRUGS!!* But hey, feel free to toss the contents of *them* all over the sodding place too!"

"No, *please don't!*" Helen suddenly chipped in with. "All the clothes in the black case are decent, clean and neatly folded. Feel free to search, but *please* don't mess them all up, they've not long since been ironed."

The youngster rolled out from under the truck and switched off his torch.

"All clear sir," he announced positively.

"And that, *commander,* is *ALL* you're gonna get from these guys today," I threw back at the chief.

I started watching both the women begin to rummage carelessly through the contents of the two suitcases, blatantly ignoring Helen's simplest of requests. One of them even managed to drop one of my expensive, neatly folded Hawaiian shirts on the filthy concrete floor, and then promptly stood on it whilst attempting to pick it back up. The other one was attempting to prise open the foot pump air cylinder, a feat that's not even remotely possible!

"I really am gonna lose my fucking temper with you lot soon!" I shouted at them angrily.

"Listen sir, madam," said the chief calmly, "why don't you just go take a seat over there and let us get on with our job in peace?"

"Because you're not doing your fucking job properly!" I shouted back at him. *"You're nothing but a bunch of sodding cowboys. And WE, Mister Dumb-Ass Customs Officer, are NOT FUCKING DRUG SMUGGLERS!!! Jesus! Do we LOOK like a pair of criminals? I mean, REALLY?"*

"There's no such thing as *'a look'* I'm afraid sir, you simply never can tell. its simply our job to carry out random checks on vehicles crossing the border, that's just what the UK government instructs us to do. And that, sir, madam, is precisely what we're doing."

"Well, as I've already said," I answered him straight back, "in my considered opinion, you're doing it in an *extremely unprofessional* manner, and I shall now report you directly to your superiors at my first available opportunity."

With that, I suddenly reached inside my open kit-bag, and pulled out a small, stubby-handled pozi-drive screwdriver. I offered it to the head muppet, and said *very* sarcastically,

"D'you know, if I really *was* trying to smuggle some type of drugs back into the UK, although God only knows what they might be exactly, coming from *Spain* of all places, but anyway, d'you know precisely where I'd choose to hide them? I'd stuff them all inside those flashing yellow lights up there on the roof of the cab. Here, why don't you get one of your *shit-for-brains* to go take *them* apart and see what they find?"

I pushed the screwdriver a little closer towards him. He ignored it entirely, however he did instruct one of his minions to climb up on the roof to make a closer inspection. I began to laugh at this point. I reached into my kit-bag once again, and pulled out both my Leatherman multi-tool and my little digital camera. I scrolled through some of the pictures that Helen and I had taken, found the series of the ones showing us actually launching the Phoenix off the back of the Foden on the slipway in Fornells, and turned the images towards the chief, shoving the camera right under his nose whilst scrolling through them one by one.

"Look," I said, growing evermore annoyed with this seemingly apparent fiasco, "if you don't believe us, take a look through these. Go on, check them all out, there's a complete record of virtually the whole of our trip detailed on there, just to prove that we're not *LYING* to you!"

He ignored me, and looked across at his ladies, who were both in the process of attempting to close down the lids of the two suitcases.

"All clear here sir," one of them announced positively.

"Okay," I said, becoming even *more* sarcastic, whilst extending a two-inch flat knife blade from the side of the Leatherman, and thrusting it handle-first towards the chief, "so, why don't you go do all the sodding tyres next then? I mean, come on, there's seven of them all told, that's gotta be one *serious* haul for you poor guys, surely?"

"All clear here sir," called the muppet sat on the roof of the cab.

"Now you really *are* being silly," said the chief condescendingly. "Put the knife away please sir."

I refolded the little blade, and chucked the Leatherman back into my still open kit-bag.

"Well," I grunted in disgust, "where exactly d'you draw the line with this kinda shit? *Eh?* I mean, why don't you go get a whole team of mechanics in here for God's sake? Take the whole fucking truck to pieces why don't you, *every single nut and bolt!* Find nothing, put it all back together, keep us locked up in here for a fucking fortnight, waste thousands of pounds of taxpayer's money, and for what? *For FUCK ALL, that's what!*"

"Its okay sir, madam," the boss-man said politely, "you're free to leave."

"WHAT??" I screamed at him. *"Can I have that in fucking writing?"*

"On behalf of Her Majesty's Customs and Excise Services, we sincerely apologise for any delays or disruptions to your travel plans, sir, madam, you are now free to continue on your way."

"Well knock me sideways with a fucking pigeon's feather," I exclaimed, lifting the suitcases back up onto the flatbed and slotting them neatly back down behind the broken fridge-freezer.

Whilst one of the younger muppets slid the long corrugated exit door open, I decided, quite wisely I'm sure, to refrain from any further sarcasm, and concentrated solely on securely re-lashing the rear load with the ratchet straps. Helen climbed back into the cab, and I passed her up the bags, which she neatly stacked back in their rightful place. Before climbing in myself I had one last little trick up my sleeve. I jumped back up onto the flatbed, and whilst pretending to double-check the tightness of the ratchet straps, I suddenly spun around, aimed the little camera at all five of the Customs gang, snapping off a couple of shots that perfectly caught all five of them in-frame together, gawking at me with mild surprise.

"That one'll suffice for the complaints procedure," I casually informed them.

I jumped up into the cab, started the engine and released the air brake, but before driving off I had one final word to say to them. I leaned out of the cab window and shouted it back across the massive tin warehouse at them,

"Random, my fucking arse! Next time, try picking on someone who looks at least halfway suspicious, learn to do your jobs PROPERLY, and stop wasting taxpayers' money winding up perfectly innocent tourists!"

And with that, I stamped down hard on the accelerator, leaving a huge cloud of black diesel exhaust hovering around the inside of the giant corrugated tin shack. *I hoped they bloody well choked on it!*

"I know they've got a job to do babe," I said to Helen, as we pulled out of the shed and joined back into a queue of vehicles heading steadily towards the *'down'* ramp, "but firstly, like you heard me say, civility costs nothing. And secondly, they need to learn to be a little more *selective* with their *randomness* policy!"

"I totally agree with you hun," Helen totally agreed with me. "To be honest, I think they were *all* out of order, every single one of them, and good on you for telling them so. So, are you really gonna file a complaint with their authority?"

"Well I've certainly caught the right image on camera to identify them all, but realistically babe, *no*, I'd only be wasting my time, and to be honest, I'll have far more important things to do than that when we get home. Mind you, I have to say, when you stop and think about it; an empty 1970's car transporter with a dead fridge-freezer strapped to the back, plus a couple of amateurs sat up in the cab? Would you not think that looked a mite suspicious d'you reckon? Or would you not even give it a second thought?"

"Hmmm . . . I suppose you might have a point there!" she smirked.

We followed the queue of traffic down the ramp, and drove onto the rear carriage of the commercial train. The vehicle in front kept moving ahead, so we followed along behind until pulling to a stop just a very short stroll from the lounge-cab we knew we had to use. As I switched off the engine I looked at my watch. 1.45pm! *Quarter to bloody two in the afternoon! Three sodding hours those wankers had kept us back there! Bloody jobsworths!* Minutes later, once we were sitting comfortably in the little driver's lounge, the train pulled steadily away from Coquelles station on the outskirts of Calais, headed down the gradual incline, and on into the deep dark recesses of the tunnel itself. After picking up speed, before we'd even had time to properly gather our thoughts back together, we were slowing once again at the start of the next incline, which subsequently led to us bursting forth back out into the daylight yet again, and then pulled gradually to a halt at the end of the line in Folkestone station. Minutes later we drove off the train, along the traffic lane towards the *'up'* ramp, and then headed directly for the M20 motorway. Three o'clock on a Tuesday afternoon was never going to be the ideal time to hit the M25, but then again, *when is?* As it so happened, it proved to be relatively quiet, and we were able to keep up our average speed of 65mph. Then, shortly before five o'clock, both as eager as each other to get back to our cosy little semi in Fishponds, we ran underneath the overhead roundabout at the top of Tormarton Hill, the M4's junction 18 turn-off for Bath. *'Hmm, okay then,'* I thought to myself, *'this'll be the very last chance I get to see what I can squeeze out of this faithful old bus, let's REALLY let her off her reins and see what she'll do!'*

"Just eight miles of motorway left babe, and its all downhill from here. Hang on to yer hat, let's see what this old girl can *really* do!"

It had become dark by then, but the traffic was exceptionally light for five o'clock on a weekday, so I gave the old Foden her head and stamped the throttle down to the floor. She very quickly ran passed the 70mph mark, and to both my surprise and delight, at the bottom of the first four mile steepest section of the hill the needle was hovering very fractionally under the eighty mark. *80mph! Good girl!* I don't think you'd find many modern commercial trucks capable of that kind of speed, they'd all seemed to have been fitted with limiters by then. *Looks like we'd picked on a real good'un after all, despite the couple of mishaps along the way!*

"Welcome home sweetheart," I said warmly to Helen, as we pulled off the M32 and headed through Hambrook towards Downend. "Successful mission accomplished, despite its trials and tribulations, so thank you, from the very bottom of my heart, for your ever-patient and enjoyable company. its been an absolute pleasure my love."

"The pleasure, my darling," Helen replied sweetly, "was all mine."

I pulled the truck halfway onto the pavement in the narrow little street just outside our house in Fishponds, so as not to block the road for the night, pulled on the brake, shut down the engine, leaned across the top of our bags, and pulled Helen close towards me. I hugged her tight for a good whole minute, then kissed her passionately on the lips. We were both feeling enormously proud of ourselves, and we sang merry tunes out loud as we jumped down with our bags, and walked back through the front door into our chilly little house. Helen headed straight for the central heating boiler, followed *immediately* afterwards by the bathroom, whilst I went back out and unstrapped the fridge and the two cases. I carried the two cases indoors, then went back and pulled all of the black bags out of the fridge. I re-lashed the old fridge, that would most likely get disposed of in our skip at work the following day, locked up, and wandered back inside with the bags, dumping them all on the kitchen floor by the washing machine.

"Cab'll be here in five minutes babe," Helen called down to me from upstairs.

"Brilliant!" I shouted back. "Where are we going?"

"Down the Railway Tavern," she replied. "I think we deserve a little celebration drink, don't you?"

"Damn bloody right I do," I replied enthusiastically. "Good move honey, I'm ready when you are!"

Ten minutes later we walked into our favourite local pub, bumped into the usual crowd of assorted good mates and close friends, and that's exactly where we spent the remainder of the evening, whiling away the hours with embellished tales of our recent adventures, and many, many pints of good old-fashioned English ale.

CHAPTER THIRTY THREE

The following day, Wednesday the 4th, was the company's first official day back at work, following their two week festive holiday break. Luckily for me there was no need for me to go in early, as my wonderful daughter Michelle, as ever, had already pre-planned all the staff's duties for the remainder of the week, and everything, in line with the company's standard system, had been written up on the board, so they all knew exactly what they had to get on with without the need to ask. As per usual I'd make a point of catching up with Michelle during the course of the next couple of days, particularly with regard to customer demands and orders received, etc, etc, and then we'd spend the Friday together writing up the board for the following week's programme of works. Week by week, with regard to the manufacturing and installation programming, that was essentially the way the company worked. It always had, since 1979, and still does to this very day.

Helen had already been given permission to take one extra day after our return, so she'd be going back in the following day, first thing on the Thursday morning. That meant she'd most likely spend all of Wednesday unpacking our bags, putting the washing on, and then food shopping, whilst I went in to work to sort the lorry out. Neither of us woke particularly early the following morning, and when we did, once we were ready, we wandered around the corner to our little local café for a quick breakfast. I'd tried to read the front few pages of the Daily Mail over my bacon and eggs, but it had meant so very little to me, seeing as we'd been completely out of touch with reality for the last couple of weeks, that I simply folded it back down on the shelf and cracked on with my scram. Once breakfast was done we walked back around to the house, I kissed Helen and wished her luck with the remainder of her day, and immediately got stuck in to the task in hand.

First thing was to clear the cab from any of our remaining personal possessions, such as the roadmap and the CD player, etc, all of which I took back indoors. Next I checked the oil and water levels once again, and was delighted to find both of them still to be perfectly spot on. I then drove the truck in to work, and parked it up on the road outside, right where it was most likely to be seen by the daily hoards of traffic passing by, as our showroom fronted onto a relatively busy suburban main road. After saying good morning and Happy New Year individually to each member of staff, and giving Michelle a huge, long, full-on emotional hug, I unstrapped the old fridge, dragged it off the flatbed, then tipped it end over end into the half-empty rubbish skip sitting on the company's forecourt. I then ran a hosepipe from an external tap, connected it up to the firm's *Mickey Mouse* little jet-wash unit and gave the whole truck a good washing down from top to bottom. I even climbed a step-ladder specifically to do the roof of the cab, which was easier than trying to scramble up the HIAB at the front of the flatbed. Jet-wash safely packed away, I then ran an extension lead from the showroom, and fully vacuumed out the inside of the cab. That would do it then. *Nice and sparkly-clean all round!* Next I went down into the factory and found half an 8x4 sheet of 2mm white Foamex, an offcut from a previous job somewhere, and using a jig-saw I cut two identical size pieces, each 3ft x 2ft, then wiped them clean using some meths soaked tissue roll. I stuck a roll of bright red hi-tack cast vinyl into the firm's graphics plotter, programmed in what I wanted it to print, and then pressed *'GO x 2'*. After weeding the vinyl I stuck the sticky-backed red lettering centrally onto each of the white Foamex boards, squidged out the water bubbles, peeled off the application tape, and stood back to admire my handiwork. I was happy enough with the results.

FOR SALE:- Foden Car Transporter all in Perfect Working Order – 3-ton HIAB – 1-ton winch – Recent Full Service – Brand New MoT – Taxed and Ready To Go – Recent Proven History – £2,600.00 ono – call in to showroom and ask for Chris – test drive welcome at any time – beautiful ride.

That should do it then! Using some Blu-Tack I stuck them up inside the cab, one board in the centre of the front windscreen, one in the middle of the rear window, so that they could clearly be seen from both directions. Then I went back into my office, called the Trade-It, and placed virtually the same ad, substituting *'showroom'* for my mobile phone number, and paid for just one week's edition. And then I went back to work. *With a vengeance!* It had begun to roll around in my head just what that trip had cost me altogether. Okay, chances were that we'd've gone off for an Xmas holiday somewhere anyway, so I could certainly disregard the £964 return flights to Malaga, as well as the majority of the food and drink that we'd had over the previous couple of weeks, which probably came to around £1,250-ish, especially if I were to include hotel costs and parking, etc. However the Foden itself stood me in at £3,200, plus the £985 tax, insurance and RAC cover, £620 preparing the Phoenix for her travels, around £725 altogether on diesel, £475 for the Chunnel, nearly £200 on motorway tolls, and £430 for the ferry. *Hey ho! Who said boating was cheap?!!?* Best I get my nose back to the grindstone I reckon, that's a lot of outlay to make up for. And selling the Foden for just £2,600, which was the genuine realistic value that I'd put on her, all things considered, wasn't exactly going to cover it all. Still, it appeared from my initial conversation with Michelle that, despite this generally being the firm's quieter time of year, we actually seemed to have plenty in the way of new orders coming in, which would certainly give me plenty to get my teeth stuck into. Plus, just knowing that the Phoenix was sat comfortably and safely at her little mooring in Fornells Bay gave me all the warmth, comfort and enthusiasm that I needed to begin building my own personal coffers back up again, ready and waiting for our next family holiday together at our beautiful little apartment in sunny Menorca. I picked up my office phone and began ringing clients, simply to say *'Hi, Happy New Year, how's business looking right now? Anything we can help you with in any way?'*

Appointment, order. Appointment, order. Appointment, order. Survey, survey, survey. This was going really well. In fact, probably one of the best starts to any year that we'd ever had. It certainly kept me running around all over the country, my feet hardly even had time to touch the ground. Until Friday that was. Fridays, whenever possible, were always spent in the office, planning the following week's works programme, and writing it up on the board. It was a bit like piecing together a complex economic jigsaw puzzle, and the busier the company became, the more complex the puzzle. But it always got done on the day. Come five o'clock, albeit sometimes miraculously, everything finally came together and slotted neatly into place, and once the board was full, and *logically* sequenced, then our work for that day was done. Board done? *Tick!* High fives all round? *Tick!* Glasses at the ready? *Tick!* Cork out of bottle it is then! *(Tick!)* And that, as the expression goes, is precisely what made *The Company* tick! With the combined consci-entious efforts of all involved, *it worked!*

Ten days later, whilst we were in the middle of piecing together the board on the Friday lunchtime, I took a phone call from the boss of one of my best clients. He asked me if I could please carry out a full survey for their usual standard scenic theming requirements at yet another Center Parcs project they'd just taken on, this time at Kempervennen near Eindhoven in Holland. *'Yes Dominic,'* I'd replied enthusiastically, *'good to hear from you, I think this'll be our sixth? Yes, I fully understand the spec, and yes, we can squeeze this in to our programme, no problem sir. I'll take care of the survey on my own. When would you like me over there?'* Dom had replied that they'd be start-ing on-site on the following Monday, so anytime during the forthcoming week would be good with him, providing we could guarantee complying with their eight week turnaround as per usual. I said I was sure we could, but I'd confirm that for definite once I'd visited the site and studied the drawings in detail. *'And yes, I'll be driving over, as always, and yes, I'll look forward to seeing you over there, most likely next Wednesday, but I'll give you a call on Tuesday to confirm so that you can reserve me a bed for two nights in one of the contractor's villas. Thanks Dom, have a good weekend.'* Great, yet another highly profitable CP project, just what I needed to get my teeth stuck into to help make up for some of my recent costly expenditure. Yes, I knew it meant taking the damned Chunnel *yet again,* but hey ho, this time, firstly, it was for work, and secondly, I'd be driving a *fast* comfortable car, as opposed to a *slow* overloaded old lorry! After I put the phone down on Dom I asked Michelle if she wouldn't mind swapping my old Shogun for her pretty little convertible Mercedes SL230, *yet again,* just for three days this time, so I could drive over to Holland and back to look at another job for Dom. After she reluctantly replied *'I suppose so! PLEASE don't bend it!',* I pulled a well-used road map of Europe out of a drawer and spread it out over my desk. 360 miles from Bristol to Eindhoven. *Plus* the dreaded Chunnel! No problem, all in a day's work! Drive over Wednesday, survey Thursday, drive home Friday, quite possibly with a passenger thrown into the equation on the return trip; that was often the way these jobs worked out. I made a few more phone calls, set a few wheels in motion, then con-tinued with planning the board for the following week, including working into it my own proposed schedule.

An hour or so later a scruffy looking middle-aged chap, in dirty mechanic's overalls, walked into the showroom and asked to see Chris. He asked me various questions about the Foden, all of which I answered with confidence, and then asked me if I wouldn't mind taking him for a quick test drive. I said that would be no problem, grabbed the keys from my office, and after unsticking the For Sale boards from the windscreens, I drove him on a ten mile round trip, out through Downend and Hambrook, down the M32 towards town, where I let her run comfortably up to 70mph, and then back up Fishponds Road, parking her back in the exact same position outside the showroom. As per usual she ran like a dream. I showed him how the hydraulic HIAB worked, then demonstrated the remote electric power winch. He told me it was *exactly* what he was looking for, said that he'd have to talk it through with his partner first, made a note of my mobile number, and left. I thought no more of it, and with the help of my wonderful staff, we completed the board by around five-fifty, then all disappeared off to the pub together. Monday mid-morning I answered a call on my mobile from the scruffy guy who'd shown interest in the truck the Friday before. He told me that he'd chatted to his partner over the weekend, and they were prepared to offer me £1,600 for it, as that's all they honestly believed it was worth. I bit my tongue, refrained from telling him exactly where to get off, and said I'd think about it. I didn't bother thinking about it at all though, I simply called the Trade-It and asked them to repeat the same advert in their next two editions, which they duly did. *Sixteen hundred quid my ass! Bloody cheek!*

Wednesday came around, and having confirmed everything with Dominic the day before, I'd got an early start in Michelle's nippy little two-seater Merc, and by 1700hrs CET I was settling myself into a twin room in a six person villa, which was also in dire need of refurbishment, at Center Parcs Kempervennen in Holland. The following morning I met up with Dom and a couple of his workforce, and we went through the designer's drawings together. None of them resembled traditional construction drawings in the slightest, they never did. They were far more just a series of artist's impression sketches. But we'd all become used to these types of images by now, and exactly how to transform them from perception into reality, and together we all set to with our tape measures, theodolites and laser-levels, until we'd compiled sufficient practical information as to the specific layout of the actual site itself in order to commence our manufacturing process. Mostly what was generally required was acre upon acre of different coloured flame-retardant canvas fabrics, which would then form the visible aspect of various roof structures. All of this needed to be pre-sewn in our factory, and then installed on-site, perfectly replicating the designer's drawings, by our excellent teams of fitters, all of whom had by now got used to this rather non-precise method of workmanship. In addition to the canvas work, the scenic theming aspect involved significant sourcing of ancient architectural artefacts, more often than not of a nautical theme, which were then used for decorative purposes to hang underneath the canvas. I'd always considered myself somewhat of an expert at collecting ancient nautical artefacts, as my wife would gladly attest to, mainly on account of how cluttered our back garden always seemed to look! However, I often found certain aspects of my collection of 'rubbish' came in extremely handy when asked, for example, to nautically theme a Center Parcs bowling alley, and actually felt quite smug with myself when taking the view that I'd genuinely made some 'money for old rope'!

Moreover, this project in particular, on top of the considerable quantity of rolls of awning fabric that we'd need to use up from our huge stocks, required a large quantity of rope-work to help part-build a new children's play area. I was certainly going to have my work cut out for the next few weeks, sourcing and purchasing the correct products, supervising the complex manufacturing process, then going through the drawings with our fitters, in an attempt to get across to them precisely what it was the designer was looking for, and how they should transform what we'd manufactured and sourced into roughly what the drawings depicted. Especially given that, firstly, we had fixed physical parameters within which to work, and secondly, as always, we had a *critical* completion date to meet! But hey, I felt fully confident that we'd achieve it. We'd managed to so far on the five previous CP projects, and this one was no different in concept. Having collated all the relevant dimensions and details required, the following morning I took a copy of the drawings with me and jumped back in the car to head back home. At the very last minute Dom asked me if I'd mind taking Mike back with me too. He'd planned to ride back with Dom, but Dom had decided to stay over for the weekend, as his own pre-planning works were as yet unfinished. I said *'of course, no problem whatsoever'*, and Mike chucked his kitbag next to mine in the boot of the little two-seater Merc, jumped into the passenger seat, and off we shot at great speed, headed on our way back through Belgium towards Calais. Come six-thirty later that evening I was dropping Mike off at his front door back in Staple Hill, Bristol. Survey completed, no dramas, just another day, *or three,* at the office!

Monday morning arrived, and I spent the week getting stuck right into my increasingly busy work schedule; writing up job-sheets, ordering materials, processing orders, survey, quote, supply; survey, quote, supply; and so it went on. The following Friday afternoon, having received not one single call to date through the Trade-It, the same scruffy mechanic chap sauntered back into the showroom, and asked me if I'd thought anymore about it yet. I said *yes,* I had, and as far as I was concerned, given what I'd spent on her altogether, along with the successful two and a half thousand mile round trip that I'd just put her through, in my opinion the Foden was well worth what I was asking for her, if not considerably more. He said sorry, but it was £1,600 or nothing, that's what his partner had told him; but he was happy to pay in cash-money, no guarantees, no paperwork, no receipt. I said '*thanks, but no thanks',* and we left it at that. I rang the Trade-It again, and booked the same ad for one more week, then rang the Bristol Evening Post and placed the identical ad with them too. Which, as it happened, cost me about five times as much as the Trade-It ad! The weekend went by again without a single call, despite the Post managing to squeeze the advert into that Friday night's weekend edition, and by the time the following Wednesday arrived, not only had no one else either phoned or called in, but most of the company's fitters, as well as a few of the neighbours, had begun to moan ever so slightly about where it was parked. Just how inconvenient it was proving to be every time we had large delivery lorries pulling in, or whenever any of them wanted to park up and load their own vans. How much longer was it likely to be staying there, and if so could I *please* go and park it somewhere else, a little further out of the way? *Please!* Which, realistically, didn't make any kind of practical sense, at least not if was going to continually keep my eye on it whilst trying to sell it. The following Friday, still without a single jot of interest manifesting itself from any other direction, the same scruffy mechanic stuck his head around the door, and asked, *once again,* if I was still sure. I called him through into my office, reiterated to him just exactly how much of a bargain he was getting, and sat at my desk whilst I watched him count out sixteen hundred quid in dirty, used twenty-pound notes. I handed him the keys, the MoT certificate and the logbook, which we'd both signed there and then, and as I reluctantly shook his grubby little hand, he pulled a large partly toothless smug grin at me, knowing full well that he'd just bagged himself an absolute bargain, mumbled '*thanks buddy',* and wandered back outside. Still, the pressures of work were fully back on right now, so the bottom line was that it was simply one less thing for me to worry about. I'd got enough on my plate at the time, what with several new contracts to run, one of them with a rather tight completion date, and in *Holland* of all places, so I guess the last thing I needed right then was to waste any more valuable office time trying to sell worn out second hand commercial vehicles that I no longer had any use for. I pocketed the sixteen hundred quid cash, grateful I suppose for small mercies. Although I must admit, I couldn't bear to face watching him drive my beloved old Foden off down the road finally, once and for all, never to be seen ever again, so I simply stayed in my office, picked up the phone, and dialled yet another potential client.

CHAPTER THIRTY FOUR

'*Forget about the old Foden Chris, its gone! its sold, its out of everyone's way, and that's all that matters. Just concentrate on work. Work, work, work, work, work, that's all you gotta do right now. Oh yeah, and then holiday! With the family! With the Phoenix! In Menorca! In the sunshine!!' Thoughts! Constant DiY mind games!! Hey ho!*

Work was actually going swimmingly well for a change. Sometimes it did, sometimes, especially during Jan and Feb, *it didn't!* But this year, so far, it certainly was. In fact, with the next lucrative CP project coming up, we had so much manufacturing to get through, following which we'd need at least four guys on-site in Holland for a minimum of a fortnight to complete the installation, that I had to have a little word in Michelle's ear to see if we could stop pushing quite so much for more new orders. Inevitably she retorted with her standard response, *'never say 'NO' to a potential customer!'* However, the least we could do was inform everyone, for the time being at least, that their order was likely to take up to six weeks to complete, as opposed to the usual three. She agreed to that being an acceptable compromise, and carried on pushing for more orders. Meanwhile, in between driving here, there and everywhere to carry out more and more surveys, I continued firstly with the monitoring of manufacturing and production in the factory, and secondly, following regular communication with Dominic in regard to on-site progress, liaising in ever increasing detail with the four of our fitters that I'd assigned to the project.

All four of them had worked on the previous five CP projects, so they already had a good idea of Dom's methodology, but I wanted them to have as good an understanding as possible as to the specific requirements relating to this new site, given that not one site so far had even come close to replicating another. Although the principles remained a constant throughout, the specifics of each site varied significantly, and in order that I didn't need to spend the whole two weeks on-site myself, directing and supervising the installation, the five of us spent a considerable amount of time together poring over the drawings. We all went through my survey notes in the minutest of detail, producing our own site-specific plans for Dom's prior approval, *by fax,* and constructing a detailed works programme as to precisely what had to go where, who was responsible for which aspects, and along with the products that were currently in production, what tools, machinery and access equipment, *etc, etc, etc,* they'd need to take over with them. And just as bloody well I did, as it was about to transpire!! I'd even produced a site-specific RAMS *(risk assessment and method statement),* faxed a copy to Dom, and provided copies to each of the fitters, along with their detailed job descriptions, and a full programme of works. All other instructions they'd be happy to take on-site directly from Dom, who, effectively as overall project manager, would remain on-site for the entire duration of the project. The fact was, they were a great bunch of guys, were our fitters. They knew what they were doing, they were all *very* good at their jobs, they'd all worked with Dom on numerous previous occasions, so they fully knew the score, and we trusted each and every one of them implicitly. So hopefully, if all went entirely according to plan, and there was no reason why it shouldn't, then all I would be required to do personally was to attend site with Dom on handover day, Monday 13th March, sign the job off, and subsequently, all being well, submit our invoice. And here we were, halfway through February, and production of *all* orders were currently running entirely according to schedule. *Spiffing!* Thursday 9th Feb I drove to London to carry out a site survey on behalf of a brewery customer of ours, for three giant 6m x 6m commercial umbrellas, with integral lighting and heating, in the rear garden of a pub in Kensington. Friday 10th Feb Michelle secured the order for the three umbrellas, then we spent the rest of the day together *'doing the board',* completing it somewhere around 5.30pm-ish, and subsequently celebrating the little successes of yet another week by sharing a bottle of Chardonnay with our friendly team of office staff.

I spent that weekend at home with Helen, both of us discussing together our assorted work commitments, and trying to work out when it might prove most practical to plan our next family holidays together. I told her that I had four guys driving over to Holland on Monday 27th Feb, and that all being well, hopefully they'd all be driving back together on Friday 10th March. They'd be taking two vans over anyway, partly because of the amount of kit they needed to carry, and partly because the two teams had slightly differing agendas. Dom would be organising all their accommodation, they'd have more than adequate float to cover their food and drink. *Well, their food at least!* And whether they chose to drive home and back for the weekend of the 4th/5th, halfway through the job, depended entirely on how well the work was coming along in line with the programme. Chances were, if neither Dom nor myself made that decision for them, they'd be perfectly capable of making it for themselves. As indeed they would if any of them needed to stay on over the weekend of the 11th/12th just to finish off. The fact was I'd prefer to be around over the course of the two week installation *(fat bloody chance, as it so happened!)* on hand, just in case I might happen to get called upon. Plus, I had to drive back over on Sunday 12th anyway, so that Dom and I could hand the job over to the Center Parcs management team first thing on the morning of Monday 13th. That part was *critical!* Helen was really happy for me, and for Michelle, and indeed for the company as a whole, for the fact that we'd managed to pull so much work in, and we were keeping everyone extremely busy. *Good times!* They were for Helen too; she'd just been awarded a small pay rise, but more importantly her firm had given her an extra week's holiday each year, beginning from the start of their next financial year on April 6th. That would *definitely* come in handy, *for sure!*

"Well done babe, that's *exactly* what we need!" I congratulated her. "That's more family time together in the sunshine, *yippee!* So what I was thinking was this. Once I've got this Center Parcs job well out of the way, give it a week or so for the guys to settle back into their usual routines at work, then somewhere near the end of March I'm gonna fly over to Menorca, on my own, just for a few days, just to check on the apartment, make sure the Phoenix is all okay, and go say buenos dias to Pedro. That sound like a good plan to you?"

"It does," Helen replied, "apart from one minor detail."

"What's that babe?" I asked.

"They don't start flying from Bristol to Mahon until the beginning of April." she replied.

"Oh," I said, remembering that there were no direct flights from the UK to Menorca whatsoever during the winter back then. "Oh well, looks like I'll be EasyJet's very first customer for that route this year then; I'll take the first available flight there, and get the next available one back. More importantly though, I think you and I should go for a week sometime in May, just the two of us together, and then when the kids break up from school for the summer, subject to clearing it with Rachel first, I think we should take Tori and Alex for a whole fortnight sometime during July. Before it gets *too* hot, as it sometimes tends to during August. How does that sound?"

"Absolutely perfect," Helen replied, "although I will add one extra comment, which I'm sure you already know anyway."

"What's that hun?" I asked.

"Its never too hot for me! Even in August!" she beamed back at me.

"I know that sweetie," I agreed. "Me neither. But you know what Tori's like. If it gets *too* hot for her, she won't go *anywhere* without a sun parasol; and even then its only if we manage to tear her away from an air-conditioning unit somewhere. Which we don't happen to have in the apartment anyway!"

"I know," sighed Helen. "Still, I'm sure she'll grow out of that one day."

"I'm sure she will," I agreed with a grin.

I checked the calendar that hung on the front of the cupboard door in the kitchen. As it so happened, April the 1st was a Saturday, and we had nothing booked for that day. In actual fact we had very little booked on the calendar for the foreseeable future. I checked with EasyJet, and sure enough, their first flight from Bristol to Mahon was indeed Saturday the 1st. So I booked it there and then. And as they'd only be flying once a week up until the next half-term school holiday, I had to book my return flight for Saturday the 8th. Hey ho, I'd have to spend a whole week out there. On my own. Alone with the Phoenix. *What a damned shame!* I drew a big smiley face on both dates on the calendar, then joined them together and wrote '*Chris to Menorca*' directly above the line. €138 return, not bad I thought, not bad at all. I then pencilled in a *potential* week towards the end of May, and told Helen that it would be subject to her confirming that she was allowed that specific time off work, then provisionally pencilled in the second two weeks in July, telling Helen that I'd have a chat with Rachel the first opportunity I got.

It wasn't our turn to have the kids that particular weekend, so Saturday night we ate out in town, and then went to the cinema. Sunday morning we had a lie-in, and then I got myself stuck into some long-overdue gardening, whilst Helen began to prepare a Sunday roast just for the two of us. I was determined to eat that in the peace and comfort of my own lounge, sat on the sofa whilst watching the four o'clock game on Sky TV, which just happened to be Man Utd v Liverpool. Which, to Helen's credit, worked out just perfectly. And to Man Utd's credit, accompanied by my own *very* noisy and over-enthusiastic encouragement, as well as several cans of Old Speckled Hen, they thrashed Liverpool 4-1. *Way to go you Red Devils!* The following weekend it *was* our turn to have the children, and when I picked them up from their mum's house early Saturday morning, Rachel confirmed that it would be fine for us to take them away on holiday during the second two weeks of July, no problem whatsoever. I said thanks, and when I told the kids exactly what it was we'd had planned for them for those two weeks, they both jumped up and down with joy and excitement all the way home. All the way from the *very top* of Fishponds to *very nearly* the top of Fishponds! Our house was all of half a mile from Rachel's house, so invariably we'd simply walk between the two. When we reached home, and their excitement calmed a little, we stuck them in the back of the car and drove to Swindon, where we all went swimming together at the Oasis Leisure Centre. On the Sunday we took them out to dinner at the Jolly Sailor, a beautiful little country pub sat right next to a lock beside a weir on the River Avon at Saltford. It was a little chilly, but it was dry, and the sun was shining, and after dinner Helen and Tori went for a pleasant little stroll along the towpath, whilst Alex and I kicked a football around in the fields. It was a great weekend. No squabbles, no injuries, no tears. *Just for a change!* Monday morning arrived, and it was time to take the kids to school. Alex was easy, he was still only nine years old, and attended Christchurch Juniors in Staple Hill. After breakfast I dropped him off by car on my way to work. Tori's journey was a little more complex. She was now eleven, and after *winging* the entrance exam, had recently started at '*Clifton High School For Proper Little Madams*', a private and *rather costly* senior school, right across the other side of town. Helen had got Tori's travel timetable down to a fine art though. Because Helen worked right in the centre of town, she dropped Tori off every other Monday morning at a bus stop right opposite the Hippodrome, where all she had to do was hop on the number twelve, and for just fifty pence she could hop off again just ten minutes later, right outside the front entrance to Clifton High, in plenty of time for assembly. That worked absolutely fine. Getting back home was a little trickier for her, as she had to get the number twelve back down to the Hippodrome, and then wait for the number six, which was twice the distance and twice the cost, to get her back up to Fishponds again, where she then had to walk all of quarter of a mile from the bus stop back to her mum's house. However, Tori seemed to have grown into a decent, intelligent and responsible young girl by this time, and as far as I can remember we'd had very little in the way of problems with her school transport regime. Helen and I had decided that we wouldn't book the flights for the May and July holidays just yet, because by then they'd be flying to Mahon twice a week, and we hadn't sat down together and discussed the finer details as to which days might suit us best, so we'd agreed to make that decision immediately after I returned from my own little jolly during the first week of April. So, Monday morning, February 20th, after dropping my youngest off at junior school, I walked into my office, some three-quarters of a mile back down the road, at pretty much precisely 9am.

Wednesday morning, February 22nd, at pretty much precisely 11am, whilst sat at my desk running through a whole set of complex job costings, my mobile phone rang. Sat on the desk right under my nose, the screen lit up with the name *PEDRO*. *I'll never forget that phone call for as long as I live!* I hit the *'answer'* button immediately.

"Hola, hola, Mister Chris? Mister Chris?"

"Si, si, hola Pedro, qué tal?" I replied, wondering why on earth he might be calling.

"Mister Chris, Mister Chris, I am having news! I am having news!"

"What is it Pedro? What news are you having?"

"Mister Chris, I am having Medicane! I am having *horrible* Medicane!"

"Oh, my God Pedro," I replied with genuine concern, "what medicine exactly? Whatever's wrong with you? What has the doctor said? What's the problem?"

"No, no, Mister Chris, is no *doctor,* is *MEDICANE!*" Pedro continued to shout at me. "Is *very, very* bad, we have muchos, muchos, how you say, *brokens!*"

"Pedro, I am not understanding you very well. What is *Medicane?*"

"Is very, very rare in Balearics, but sometimes is happens. We has happens one times before!" he continued, his voice becoming sadder by the minute. "Medicane is, how you say, *hurricane, but in Mediterranea!*"

"*WHAT!*" I shouted down the phone at him. "A *Mediterranean hurricane is a MEDICANE!* I've never heard of one of those before. How bad a hurricane Pedro? I mean *Medicane! Pedro? How bad exactly?*"

"Winds *VERY, VERY* bad," he continued. "Is no Tramontana this time, is coming from *EVERY* directions, is worst Medicane we have seen in

Balearics for maybe fifty years. *Muchos, muchos things are broken!* We have lost many, many trees. Some peoples are losing roofs from thems houses. Even one of the ferry boats, it go from Menorca to Majorca every day, it has, how you say, *capsize,* si, overnight, on its mooring in Cala Ratjada, some peoples is even getting hurts a little bits."

"That was in *Majorca* Pedro, how's everything in *Menorca?*" I asked anxiously.

"Is *very, very* bad Mister Chris. I am having *many, many* boats have sink on their moorings in Mahon. Even their *moorings* have sink too, many pontoons, they *ALL* broken!"

"And Fornells?" I asked, with considerable trepidation.

"Fornells Bay is *very, very* bad Mister Chris. The visitor's pontoons, they are all gone, mostly they break to little pieces. In the harbour there are three fishing boats that are sinked, and three more that is broken over repairs. Even the servicios, how you say, *toilets building?* This is all in the water at entrance to harbour, is brokens *everywhere!*"

"Go on then Pedro," I continued reluctantly, "give me the bad news on the Phoenix then."

"Mister Chris, I so sorry, is nothing I can help. Your Phoenix she is gone! She has gone to other side of bay, behind island, and she too is all broken up against the rocks. She in *VERY* bad way I thinks!"

FUCK! FUCK! FUCK! FUCK! FUCK! FUCK! FUCK!

And no *FUCKING* insurance either!!!

FUCK! FUCK! FUCK! FUCK! AND TREBLE-FUCKING-FUCK!

"Any chance you could go take a look at her for me please Pedro? See if its possible to tow her back over to the harbour so I can maybe make some repairs?"

"Is no way Mister Chris, I very sorry. Phoenix is up on rocks somewhere behind Isla Lizard, I am not thinking she can be repaired, and is no possible for me to get there anyways. She too far away, she too far gone, and I tearing out my hairs with too many other works, and over one thousand peoples, *including El Mayor de Mahon,* they *ALL* shouting me to helps. But I am only one man! What I can do?"

"Hmmm, yes, well, worst storm in over fifty years eh; I can sympathise with your predicament right now Pedro. But as for my poor little Phoenix, *what the fuck? Is that just my fucking luck OR WHAT?*"

I was beginning to get angry now, however, there was clearly no point in getting angry with Pedro, the situation wasn't his fault in any way, so I simply directed my anger solely at myself. *Especially* for leaving the Phoenix in the water with no *sodding* insurance. *SURELY I should've known better? You'd've thought? SURELY?!!?* I'd never even heard of a *Goddamned MEDICANE!!!*

"So, if you can't get over to her Pedro, what the hell chance do I have exactly? And if, as you suspect, and I have no reason to doubt you, she really is as badly damaged as you reckon, then *fuck it,* we'll just leave her be where she lies then, eh? Yet another Menorcan shipwreck for the local hooligans to ravage and plunder over the forthcoming months. Yeah, *fuck it,* just leave her be Pedro."

"Oh, no, Mister Chris," Pedro continued, "is no possible, *no, no, no!* This land of Fornells Bay, this is all '*Reserve de Biosphere*'. Is all, how you say, *protected* land. You cannot leave your Phoenix where she is sticking, you will be getting *fine of €50,000* for the littering of the reserve. So I sorry, but you will have to be moving her somehow. El Mayor, he has already informed me of this to be the case. And with everyones too! But for most everyones, they are mostly having some seguro, how you say, *insurance papers,* for to be helping them with some costings. This I am knowing you are not have, but I sorry, I *very, very* busy, and I *only one man!*"

WTF?!!? So, Pedro can't get himself across to the Phoenix, but somehow, *I HAVE TO!!*

"Well, at least thanks for calling and letting me know the situation Pedro, you're a good man. And I've no idea right now how I'm going to do it, but one way or another I'll get over to see you sometime next week. Don't worry, I'm a pretty resourceful kinda guy. I'll figure something out; *where there's a will, there's a way!*"

"Gracias Mister Chris. I sorry I cannot help much, but I see you soon anyways. Adios amigo."

FUCK! FUCK! FUCK! FUCK! FUCK! FUCK! FUCK! Best I go research some *sodding* flights then!

CHAPTER
THIRTY FIVE

To say that my mind was reeling at this point is probably somewhat of an understatement! It would be more accurate to describe it as being almost totally blown! However, only *almost!* After all, I *was* the boss, and *someone* had to keep their shit together! That someone, as always, being *me!* I pushed my paperwork to one side, at least that particular job could wait for the time being. I then wandered into Michelle's office muttering *'shit-fuck-bugger-bollocks!'* to myself as I went.

"Whatever's the matter dad?" Michelle asked, clearly concerned. "I heard you on the phone to someone just now. I'm guessing it was Pedro, what on earth's happened?"

I sat down opposite her desk and explained to her about the *Medicane* that had recently occurred in Menorca, and the current situation with regard to the Phoenix. I told her that I was *extremely* anxious to get over there as quickly as possible. Firstly, to see if it was at all possible to salvage anything, including *possibly* even the boat itself. Secondly, to recover the boat from precisely where it had landed up, as this was *apparently* deemed to be entirely my responsibility. Thirdly, the sooner I get the job done and out of the way, the better, before the situation potentially became even worse. And fourthly, if I didn't salvage the wreckage of the Phoenix with immediate effect, I'd most likely start building a bad reputation for myself in the Fornells Bay area, and I really didn't want to live with that level of embarrassment whenever I visited our little home there in the future. Oh, and there was probably a fifthly and a sixthly too, but like I said, my mind was still reeling. I was trying my best to weigh up, prioritise and balance my immediate responsibilities; between managing the Center Parcs project that we had on at the time on the one hand, and clearing up the mess I'd allowed to happen in Fornells Bay as quickly as possible on the other. I asked Michelle how she'd feel about me not being around for the next week or so, given how much work the company had on at the time; *if,* and it was a big *IF,* I could manage to work out some kind of practical way of getting over there. She confidently confirmed that all her orders were perfectly under control, her and Dave would be quite capable of putting the board together on whichever Fridays might apply, it all came down to how confident I felt about letting the CP job run itself in my absence. I told her that the manufacturing side of it was well under control, all aspects running entirely according to plan, there wouldn't be any delays with materials or anything, but I felt maybe we ought to convene a meeting with all four of the fitters, the six of us sit down and talk it all through together *ASAP,* before I make a final decision.

Later that afternoon, by arrangement, the fitters all returned to the office, and we sat around a table together, coffees in hand, discussing in detail, once again, the logistics of the CP job in Holland. I explained my current predicament, promised *faithfully* that I'd make the handover meeting on-site with Dom on Monday the 13th, and said that the quicker I packed myself off to Menorca the earlier I could get myself back to work again. I said I was feeling, although *praying* would be a better word, *quietly confident,* that with Pedro's help and guidance, I could achieve a rescue mission within a week or so, and providing they all felt confident enough to complete the Dutch CP installation without needing to rely on me having to attend, then I'd really like to get gone at my earliest available opportunity. Roland, being the most senior of the four fitters, went through the drawings one more time with me, the others watching intently, and then began asking a series of highly relevant questions in relation to the manufacturing side. I satisfied each and every point as he raised them, and as soon as he felt confident that everything would be ready on time, he turned to me and said,

"Don't you worry yaself boss, we've got it covered. We know what we're doing, and we'll have it all done in time. No problem, you just go do whatever it is you gotta do, leave CP and Dom to us, we'll be fine."

The other three fitters all agreed, and after thanking them, telling them all how much I appreciated their efforts, and how proud I was of their abilities, and promising them all an *extra large* bonus if they completed the job on time *without* any hiccups. *On top of their inevitably HUGE amount of overtime hours that we'd have to cover as well!* I reminded them all that, in the event of any specific on-site queries, I most likely wouldn't be available by phone whilst wearing my *sodding* wetsuit! Michelle concluded that between herself, Dave, Dominic, Roland and the rest of the team, they'd all cope admirably, and I should simply forget about work altogether, and go fix whatever it was I needed to fix. For once in my life I was lost for words. Which was probably just as well, because by then I was almost in tears anyway. All I had to do next was tell Helen. *Oh, joy of joys!!*

I sat back in my office, gave up concentrating on work entirely, picked up the phone and began researching flight options. As it turned out I could get an EasyJet flight from Bristol to Madrid first thing the following Monday morning, Feb 27th, coincidentally the very same day the guys were programmed to drive over to Eindhoven! Then, on the same Monday lunchtime, there was an Iberia flight available from Madrid to Mahon. And in view of the fact that it was *imperative* that I drove myself from Bristol to Eindhoven on Sunday March 12th, *luckily,* I managed to find a similar reverse trip available on Friday the 10th, Iberia Mahon to Madrid mid-morning, EasyJet Madrid to Bristol departing around teatime. I pulled out my credit card, a *little* of which had been cleared by then, but not a lot, and spent the next hour booking all four flights whilst they were still available. And if I failed to complete the task in hand in the allotted timescale, whatever the task might turn out to be when I got there, well then so be it. I'd just have to go back and continue with it another time, like maybe the first week in April for example! *Humph!!* I wandered back into Michelle's office, kissed her on the cheek, and thanked her for her constant unwavering help and support. I then told her that I'd be around to help with the board this coming Friday, but that I'd be flying to Menorca on the Monday, returning eleven days later on the 10th, in order that I could drive over to meet up with Dom on Sunday the 12th. She stood up, threw her arms around me, hugged me tight, and consoled me with the words,

"Don't worry dad, I'll take care of work, everything here'll be just fine, you'll see."

Tears began rolling down my face, and I reached across for a box of tissues sat on the side of her desk in the hope that she wouldn't notice. I suspect though, just as she hugged me even tighter, that she probably had. I kissed her lightly on the forehead, said my goodbyes for the evening, drove my scruffy old Shogun back home, and sat on the sofa waiting patiently for Helen to arrive.

She pulled into the drive at her usual time of six o'clock, and the minute she walked through the front door I threw my arms around her and burst into tears, *yet again!*

"What on earth's the matter Christoff?" she asked me in total shock. *"Has somebody just died?"*

"Not some*body* babe," I eventually replied, choking back the last of the tears, "some*THING!* Or at least I'm pretty sure it has. The Phoenix, I'm afraid. Pedro called, she's been wrecked in a storm."

Helen just stood there in stunned silence, her mouth agape. I walked her through to the lounge, helped her off with her coat, sat her on the sofa, and began to explain to her everything that Pedro had described to me. By the time I'd finished she was almost in tears herself. I told her that I'd already booked return flights from the 27th to the 10th.

"I'd very much like to go get this problem cleared up sooner rather than later babe, but I really have no idea what I'm likely to find until I get over there, because Pedro hasn't managed to get anywhere near the boat. She was washed up on the rocks right across the other side of the bay, and by the sounds of it there's wide-scale damage right the way across *all* the Balearic Islands, so Pedro's right up to his arse in alligators right now. Of course, its entirely possible that I can save the Phoenix, maybe carry out a few repairs here and there. After all, she's a tough old bird, so you never know, I *might* be able to salvage her. *However,* well, from the way Pedro described it, and knowing exactly how sharp and rough those volcanic rocks that surround Menorca's bays are, well to be honest, I'm not realistically holding out a whole lot of hope. But hey, who knows eh? Never count your chickens and all that shit! And talking of *shit,* if it really does come down to it, and it turns out that I *can't* save her, bearing in mind that none of this will be covered by her current insurance conditions, then I'll have no option other than to accept the usual once again."

"The usual being what exactly?" Helen asked, still wiping away a few tears. *"SHIT HAPPENS!!"* I answered cynically.

I called Pedro and told him to expect to see me sometime on the 28th, after I'd carried out my own recce of the situation. I also needed to check there was no damage to our *own* apartment before doing anything else. Helen started making the tea. I poured myself a treble brandy and sat on the sofa with my feet up. I switched on the telly, hurriedly skipped past Eastenders until I found a half decent soccer game, *Millwall versus Brentford,* then poured myself another treble brandy. *Fuck it!* The following day I went into work, and spent virtually the whole day ensuring that every minuscule detail was fully taken care of for the imminent CP project. Then on Friday I went in again, and come five o'clock Michelle, Dave and I had successfully completed the board together. Not a bad couple of days I'd thought, considering just how much my mind was constantly wandering all the time.

Something had failed, something must've broken, what the heck could it have been? How did she get across the other side of the bay? Surely she can't have dragged the sinker across? How much damage? How exactly was I going to recover her? So many sodding questions!!! God my head hurts!!!

That weekend wasn't exactly one of the *most* enjoyable I'd ever had! My head was *still* spinning, and *not* from the brandy I might add! I studied some maps and charts of the eastern coastline of Fornells Bay, wondering how the heck I was going to even *find* the Phoenix. I reviewed some historical weather reports for the Balearic region of the Mediterranean, and felt absolutely *gobsmacked* when I discovered just how powerful this particular Medicane had been. Wind speeds measured, both on Menorca and Majorca, in excess of 150mph around the *'eyewall'* of the storm. *Shit the bed!* That's equivalent to a Category 4 hurricane in the Caribbean, that's just one step down from the *maximum! How big will the waves have been exactly? How high up out of the water will she have ended up? How the heck am I going to get her back afloat again? ON MY OWN!!* And now its the beginning of March, the coldest time of the year at night and the water's going to be *bloody freezing! 'Oh come on Chris, stop bloody moaning. Like you said, sometimes shit happens, just get on and deal with it!'* At least there was one thing I knew I could always count on. *My own ingenuity!* If anyone could pull this one off, it was *me!* God only knows how I'd been fool enough to allow it to happen in the first place, but it was my fault and mine alone; *ALL* entirely down to me, so I'd *damned well* have to go and put it *ALL* right. My confidence and determination steadily began to build. *'Failure is NOT an option!'* I began packing a case. Luckily my wetsuit was already over there, but I'd need to take some extra warm clothes with me, some decent walking boots, and some older stuff that I could simply chuck out after I'd messed it all up. I was pretty sure that some aspects of this task ahead of me were going to be decidedly iffy, if not entirely dangerous altogether!

Six o'clock Monday morning, I kissed my wife goodbye, told her not to worry about me, I'd be just fine, and set off for Lulsgate Airport, or Bristol International, as its known today. I parked the Shogun in long-term parking, and checked my bag in at an EasyJet counter. Ten-thirty Spanish time I checked my bag into an Iberia counter at Madrid Airport. One o'clock lunchtime, the beginning of Spanish siesta time, I threw my case into the back of a 5-door Peugeot estate hire car, drove out of Mahon airport, and took the road to Fornells. I didn't bother stopping at the Repsol halfway there for provisions, especially when I noticed it was shut and taped off, mainly due to the canopy above the fuel pumps having gone missing. I was *way* too anxious to find out exactly what had happened to the Phoenix to take that much notice anyway. What had gone wrong exactly with all of my *so very carefully* thought out and well-executed plans? I drove the brand new Peugeot straight down the little lane towards Ses Salines, pulled up on the grass verge at the top of the narrow shingle beach, and climbed out of the car. So, here I was then. *The moment of truth!* What the *FUCK* had gone wrong? I looked out across the water. It was flat calm, and shimmering azure blue beneath the bright sunshine in a perfectly cloudless blue sky, simply *impossible* to imagine how it might have looked a couple of weeks ago. Other than the fact that I'd noticed a significant amount of trees down along the way there, and a *huge* amount of assorted debris washed up into the reed marshes way off to my right, it was still, *almost,* a picture of perfection. But only *almost!* Slowly but surely I began to notice more and more things out of place. Like scaffolding that had been up previously, but now wasn't. And scaffolding up now, where previously there'd been none. That kind of thing, and lots of it. *'Lake Placid my fuckin' arse!'* I began thinking to myself. I wandered down across the beach to the water's edge, and there, some fifty yards in front of me, sat perfectly motionless, was my large, round, red plastic mooring buoy, with its stainless steel ring still safely and securely attached to the top of it. *That plan had worked okay then!* There was nothing wrong with the sinker mooring, that was all still perfectly intact. I cast my eyes across the bay, shielding them as I squinted through the bright sunlight, and just to the south of Lizard Island, around a mile or so from where I was standing, I could clearly see the outline of the Phoenix, lying on her side, washed up onto the rocks amongst another huge assortment of debris, some distance away from the water's edge. So that would also be about a mile or so's trek then, across rough, boggy private farmland, in order to reach her from somewhere back along the main road a short way. *That sure as hell wasn't going to prove simple!* As I turned to walk back to the car I noticed something else out of place. The dilapidated old wooden jetty, most of it was gone! Half a dozen or so of the upright wooden piles were still roughly in place, mirrored perfectly in the dead calm waters, but the board-walk itself, *totally vamoosed!* As indeed had all the other little fishing boats moored to similar sinkers around the bay, although maybe their owners had all found the time to remove them from the water before the storm hit, who knows? They certainly weren't just pulled up onto the beach though. Hey ho! I climbed back into the car and drove on into Fornells Town, pulled up at the very top of the concrete slipway, got out and literally stared all around me in disbelief. *The whole toilet block was in the sea!* The visitor's pontoons had *gone!* The entrance to the harbour was almost completely blocked with both sunken and floating debris. Half the fishing boats inside the harbour itself appeared to be just a jumbled up entanglement of smashed up white painted planking. One of the larger boats that had been chocked up on the hard for the winter had collapsed, rolled onto her side and splintered all across the concrete paving, and probably worst of all, the entire roof of Es Pla restaurant was lying in a thousand smithereens all over the harbourside car park, which itself, out of necessity, had been entirely cordoned off. *Oh dear, oh dear, oh dear, what a bloody mess!* Still, my job, here and now, was simply to clear away my *own* mess. The local authorities would undoubt-edly take care of the rest. I jumped back in the car and drove the couple of miles around the lanes to our pretty little Apartmentos Tamarindos, care-fully manoeuvring around half a dozen trees along the way that were still partially blocking the road; but thankfully only partially. I pulled up in the car park in front of the apartment, grabbed my bag, unlocked the door and walked inside. Other than the fact that it was damned cold, thank-fully there didn't appear to be any damage anywhere. I switched on the electricity, and was extremely pleased to notice that Jaqueline, our wonder-fully efficient local management agent, had already had the fridge-freezer replaced with a brand new identical one. I wondered for a brief moment how much that will have added to my account, then let the thought drop. I then took all three convector heaters out of the wardrobe, sat them in the middle of each room, set them all to 'seven', and left all the internal doors open. It was roughly 2.30pm, so I reckoned I still had enough daylight left to somehow get myself over to the Phoenix, work out some kind of plan of action, and get myself back to the car again, without getting shot at, injured, crushed or mashed along the way. I opened my case on one of the kid's beds, and changed into some more suitable clothing. Three thin layers on top, covered by an old, waterproof, fleece lined cagoule, heavy duty denim jeans tucked into a shin high pair of waterproof walking boots, and a pair of leather gloves, just in case. *Just in case of what, I had absolutely no idea!* On my way back towards the car I wandered very briefly around our little complex, including down by the pool, and was very pleased to note that, thankfully, we appeared to have escaped pretty much all in the way of storm damage ourselves. Albeit the pool quite clearly needed emptying and thoroughly cleaning out, that too was full of debris and detritus, however, at least nothing appeared to be damaged or broken. *Hooray for small mercies!* I grabbed a torch and my camera, again just in case, checked my phone was fully charged, jumped back in the car and headed back towards Ses Salines.

I took the main left turning back towards Mahon, and after about a mile, when I was fairly sure that I'd passed the salt plains and the reed marshes at the southern end of the bay, I found a suitable lay-by of sorts, pulled the car over, and parked it up where it wasn't obstructing the gateway to the fields beyond. I locked the car, climbed over the gate, walked a hundred yards or so into the middle of the long, damp, green grassy field, then stood still and looked all around me, trying to get my bearings. There was absolutely nothing in the way of recognisable landmarks, however, with the weak sun behind me over my left shoulder, and my own ever-confident sense of direction firmly locked into my mind, I set off in a roughly north-north-westerly direction, knowing that somewhere along the way, I knew not where, eventually I was bound to come across the wild, rocky easterly shoreline of Fornells Bay. The going was pretty tough to be fair. The sodden grassy field ended some hundred yards later bordered by a tall, nasty, spiny blackthorn hedge, the only way around it being by way of a boggy marsh in the bottom left hand corner, where I part-tore my jeans on a tangle of trodden-down barbed wire whilst trudging through it. Grateful for the leather gloves I'd brought along, the next field led me up into some dense woodland, where many trees had recently fallen, entangling their branches into a forest of bramble bushes, some of which I was able to skirt around, others which I simply had to beat a pathway through the middle of. At the end of the woodland I came across another rusty old barbed wire fence, the other side of which was an old disused track that looked as if it might lead somewhere promising. I scrambled through the barbed wire, only to turn and notice a dilapidated old wooden board, still nailed to the side of a tree, with the words '*Estrictamente Propiedad Privada – Mantener Fuera*' still faintly visible painted on its face; '*Strictly Private Property – Keep Out*'. Hey ho, *shit happens!* I carried on down the old track to my left, which ended a short while later at a series of very old, tumbledown, derelict farm buildings. I carried on through what was obviously, once upon a time, a working farmyard, at the end of which was yet another spiky blackthorn hedge sat atop a small embankment. With no noticeable way around *or* over it, I scrambled through underneath, still managing to tear the back of my cagoule somewhat in the process. '*Ouch! Thank God again for these tough old gloves!*' The other side of the hedge was an open boulder field, vaguely resembling the landscape you'd expect to find littering the base of an extinct volcano, and as I picked my way carefully over and around the huge rough rocks, I found myself approaching the crest of a vast, open, treeless hill. And upon reaching the top of the hill, there, spread out peacefully and beautifully before me, was the whole of Fornells Bay, in all of its splendid glory, basking in what little remained of the steadily lowering sunshine. And there, just a few hundred yards down across the boulder field, away over to the right, lay the Phoenix herself. She was lying on her side, probably some twenty feet from the water's edge. I was effectively staring right down on top of her roof, as if getting a perfect aerial view from a helicopter. *Not that I had a bloody helicopter of course, although there and then I kind of wished I had!* But it was all wrong! She looked sad, broken and stuck! My heart sank, tears began to well up yet again, and I felt a deep sense of despair beginning to grab a hold of me. '*Come along you silly old sod, pull yaself together now! At least you've found her, and now you've got a job to do! And not an easy one at that either, by the looks of it, so let's go get stuck in. We're on a time limit, remember?*' Yeah, I'd found her alright, and got myself straight over to her too, although I'm sure there had to be an easier way back. But hell, what a bloody mess! I scrambled the last couple hundred yards down across the boulder field, then jumped down onto what amounted to a very small sandy beach. I placed my hand on the Phoenix's foredeck, and between the tears I muttered out loud, '*I'm SO sorry old girl; so VERY, VERY sorry! I didn't mean for this to happen, I REALLY didn't!*'

And then, as if I'd suddenly been kicked right up the backside, I swallowed my pride, wiped my eyes, and put my *determined* head back on. I grabbed a hold of the anchor chain that was hanging motionless over the front of the bow. The locking mechanism on the foredeck hadn't failed, the chain was still clamped securely in place, with the remainder of its length still sat in the chain locker. I lifted up the free end of the chain. *It was the padlock that had failed! THE FUCKING PADLOCK!! Fifty fucking euros-worth of solid, stainless steel HIGH-FUCKING-SECURITY shitty sodding padlock! Jeez, why hadn't I just used an ordinary sodding shackle instead? Still, from everything I'd heard and seen so far, I guess something else would probably have given way instead. Hey-fucking-ho!!*

It had taken me over an hour to fight my way across land to this Godforsaken stretch of coastline. By now it had just gone four o'clock, the sun was beginning to dip over the horizon across the other side of the bay, and I *needed* to come up with *some* kind of plan. The Phoenix was laying on her side, her bow stuck across the smooth sloping boulders, and her stern resting against a small patch of soft yellow sand. But sticking right through the port side of her hull was a *huge* rock. The hole through the side of the hull was around seven feet long, centred amidships, and around four feet high, stretching from a foot or so above her keel to a foot or so below her port gunwale. And the top of the rock itself, the majority of which was clearly just a part of the shoreline, was still stuck inside the hole. Somehow I was going to have to roll her over onto her starboard side, just to get her off that horrible jagged rock. As I walked around the other side of the hull, the first thing I noticed was a tree! *A whole bloody tree!* Probably around thirty-five feet in length, with a solid trunk that I'd reckoned, at its critical point, where it was firmly wedged up underneath the starboard hull of the Phoenix, had a diameter in the region of around two feet. *What a bloody state to get into!* There was no way the Phoenix was going to float upright, with that massive hole through her side, and there was ten tons of old tree wedging her firmly against the rocks, preventing me from rolling her over *anyway! Shit-fuck-bugger-bollocks!* I walked around behind her and examined her stern-gear. Her rudder stock was bent up at what appeared to be an irreparable angle, and her bronze propellor, still fastened securely to the end of a slightly bent prop shaft, had one of its three blades sheared off. The tonneau cover that had covered the aft deck had disappeared altogether, nowhere to be seen. I climbed aboard and leant against the aft seating, just as three or four giant rats scuttled off out through the hole in the hull. That made me jump a little, given that everywhere around at that moment was so amazingly peaceful. There wasn't a breath of wind, and not a single sound coming from anywhere. Not even the sound of birdsong! *Rats! Yuk!* The first thing I noticed inside the aft deck was that the rock had pushed its way so far through the side of the hull, that it had hit the side of the engine, and smashed it off of its mountings. It was still in-situ, with its gearbox firmly attached to the bent prop shaft, and who knows, it may even work again one day, but there was no way it would ever be powering this particular vessel ever again. I was sad to say, in fact, *EXTREMELY SAD TO SAY,* that in my considered opinion, she was very clearly damaged beyond repair. Still, *how the heck, in a month of bloody Sundays, am I going to get her off this sodding beach! Think Chris! THINK!!*

I climbed through the broken cabin door into the forecabin, and started to look around for some of my equipment that I'd stashed aboard. That's when I realised that it wasn't the rock that had smashed the door off, it was probably some of the local kids. *Skivvies! Fuckin' pirates!* She'd been looted! The seat cushions had been tossed to one side, the lockers forced open, and as far as I could make out anything of any value had gone. *Bastards!* Tools, ropes, anchor, waterproofs, and most importantly of all, *my sodding grab bag!* Well, there's another grand's worth of kit gone down the Swannee then, *at least!* Ironically, the little shits had left the fenders aboard. *Whoopee-fucking-doo!* And a life-ring. And a flagpole, with a tatty old red ensign attached to it. And even the battery. And I suspected that the anchor chain would've proved too much to manage. *Wow, lucky old me!* Or maybe they'd planned to come back for more another day, *who knows?* I gave up thinking about all the missing equipment, it was only going to depress me even more. I had to stay positive, and put some kind of rescue plan together. *Think Chris, THINK!* I climbed back out of the poor broken old Phoenix, walked some twenty feet or so down to the water's edge, where there wasn't even the tiniest of ripples, and plonked my ass down on a particularly smooth rock, my boots wedged firmly into the damp yellow sand. I stared long and hard at the Phoenix, and the dreadful predicament that I'd sadly allowed her to get herself into. *Think Chris! Where there's a will, there's a way! Wherever there's a disadvantage, turn it into an advantage! Turn every negative into a positive! An obstruction needn't necessarily be an obstruction, it can be given a purpose, made into something that'll help, as opposed to hinder! THINK!!!* So I sat there and I thought. *Failure is NOT an option!!* And then I thought some more. And then some more. And as it began to get dark, and I began to wonder if I was even going to be able to find my way safely back to the road again, a plan slowly but surely began to formulate itself deep within my stupid little sponge of a brain. *'I think I've got it!'* I said to myself aloud. *'Pedro, mañana mi amigo, I need to avail myself of some of your precious specialised equipment, por favor!'* I jumped up off the flat-topped knobbly-sided rock that I'd been sat on, right at the water's edge, some twenty feet away from where the keel of the Phoenix was firmly wedged underneath the trunk of a giant tree, her port-side hull smashed to pieces over a huge rock, and stared evermore carefully at the lay of the land, the barnacles attached to *some* of the rocks, and the line of seaweed that was strewn from one end of the small patch of sand to the other. I strolled back over to the Phoenix, gave her a good firm pat on her canoe-shaped stern, and confidently said to her aloud, *'Don't you worry yourself now my love, we'll have you out of here in no time, you'll see!'* I then pulled my torch out of my pocket, switched it on, and began climbing *carefully* back across the boulder field towards the derelict farm buildings. I crawled underneath the prickle hedge, tearing yet another small rip in the back of my old fleece lined cagoule, and upon reaching the clearly disused old track the other side of the farmyard, I turned left, and some fifteen minutes later I arrived back at the road. I climbed gingerly over an old wooden gate that was well wrapped in more rusty old barbed wire, ignored the faded old wooden sign, that simply had the word *'PRIVADO'* barely visible on it, and headed off down the road towards the car. Another fifteen minutes later and I was driving back towards the apartment in Tamarindos. *I had a plan!*

Later that evening, after I'd showered, changed, and remade our double bed using *both* of the sleeping bags that I'd left on top of the wardrobe some two months previous, on account of how damned cold I knew it could get during the night at that time of year, I jumped back into the car and drove up to Marco's, just up the hill a little way. I parked up, walked up the path, in through the front door, which I just *knew* would be open, and ordered myself a large cerveza at the bar. I then called Helen, gave her the bad news, along with a brief rundown as to how I felt I might be able to partially resolve the situation, then wished her a pleasant night's sleep, and blew her a kiss. I hung up, and then called Pedro. I reeled off a list of all the equipment that I was going to need to borrow from him, or *hire from him,* as it turned out, and asked if it was possible for him to have all of that ready and available for me the following day. He said that he could, no problem, but it would most likely take him until lunchtime to sort it all out; could I come and collect it *after* lunch, por favor. I said fine, no problem, but I needed a RIB too, preferably with at least a 40hp outboard on the back, and my hire car didn't have a tow bar on it, so I couldn't come collect that exactly. He said *'no problemo Mister Chris',* one of his work RIB's was already in the water in Fornells harbour, he'd been using it to drag some of the floating debris away from the harbour's entrance. In fact, he'd managed to clear sufficient of a gap past the wreckage of the toilet block so as to be able to get in and out of the harbour, and as his four-meter Zodiac RIB did indeed have a 40hp Mariner on the back, and the tank was still at least three-quarters full of fuel, he'd give me the keys to that too when I collected the rest of the equipment. He said there's no way of mistaking the RIB, it had *Pedro's Boat Centre* written in large white letters all down both sides of it. I thanked him profusely, hung up, and ordered a basket of chicken and chips from behind the bar. I was *exhausted!* I was sad and depressed, and I felt both hungry and tired. *Very tired!* I finished my food, necked my second pint of lager, paid and thanked Marco, telling him that I'd probably be seeing him again the following day. And the next. And probably the next too! And then I headed off home to bed, still tired, still exhausted, and *still* depressed.

Hey ho Reason, you reap what you sow, learn to deal with your own stupid mistakes!

CHAPTER
THIRTY SIX

Twice I woke up during the night. The first time to drag another of the convector heaters into my bedroom, the second time to turn them both fully up to *'ten'*. Chilly *or what?* The place hadn't been heated for nine weeks, it was *bloody freezing* at night, despite me using *both* sleeping bags. I felt a little better when I awoke the next morning. I can't remember whether I was feeling a lot more positive, or just a little more cynical, but I was certainly filled with determination, and seemingly more prepared to accept the situation for what it was. *My loss, but at least no one had got crushed or mashed. Yet!!* I had no fresh food in the apartment as yet, but I wasn't bothered particularly, I'd have something to eat and grab a few provisions once I'd driven into Mahon to meet up with Pedro. I dressed, pulled on an old pair of trainers, and walked outside into yet another sunny cloudless sky. Blimey, *ten o'clock!* Ah, but it was only nine o'clock really, *wasn't it?* CET/GMT, I'd grown accustomed to the constant time adjustment scenario; although it still always threw me a little on the first day. I drove into Fornells and parked up near the top of the slipway. The wall that ran off to the right, and the flat area of hard-standing scrubland adjacent to it, was exactly where I was proposing to have the Phoenix lifted from the water. *As, when and IF I could get her back over there!* I couldn't even see the Phoenix from where I was stood, she was hidden from view by the southern tip of Lizard Island. Once I'd walked a quarter of a mile down the road in the direction of Ses Salines though, she came into view, and again I'd estimated around a mile and a half from her to me. *Shit, this was gonna be a damned tricky operation!* I walked back to the concrete slipway, and right down to the water's edge, which was as calm and still as a millpond. A critical part of my plan immediately became apparent.

The tide was out! Whoever tells you that the Mediterranean has no tides is simply *wrong!* Don't believe them! Sure, Mediterranean tides are *generally,* to all intents and purposes, *negligible,* however they most certainly *do* exist. The Med has neaps and springs, just like all the oceans do, but its daily cycle varies hugely from that of the Eastern Atlantic, and the shores of the UK, and its mean range, which more often than not goes entirely unnoticed by virtually everybody, also varies enormously, depending on whereabouts in the Med you are. Some parts of the Med have a mean tidal range of as little as five inches, other areas can reach up to double that. I had no idea whether we were on neaps or springs at the time, or indeed precisely what the mean tidal range even *was* in Menorca, because it wasn't generally something one needed to know, but judging by the visible dry-slime area at the very bottom of the slipway, and relating it to the high seaweed tidal marks that I'd noted along the sand the previous evening, I'd reckoned on at least six inches of tide rise and fall currently between high and low water, and I was pretty damned sure I was going to be relying on that very small increase to make all the difference in helping me to get the Phoenix refloated. *If, that was, she'd even float at all!* I jumped back in the car and headed off towards Mahon.

I walked into Pedro's marine chandlery store shortly after noon, and one of his young mechanics told me that he was out and about somewhere, but that he should be back fairly soon. I said no problem, I'd be waiting in the little café next door for him. I wandered into the café and ordered myself some breakfast. Tortilla con papas frites, y café con leche. Pedro walked in some thirty minutes later, and after a warm, lengthy and *powerful* handshake, I ordered two more coffees.

"Mister Chris," Pedro began, "I am very please for to be seeing you, but I am very, very sad for to be seeing your Phoenix how she is lying. Is going to be *very, very* difficult for you to be collecting her back to the Fornells harbour. But I help you as much if I can, maybe. But I am being *very, very* busy man right nows. How bad is you are thinking the damages are to be Mister Chris?"

"Well Pedro," I said a little negatively, "its definitely gonna be touch and go. But I've been down to look at her, I walked across the fields and down through the old farmland yesterday afternoon, and I'm pretty sure I've come up with a half decent plan of action."

I didn't bother telling him about the massive gaping hole in the port-side of the hull, that would only have stressed him out even more. It was bad enough *me* being stressed out right now, let alone inviting him to join in too. What I *did* tell him about was the failure of the *sodding* padlock though. I even suggested that maybe I should have left her at anchor, instead of locking her to her sinker.

"Mister Chris," Pedro replied sympathetically, "whatever you would have did, it would not have worked. Your Phoenix, she would be broken over the rocks in any case. If you leave at anchor, she drag her anchor, like many other yachts, there is muchos, muchos damages to many, many boats at anchor all around our islands. Some they are now being lost *forever!* And if you fix her better ways to the sinker, I know something else it would be breakings, most likely that, how you say, *red plastico booy!*"

"Buoy!" I politely corrected him. *"Booy* sounds *horribly* American!"

"Is no matters," he continued sadly, "our waves that we were seeing around our coast, they are being just *ridiculous!* Like as to the biggest waves ever we have seen! *Is CRAZY!* And even in the bay of Fornells, your Phoenix, she was mooring in one and a half metres of water, si, but the waves here in this part of the bay, they are making like two metres high. And they coming from *every* directions. Your Phoenix, she is keep hitting the bottom of the sea, on the muds. She *very, very* strong boat, most people's boats they are breaking into many pieces, the Phoenix she just breaking one thing, then she banging on rocks in wind and waves. Wind and waves *CRAZY! Most* peoples, they all mucho frightened, they are just staying indoors, but some they are losing parts of their houses too. We have *muchos, muchos* damages all over islands. But what I do Mister Chris? *I ONLY ONE MAN!!"*

"I know Pedro, I know," now seemingly my turn to sympathise. "Listen mi amigo, providing you have got all the equipment I have asked for, and you're happy for me to keep it all for a few days, then like I said, I have a plan, and hopefully I can pull it off."

"I do, is all here, in auto-van outside. But I worry now, you say is only *half decent* plan, no?"

"Trust me amigo, where there's a will, there's a way, I'll make it work, you'll see. However, I shall need some very *critically-timed* help from your good self, at the *exact* time I'm ready, if you wouldn't mind, por favor?"

"Okay Mister Chris, I see what I might do, what is help for?"

"I'll call you first on your mobile, just to let you know that I'm on my way, then I shall need you to be ready and waiting with your seven-ton mobile crane, sitting at the water's edge on the hard-standing next to the slipway, strops already lowered, in preparation for lifting the Phoenix straight out of the water the *very minute* I get her back across to the quay wall. This will be okay with you please my friend?"

"Yes, is okay, but this seven-ton mobile crane of mine, it is costing *muchos* euros for to be using. Especially for me to be bringing all way overs to Fornells!" Pedro politely informed me.

"Yeah," I countered back at him, "but not quite *fifty-fucking-thousand euros* though, is it my old mate?!!?"

"Si, si, Mister Chris, I am seeing what you are mean. Is okay, when you are needing crane you must be telephoning me the night before, so I can arrange timings please."

"No problem Pedro, I'll call you well in advance, and give you plenty of notice." I confirmed. "Now, can we go load the kit into the back of my car please, I think I've got a bit of a busy schedule ahead of me, and I'd like to make a start on it today, if at all possible."

"Si, si, Mister Chris, no problemo."

I paid for the breakfast and the coffees, and we walked out of the little café and along the pavement to Pedro's tatty old white Seat works van. I backed my car up to the back doors of his van, so that we didn't have to lug the stuff too far, some of it being just a tad heavy. As we transferred each piece of kit from his van to my car, I mentally ticked each item off my list one by one:-

Petrol-powered 50 gals per min water pump, with *extra long* hoses. *Tick!*

Petrol-driven chainsaw with 18" blade and *recently-sharpened* teeth. *Tick!*

5-ton Tirfor-winch with *extra long* cable and strong hooks. *Tick!* I'd asked for a 10-ton Tirfor, but he only had a 5-ton one available. Hey ho, I'd manage!

Three *extra long* heavy duty ratchet straps, with decent hooks each end. *Tick!*

Two spare 1-gallon cans of 2-stroke petrol. *Tick!*

One *extra long* heavy duty tow rope. *Tick!*

Two coils of mooring line ropes. *Tick!*

One lightweight tool box with an assortment of basic tools. *Tick!*

An *extra long* security cable and padlock, so I could lock it all up overnight. *Tick!*

Oh yeah, and the keys to the RIB. *Tick!*

"I think that just about does it," I concluded. "Thanks Pedro, I'll keep in touch and let you know how its going. One thing I must tell you my friend. I have my flights booked back to England on Friday the 10th coming, and I absolutely *cannot* afford to miss them."

"Very Good Mister Chris," Pedro warmly crushed my hand once again. "I am wishing you all the very best with your rescue project, and hoping very much that you are keeping yourself safe."

333

"Gracias mi amigo," I ended our little tête-à-tête with, "y adios; hasta la proxima!"

I jumped in the car and drove back to Fornells, once again stopping at the top of the wide expanse of concrete apron at the top of the slipway. *'Now, where exactly is Pedro's Zodiac?'* I thought to myself, as I ducked under the cordoned-off *'keep-out'* tape, and wandered along the inner harbour's quay wall. I soon spotted it, tied up to a cast iron ladder that ran down the inside of the wall, right over in the far corner of the harbour, but on the road side, as opposed to the harbour wall side where the majority of the jumbled up assorted wreckage was still lying afloat. Or at least, *mostly* afloat! The RIB was easily accessible, and I'd be running it through the clearing in the flotsam at the harbour entrance, and around to the slipway where I could more easily load the equipment aboard. I checked my watch. It was two-thirty in the afternoon. Not exactly the best time of day to begin a project of this magnitude; *and danger!* I think I'd best leave all the kit in the car for the time being, and make an early start first thing the following morning. I drove into Mercadal, the closest municipal town to Fornells, and walked into the local Consum to buy some basic provisions. Bread, butter, cheese, milk, bacon, eggs, etc, etc. Oh yeah, and needless to say, most importantly of all, peanut butter, and a dozen cans of San Miguel lager. I then drove back to Tamarindos, and spent the remainder of the afternoon netting debris and flotsam out of our gorgeous newly-tiled swimming pool. Later that evening I showered, changed, and ate the most basic of meals once again at Bar Marco.

09.00hrs CET, Weds 1st March. Breakfast done and dusted, warm scruffy clothes donned, old trainers tightly laced, I climbed down the ladder and jumped into Pedro's Zodiac. I primed the manual outboard with fuel, she started first pull of the cord, and I ran her around to the side of the slipway, re-mooring her where the fuel pontoon used to sit, yet another thing that had also disappeared off down the coast somewhere! I had nine full days in which to get this job completed, and I was feeling pretty positive about it. I just prayed that yet another one of my cunning little *Chrissy-plans* was going to come together okay, because if it didn't, *God only knew* what the final costs were likely to run to. But hey, *stay calm, stay focused, and stay positive!* So that's exactly how I was. So, day one, clear all unnecessary items and remove all excess weight from the Phoenix. All I needed for that was the toolbox, which I removed from the car and placed on the floor in the RIB. I then ran the RIB across the bay, which, at thirty knots or so, took all of four minutes, lifted the outboard, and beached her on the small patch of sand. I ran the painter around a rock, tied it off, and scrambled across to the Phoenix. Fingers crossed that the tide was *out,* because it was still a good twenty feet from the water's edge to the hull of the boat. However, the line of drying seaweed scattered across the sand was only ten feet from the keel, so all being well, once the tide rose to its highest, that would make the distance I had to haul her with the Tirfor-winch significantly less. I set to, removing every remaining loose item from the boat. Cushions both fore and aft were first, most of them still lying upturned and sodden. I then grabbed a couple of spanner's and removed the battery, and even spent some considerable time undoing the huge castle nut and removing what remained of the propellor. The prop didn't actually weigh very much, even though it was bronze alloy, but having it off the shaft and out of the way would hopefully make it considerably easier to drag the hull down over the rocks, and subsequently across the sand. *All four and a bit sodding tons of her!* Next I removed the anchor chain, pulling it out across the foredeck after releasing the clamping mechanism, and snipping through the bitter end inside the chain locker with a Stanley knife. That long old chain really *was* heavy, and I dragged it across the sand, heaved it up into the RIB, and sat it on top of the sodden seat cushions. Four large old plastic fenders, one life-ring, and a flagpole with ensign, all in the RIB. Then I started going through each of the lockers a little more carefully. I found nothing of any value, little in the way of weight, however a significant amount in the way of filthy bilge water. *'Well, if it ain't runnin' out, then it ain't comin' in!'* I thought to myself. That could wait until I had the pump up and running. I grabbed a few more tools, and removed the sea toilet from its mounting in the tiny heads closet, then lowered it down onto the rocks with the cut length of rubber hose that was still attached. I then punched a hole through the bottom of the fresh water tank, and let what little remained inside drain into the bilges. The quarter of a tank of diesel fuel, unluckily for me but *extremely* luckily for the environment, *thankfully,* all seemed to have remained safely inside its stainless steel tank, as indeed had the engine oil within the sump of the marginally damaged little Ford diesel engine. *Again, forever grateful for small mercies!* I threw the smashed-off door to the forecabin out onto the beach, scrambled out over the aft deck, then carefully placed the door and the toilet into the RIB.

I then sat back down on the flat-topped rock, and gave considerable further thought to my plan of action. Ultimately I had no idea whether it was likely to work or not until I tried it, and I knew that step two, dealing with the huge tree, was going to prove a critical aspect. As indeed was winching the boat back towards the water. I began clearing some of the loose rocks and boulders out of the way, heaving them one at a time way over beyond the bow. I'd be attempting to drag the Phoenix stern first back towards the water, and because of the lay of the land, and the specific location of certain outcrops of rock, I was beginning to feel gradually more confident that I could achieve this part. The more critical question however, was *could I actually manage to keep her afloat all the way back across to Fornells harbour? With a massive gaping hole in one side of her hull?* 'Only one way to find out I'm afraid Chris. *Suck it and see!*' I untied the RIB's painter, shoved her back off the little patch of sand, fired up the engine, and plodded slowly back across to the slipway just outside the harbour. I tied her up, then dragged each item of scrap one at a time up the slipway, and stacked them up in a neat pile where the bins used to be, just behind where the toilet block also used to be. The anchor chain was the last thing to drag up the slope, that old lot not proving quite so easy, but eventually I managed to pile it all up again on top of the sodden seat cushions, and left it there, thinking that if anybody fancied stealing it they were welcome to it. I then tied Pedro's RIB back up in the corner of the harbour, and drove back to Tamarindos to make myself some tea. That would do for the day, and I already had the following day's plan firmly fixed in my mind. I made myself a peanut butter sandwich, switched on some easy-listening music, put my feet up on the sofa, and cracked open a nicely chilled can of San Miguel. A plastic basket of chicken and chips at Marco's would most likely be next on the list.

The Phoenix lies wrecked upon the rocks

CHAPTER
THIRTY SEVEN

Thursday the 2nd. Breakfast done, I dressed in the same scruffy old gear, grabbed the chainsaw, the ropes, the ratchet straps and the Tirfor-winch out of the back of the car, placed them carefully into the RIB, along with one spare can of fuel, and headed off, this time under a rather dull and cloudy sky, across the bay towards the southern end of Lizard Island. Hidden from view a little further behind which lay my beloved but badly broken Phoenix, unceremoniously washed up on the rocky shore. I secured the RIB and carried the equipment ashore. There was very little in the way of breeze, despite it being overcast, but as no sunshine had yet appeared it still remained pretty chilly from the overnight low. No matter there though, I had a good idea that what I had next on my agenda would keep me sweating, no matter *what* the weather! I checked the petrol in the chainsaw, pulled the cord, and powered it up. *Vroom Vrooooooom! I LOVE working with a chainsaw!* It wasn't the biggest chainsaw I'd ever used; an 18-inch blade versus a 24-inch tree trunk. But it was all I had, so I'd *have* to make it work. And work it most certainly did, albeit probably the hard way. I had to cut down from the top, up from the bottom, then in from the side to make any *serious* impression, but after slogging away at it for half an hour or so, I managed to cut all the way through the thickest section of trunk. The second cut, where the trunk was still almost just as thick, I made about seven feet away from the first. I then spent some considerable time trimming all the broken branches and dead knots from all around the circumference of this seven-foot section of tree, after which, once I'd cleared one or two more large rocks out of the way, I was able, with somewhat of a struggle, to roll it down across the rocky outcrop, across the sand and on out into the water. I kept on rolling until it was roughly about half submerged in a foot of water, still weighed heavily down into the sand underneath. This now allowed me to see right underneath the hull of the Phoenix, whereupon I noticed, with just a *modicum* of shock and horror, that her keel was broken. Not broken to such a degree that it would prevent me from continuing with my plan, but certainly sufficiently cracked so as to *definitely* render her unfit for any kind of economical repair. Once again I stared at her with a tear in my eye, patted her gently across her stern and sighed aloud *'sorry sweetheart!'* The words of a line from the title track of Elton John's album Madman Across The Water kept echoing over and over through my mind, as indeed they are right now as I sit here writing this sad story. *'I can see, very well, there's a boat on the reef with a broken back, and I can see it very well. Take my word I'm a madman, don't you know. So is it in your conscience that you're after, another glimpse of the madman across the water.'* I doubted very much if anyone could *glimpse* me where I was, partially shielded from Fornells Town by the shores of Lizard Island, although to be honest I'd given up caring by then. If the truth be known, I'd given up caring about a lot of things at that moment in time. *Get on with it Reason, FFS!* I fired up the chainsaw again; although no one could see me, they sure as hell could *hear* me! It took me another two hours or more to cut the remaining two thirds of the tree up into pieces that were small enough to carry off around the front of the boat, and chuck across the pile of rocks and boulders that I'd already thrown over there the day before, well out of harms way. Next, I took one of the ratchet straps and threw it over the roof of the Phoenix, fastening the hook securely underneath a solid deck cleat, that was located amidships on the port-side walkway. I needed to roll the Phoenix over so that her starboard-side hull would be lying on the smoother surface of the sloping rock-face, pulling the gaping hole in her port-side hull clear of the jagged rock that was currently sticking inside her, its tip wedged into the side of the engine. I joined another ratchet strap to the end of the first, wedged my feet firmly against a solid rocky outcrop on the seaward side, and pulled with all my might. She didn't budge an inch! Okay, *Plan B it is then!* I took the heavy duty tow rope, and tied it around another solid rocky outcrop, this time a little further away. I then attached the short-cable fixed end of the Tirfor-winch to the loop of rope, and the steel hook on the long end of the 5-ton cable to the hook on the end of the ratchet strap. I pulled the slack cable through the winch, clamped it down, and then began cranking the handle. It wasn't overly difficult to crank, and inch by inch the Phoenix gradually rose upwards and off the rock that she was seemingly stuck over. Several more cranks, one inch of movement at a time, and before I knew it she was sitting perfectly upright, balancing precariously on her cracked keel. And then, suddenly, just as she reached her tipping point, there was an *almighty THUMP! CRASH! SCRAGE!* And then she rolled over onto her starboard-side hull, and slid another foot or two down towards the sand. *That was great!* But there was still an awfully long way to go to get her anywhere near the water! I was hoping maybe the water could come a bit *nearer to her!* Still, at least I was getting *somewhere,* things seemed to be going *roughly* according to plan. I'd had enough for the day though, so I loaded all the kit back into the RIB, headed back to Fornells, packed it back in the car, secured the RIB back at its mooring, and drove back home. Hey ho, another day tomorrow.

Friday the 3rd. I suspected I might have to get partially wet today, so I pulled my wetsuit bottoms on, then donned some old neoprene socks inside my trainers; that water was *dreadfully* cold. The weather was looking decidedly worse too, so I threw my now-torn old fleece lined cagoule on over my three T-shirts, then set off once again for the slipway, gloves in pockets. This time I loaded *all* of the kit into the RIB, including the cable-lock, and set off steadily across the bay. On reaching the Phoenix I tied up, then humped everything ashore, the heaviest of all being the caged petrol-driven water pump. I checked the tank for fuel, primed the pipes with seawater, then hoisted it up into the aft seating area, wedging it upright firmly between the floor and an empty seat-locker. I reached inside the locker, and shoved the end of the '*IN*' hose as far down as I could push it, right into the deepest pool of water that had collected inside the stern, then hung the '*OUT*' hose over the side of the deck. I fired up the little petrol engine, the water started pumping immediately, and within less than a minute the pipe was sucking air. *Well that worked okay then!* I switched it back off, jumped out, and set it down to one side, well out of the way. Now began one of the hardest parts! I took the tow rope, and waded out into the water until I was almost up to my waist, whereupon, immediately astern of the centreline of the Phoenix's hull, I found the very end of the solid rocky outcrop, with a firm, tough, knurled lump of rock some two feet under the surface of the water. I made a lasso with the tow rope, reached down under the water, and tightened it around the solid knurled rock. I strained against it, happy that it was fastened securely, then tied a bowline in the other end, to which I fastened the short-cable end of the Tirfor-winch. I waded back ashore, grabbed a ratchet strap, and took two turns around the top of the rudder-stock. I hooked another ratchet strap to both hook-ends of the first one, then hooked the winch's long-cable end to the hook the other end of that. I shortened the ratchet straps as much as possible, and lengthened the Tirfor-winch cable as far as it would go. I then waded back out to the rocks, took up the slack, and began cranking. At first it was relatively easy, and inch by inch I began dragging the hull of the Phoenix down over the lower slope of the rock-face. Backwards/forwards, backwards/forwards; if anyone reading this has ever used a Tirfor-winch before, then I'm sure you'll *fully* understand where I'm coming from! Backwards/forwards, until, very gradually, one inch at a time, the starboard-side hull of the old girl was finally off the rocks, and laying flat on firm damp sand. So all I had to do now was keep going until she was dragged, one inch at a time, into water that was deep enough to float her. And now I ran into a bit of trouble. Firstly, now that she'd moved, and the tree was gone, I'd discovered that she had more than just the one hole. Although the others were relatively small, they'd end up underwater for sure, so just as well I'd opted for the *50-GPM* water pump! Secondly however, now that I was dragging the hull across flat wet sand, the going with the Tirfor-winch had become ten times harder, and now, not only was I *really* having to put my back into it, but I was doing so in around two feet of seawater. I slackened the cables and swapped the Tirfor around the other way. I also did away with the second ratchet strap, so that now the Tirfor was much closer to the boat, and it was only my feet that were getting wet. But it was still *extremely* hard going, and still a *very* long way to go. And *still the tide was out!* But hey, that could wait for the time being, I wasn't yet ready for deeper water. I continued to strain over the Tirfor. Backwards/forwards, backwards/forwards, backwards/forwards, it was never-ending. But at least she was moving. *Not far mind you!* But she'd moved. And then, halfway through the afternoon, all of a sudden my strength gave up. *I was knackered!* I'd had enough! Time to pack up and come back tomorrow, I'd thought. So I stopped. I left the Tirfor tensioned in-situ, I cable-locked the water pump to the deck of the boat, I chucked the remaining gear back in the RIB, untied her, and headed back towards town. I knew when enough was enough, and the last thing I needed right then was to go putting my back out, or some other such careless injury. I packed the kit in the car, moored the RIB, then drove home and took a very long, very hot shower. After drying and dressing, I cracked open a can and slumped on the sofa to one of my favourite songs by Bon Jovi. *'Woah, woah, we're halfway there. Woah, woah, livin' on a prayer!'* How *very* appropriate!

Saturday the 4ᵗʰ. Coffee and eggs, that was sufficient, and then I just got stuck straight back in, as per usual. And no, it wasn't much fun pulling wet wetsuit trousers on either! Such is life! I was kind of hoping that I wouldn't need to use the chainsaw yet again, so I left it tucked underneath the passenger's seat in the car. The remaining gear I took back across to the other side of the bay, and was extremely pleased to note that nothing had been disturbed. So, body restrengthened with suitable nourishment, including amongst other things, a bottle of red wine with last night's dinner, and a large plate of scrambled eggs for breakfast, I set to work once again. Backwards/forwards, backwards/forwards, backwards/forwards. And then I began to scratch my head a little. Had the Phoenix began moving forwards *quicker* than she had been up until now? Was she actually moving *two* inches per pull instead of one? *NO! Finally,* the tide had begun to rise! Back/forth, back/forth, come on now Chris, get yaself a rhythm going here. *Damn this was hard work!* But I kept it going all the way up until lunchtime. *Not that I actually had any bloody lunch with me!* Oh well, food could wait, work comes first! So, come around one-thirty-ish, between myself and Señor Tirfor, helped along admirably by the marginal increase in the level of the water, we'd managed to drag the Phoenix along on her starboard-side flank altogether some thirty feet, out into approximately twelve inches of water. She was beginning to take water onboard again via the series of smaller holes punched through various different places around her hull, but I wasn't overly concerned about that, the most important thing was the fact that the gaping seven-foot by four foot hole in the port-side of her hull was still way above the waterline; thanks to her laying on her starboard side.

Okay, so the next part's the clever part! I'd managed to drag the Phoenix out more or less level with the seven-foot length of tree stump that I'd cut and left half submerged. As the tide had risen a little, this made the hefty old log considerably easier to roll, although I wasn't entirely sure at what height it was likely to float, if at all. I rolled the trunk right up to the Phoenix, so that it was wedged firmly amidships underneath her starboard-side rubbing-strake. I then took a ratchet strap, buried my arms deep underwater so that I could tunnel underneath the huge log, and pulled the metal-hooked end of the strap through from the other side. I hooked the strap back onto itself, tightening it around the exact centre of the trunk, then stood on top of it and tugged, just to make sure it was totally securely fastened. I then connected the loose-end hook to the free end of the other ratchet strap, re-connected that to the deck-fittings on the port-side of the boat, then ratcheted the straps up as tight as they'd go. They weren't powerful enough to lift the tree trunk up off the bottom, but if anything, as and when the depth of water were to increase, if the tree trunk were to slip lower into the water, then all that would achieve would be to float the Phoenix further over onto her starboard side. *All good!* God forbid the bloody log should decide to sink though, that could potentially spell *disaster!* So, all I needed now was considerably deeper water, plus a tow rope! I kept my eyes closely on the level of the tide, however, sadly, I'd noticed it gradually beginning to recede. I'd made a mental note though; I'd reckoned it was probably at its highest at around 2pm that afternoon. And making a rough assessment as to how the water level had behaved over the previous few days, I was going to take an educated guess as to the fact that, mañana, at around 3pm-ish, it may even be an inch or so higher than it was today. *Fingers crossed yet again!* And that, as they say, was the best I could hope for! Because one more inch of water level height would take it right up to the drying line of seaweed, so that was it. *Maxed out at six inches above low tide. It was now or never!* Or rather tomorrow or never.

I called Pedro, who answered immediately, and asked him if he could get his mobile crane over to Fornells, and set it up at the water's edge, for sometime shortly before two o'clock tomorrow lunchtime. I happened to mention that I was figuring on high tide being somewhere around three o'clock, although I'm really not entirely sure whether he had the faintest idea what I was on about or not. Either way, he said,

"Si, si, Mister Chris, good luck, I am being there awaiting for you with crane ma*ñana for one o'clock times*. I am hoping for you it will be works!"

I was done with the Tirfor; the two ends were almost touching, and there were no other suitable rocks available to attach it to, so there was no way I could drag the Phoenix any further than where she'd managed to finish up at. I slackened off the cables, disconnected everything, placed the Tirfor and the spare ratchet strap back in the RIB, then removed the tow rope from the furthest out submerged rock, which was now only a metre or so away from the Phoenix's bare-ended prop shaft. I stood back and examined the result of the preparations to yet another cunning little *Chrissy-plan,* and prayed to God that it'd work! I'd have forty horses of towing power with me, so all I needed now was adequate water depth around the hull, and a bloody miracle to keep the trunk floating at precisely the right height, so as to float the Phoenix *right over on her side,* keeping the gaping hole in the side of the hull high and dry. The 50-GPM water pump should take care of the rest of the water ingress, right up until Pedro's crane safely lifts her from the water. I stood back, attempted to sum the situation up, and grimaced instead of smiling. *What could POSSIBLY go wrong?!!?*

Sunday the 5th. No I *didn't* bother going to church first, although as I stood at the edge of the slipway staring out across the bay, I did say a little prayer to myself. Actually, to be perfectly honest, it was a *massive* bloody prayer! I drove into Mercadal, found myself a little café and ate some breakfast. I was feeling somewhat nervous to say the least. What if it all went horribly wrong? What if she sank halfway back across the bay? How much would *that* rescue operation finally cost me? *Dammit!* I needed to keep myself busy, just to stop all those negative thoughts from running through my head. I finished my breakfast, stocked up on a few more provisions from the Consum, and drove back to the apartment at Tamarindos. At least the sun was shining once more, and still there was very little wind, that would certainly help the situation. I pulled my wet wetsuit bottoms back on, and just in case things started to go horribly wrong, I pulled the jacket on too. I pulled my cagoule over the top, laced up my wet neoprene-lined trainers, and drove back to the slipway. Just as I brought the RIB around to the side of the slipway, Pedro appeared, and steadily began edging his bright red, smart-looking mobile crane across the hard-standing towards the water's edge.

"Mister Chris, Mister Chris," he shouted over to me through the open door of the powerful 7-ton brute, "I will be ready waiting for to be lifting your Phoenix, *you go, you go,* tide will soon be good."

Ah, so he *did* understand the local tides then. That was good to know, I thought I'd worked out that little trick all on my little lonesome.

"Buenos dias Señor Pedro, qué tal?" I shouted back at him, just as one of his work colleagues pulled alongside the crane with a car transporter. Very, very similar in fact to my old Foden; *although considerably newer!* "I will go now, I have everything ready to roll, hopefully you will see me come from around the back of the island very soon."

"Es bueno Mister Chris, you are being very careful now, por favor," he shouted back, as he began sorting through assorted types and lengths of strops that he could suitably attach to the crane's hydraulically extendable boom.

I set off across the bay at high speed, with nothing else aboard other than the tow rope, a large roll of gaffer tape, and a new Gerber multitool, both of which I'd paid quite a lot of euros for in Pedro's chandlery. When I reached the small patch of sand across the other side of the bay, the Phoenix was still sat there, laid right over on her side, looking as sad and forlorn as ever. A lump began to rise in my throat, but I choked it back down and began concentrating on the gradual rise of the minuscule little incoming tide. She was still sat in around twelve inches of water, as also was the seven-foot length of tree trunk that was tightly strapped over the top of her coachroof to her starboard side, which she simply appeared to be leaning against. I removed the cable-lock from the water pump, then fixed the pump's cage securely into its current perfect location using half a mile of gaffer tape. I then made sure the water inlet pipe was pushed as far down into the bilge as possible, and gaffer taped that into place too. I grabbed an old plastic container out of the mass of debris, that still littered the small patch of sand forward of the Phoenix's bow, filled it with seawater, then poured it down the pump's outlet pipe in order to prime it. I then gaffer taped the outlet pipe at a suitable angle pointing overboard, pulled the starter cord, and up the sweet little petrol motor started. Immediately the water that was still lying in the bilges, still seeping in through various smaller holes punched through the hull, where I couldn't actually see them, began arcing up through the air at an alarmingly fast rate, splashing back down into the sea over the starboard side of the aft deck. Minutely, almost imperceptibly, the Phoenix appeared to raise herself fractionally higher in the water, although she was still very firmly sat on the bottom; as also was the heavy section of tree. However, the water level was still clearly rising, and the water pump was very clearly still ejecting somewhere approaching its fifty gallons per minute out over the side of the hull. Shortly after two-thirty the pump stopped pumping, even though its engine continued to run, which clearly indicated to me that the Phoenix was empty of water. And the tide certainly wasn't going to rise any further, it had already risen by *two inches* already, and now it had levelled off. This was it then. *This was my opportunity. SHIT OR BUST! As they say!* I tied one end of the long tow rope to the Phoenix's rudder-stock, the other end to the RIB's ski-ring, which was bolted through the solid rear transom, backed the RIB away from the beach, took up the strain, shut my eyes and prayed. *The moment of truth, Mister Chris!* I pushed the throttle forward. Then I pushed it forward a little more. Half revs, *nothing!* A little more, three-quarter revs, *nothing!* Full throttle, maximum revs, *still nothing!*

It wasn't looking much like the Phoenix was going to budge. In fact, she hadn't even shifted a single millimetre! She was lying on clear flat sand, in around fourteen inches of water, her bilges were very obviously empty, she had forty horses tugging away at her, albeit granted they were only two-stroke horses, and it wasn't looking like she was going *anywhere!* I kept the RIB's Mariner engine running flat out. I even put my feet up on the dashboard, and sat there with my arms folded for a good five or six minutes. *Nothing! Absolutely bugger all in the way of shiftage!* I throttled back, spun the RIB around, ran her up on the beach with the outboard raised, hopped out, and switched off the water pump. I pulled my phone out of my inside cagoule pocket and dialled Pedro's number.

"Si Mister Chris, qué tal?" he answered immediately. "What is happen? How is you go?"

I answered his questions with the one and only thing that sprang to mind, *"WE'RE GONNA NEED A BIGGER BOAT!!!"*

"How are you meaning?" he asked.

"I'll come see you and explain," I answered.

I untied the tow rope from the RIB's ski-ring, pushed her out, dropped the engine, yanked the cord, spun her around, and shot back across the bay to the slipway. I moored her up alongside, jumped out, and walked up to where Pedro was stood next to one of his crane's four foot high tyres.

"Okay mi amigo," I began in desperation, "the Phoenix *WILL* float. She's currently lying in around thirty-five centimetres of water, and she's sitting flat on the sand, but I'm afraid forty horsepower simply isn't enough to drag her off into deeper water. Realistically I'm gonna need more like *four-hundred* horsepower, not just *forty!*"

"Oh dear Mister Chris, is not being good," Pedro said, staring at the ground whilst kicking a couple of loose pebbles through the coarse grass. "I'm afraid I am not having four-hundred horses anywheres for you to be using."

"Oh dear," I said, shaking my head sadly. "Oh dear, oh dear, oh dear."

"But I am having FIVE-HUNDRED horses!" he exclaimed proudly, looking up with a huge grin across his face. "Around in Port d'Addaia I am having moored my boat the *Thunder*. She is having two Cobra turbo-types petrol engines, each one being of two hundred and fifty horses. Also, these engines they are four-a-strokes, no two-a-strokes liking on RIB, so they are being more like, how you say, *fifteen* times bigger the powers of RIB. Is will be good, but I must tell you, she use muchos, muchos gasolina, you must

being most careful with her. I can bring her here to slipways in Fornells by sometimes tomorrow, I am not really knowings when; I *very, very* busy man! But then you can use my Thunder sometimes on Tuesday, and I can comings to use crane at same time. And also, this I am knows, the water-tide, it will be maybe little bit highers on Tuesday afternoon, so is good for you too. Crane is okay for staying here meanwhiles. How is soundings with you Mister Chris?"

"Sounds bloody marvellous Pedro!" I thanked him profusely. "I'm good with big boats, powerful ones too, I have muchos, muchos experience. *However,* I'd very much appreciate it if you'd give me a brief lesson in how to treat her first please, before I go running her into shallow water, or risk damaging her at all. Just give me a quick run-down on the controls first, before I take her out please. Is good no?" I was beginning to pick up a little of Pedro's perfect Spanglish by now.

"Is no problemo Mister Chris," he continued, "I know you good with boats. You just no good with *bastardas tormentas españolas!*" He dug me playfully in the ribs just a *might* too hard. Luckily I was still wearing my wetsuit, otherwise it *possibly* may have hurt. I forced a smile back at him.

"Thunder, she will be right here by tomorrow night, I comes to meet you here by eleven-hundred hours Tuesday mornings for to show you her workings. Is good no?"

"Is perfecto Pedro, muchos gracias, I see you on Tuesday."

He climbed into the driver's seat of his clever hydraulic-ramp car trans-porter, his colleague already sitting in the passenger seat, backed it around over the hard-standing, then drove off back in the direction of Mahon, tooting his horn and throwing a friendly wave out of the window as he left. I moored the RIB back where it belonged, pocketed the keys, and drove back towards the apartment to change into something a little more com-fortable. Touch wood I'd not be needing the RIB again!

CHAPTER
THIRTY EIGHT

Monday the 6th. I'd driven into Mercadal the evening before, gorged myself on delicious spit-roasted suckling pig at The Windmill, which had cost significantly less than I'd expected, then pretended to join in with some kind of deep and meaningful conversation, relating mostly to storm damage I'd guessed, with a bunch of do-gooders in a Spanish local's bar. Realistically I'd had no idea what they were talking about, nor they me, however we'd all ended up in agreement with each other anyway, regardless of whatever the subject may *actually* have been about; and muchos, muchos cervezas were consumed by all. The drive back home afterwards was a little *iffy*, to say the least, however there was literally no other traffic *whatsoever* on the roads at that time of night/year anyway, let alone pedestrians, and I'd managed to keep my wits about me more than adequately for the brief little trip back home. Needless to say, I'd collapsed into bed somewhat exhausted, following my week-long efforts, and considered that I'd earned myself the lie-in that I took the liberty of the following morning. Thankfully, after a whole week of leaving all three convector heaters switched on, the little apartment was starting to become a tad cosier. When I finally awoke late on the Monday morning, I took another long hot shower, then cooked myself a full English breakfast for lunch. I spent the rest of the afternoon on the phone to both Michelle and Dominic, catching up on progress over at Center Parcs Kempervennen. Apparently, everything was going entirely according to plan. In fact, so much so that two of our fitters had actually driven home on the afternoon of Friday the 3rd to spend the weekend with their families and kids, driving back over again on the following Sunday afternoon. All of which, *quite clearly*, would get added on to their weekly time-sheets, however, at the end of the day, *ALL* labour and materials would get costed into the job anyway, appropriate mark-ups would be applied, as and where I saw fit, and providing the final invoice came in at under my initial *guesstimated* budget, which it *always* did, as I always well *over-guesstimated* in the first place anyway, then Dom would be happy, CP would be happy, and all being well, the company would make sufficient, if not significant profit. It generally worked out pretty well with Dom and CP, it was an ongoing contract that I was not only particularly proud of, but genuinely cared about a huge amount. So, not missing my flights home on the forthcoming Friday was absolutely *imperative,* I simply *had* to meet up with Dom on the following Monday morning. Just to doubly reassure myself all was well I called Roland too, but all I got from him was his usual response, '*Just chill boss, everything's cool!*' Cheers Ro, you're a superstar! I wandered up to Marco's later that evening, and just for a nice change I ate chicken and chips in a plastic basket. As usual it was . . . *average!* However, a couple of small Estrellas helped it on its way, and I retired to bed for yet another early night. I knew I didn't have a particularly early start the following morning, but I most certainly wanted to be fully fresh and focused. I fell asleep to Pink Floyd's Dark Side Of The Moon, thinking, as I so very often did, '*You lock the door, and throw away the key, there's someone in my head, but its not me!*' Amongst myriad other meaningless '70's hippy paranoia!

Tuesday the 7th. I awoke with a clear head, a positive mental attitude, and a driven determination to successfully complete the task in hand. I showered, scrambled some eggs for a quick brekkie, accompanied by toast and coffee, pulled on my wet wetsuit gear once again, *just in case,* then drove around to the slipway by Fornells harbour. It was a little before 10am; I had an hour to kill before Pedro arrived. I parked the car well out of harm's way, climbed out, and walked across to the side wall of the slipway. And there, to my astonishment, moored alongside, sat what looked very much to me like an old cruiser-class offshore-racing powerboat. She was probably thirty-six feet long, and sleek, *very sleek,* clearly all power and muscle, with virtually nothing in the way of accommodation; other than possibly that to match what the Phoenix had once boasted. She had no windscreen to speak of, and virtually nothing in the way of equipment or fittings aboard, other than stainless grab-rails along either side of her long foredeck, and an oversize CQR anchor protruding from the front of her understated pulpit. The only differences between her and a professional racer that I could immediately identify, were firstly the lack of colourful decals or advertising plastered all over her. She was just plain matt white all over, top, bottom and sides, with her name *THUNDER* printed just once in small, subtle black letters low across her stern. And secondly, despite Pedro's efforts at protecting her from touching against the concrete wall with a pair of large white fenders, she'd quite clearly been, how shall I say, *'well used'* over the years. She was all perfectly intact, not exactly bashed around at all, just clearly *'well used!'* The next thing I noticed were her long-pitch, stainless steel, Arneson surface-piercing props, protruding aft of her rear transom, gear that would most definitely give her a *serious* turn of speed. And lastly, as the penny dropped, I noticed that she didn't even have *Pedro's Boat Centre* printed anywhere on her. In fact, if I were to sum up the overall appearance of the Thunder in two words, I'd've described her as *bland and inconspicuous! 'Hmmm . . .' I thought to myself!* Still, her controls looked relatively simple to master, and I'd driven similar types of craft many times in the past anyway, so providing she responded to her controls in a *normal* manner, I wouldn't find any difficulty driving her. All I really needed to know was what her stern's draft was, and how close to the shore it would be safe for me to reverse her. Shortly before 11am Pedro and his colleague arrived, once again reversing the car transporter up to the water's edge adjacent to the crane. Pedro hopped down from the truck, and greeted me yet again with an overly-firm warm handshake.

"Buenos dias Mister Chris, you are being fine today? Este mi amigo Oscar, I am needing him here for to be helping me with getting strappings around your Phoenix when you are pull her back to this place. As you can seeing, water by this side of wharf here is quite very deeps, so Oscar he helps me good. You have looked my Thunder, no? Is good boat for job, no?" Pedro grinned somewhat knowingly.

"Buenos dias Pedro," I replied, attempting to extricate my crushed hand from his ridiculously powerful grip. "Y Buenos dias Oscar, qué tal?" I offered to his young helper, shaking his hand too, and realising to my horror that this time the shoe was on the other foot. Or rather the glove was on the other hand? *Or whatever!*

"Si, bien Mister Chris, gracias," Oscar replied courteously, gently rubbing his right hand with his left.

"Okay," Pedro continued, walking diagonally across the slipway with me towards the Thunder. "You are seeing one of these type boats before Mister Chris?"

"Many years ago Pedro," I began, about to give him a fully qualified reply, "I used to help out with a cruiser-class offshore racing team that was both owned and sponsored by a Bristol-based company called Wonderfire. Their boat was a thirty-six foot Bonito, which *also* had 250hp Cobras linked to Arneson surface-drives, and we played around with so many different pitches of propellor that at one time we even managed to get her up to 135mph, once we found some *very* calm seas somewhere. However, with those particular props she had no low-speed performance whatsoever. Anyway, the point being, I never raced with her, but I drove her many times in testing and practice runs. So yes, I have plenty of experience piloting vessels of this nature."

"Okay Mister Chris," Pedro continued, "this very good for to hear. I must tell you now that these propellers, they no built for speed, they built for *power!* The Thunder, she have a top speed of maybe only one hundred thirty *kilometres* per hour, not so fast like your Wonderfire, but at low speeds she *very, very* powerful!"

"*Great!*" I replied. "That's *exactly* what I need to drag the Phoenix off the sand, and back out into deeper water. Most importantly Pedro, what I need to know is her maximum stern draft, as in how close to the shore can I back her up exactly?"

"She have surface-drives," Pedro answered, "so her draft at stern only maybe seventy centimetres. *BUT,* you must not be taking her too close to beach, *especially near some of rocks,* because already I am changing these propellers two times so far just in this one year! So you must be jumping into waters at up to around your waistline when you are getting to beaches. I am please for see you are having on wetsuit!"

"Don't worry buddy," I said confidently, "I know exactly what I'm doing, as well as how damned cold this water is right now. However, I would appreciate a brief lesson first though, if you don't mind. Even though they might all look the same, they *definitely* don't all handle the same. Could I take her for a one-off spin around the bay first please, with you aboard sat next to me? Will be okay por favor?"

"Si, si, of course Mister Chris," Pedro confirmed enthusiastically. "Jumps onboard now, I am showing you how she is workings."

I stepped aboard the Thunder, and slid across into the passenger's bolster seat. Pedro hopped aboard with the keys, and fired up both the engines. *Wow*, what an awesome *growl* the pair of them made. Oscar then kindly cast off her mooring warps for us, throwing them both aboard for me to catch and stow, then Pedro eased both throttles into forward gear, and we slid gently away from the vertical wall along the side of the slipway. I reached across behind Pedro's seat and pulled both fenders aboard. A few seconds later Pedro turned to me and said,

"Right, Mister Chris, I am showing you nows what my Thunder she can be doing."

He pushed both throttles fully forward together, the twin Cobras literally spat thunder out of their exhaust cowlings, which immediately seemed to echo around the silence of the peaceful bay, totally destroying any semblance of tranquility, and off we shot at a ridiculously fast pace on possibly one of the fastest accelerating vessels I've ever had the pleasure of enjoying. Pedro continued on roughly a straight due southerly course, and shortly before we reached Ses Salines some two minutes later, the speedometer was clearly reading just over 50 knots. *Slightly under sixty miles per hour!* Pedro throttled back as we approached the shallows around Ses Salines Bay, and as we settled back down off the plane he turned to me and said,

"Okay Mister Chris, this was how I *NOT* want you to be driving my Thunders!"

I looked at him and smiled, telling him quite firmly that that was *NOT* the purpose I was using her for. I'd most likely be dragging the Phoenix across the bay at just *one knot,* if that even, and praying to God that she didn't sink along the way. Pedro pointed out the large red plastic mooring buoy, bobbing around in the wash that we'd just created, some fifty yards off the beach.

"This your sinkers booy?" he asked, still pointing towards it.

"BUOY!" I corrected him once again. "Yes. At least it *was.* I obviously don't have a use for it anymore though, do I! So I guess its over to you now mi amigo."

"I am knowing some peoples who will be using it. It is looking *very* good, and is surviving huge Medicane with no problems. Many moorings like this, they now all gone because of storm waves. I think this one very good for some local's fishingmens. So, now you drive boat please Mister Chris, you take me over nearby to your Phoenix, por favor, so I am looking your problems, then you takes me back to slipway, I seeing how goods you are driving my Thunders, and then, if I think okay, you droppings me off so I am manning crane, and you goes to get her to me. You are being ready?"

We swapped seats so that I was at the helm, whereupon I immediately pushed the starboard engine-throttle into forward gear, and pulled the port one back into reverse, spinning the Thunder around one hundred and eighty degrees in her own length. Then, just as her bow pointed directly at the southern tip of Lizard Island, I pushed the port throttle into forward too, and allowed us to chug along gently at around four knots, with both engines set to tick-over. Pedro was already clearly impressed with the way I was handling her, and began concentrating more on spotting how the Phoenix was lying, as opposed to monitoring my driving skills. Not that he'd needed to monitor them at all, I'd felt entirely comfortable with the controls, and perfectly confident in my ability to handle what was clearly a genuine *beast of a machine!* As we neared the Phoenix I set the controls to neutral, and allowed the Thunder to drift in a little closer to the shore. Pedro stared at the Phoenix, noting the way the bulk of the sawn tree had been strapped right across her coachroof from just underneath her starboard gunwale, forcing her to float right over on one side. He spotted the way the water pump had been set up, and below it the long tow rope attached to her rudder-stock, its free end coiled up on the sand just above the *'high-water mark'*, the line of dry seaweed halfway up the little patch of sand.

"Okay Mister Chris," Pedro said positively, "I can seeing you have muchos problemos here, but I am thinkings you have been making preparations in very good ways. So, when you brings my Thunders back to here, using her anchor please for not to be getting too close to beach. And then, when tides they reached up to that, how you say, *seaweed* marks, then tow rope is plenty long for to reach this ring here at stern of Thunder."

Pedro pointed out a purpose-made tow ring secured firmly through the top of the rear transom, high above the sharp steel blades of the surface-piercing props. He then showed me how the hydraulic anchor release and retrieve mechanism worked, which thankfully was conveniently located *inside* the cockpit, and finally made the point of telling me to tie the tow rope tight, with no slack or sag between the Thunder and the Phoenix, otherwise I'd run the risk of the prop blades slicing through the rope. I nodded and said yes, I fully understood where he was coming from.

"Please Pedro," I then half begged him, "I'm not *entirely* sure I'm gonna pull this off right now, I'm beginning to feel the collywobbles somewhat, but one thing I *am* sure of, I'm only gonna get the one shot at it, *that's it!* There'll be no second chances, and no going back either. So its absolutely critical, por favor, that you and Señor Oscar are *ABSOLUTELY 100%* ready for me with the crane, and the correct strops, when I get back over there."

"What is *collywobbles?*" Pedro asked, handing me a seriously sharp fish filleting knife.

"No matter," I replied, "just a silly English expression. What's the knife for?"

"If Phoenix all goes under waters on ways over here, you are reachings behind back of boat and cuts the towing rope. Is *MUY IMPORTANTE!*"

"Si señor, entiendo perfectamente!" I replied in almost perfect Spanish. "I totally understand. Oh, and one more thing, por favor mi amigo." I added.

"Si, what is?" Pedro asked.

"Would you mind *awfully* if I gave the Thunder a little turn of speed on the way back?"

"No problemo Mister Chris, but you must be going *slows* when we get nearing to Fornells."

I looked at him, grinned sneakily, and clunked both throttles into forward gear. After pottering out into slightly deeper water, I suggested he might like to sit tight and hang on to the grab-rail on the dash. I then pushed both throttles fully forward, slamming both of our bodies back into the padded bolster seats with a stunning amount of G-force. I banked the Thunder sharply around the south shores of Lizard Island, and as Pedro clung to the grab-rail tightly with both hands, gritting his teeth somewhat, I headed off towards the cliffs at the entrance to Fornells Bay at somewhere approaching fifty knots. The water was calm, the sun had peeked out from behind a cloud, the air was clean and fresh, and just for those couple of minutes, for the first time in the last fortnight, *I FELT GOOD!* However, that was simply because I had a serious muscle-toy to play with for a few moments. Nonetheless, I savoured those few moments to their fullest potential. Some way after we passed the entrance to Fornells harbour, and headed a little further on out towards the open sea, Pedro stared across at me as if to wonder where the heck I was going. With that I throttled back a little, and spun the Thunder in a tight fast arc back towards the harbour. As we approached the harbour entrance I throttled back even more, and as we settled back down off the plane, with the long vertical wall to the side of the slipway just some hundred yards or so directly ahead of us, I shouted to Pedro *'Fenders over to starboard por favor!'* Pedro immediately reached around behind me, and threw the still attached fenders over the side, whereupon, after he'd sat back down, I'd spun the wheel around to port, gunned the starboard throttle forward a little, spun the wheel back to starboard, and clunked the port throttle into reverse, then gunned the revs momentarily on the port engine. I then quickly set both throttles to neutral, centralised the steering, stood up, and grabbed both mooring warps with one hand, then threw them both ashore, just as the Thunder glided elegantly sideways up against the wall, the fenders taking all the impact of my seemingly well-practiced, perfectly executed manoeuvre. Oscar was standing there waiting to take the mooring warps, and he tied them individually to the steel railing that ran down the left-hand side of the slipway. I switched the engines off, and looked across at Pedro with a grin on my face.

"Mister Chris," he said, clearly impressed with my parking ability, "I am seeing clearly that you have drive fast boats like this before, you are being very good with handlings of them."

"Gracias mi amigo," I answered with a degree of both pride and modesty, "I guess me and boats just naturally go together. Or at least *SOMETIMES* we do! Anyway, she's a beauty, maybe one day I'll be able to afford something like this myself. In the meantime, sadly, I now have some urgent business to attend to."

"Si Mister Chris," Pedro agreed. "I am thinking that best timings for highest waters will be around three o'clock, and is now already nearing two o'clock, so I think maybe is best if you takes my Thunders with you now, and go prepares for to getting ready for tow. Oscar and I will be await here with preparing Thor correctly for lift."

"Thor?" I queried.

"Thor is name of crane." Pedro said proudly.

"Oh, I see," I said. "Okay, wish me luck my friend, I'll be back in an hour or so with the Phoenix."

"Buena suerte Mister Chris," Pedro called after me, as I climbed back into the Thunder's driver's seat.

I fired up the engines, Oscar untied and threw me the mooring warps, and I chugged slowly away from the quayside leaving both fenders still hung over the side. I ran the Thunder across the bay at a relatively sedate speed, swung her around the south end of the island, and allowed her to drift gently into around six feet of water, some thirty yards or so directly off the patch of sand that the Phoenix lay on. I immediately hit the anchor-release switch, automatically releasing the CQR from its cradle right at the very front of the long pointed bow, which splashed down into the water, dragging a couple of metres of anchor chain along with it. I pulled the port throttle into reverse, gradually running astern whilst feeding out more chain, then hit the chain-lock switch, set the anchor, and returned the port throttle to neutral. I switched the engines off, then immediately jumped over the side into one metre of chilly water, right up to my waist, precisely as planned. I waded ashore, grabbed the coil of tow rope that was attached to the Phoenix, ran it back out to the stern of the Thunder, and looped it through the tow ring. I pulled tight on the rope, tensioning it between the Phoenix and the Thunder, and taking up even more slack as the Thunder's anchor chain lifted a little and I pulled her towards me. When I was happy with the positioning of everything, I tied the tow rope off tightly to the ring, throwing the spare loose end over the transom and into the back of the boat. I measured the depth of water at the Thunder's stern. It was tight; there was only about five or six inches of water underneath the bottom of her props, but I felt confident that was adequate; and anyway, if she *dug in,* then she'd only be digging in to fine sand, so all being well that wouldn't cause any damage. Plus, I'd come up with yet another little *Chrissy-plan.* Plus, the tide was still coming up anyway, so all good! I waded back ashore, checked all around the rocks first to make doubly sure that I hadn't left anything behind, then climbed inside the Phoenix to check on the water level. It was 2.30pm, and I reckoned the sea level had about another half inch to rise until it reached the rough line of seaweed. *'Every little helps,'* I told myself. *'Be patient Chris, wait for the right moment!'* The Phoenix was now lying in almost fifteen inches of water. *Would it be enough? Were the Thunder's engines going to be powerful enough to cope? Could I finally manage to drag the Phoenix off the rocks?* I analysed the situation once again. There was around twenty feet of taut tow rope connecting the stern of the Phoenix to the stern of the Thunder, and everything, as far as I could tell, was set as perfectly as I could possibly make it. *'Patience is a virtue Chris, and every inch counts.' Or at least, so I'd been told on numerous occasions!* I checked my watch. Quarter to three. That was it then, it wasn't going to get any higher, so it was *now or never, shit or bust, LET'S DO IT!*

I primed the water pump, pulled the cord, and started the little petrol engine. Immediately water started arcing into the air and out over the gunwale, as the pipe steadily drained the bilges. As the fountain of water continued to gush over the Phoenix's stern I waded back out to the Thunder, climbed aboard, and started up both her engines. I pushed both throttles into forward gear, then set them to about a quarter revs, but nothing moved. The props bit into the water, skimming the top layer of sand, and sending a plume of spray towards the beach, but the Phoenix remained stuck fast. Half revs, and an even higher plume of spray, but still no movement. Three-quarter revs, and the huge gush of water from the Thunder's rapidly spinning props was now spraying water and sand all over the aft deck of the Phoenix. *Okay, time to activate Chrissy-plan number one-hundred-and-bloody-something-or-other!* Why rely solely on the Thunder's props, when effectively I had another *'Tirfor-winch'* ahead of me? I left the throttles set on three-quarter revs, and whilst keeping my finger pressed firmly down on the *anchor-retrieve* button, looked behind me, and gawked in sheer amazement as the Phoenix began to slide slowly but surely along the sandy bottom, and steadily further out into deeper water. *'ITS ONLY GONE AND BLOODY WELL WORKED RODNEY!'* I shouted to myself above the noise of the screaming engines. Not only that, but the deeper the water gradually became that I was slowly dragging the Phoenix out into, the lower the tree trunk sat, and the more it began to roll her over onto her side. Now, that was all well and good for keeping the gaping hole in the hull well above the waterline, but I just prayed to God that the tree trunk wouldn't sink altogether. Just as the big old CQR anchor clunked back into its steel cradle at the front of the bow, I released my finger from the anchor-retrieve button, and throttled back on the engines ever so slightly. The Phoenix was still sliding along sand, dragging the huge tree trunk alongside her, but at least she was still moving, and getting into increasingly deeper water as she came. I throttled back a little more, and as the Phoenix's hull finally kissed goodbye to the sandy bottom, the tree trunk settled at around seven-eighths submerged. *Perfect!* The only thing I couldn't tell was how quickly the old girl was filling up, relative to how well the water pump was coping with emptying her back out. I throttled back to around one-quarter revs, dragging the Phoenix along backwards behind me, laid right over on her starboard side, and kept one eye firmly fixed on the long, sharp-bladed fish filleting knife sat on the passenger seat next to me. We rounded the southern end of Lizard Island, staying well away from the shallows, and began heading directly back towards Pedro's crane, Thor, at somewhere approaching one knot. I looked back at the Phoenix again, and made a mental note of the fact that her starboard-side rubbing strake amidships, directly above where the log was strapped, was running along at about one inch above the surface of the water. *I didn't feel comfortable!* I felt nervous, the collywobbles had set in once again, and I was very close to that horrible feeling of *dread*. One mile to go, at just one mile per hour! I honestly couldn't see her lasting a whole hour! The water pump was doing its job admirably, but even at 50-GPM I just couldn't see it coping with the influx for that length of time. I increased the revs a little, but it didn't appear to make very much difference to our speed through the water.

Ten minutes went by, and as I stared carefully at the attitude of the Phoenix some twenty feet behind me, I couldn't help but notice that the starboard rubbing strake amidships was now dragging *through* the surface of the water. *The water pump wasn't keeping up!* I pushed both throttles forward to half revs, whereupon we increased our speed to somewhere around one and a half knots! *One and three-quarter miles per hour! And still three-quarters of a mile to go!* I kept our speed and course steady, shut my eyes and prayed. The simple fact of the matter was, praying was *all* I could do. I opened my eyes and stared once again at the knife. *NO, come on, we can DO this!* With every minute that went by the Phoenix appeared to sit increasingly lower in the water. No it wasn't just my damned imagination, not only was the surface of the water now well over the starboard-side gunwale, is was also getting ever closer to the bottom of the gaping hole on the port side too. *Come on guys, PLEASE, just ten more minutes!* I could clearly here Thor's engine running now, even above the thumping of the Thunder's twin Cobras, we were that close. I could plainly see Pedro sat at the controls in the cab, and Oscar balancing precariously atop the centre of a large H-shaped steel boom that was hanging from the crane's chain hook, directly above the water. Slung below the boom, attached to all four points of the huge 'H', were two heavy duty webbing strops, identical to those used on a standard travel hoist. *Five more minutes to run!* Oscar was gesticulating at me, clearly indicating that he wanted me to somehow try and drift the Phoenix directly in to the underside of Thor's spreader-boom starboard side to, so that the log was up against the wall, and the gaping hole was facing seaward. I gave him a quick thumbs-up, and quickly transferred the Thunder's fenders from starboard to port. I'd reckoned on there being only just sufficient space for me to drift the Phoenix to that exact position before the anchor projecting over the front of Thunder's bow crunched nastily into the solid, vertical concrete wall at the southern end of the wide slipway. I'd got *one chance only* of getting this right. And a thousand chances of *fucking it all up!* I throttled back to tick-over, and aimed Thunder's sleek bow directly towards the wall beneath Thor's vertical chain. 100-feet, 75-feet, I pulled the throttles back to neutral. 50-feet, 25-feet, wheel straight, port throttle ahead, starboard astern, and the Thunder spun her bow around to the right. Both throttles to neutral, and I allowed Thunder's fenders to bounce off the wall, before nudging her slightly forward out of the way. I pulled her up just a couple of feet before her CQR crunched into the concrete, then spun around just in time to see the heavy log strapped to side of the Phoenix touch firmly up against the wall, with the Phoenix's coachroof graunching along the top of the wall itself. Oscar was immediately right on the case. Like a professional steel erector, or an agile little monkey even, he looped one strop around the underside of the Phoenix's bow, and whilst I *very* quickly untied the tow rope from the ring on the transom of the Thunder, in order to free it up, he sprinted across to the other end of the swinging H-frame, and looped the other strop around the underside of the Phoenix's stern. He double-checked both strops for position, then, still sat astride the centre of the H-frame, gave Pedro the thumbs-up. Pedro began hoisting, and very, very gradually the Phoenix lifted up and out of the water.

'HALLE-FUCKING-LUJAH!!!' I screamed aloud excitedly.

Neither Pedro *nor* Oscar took their eyes off the ball for one second. The moment the Phoenix's hull was some twelve inches off the surface of the water Pedro halted Thor's steady lift, and allowed her to hang there, seawater pouring from half a dozen fist-sized holes punched through both sides of her hull. Ironically, the moment the crane's strops had taken the strain and supported the weight of the Phoenix, the water pump had suddenly stopped. It turned out sometime later that it had completely run dry of fuel. Purely by chance, its timing on that couldn't have been judged any closer to perfection, albeit entirely accidentally. Pedro allowed the Phoenix to hang in position until the remainder of the water inside finished draining from the hull, then lifted her still higher, slowly swung Thor's boom around by ninety degrees, then lowered her down until she rested lightly atop the transporter's flatbed. Oscar swung down from the H-frame, and following a brief discussion both he and Pedro agreed that the tree stump was interfering with the balance of the Phoenix on the back of the truck. Oscar then climbed back up onto the Phoenix's coachroof, and released the pair of ratchet straps that had secured the one-third of a tree in position. He then jumped down, and between the two of them they manhandled the log out of the way. Pedro then fully craned the entire weight of the Phoenix down onto the back of the transporter, laying her down on her still-solid starboard hull, her cracked keel and the gaping hole through her port side clearly visible to me from where I was stood. As I watched intently from the cockpit of the Thunder, as the poor little truck's rear-axle springs bottomed out, I couldn't help but notice one other thing. The bow of the Phoenix overhung the rear end of the flatbed by at least seven feet. Almost one third of the entire length of the boat. Their little transporter was quite clearly somewhat *smaller* than my old Foden. Still, the Phoenix was obviously sat aboard securely enough, and it wasn't as if they had very far to go exactly! Just for a change, that particular issue wasn't my problem! I watched as Pedro and Oscar manhandled the heavy log back up onto the front of the flatbed, then turned and fired up the Thunder's twin Cobras once again. I left Pedro and Oscar to strap their newly acquired load securely to the little truck's flatbed, including the heavy water-sodden log, which they'd clearly decided to keep, and backed the Thunder away from the quay wall. I reversed her out into the bay, moved her fenders across to her starboard side, spun her full circle, and ran her around to the other side of the slipway, mooring her back up *precisely* where Pedro had first left her. I secured her warps, then wandered back over to Pedro and handed him the keys. I also handed him the keys to the RIB, which I'd also left *precisely* where I'd found it, and for what it was worth, I handed him the keys to the Phoenix too, explaining to him with great sadness that she was now all his. I then pointed out the pile of stuff that I'd removed from the Phoenix in order to lighten her load, including the couple of hundred quids-worth of anchor chain, and he said he'd most likely have all that picked up when he returned to Fornells in a few days time to collect his beloved Thor. He then hurriedly told me that they really should get gone as quickly as possible. It was past five o'clock by then, we'd been stood there chatting for a while in semi-darkness, and he had no flags or trailer-board available to hang on the bow of the Phoenix, which was blatantly overhanging the back of his transporter by way too much. The three of us all congratulated each other on a job *extremely* well done, Oscar hopped up into the passenger seat of the truck's little cab, and I winced once more as I shook hands with Pedro yet again, thanking him profusely for his incredible amount of help, and informing him that I'd see him at his chandlery store the following morning when I dropped the remainder of his equipment back, and settled up his account.

"Gracias Mister Chris," Pedro called back to me as he turned and walked towards the truck. "You very good man, muchos clever man too, this job is making much too difficults for me, so very, very well done. Hasta mañana mi amigo, y adios."

"Ciao Pedro," I called back, as he climbed up into the driver's seat.

He started the engine, then drove cautiously across the hard-standing and out onto the road, switching the twin revolving yellows on the cab roof on as he went. As he and Oscar both briefly threw a quick wave out of their windows at me, I walked across to the middle of the road, stood there and waved back, then blew a heartfelt kiss towards the poor old Phoenix.

"I'm sorry for all the pain and suffering that I've allowed you to go through old girl," I called aloud after her, "but at least I haven't left you entirely stranded in the middle of nowhere, I suppose that was the very least I could do for you. Te veré de nuevo mañana mi niña bonita. Buenas noches."

Following which, once again with tears in my eyes, I wandered back to the car, then drove back to my cosy little apartment in Tamarindos in order to calm and warm my shaking and shivering body under a steaming hot shower. I don't remember whether it worked or not, although I doubt if it had!

CHAPTER THIRTY NINE

Wednesday the 8th. I'd already finished up the eggs and bacon that I'd bought a few days previous, so following peanut butter on toast for breakfast I wandered out onto the tiny little front terrace, sat on top of the old wooden pub garden table that had once belonged to the Railway Tavern in Fishponds, and dialled Pedro's mobile number. It was grey, dull and cloudy, the wind had freshened somewhat, and I still had the shivers and shakes from the day before, although I suspected that had nothing to do with the temperature. Pedro answered on the tenth ring, and I asked him what would be a good time of day to catch up with him.

"Hola Mister Chris," he replied, clearly out of breath, "I *very, very* busy, I only one man!"

"I know that Pedro, you must be up to your eyes in it these days," I sympathised. "Anytime's good with me though, I'm not flying 'til Friday morning, so whenever you can find a few moments between now and then we need to catch up over a few things. Like *payment* for example?"

"Ah, si, comprende señor," he replied, suddenly seemingly a little less out of breath. "Mañana I will be stops for siesta times to be eat in café-bar next to workshop. You are comings to chandlery, and then we are goings to eating our lunches together. One o'clock times yes? Is good for you Mister Chris?"

"Si, si, Pedro," I answered him positively, "esto es bueno. I shall bring all your equipment back shortly before, and then we are going for having lunches together at one o'clock. Hasta mañana mi amigo."

Damn; his vocabulary and accent were becoming annoyingly catching! I hung up before my impersonations became mildly embarrassing. What to do, what to do? I was feeling a little lost. Actually, if the truth be known, I was feeling *VERY* lost! All that effort, followed by all that effort, and for what exactly? Very clearly for nothing. Absolutely nothing to show for it whatsoever! *'Hey ho, get a grip Reason,'* I scolded myself, *'sometimes shit just happens, get over it!'* I thought about it a little more. *'Yeah, maybe. But usually when it does its covered by a sodding insurance policy, you blithering idiot!!'* I felt an argument with myself coming on, somehow between my heart and my head, so I wandered back inside and put some happy music on the stereo instead. Rod Stewart's *Never A Dull Moment,* that seemed to suit for the time being, although the thought did run through my mind at the time, if I were to become *totally* cynical about the situation, maybe a little later I'd go for Supertramp's *Crisis? What Crisis?* In actual fact, a little later, I didn't go for that at all. I went for a walk instead. Dressed in jeans and trainers, a sweatshirt and my trusty old ski jacket, I took the rocky coastal path into Fornells Town, turned right, and walked along the road beside the bay towards Ses Salines. I spotted various builders, contractors and handymen along the way, all desperately trying to make good the assorted devastating storm damage in time for the forthcoming summer tourist season, but other than that the bay was as calm and peaceful as ever. I wandered off the beaten track and along the water's edge, past the remains of the old wooden jetty at the top end of Ses Salines village, and on down to the little shingly beach towards the bottom end of the bay that, over the last year or so, I'd come to know and love so very well. I sat myself down on the upturned hull of a very old, small, clinker-built wooden dingy, which, although its relatively new-looking painter was securely tied around the base of a sturdy old Tamarind tree, didn't actually look as if it belonged to anyone. I stared out across the bay, firstly at the tough old red mooring buoy gently swaying around in the light breeze, some fifty yards offshore, and then beyond the southern tip of Lizard Island opposite to the far side of the bay, where the Phoenix had ended up after breaking loose from her mooring, some mile or so away, and I just sat there, totally dumbfounded. *How the hell had that even happened? All because of a cheap Chinese padlock? WELL IT WASN'T FUCKING CHEAP! And it wasn't fucking Chinese either, otherwise it wouldn't have had a CE mark stamped next to the maker's name on the back!* I still couldn't believe it! I'd moored the Phoenix here during what I'd estimated was a northerly Force Ten gale, and this part of the bay was as flat as a millpond. *FUCKING MEDICANES!!!* Pedro had told me that the storm had whipped the seas up from every conceivable direction into a massive frenzied cauldron, and conditions right here were such that the Phoenix's hull would've been smashing against the bottom, as well as either pulling her bow under the waves or lifting the sinker right up off the bottom. One way or another something would've given, and in some ways I suppose I could count my lucky stars that it was what it was. *'She very tough boat, your Phoenix!'* If the padlock hadn't given way, given the power of the *record-breaking* Medicane on that fateful day, its entirely possible she could've dragged her sinker across to the centre of the bay, and *then sunk,* maybe even in *very* deep water! *And then what?* How much would *that* rescue mission have cost me exactly? It didn't bear thinking about. In actual fact, none of this bore thinking about; *especially* the fact that I'd allowed it to happen without any *Goddam insurance!* Nevertheless, I still just sat there, head in hands, entirely dumbfounded. The reality of it all hadn't entirely sunk in by then. *FUCKING MEDICANES!!!* I've no idea exactly how long I'd sat there for, throwing little pebbles into the sea, and generally sulking to myself. Maybe I was going through some form of grieving process, who knows? All I know is that by the time I stood back up I was shivery cold, and hungry, and beginning to think a little more positively about trying somehow to put this whole episode behind me. I began wandering back towards Fornells, hoping that once I got there maybe I'd find a bar open somewhere in town. Anywhere other than dreary old Marco's place! Fortunately for me, although possibly not quite so fortunately for my wallet, the Hostal La Palma at the top of the town square, Plaça s'Algaret, was not only open, but was busy with many locals, y muchos musico joyosa appeared to be coming from their little jukebox in the corner. And that, as they often tend to say in Fishponds on a Sunday morning, is more or less the last I remember about that particular night.

Thursday the 9th. I awoke early with a hangover, downed a pint of tap water, and went back to sleep again. The next time I woke up I felt fine, until I peeked at my watch, whereupon I began to worry about being late for my pre-arranged meeting with busy old Pedro. I jumped in the shower, dressed myself quickly in the same set of clothes that I'd found strewn all across the lounge floor, jumped in the car, and set off towards Mahon. Along the way I couldn't help but wonder how the hell I'd managed to get myself back home the night before. Oh well, I guessed it'd come back to me in due course. I pulled the car up outside the entrance to Pedro's chandlery store, lifted the hatchback, and walked inside carrying the water pump, its little fuel tank still devoid of 2-stroke.

"Ah, Mister Chris," Pedro called from somewhere near the back of the store, "you can leavings pump on floor by shelvings here, I comes now to help with rest of things."

Together we offloaded the remainder of the equipment from the back of the hire car, including one empty fuel can, the entire contents of which I'd needed for the chainsaw, and one full can, some of which I really *should* have topped the water pump up with before setting off with the Phoenix in tow. *'Hey ho, whatever! Mission accomplished anyway!'* I'd thought to myself. I was way beyond caring by that point! Just as I locked the car up, again unnecessarily, Pedro informed me that it was nearly one-thirty, and he'd got a table booked for one o'clock, so *ideally* we should get a bloody move on! We took our seats at a table in the little café-bar next door, and Pedro immediately ordered half a dozen assorted tapas dishes, a bottle of Rioja, and a jug of table water. I was quite grateful that the table water arrived immediately, and initially I wasn't overly looking forward to the red wine. Having said that, once the tapas dishes arrived, most of which were swilling around in *way* too much garlic sauce, not to mention chilli sauce and olive oil, I'd actually become rather grateful for the Rioja too, and forced myself to swill each mouthful of food down with a generous gulp.

"Mmm, this food's delicious," I lied blatantly to Pedro, then forced my last mouthful of Rioja down. "Anyway, that's enough for me thank you my friend, I already cooked myself a large breakfast earlier this morning," I lied once again.

"Postres? Café?" Pedro asked.

"No, no, gracias," I replied, "I really think we should get down to business now, I still have things to do today," I lied yet again. "I'm flying home tomorrow morning, so I'm kind of running out of time right now. I must say though, Señor Pedro, mi amigo, I simply don't know what I would've done without you. You have been *SO VERY, VERY HELPFUL,* with all of your time and your equipment, *especially* your wonderful vessel the Thunder. I know I wouldn't have been able to salvage the Phoenix at all without your help, and Oscar's help too for that matter, and that's a fact. When it comes down to saying thank you, I simply don't know where to begin. So I must pay you for your efforts, but again I don't know where to begin. And I sure as hell have no idea how to put a value on the time and efforts that you've personally devoted to helping me out of the crazy predicament that I managed to get myself into. So Pedro, my friend, where exactly do we start?"

"Is okay Mister Chris," Pedro began, "I am not being required to charging you IVA on these things that I am loaning for you, so I can make the bill however I am wanting. Last night I am sitting down in my office, in my house, and I am workings it all out for you. My time is my time, and mostly I am *only one man!* But it is you that is clevers, you are achieving all difficult parts on yourself. So, some equipment, is littles. And then the Thunder, and my Thor, I am adding all this together, and then I am thinkings that I must try to help Mister Chris in some ways, because he is no having, how you say, *insurances.* So, I am making my price rounding down to simples figure, especially to be helpings for you. So, if is okay you can just be giving me cash of three thousand euros por favor. Is good for you Mister Chris?"

Well, *'FUCK ME SIDEWAYS WITH A NUCLEAR-TIPPED BALLISTIC MISSILE!'* was my initial thought! My second thought was, *'Where the hell am I gonna get that kinda cash from this late in the day?'* And my third thought, well, to be honest, that's probably *unprintable!* I gulped, twice, then looked Pedro straight in the eye and said,

"Sounds *extremely* fair to me my friend, and thank you once again, *from the heart of my bottom,* for all your help. D'you have any idea what time the Bank of Sa Nostra in Mahon stays open until today? I'm gonna have to pay them a little visit I'm afraid, I don't tend to carry that sort of cash around with me. Uh, like, *not ever!*"

"Is okay Mister Chris," Pedro continued nonchalantly, "I thinks is stays opens until maybe eight o'clocks tonight, so is plenty of times for you. Anyways Mister Chris, I must just say you now, mañana my colleague Carlos, he takes me and Oscar over to Fornells in one our vehicles, then Oscar he drive my Thor back over here to yard in Mahon. Me, I drive Thunder back to Port d'Addaia, Oscar he collect me in vehicles and brings me back Mahon. Then we *all* back Mahon, so is all good. And, I am also saying, we tries to do all this in *light of day,* because last night, when I am bringing Phoenix on back of truck, only just before we getting Mahon, we are getting stopped by, how you say, *traffic police!* They are saying boat is too big, lorry is too small, and end of boat is having no lightings. I think maybe they were trying to give me ticket, but I give them big arguments instead!"

"Oh dear, that was a little unfortunate," I muttered *nonchalantly!* "Anyway, must dash, gotta go get my passport from Tamarindos before I can draw *that much* money from the bank. Toodle-pip, back in a couple of hours or so."

I jumped in the car, and sped off back towards Fornells to find my passport. In all honesty, I wasn't entirely sure I wanted much in the way of in-depth conversation with Pedro about *any* of the issues he'd just raised. *Particularly* the bit about the police, we'd have had *way* too much in common over that one! And frankly, I didn't have the time anyway. Although to be fair, the more I thought about it, the more I began to accept that €3,000 cash probably wasn't altogether that bad a deal anyway, *especially* considering the maximum fine I could potentially have received as an alternative. Plus, God forbid, what if she *had* sunk in the middle of the bay? *What then?* So hey, after all, I suppose €3,000 did equate to *only* £2,000. *Two thousand sodding quid! ONLY!* I wasn't even sure whether there was that much money in my Sa Nostra account anyway! I guess I could've put it on one of my other *unused* credit cards, but then I'd've had to pay 20% IVA, yet another four hundred quid on top! I grabbed my passport from my kitbag, and as I drove back towards the centre of Mahon, with just a *few* butterflies in my stomach, I casually wondered how long it might take to get an overdraft application approved. However, on arrival at Sa Nostra, *fortunately for me,* although my account held a little *under* €3,000, one of the managers graciously allowed me to draw the full amount, on the basis that my next one hundred euro direct debit was imminently due in anyway. I thanked him profusely, jumped back in the car, and headed back towards Pedro's chandlery store down alongside the harbour.

I handed Pedro over his three thousand euros cash in crisp, new, fifty-euro notes, and watched whilst he counted it out on the glass counter top right next to the till, then fold it and shove it deep in his trouser pocket.

"Muchos gracias Mister Chris," he said with a warm smile, "you very good man. Also, you are being very clever man. I know is very sad over your Phoenix, but most peoples they are just paying me to do the rescues and make good all their damages. Somes are easy, somes are very hard, but your Phoenix, for me she impossibles. So, you very *clever* man, and I very *busy* man. So now I must go to help with big yacht that is broken and sinked in the harbour here in Mahon. Adios Mister Chris, I am hopings for to be seeing you again one day soon, and also hopings for you to be having safe flight home."

"Gracias Pedro," I replied, "I can't exactly say its *all* been a pleasure, but hey, I couldn't have done it without you, that much I know. So tell me, por favor, before I go, where exactly have you put the wreckage of the Phoenix? Can I go take one final look at her please?"

"Si, si, no problemo mi amigo. Your Phoenix she is now sit on old trailer over in yard by cranes, close to edges of water. You are knowing where we put old trailer? Is okay if you goes to see, yard is no closed. Just be carefuls of water, por favor, yard is having muchos of rubbish, and not many, how you say, protect by railings. Buena suerte Mister Chris, y adios."

We shook hands one final time, and I walked back to the car, whilst carefully trying to reset the knuckle joints in my right hand. I started the Peugeot, drove around to the other side of the harbour, parked up just outside the gin factory, and walked across the road into Pedro's cranage yard. Across to my left was *'Big Crane'*, and over to my right was *'Little Crane'*. Not that Little Crane was *little* by any stretch of the imagination! Parked in the long grass between Little Crane and the tall steel security fencing, was the old yard trailer, and there lay the Phoenix, sitting perfectly upright on top of the rusty old trailer. I stared across at her from a slight distance, looking directly at the front of her bow, and just for a moment she looked *exactly* the same as the day I'd first bought her all those years ago, some twelve hundred and fifty miles away from where she was now sat. I shut my eyes and pictured the scene in Uphill. I opened them again, and yep, pretty much *identical!* If I hadn't known better, I'd've said there and then, *'Yes please, I'll take her'.* But I *did* know better. *Much better!* I walked across through the long grass, and all around her for one final time. Clearly, upon closer inspection, sadly *no one* would have bought her. I peered through the gaping hole in her port-side hull at her little Ford Diesel engine, that sat twisted and askew across the broken flooring in the aft deck, and resigned myself to the fact that, unfortunately, she was fit solely for the skip. I stood on the frame of the trailer, reached up, and gently kissed the centre of her prow. *'Farewell old friend, and once again, my sincere apologies!'* I jumped back down, turned my back on her one last time, and strolled purposefully back to the car. For the past ten days I'd felt entirely as if I'd been living in a dreamworld. Now it was time to go pack up my kit, and prepare for the flight back to reality.

Friday the 10th. Peanut butter sandwiches for breakfast again. I *hated* wasting food, although sometimes I guess there's little in the way of choice. I finished most of the milk via three strong cups of coffee, then binned any remaining perishables. I placed the three convector heaters neatly back in the wardrobe, folded the sleeping bags back up on top of it, and briefly ran the vacuum around the whole apartment. I shuttered the windows, flicked the main electricity trip switch to *'OFF',* locked the front door, and carried my bags to the car. *'Adios Tamarindos, hasta la proxima!'* I then drove to the airport, handed the keys back to the hire car office, checked in my bag, and one hour, one coffee and two croissants later, boarded the 11am Iberia flight to Madrid. Later that afternoon I boarded my pre-booked EasyJet flight back to Bristol, satisfied passport control upon landing, retrieved my baggage from the sparsely-loaded carousel, walked across to my old Shogun located in long-stay parking, and drove back to Fishponds. As I pulled into the front drive of our little 3-bed semi, Helen stepped out of the front door to greet me. I threw my arms around her, and gave her the biggest hug I'd given her since our wedding day. Once again a tear began to roll down one cheek, that one alone setting Helen off too.

"Come on sweetheart," I said, my voice full of emotion, "it was a successful mission, I achieved precisely what I set out to achieve, let's go down the pub and celebrate."

"I don't think *celebrate* is the right word exactly," Helen replied, sniffling a little whilst drying her eyes. "Let's just go down the pub and get drunk!"

"Damned good idea," I agreed enthusiastically. "What could *POSSIBLY* go wrong?!!?"

I spent the Saturday morning sorting out my dirty laundry, packing another overnight bag ready for my *hopefully very brief* trip to Holland, and filling Helen in on some of the finer details from the previous ten days. We'd both agreed, there and then, that we simply needed to put the whole episode down to just one of those unfortunate experiences that life tends to throw at you every now and again, leave it all behind us, and move on with our lives. *'Onwards and upwards!'* I'd declared positively. Saturday afternoon I drove over to Michelle's, and spent the next few hours going through work stuff. *Thankfully* she had *everything* completely under control, although by the looks of it the strain was beginning to show just a tad.

"I just don't know how you manage it dad," she exclaimed, "running all these jobs from here to Timbuktu, all at the same time; its a complete bloody nightmare sometimes!"

"I'm beginning to get used to nightmares these days sweetheart," I replied knowingly. "Anyway babygirl, I'll tell you *exactly* how I manage it. There's only *one* way I cope with this business, and that's simply because of *you!* If you weren't here to help run it with me, then I can assure you I *wouldn't* cope, its as simple as that."

We gave each other a *huge* hug, then she filled me in on the progress of the Center Parcs job in Holland. Everything had gone exceedingly well.

Two of the fitters had completed their roles and driven back Thursday afternoon, Barry and Roland had stayed on to finish up some minor snagging issues and driven back late last night, and Dominic was *extremely* happy, and looking forward to seeing me tomorrow evening in order that we could hand the job over first thing Monday morning. I swapped cars again with Michelle, electing once again to drive her fast little Merc over to Eindhoven, and I kissed her on the cheek, said goodbye, and drove back home. Later that evening I took Helen out to a beautiful little oldie worldie country pub, with a thatched roof and a huge open log fire, and we enjoyed a perfect Chateaubriand for two together by romantic candlelight.

The following morning I showered, and dressed *'smart but casual'*. My wonderful wife and I sat in the kitchen and ate breakfast together, following which I kissed her goodbye, threw my overnight bag into the boot of Michelle's little car, and set off, once again via the Chunnel, towards Kempervennen. Seven hours later, after clearing CP's security gate, I pulled up outside Dom's *contractor's* villa. Dom stepped outside to greet me, and warmly shook my hand, congratulating me on yet another *'refurb and upgrade'* job extremely well done. I informed him that the majority of it had been overseen by my highly capable daughter Michelle, but didn't elaborate further as to my own precise whereabouts throughout. He asked me to pass on his gratitude to her too, for her superb efforts in completing a job well done. We walked the Parc together, inspecting and discussing in detail each and every aspect of both our's and the other sub-contractor's installations, and jointly came to the conclusion that the overall effect was indeed tremendously impressive. *High fives all round,* we both agreed.

"Let's just hope that CP's management team are in full agreement with us tomorrow morning." Dom stated a little nervously.

"I know there's a huge amount of money riding on the result of this overall project Dom," I replied to him with an air of confidence, "but frankly I can't see that you've got anything to worry about. In fact, I'd go as far as to say that what's been achieved on this particular CP install, in my humble opinion, is basically *above and beyond the call of duty!* For what its worth."

"Well thank you Mister Reason. In actual fact that's worth a lot! I just hope the bosses agree with you!"

Dom showed me to my own private bedroom, and after grabbing my bag from the car I turned in for the night. The following morning, at 8am *sharp,* I found myself standing alongside two other smartly-dressed sub-contractors. The three of us stood just behind Dom whilst he shook hands with four of CP's top brass. Once again we walked the Parc, this time all eight of us, instead of just Dom and I, the three of us subbies following along silently and obediently behind Dom, whilst he answered a barrage of questions thrown at him from all angles by every one of the CP management team. The whole process took roughly an hour, at the end of which the bosses *appeared* to be nodding their heads in acceptance, and Dom shook hands once again with all four of them. After the four bosses had left, Dom turned to the three of us and proudly announced,

"*PROJECT APPROVED!* Congratulations on a job well done chaps. All good, everyone's happy, so very soon we *all* get paid! *Good stuff!* So, you all know the score. Invoices in to me at *under budget* please, within the next seven days. Thank you all kindly for your attendance, there are no further snagging issues to take care of, so on that basis we're all free to drive off home. Oh, just one other thing before you all leave; I thought I'd best give you all fair warning. The next CP project begins in eight weeks time! Elveden Forest, which, for a change, *is in the bloody UK! Hoorah!*"

We all cheered, and shouted *'well done'* to each other, there was much patting of backs and shaking of hands all round, and a heartfelt round of applause for Dominic and his professional project management skills. I thanked him personally, particularly for the profitability of the work that he continued to put our way, told him that we'd all be very much looking forward to the next one, then grabbed my overnight bag out of my room. I threw it back in the boot of the little Mercedes and drove back home to Bristol with my head held high. *'So you see Chris,'* I casually muttered to myself somewhere halfway along the northern coast of Belgium, *'things CAN go right sometimes!'*

The following day I decided to go in to work just a little later than usual, probably around mid-morning, as I had some tidying up to do, as well as some of my own personal paperwork to go through. Helen had left for work early, as per usual, and I'd made myself a coffee, boiled a couple of eggs, burnt a couple of slices of toast, and sat at the kitchen table with crumbs and papers strewn all around me. An hour or so later I heard the letterbox clang as the postman dropped in the mail. I picked it up from the floor in the hallway, and wandered back into the kitchen. Two for Helen, one for me. 'She *always* gets more than me!' I thought to myself. But there again, most of mine *did* go to work rather than home. I left hers on the side, and stared at the face of the envelope addressed to me. *'Strange!'* I remember thinking. *'Its got RAC written across the front in large blue letters, what on earth can it be?'* I tore open the envelope, removed the contents, and laid it out flat on the table in front of me. It was an invoice. *A bloody invoice!*

To: Manned emergency commercial recovery services upon request :-

Call-out to Foden transporter from Abbeville, France – £488.70

Call-out to Foden transporter from Montpellier, France – £1,098.64

Total outstanding £1,587.34 (Payment required within 30 days. Thank you for your custom)

Epilogue

I knew I had an EasyJet flight to Mahon booked and paid for on April the 1st, but I didn't bother showing up for it. I didn't bother telling them either, so April Fool's on them. Ha ha, *but not really very funny!* I had no reason to return to Menorca at that particular time, especially on my own. More importantly though, and more than just subconsciously too, I felt that I had a considerable loss to make up for somehow, and the best way to do that was simply to keep my head down and work. *Work, work, work!* And so I did, I just carried on working. The overall loss, to be fair, I'd considered to be considerably more than *considerable!* Realistically, in my eyes, it was simply *unacceptable!* Overall I'd guessed at somewhere in the region of £20K. *Twenty thousand sodding quid!* Seriously, I could ill afford that level of wastage in my life, and although I'd felt at the time like it was going to take a month of Sundays to make up for it, all I could think of to remedy the situation, and realistically all I ever actually *knew,* was simply to keep my nose to the grindstone. So I worked and I worked and I worked. And then, all of a sudden, I landed a new contract. Refurbishing and re-branding a large proportion of Nat West and RBS banks throughout the UK and associated dependencies. So that meant visits to not only most towns and cities across both England and Wales, but also to Jersey, Guernsey, the Isle of Wight, Isle of Man and Gibraltar. *'Gib should be a good'un,'* I immediately thought to myself. *'We've got friends living over there, let's see how we can work this one to our advantage then, IF the opportunity presents itself!'* And a few weeks later, present itself the opportunity most *certainly* did! During the first week of May I drove to Thetford in Norfolk to meet Dominic once again, whereupon we surveyed together, and budgeted for, the next forthcoming refurb and upgrade to a variety of areas throughout Center Parcs in Elveden Forest. Following which, not long after costing the job, receiving the purchase order, and subsequently getting production underway, I took a call from my new client, a large UK-based interiors company, asking me to programme in a survey visit to all three appointed branches in Gibraltar at my earliest available opportunity. *'Well hey, Mister Chrissy-boy, maybe it wasn't gonna take a month of Sundays after all!'* After completing the board the following Friday, as always with Michelle and Dave's *essential* input and assistance, I whistled a merry little tune to myself on the way home from the office that evening. *'We're leavin', on a jet plane, don't know when we'll be back again. Leavin', on a jet plane...*

"Hi honey, I'm home!" I called out cheerfully as I walked in through the front door.

"Just getting changed babe," Helen shouted down from upstairs, "I'll be down in a mo."

I strolled into the kitchen and poured myself a tall spiced rum and ginger ale over crushed ice, knocked up a similar mix for Helen with infused gin and elderflower tonic, then stuck Hotel California quietly on the stereo in the lounge, in an attempt to rid myself of my newly acquired earworm. Helen ambled into the lounge a few minutes later, dressed in tracky bottoms and a baggy sweatshirt, and I handed her the G&T and asked her if she'd had a good day at work,

"Pretty average for a Friday, as ever," she replied in a dull monotone. "In fact, probably slightly below average, if I'm honest. I guess the word *mundane* would suit better. How was yours?"

"Well, as it so happens..." I began, as we both took up our usual comfy positions on our respective sofas.

I told her that I'd received the go-ahead from Dom for CP Elveden, with handover scheduled for the beginning of the second week in July. I then began explaining to her some of the more detailed technical specs required for the new NW and RBS roll-out project, such as bomb-blast safety film, manifestation and signage replacement, etc, etc. Following her second yawn, once I'd deliberately and successfully managed to bore her out of her wits, I looked her straight in the eye, and with a cheeky little grin I suggested,

"So honey, I know you've got a week off work coming up very soon, and I know we'd both planned to go over to Menorca together, but right now I'm still feeling a little sad and disillusioned with Fornells. So what say, just for a change, we go spend the week with Sam and Sarah instead?"

"WHAT??" she snapped at me in surprise. *"In Portishead??"*

"No, dafty," I said reassuringly. *"In Gibraltar!"*

"Oh God, yeah, I'd forgotten they'd moved over there after the wedding," she remembered suddenly. "Wow, that would *certainly* make a nice change, I've never been to Gibraltar before. But why babe? Why the sudden change of plan? And why Gibraltar? We were out with Sam and Sarah in Bristol not long ago anyway. Why the change of heart exactly? Surely the loss of the Phoenix hasn't affected you *that* badly? I mean, not to the point of never wanting to go to Menorca ever again? *Surely?* Please tell me that's not the case? *Please!!"*

"No, don't panic sweetie," I replied, in an attempt to sooth her concern. "Yes, losing the Phoenix *has* affected my perception of Menorca, in fact probably most of the rest of the Med too, if I'm honest. And yes, realistically I suppose, to a fairly dramatic degree. But certainly not to the point of never wanting to go there ever again. No babe, not even close. In fact, come the school summer holidays, like I've already promised everyone, we're gonna take Tori and Alex over to Tamarindos for the second two weeks of July, and there sure as hell ain't nothing gonna change that. The loss of the Phoenix is my problem, and mine alone. I'll deal with it in my own way, and in my own good time, but I certainly won't let it affect the rest of the family in any way whatsoever, so don't you go worrying yaself about that one."

"Okay," she said, relaxing once again. "So why Gibraltar?"

"Well, you know me babe," I continued with my suggested plan of action. "Never one to miss an opportunity to kill two birds with one stone exactly, am I? So, the first Nat West project has just come through, and guess where? Yep, you've got it in one. *Gib!* So are we on? Can we make it a kind of a working holiday, please? Three branches, probably just a couple of hours at each, one a day, what d'ya reckon? I mean, I've gotta go anyway, so financially this just kinda makes sense. So shall we?"

"Okay," she replied cheerfully, "Gibraltar it is then. Watch out Sam and Sarah, *here we come!"*

Great! That put my mind at rest. Finally, all being well, I had the opportunity to maybe make a small *profit* out of going somewhere on holiday. Certainly not an opportunity to be sniffed at, that was for sure. I immediately set the wheels in motion. Drive to Heathrow and fly BA direct to Gib? Or fly EasyJet Bristol to Malaga, hire a car and drive to Gib? The travelling distances were almost identical, but I opted for the second option on the basis of it being *significantly* less in cost. So, fly/drive we did, and checked into a small cheap hotel, oddly enough called The Bristol, the majority of the cost of which was going to be covered by the main contractor that I was working for at the time. Sam and Sarah were *extremely* pleased to see us, and on top of successfully completing my three extensive surveys, a *very, VERY* jolly time was had by one and all. One week of glorious sunshine, far too many Barbary Apes, and way too many John Collins cocktails later, we hugged, kissed and bade fond farewells all round with our two dearly beloved friends, drove back to Malaga, and took the return EasyJet flight back home. *Now that's what I call a successful trip!!*

Then back to the grindstone! Survey, manufacture, install. Survey, manufacture, install. Ad infinitum. *Still to this very day in fact!* But it was going well. Actually, *very well indeed!* How ironically the way things turn out sometimes. On a personal level, I'd had probably one of the worst starts to a year ever! On a business level, the company was having probably one of its best starts to any year ever! Still, '*don't question it Chris, just go with the flow!'* And flow it most certainly did! By the end of May everything had been produced and packaged in preparation for the CP Elveden project. And by the end of the first week in July the installation had been successfully completed. Early the following Monday morning I'd driven to Thetford in order to meet up with Dom, and get the job signed off in the usual manor and yet again. *Tick!* In the meantime, all products required for NW Gib were in the process of being either manufactured or outsourced, although once again it was looking very much like I'd be absent from work whilst that particular installation was being carried out. Roland and Giles had been tasked with that specific project, both of them already having vast experience in installing the diversity of products specified within the contract. *Hence one of the reasons why we'd won the contract in the first instance!* Having briefed them both exhaustively on every individual aspect down to the minutest detail, both Michelle and I felt one hundred percent confident in their honesty, their conscientious reliability, as well as their ability to perform under the demanding pressures of ever-tightening completion dates. As it turned out, thankfully we were right to trust our instincts. Yet another job ticked off! First class performance, on time, every time. *Well done R&G!! Channel Isles next please!!* Meantime, back on the *Reason Ranch,* schools were out, and both Helen and I were devoting more and more time to Tori and Alex, whilst at the same time preparing for our forthcoming fortnight family holiday back in sunny Menorca.

I'd booked EasyJet flights for the four of us on the second Saturday in mid-July, returning two weeks later on the last Saturday of the month. Bristol to Mahon returns, times four during the school summer holidays, £960 in total. Pretty damned reasonable I'd thought at the time. Not that this particular holiday was about money. It was purely about relaxing and enjoying ourselves, just like we'd *always* done. Alex was ten years old by then, and both he and Tori were becoming increasingly more excited by the day, the closer we got to our departure date. Tori considerably more so than Alex, despite her *dreadfully* irrational fear of flying, on account of the fact that it was her twelveth birthday on the 28th of July. So we'd all be celebrating that together whilst we were over there, two days before we were due to fly home. Little did she know, but I'd already booked a table for the evening in her *'very favouritest restaurant in the whole wide world!'* Then suddenly, before we even knew it, there it was. The Saturday was upon us, and up to Bristol Airport we all trapsed, baggage in hand, leaving the old Shogun once again in long-term parking. Following significant comforting of Tori's jangling nerves, by dragging her around every available toy and sweet shop throughout airport departures, we eventually took our seats on the Airbus A319 for the two hour shorthaul flight to Mahon. Or *'The Easier Route Du Soleil'*, as I'd begun referring to it as by then. Tori ceased panicking once we reached altitude, and remained calm for the whole duration of the entirely uneventful and turbulence-free flight. Upon landing at Mahon we stepped off the plane into beautiful, cloudless blue skies, and a rather gorgeous thirty-three degrees of sunshine. *Just what the doctor ordered!* We collected a family hatchback from Autos Victoria just outside the airport, and drove immediately to Tamarindos, stopping briefly along the way at a little shop in Fornells to pick up some basic essentials, such as milk, bacon, eggs, cheese and water, etc. As we'd passed the Repsol fuel station along the way, it was good to see that they'd managed to get it open again, having successfully reinstated the canopy above the pumps, and cleared away the huge piles of debris. I pulled the hire car into the car park in front of our little apartment, and the kids jumped straight out and ran off excitedly to go play around the pool, and down by the sea on our very own little pebbly beach, leaving Helen and I to unlock, carry in the baggage, and sort through the clothing, packing everything neatly away into the appropriate drawers and wardrobes. The minute we'd finished unpacking, both Tori and Alex suddenly reappeared and demanded their swimming cossies, as they both wanted to go jump in the pool. I pulled them from their top drawers, threw one to each of them, then pulled a pair of colourful lilos out from a cupboard, blew each of them up, carried them down to the pool, and threw them in. Tori and Alex were in their element. The water was warm, the weather was hot, the sun was shining, and before we knew it both Helen and I were throwing ourselves into the pool too. *Our own little piece of family bliss!*

We spent the next fortnight simply doing what we'd always done in Menorca, relaxing in the sunshine and having a laugh together. We spent days at some of our all time favourite beaches, such as Cala en Porter and Cala Galdana, sunbathing, snorkelling and playing ball. We walked out to the Cap de Cavalleria lighthouse, where the sea was as calm as I'd ever seen it, and we climbed to the monastery at the top of Monte Toro, where from Menorca's very highest point you could *almost* see from one end of the island to the other. We drove into Ciutadella, on Menorca's far western shores, and spent the day sightseeing, buying little trinkets in the pretty little touristy stores along the way, and on the Saturday of our first weekend there we visited Mahon's street markets, let the kids go pony riding around the old square, and walked around the walled city for a while, marvelling yet again at its wonderful architecture. We then drove down to Es Castell, where I'd booked a table at Dinkums for the evening. The following day, I left Helen and the kids playing together in and around our own pool, and drove down to the harbourside in Mahon on my own. I parked up alongside the gin factory, and walked across the road into Pedro's yard, where the two giant static cranes stood alongside the quay wall. To my left stood Big Crane, and over to my right, still laying there amongst the tall straggly grass inbetween Little Crane and the security fence, was my poor old Phoenix, sitting upright on her scruffy old yard trailer, looking entirely lost and forlorn. I took a steady wander through the grass, and gave her a very brief once-over. Nothing appeared to have changed, she was still my same sad old girl that I'd once devoted so much time and energy to. No difference. Until, that was, I peered inside her through the huge hole in her hull. Her engine and gearbox were no longer there. They'd were gone. *'Hmmm...' I thought to myself!*

During the short drive back to Fornells I simply told myself to get over it. *'Let it go mate, she ain't your old girl any longer!'* So I did; I dropped all thoughts of the Phoenix from my mind entirely, and concentrated once again on simply entertaining my family and having fun. *I'd had to go take a look though, I simply couldn't help myself!*

Helen had made lunch for herself and the kids when I got back to Tamarindos, but I'd said that I wasn't particularly hungry, and took myself off for a long swim in the sea from our own little pebbly beach, just down passed the pool. Later that afternoon we drove into Mercadal to do a little more grocery shopping, then ate out on the front terrace of The Windmill just as it was beginning to get dark.

For Tori's birthday on the 28th we drove to Son Bou, and spent the morning playing on the beach, *well away from the nudist area at the very far end,* and swimming in the warm calm sea. I'd even bought Alex a little kiddies polystyrene surfboard, so that he could go play with the waves, which were only all of six inches high, but he'd had great fun with it anyway. We spent the afternoon looking around Son Bou's fascinating little gift shops, buying more little trinkets and holiday T-shirts. Tori found a beautiful little necklace in a jewellery store that she fell in love with. It was a colourful round Mandala stone, encased in silver with a black leather cord. She begged and pleaded with me to buy it for her, which, seeing as it was her birthday, naturally I did. The fact was, I would've bought it for her *anyway,* but I never let on to that. She fell in love with it the minute I tied it securely around her neck. Later that evening the four of us walked into Tori's *'very favouritest restaurant in the whole wide world',* Son Bou's famous Hawaiian Bar, where I'd already pre-booked a table. Both kids jumped up into one of the bamboo double-cushioned basket-style seats, that were hanging suspended from the roof joists by strong metal chains, and swung there gently whilst sucking lavishly adorned fruit mocktails through colourful four foot long plastic straws. The food wasn't exactly first class, but the setting, surrounded by wicker peacock chairs, vases full of ornate feathers, and tame parrots and cockatiels screeching noisily from giant bamboo cages, was really quite stunning, and the atmosphere was simply electric. One of the things that Tori loved the most was the fact that all the young girl waitresses wore rollerblades, and swished around the place at high speed, snatching up empty glasses and replacing them with full ones as they passed by, often before you'd even asked! We all sat, and swung, and greatly enjoyed our meals, listening to the sounds of an old Spanish guy sat on a high stool over in the far corner, playing guitar, and attempting to sing Hawaiian-ish-type songs. It was one of those *most* memorable evenings that not one of us will ever forget, regardless of the fact that we've returned many times since.

The following day, the last full day of our wonderfully sunny fun-filled fortnight, after an early home cooked English breakfast, I packed towels and clean clothes into a couple of beach bags, and the four of us set off along the rocky little coastal path towards Fornells Town, the kids dressed in just their swimming cossies, whilst wearing tough-soled water shoes. Around halfway there we stopped off at our usual little inlet for a swim in the sea. Tori picked her way carefully across the rocks, and gradually lowered herself into the water. Once she'd just about reached waist depth, entirely predictably I might add, Alex threw himself bodily from the top of the highest rock he could find, splashing into the water right in front of her, and soaking her from head to waist. She immediately screamed abuse at him, but it went completely unnoticed, he was somewhere deep down in the depths by then. I literally laughed my socks off, then threw off my T-shirt too, dived in and joined them. Helen sat on top of a rock at the water's edge, merrily snapping off photos with my little Olympus, whilst Tori swam around the surface, trying her best not to get her long flowing locks *too* badly drenched, and Alex and I dived for shells deep down on the sandy bottom. *Happy times indeed!* After drying ourselves off sometime later we continued on our way along the little rocky path into Fornells Town. Upon reaching the harbour we walked across to the top of the slipway. The first thing I noticed was that the harbour itself had been completely cleared of all debris. It appeared to be just as tidy and pretty as it had ever looked, and thankfully for us the toilet block had been fully reinstated. We used it to change into more suitable clothing, then walked across to the near end of the quayside. The fuel pontoon and the visitor's pontoons had all been replaced. *Good work Pedro!* Although sadly, the roof was still missing from the Restaurant Es Pla, which looked very much like it would remain closed for the remainder of that particular season. Other than that, Fornells Town was its normal, pretty, thriving, buzzing, gorgeous self, no different to the way we'd always known it during any other summer, and the long row of safely moored white painted fishing boats still sat there, proudly bobbing around, all looking as pristine as ever. We crossed the road that ran along the harbourside waterfront together, and began to read some of the menu boards located at the entrances to each of the long row of high-quality fish restaurants with steadily increasing interest. Eventually we settled on one that appeared to cater well for adults and children alike. I was pretty sure we'd all eaten in that particular one at some point previously anyway! We took our seats together, underneath a pretty little yellow and white striped sun parasol, at a table for four on the front sun terrace. A waiter came over immediately, and I ordered a large jug of sangria for Helen and myself, a Fanta naranja for Tori, and a coke for Alex. A few minutes later the drinks arrived, along with a small dish of olives and some bread. Helen and I sat there picking at the olives, savouring the sangria, and just people watching, whilst simply soaking up both the sunshine and the atmosphere. Needless to say both Tori and Alex necked their drinks in short shrift, then asked if they could please go buy ice-creams from the little van parked along the other end of the harbourside waterfront. I said they could, gave them a couple of euros each, and told them both, in no uncertain terms, to *mind the road, and stay well away from the water's edge!* Both of which I knew full well they'd sensibly comply with. Although I must admit, whilst Helen began looking through the menu with ever growing interest at the various assorted lobster dishes on offer, I simply kept my eyes on the kids. They were both good kids however, and I just sat and watched whilst they simply paid for their ice-creams, then ambled back slowly along the waterfront together, eagerly devouring them as they went. They both walked a little way beyond where we were sitting, then mingled in with a small crowd of tourists, with young children in pushchairs, who were throwing pieces of bread into the harbour to feed the fish, most of which were being stolen by a small flock of seagulls before the fish could even get anywhere near them. A few minutes later, after finishing their ice-creams, the kids crossed back over the road, and wandered back to our table. Alex sat down, and started looking at the kiddies section on one of the menus, but Tori turned to me excitedly and exclaimed,

"dad, dad, I've found something *really interesting!* Come take a look with me, *please?"*

"Okay, okay," I replied, standing up and grabbing a hold of her hand, "What is it my love? What have you found that's so interesting exactly? Over by the harbour is it? Come along then babygirl, let's go take a look-see."

I kept a tight hold of Tori's hand whilst she led me back across the road towards the harbour, despite the road generally being traffic-free anyway. She tugged enthusiastically at my arm, leading me back around to the place where, a few moments earlier, the other folks with their kids had been trying their best to feed the fish in the harbour. Tori stood in the centre of the walkway with her back to the water, and tugged gently at my arm again, pointing excitedly directly ahead of her. Fastened securely to the rustic black railings that ran along the right-hand end of the quayside, inbetween the walkway and the car park, was a large wooden notice board, with an assortment of colourful posters and adverts pinned all over it.

"Look dad, look at what that one says," Tori exclaimed, her eyes lighting up as she turned her pretty little face towards me. "Can we take one out sometime, *please?* Like, next time we come here, like half-term maybe? *Please dad, can we, please?"*

I stared closely at the specific poster that had so very obviously caught Tori's eye.

MOTORISED FOUR-PERSON FISHING BOATS FOR HIRE – SELF-DRIVE AROUND FORNELLS BAY

ONLY €15 PER HOUR OR €60 PER DAY – FUEL INCLUDED – JUST CALL AND ASK FOR MANUEL

'Hmmm . . .' I thought to myself!

Acknowledgements

Commercial

Bristol Marina. Euro Tunnel. EasyJet. RAC European Assistance. Autos Victoria. Menorca-Sun. Iberia Airways. Trasmediterranea Ferrys. Artistic Blinds. The Set Connection. Pedro's Boat Centre.

Personal

Martin Brown, for his constant patience in helping me to correctly format *Word*.

Lizzie Barrett, for a significant amount of editing and proof-reading.

Mandy Smith, Brian and Rita, for a most welcome and entirely unforgettable Christmas.

My father John Reason, for giving me the inspiration and courage to tackle life's adventures.

My daughter Michelle, for holding and managing the fort with such ability and professionalism.

My daughter Tori, for stating the bleeding obvious right at the end instead of before I started.

My son Alex, despite being only nine years old, for being there when I needed him the most.

And lastly, an extra special massive *THANK YOU* to my long-suffering but wonderful wife Helen, for her help, patience and tolerance during the majority of my crazy escapades, and her willingness to share her company with me, not only throughout them, but also throughout the rest of my life.

Author's Note

I was *told* to write a book, by a great many people. Not least of whom were my GP, various medical consultants, my physiotherapist, my solicitor, my accountant, my mortgage advisor, my insurance broker, and by no means least my bank manager! So here it is, *The Phoenix,* my very first attempt, and potentially the first in a series? Maybe I should just let you, *The Reader,* make that call for me!

I could certainly write a great deal more, I've definitely had more than my fair share of *Momentary Lapses of Reason;* albeit I'd endeavour to make the rest significantly shorter than this one! Nevertheless, I have a more than adequate repertoire of life's little mishaps over the years indelibly stamped deep within my memory, along with a seemingly new found urge to put pen to paper.

That aside, despite my tragically long list of life's mistakes and errors of judgement, the truthful fact still remains to this very day that I harbour only one single regret. That being, you may or may not be surprised to learn, the simple fact that I never got to see Freddie Mercury and Queen play live. Which just goes to show, our paths through life are all about learning, and not about regrets.

Very shortly after Freddie's tragic death I made a big point of attending my all time favourite band's best ever performance, namely Pink Floyd's awesome *Pulse* show at Earl's Court in 1992. The point I'm trying to make is that we should only ever live to regret something if we make the same mistake twice. Once is simply a learning curve. Twice is pure stupidity. And if you're smart enough to learn from other people's mistakes, then maybe you can go through life with no regrets whatsoever.

There are many lessons to be learned from the mistakes that I personally made that prompted me to pen this true story. I won't detail them, if you're clever enough you should easily be able to work them out for yourself. And when you have, hopefully, you'll manage to avoid making the same mistakes that I have. Which, in itself, makes the telling of my own story all the more worthwhile.

Anyway, if you happen to have enjoyed my very first effort, then please could you email a massive thumbs-up to my publisher. Or if you'd prefer that I stopped, well, just come and find me, snatch this damned pen out of my hand, and let me crack on with something entirely different instead.

Thank you.

EPILOGUE

I knew I had an EasyJet flight to Mahon booked and paid for on April the 1st, but I didn't bother showing up for it. I didn't bother telling them either, so April Fool's on them. Ha ha, *but not really very funny!* I had no reason to return to Menorca at that particular time, especially on my own. More importantly though, and more than just subconsciously too, I felt that I had a considerable loss to make up for somehow, and the best way to do that was simply to keep my head down and work. *Work, work, work!* And so I did, I just carried on working. The overall loss, to be fair, I'd considered to be considerably more than *considerable!* Realistically, in my eyes, it was simply *unacceptable!* Overall I'd guessed at somewhere in the region of £20K. *Twenty thousand sodding quid!* Seriously, I could ill afford that level of wastage in my life, and although I'd felt at the time like it was going to take a month of Sundays to make up for it, all I could think of to remedy the situation, and realistically all I ever actually *knew,* was simply to keep my nose to the grindstone. So I worked and I worked and I worked. And then, all of a sudden, I landed a new contract. Refurbishing and re-branding a large proportion of Nat West and RBS banks throughout the UK and associated dependencies. So that meant visits to not only most towns and cities across both England and Wales, but also to Jersey, Guernsey, the Isle of Wight, Isle of Man and Gibraltar. *'Gib should be a good'un,'* I immediately thought to myself. *'We've got friends living over there, let's see how we can work this one to our advantage then, IF the opportunity presents itself!'* And a few weeks later, present itself the opportunity most *certainly* did! During the first week of May I drove to Thetford in Norfolk to meet Dominic once again, whereupon we surveyed together, and budgeted for, the next forthcoming refurb and upgrade to a variety of areas throughout Center Parcs in Elveden Forest. Following which, not long after costing the job, receiving the purchase order, and subsequently getting production underway, I took a call from my new client, a large UK-based interiors company, asking me to programme in a survey visit to all three appointed branches in Gibraltar at my earliest available opportunity. *'Well hey, Mister Chrissy-boy, maybe it wasn't gonna take a month of Sundays after all!'* After completing the board the following Friday, as always with Michelle and Dave's *essential* input and assistance, I whistled a merry little tune to myself on the way home from the office that evening. *'We're leavin', on a jet plane, don't know when we'll be back again. Leavin', on a jet plane ...'*

"Hi honey, I'm home!" I called out cheerfully as I walked in through the front door.

"Just getting changed babe," Helen shouted down from upstairs, "I'll be down in a mo."

I strolled into the kitchen and poured myself a tall spiced rum and ginger ale over crushed ice, knocked up a similar mix for Helen with infused gin and elderflower tonic, then stuck Hotel California quietly on the stereo in the lounge, in an attempt to rid myself of my newly acquired earworm. Helen ambled into the lounge a few minutes later, dressed in tracky bottoms and a baggy sweatshirt, and I handed her the G&T and asked her if she'd had a good day at work,

"Pretty average for a Friday, as ever," she replied in a dull monotone. "In fact, probably slightly below average, if I'm honest. I guess the word *mundane* would suit better. How was yours?"

"Well, as it so happens ..." I began, as we both took up our usual comfy positions on our respective sofas.

I told her that I'd received the go-ahead from Dom for CP Elveden, with handover scheduled for the beginning of the second week in July. I then began explaining to her some of the more detailed technical specs required for the new NW and RBS roll-out project, such as bomb-blast safety film, manifestation and signage replacement, etc, etc. Following her second yawn, once I'd deliberately and successfully managed to bore her out of her wits, I looked her straight in the eye, and with a cheeky little grin I suggested,

"So honey, I know you've got a week off work coming up very soon, and I know we'd both planned to go over to Menorca together, but right now I'm still feeling a little sad and disillusioned with Fornells. So what say, just for a change, we go spend the week with Sam and Sarah instead?"

"WHAT??" she snapped at me in surprise. *"In Portishead??"*

"No, dafty," I said reassuringly. *"In Gibraltar!"*

"Oh God, yeah, I'd forgotten they'd moved over there after the wedding," she remembered suddenly. "Wow, that would *certainly* make a nice change, I've never been to Gibraltar before. But why babe? Why the sudden change of plan? And why Gibraltar? We were out with Sam and Sarah in Bristol not long ago anyway. Why the change of heart exactly? Surely the loss of the Phoenix hasn't affected you *that* badly? I mean, not to the point of never wanting to go to Menorca ever again? *Surely?* Please tell me that's not the case? *Please!!*"

"No, don't panic sweetie," I replied, in an attempt to sooth her concern. "Yes, losing the Phoenix *has* affected my perception of Menorca, in fact probably most of the rest of the Med too, if I'm honest. And yes, realistically I suppose, to a fairly dramatic degree. But certainly not to the point of never wanting to go there ever again. No babe, not even close. In fact, come the school summer holidays, like I've already promised everyone, we're gonna take Tori and Alex over to Tamarindos for the second two weeks of July, and there sure as hell ain't nothing gonna change that. The loss of the Phoenix is my problem, and mine alone. I'll deal with it in my own way, and in my own good time, but I certainly won't let it affect the rest of the family in any way whatsoever, so don't you go worrying yaself about that one."

"Okay," she said, relaxing once again. "So why Gibraltar?"

"Well, you know me babe," I continued with my suggested plan of action. "Never one to miss an opportunity to kill two birds with one stone exactly, am I? So, the first Nat West project has just come through, and guess where? Yep, you've got it in one. *Gib!* So are we on? Can we make it a kind of a working holiday, please? Three branches, probably just a couple of hours at each, one a day, what d'ya reckon? I mean, I've gotta go anyway, so financially this just kinda makes sense. So shall we?"

"Okay," she replied cheerfully, "Gibraltar it is then. Watch out Sam and Sarah, *here we come!*"

Great! That put my mind at rest. Finally, all being well, I had the opportunity to maybe make a small *profit* out of going somewhere on holiday. Certainly not an opportunity to be sniffed at, that was for sure. I immediately set the wheels in motion. Drive to Heathrow and fly BA direct to Gib? Or fly EasyJet Bristol to Malaga, hire a car and drive to Gib? The travelling distances were almost identical, but I opted for the second option on the basis of it being *significantly* less in cost. So, fly/drive we did, and checked into a small cheap hotel, oddly enough called The Bristol, the majority of the cost of which was going to be covered by the main contractor that I was working for at the time. Sam and Sarah were *extremely* pleased to see us, and on top of successfully completing my three extensive surveys, a *very, VERY* jolly time was had by one and all. One week of glorious sunshine, far too many Barbary Apes, and way too many John Collins cocktails later, we hugged, kissed and bade fond farewells all round with our two dearly beloved friends, drove back to Malaga, and took the return EasyJet flight back home. *Now that's what I call a successful trip!!*

Then back to the grindstone! Survey, manufacture, install. Survey, manufacture, install. Ad infinitum. *Still to this very day in fact!* But it was going well. Actually, *very well indeed!* How ironically the way things turn out sometimes. On a personal level, I'd had probably one of the worst starts to a year ever! On a business level, the company was having probably one of its best starts to any year ever! Still, '*don't question it Chris, just go with the flow!*' And flow it most certainly did! By the end of May everything had been produced and packaged in preparation for the CP Elveden project. And by the end of the first week in July the installation had been successfully completed. Early the following Monday morning I'd driven to Thetford in order to meet up with Dom, and get the job signed off in the usual manor and yet again. *Tick!* In the meantime, all products required for NW Gib were in the process of being either manufactured or outsourced, although once again it was looking very much like I'd be absent from work whilst that particular installation was being carried out. Roland and Giles had been tasked with that specific project, both of them already having vast experience in installing the diversity of products specified within the contract. *Hence one of the reasons why we'd won the contract in the first instance!* Having briefed them both exhaustively on every individual aspect down to the minutest detail, both Michelle and I felt one hundred percent confident in their honesty, their conscientious reliability, as well as their ability to perform under the demanding pressures of ever-tightening completion dates. As it turned out, thankfully we were right to trust our instincts. Yet another job ticked off! First class performance, on time, every time. *Well done R&G!! Channel Isles next please!!* Meantime, back on the *Reason Ranch,* schools were out, and both Helen and I were devoting more and more time to Tori and Alex, whilst at the same time preparing for our forthcoming fortnight family holiday back in sunny Menorca.

I'd booked EasyJet flights for the four of us on the second Saturday in mid-July, returning two weeks later on the last Saturday of the month.

Bristol to Mahon returns, times four during the school summer holidays, £960 in total. Pretty damned reasonable I'd thought at the time. Not that this particular holiday was about money. It was purely about relaxing and enjoying ourselves, just like we'd *always* done. Alex was ten years old by then, and both he and Tori were becoming increasingly more excited by the day, the closer we got to our departure date. Tori considerably more so than Alex, despite her *dreadfully* irrational fear of flying, on account of the fact that it was her twelveth birthday on the 28th of July. So we'd all be celebrating that together whilst we were over there, two days before we were due to fly home. Little did she know, but I'd already booked a table for the evening in her *'very favouritest restaurant in the whole wide world!'* Then suddenly, before we even knew it, there it was. The Saturday was upon us, and up to Bristol Airport we all trapsed, baggage in hand, leaving the old Shogun once again in long-term parking. Following significant comforting of Tori's jangling nerves, by dragging her around every available toy and sweet shop throughout airport departures, we eventually took our seats on the Airbus A319 for the two hour shorthaul flight to Mahon. Or *'The Easier Route Du Soleil'*, as I'd begun referring to it as by then. Tori ceased panicking once we reached altitude, and remained calm for the whole duration of the entirely uneventful and turbulence-free flight. Upon landing at Mahon we stepped off the plane into beautiful, cloudless blue skies, and a rather gorgeous thirty-three degrees of sunshine. *Just what the doctor ordered!* We collected a family hatchback from Autos Victoria just outside the airport, and drove immediately to Tamarindos, stopping briefly along the way at a little shop in Fornells to pick up some basic essentials, such as milk, bacon, eggs, cheese and water, etc. As we'd passed the Repsol fuel station along the way, it was good to see that they'd managed to get it open again, having successfully reinstated the canopy above the pumps, and cleared away the huge piles of debris. I pulled the hire car into the car park in front of our little apartment, and the kids jumped straight out and ran off excitedly to go play around the pool, and down by the sea on our very own little pebbly beach, leaving Helen and I to unlock, carry in the baggage, and sort through the clothing, packing everything neatly away into the appropriate drawers and wardrobes. The minute we'd finished unpacking, both Tori and Alex suddenly reappeared and demanded their swimming cossies, as they both wanted to go jump in the pool. I pulled them from their top drawers, threw one to each of them, then pulled a pair of colourful lilos out from a cupboard, blew each of them up, carried them down to the pool, and threw them in. Tori and Alex were in their element. The water was warm, the weather was hot, the sun was shining, and before we knew it both Helen and I were throwing ourselves into the pool too. *Our own little piece of family bliss!*

We spent the next fortnight simply doing what we'd always done in Menorca, relaxing in the sunshine and having a laugh together. We spent days at some of our all time favourite beaches, such as Cala en Porter and Cala Galdana, sunbathing, snorkelling and playing ball. We walked out to the Cap de Cavalleria lighthouse, where the sea was as calm as I'd ever seen it, and we climbed to the monastery at the top of Monte Toro, where from Menorca's very highest point you could *almost* see from one end of the island to the other. We drove into Ciutadella, on Menorca's far western shores, and spent the day sightseeing, buying little trinkets in the pretty little touristy stores along the way, and on the Saturday of our first weekend there we visited Mahon's street markets, let the kids go pony riding around the old square, and walked around the walled city for a while, marvelling yet again at its wonderful architecture. We then drove down to Es Castell, where I'd booked a table at Dinkums for the evening. The following day, I left Helen and the kids playing together in and around our own pool, and drove down to the harbourside in Mahon on my own. I parked up alongside the gin factory, and walked across the road into Pedro's yard, where the two giant static cranes stood alongside the quay wall. To my left stood Big Crane, and over to my right, still laying there amongst the tall straggly grass inbetween Little Crane and the security fence, was my poor old Phoenix, sitting upright on her scruffy old yard trailer, looking entirely lost and forlorn. I took a steady wander through the grass, and gave her a very brief once-over. Nothing appeared to have changed, she was still my same sad old girl that I'd once devoted so much time and energy to. No difference. Until, that was, I peered inside her through the huge hole in her hull. Her engine and gearbox were no longer there. They'd were gone. *'Hmmm . . . I thought to myself!*

During the short drive back to Fornells I simply told myself to get over it. *'Let it go mate, she ain't your old girl any longer!'* So I did; I dropped all thoughts of the Phoenix from my mind entirely, and concentrated once again on simply entertaining my family and having fun. *I'd had to go take a look though, I simply couldn't help myself!*

Helen had made lunch for herself and the kids when I got back to Tamarindos, but I'd said that I wasn't particularly hungry, and took myself off for a long swim in the sea from our own little pebbly beach, just down passed the pool. Later that afternoon we drove into Mercadal to do a little more grocery shopping, then ate out on the front terrace of The Windmill just as it was beginning to get dark.

For Tori's birthday on the 28th we drove to Son Bou, and spent the morning playing on the beach, *well away from the nudist area at the very far end,* and swimming in the warm calm sea. I'd even bought Alex a little kiddies polystyrene surfboard, so that he could go play with the waves, which were only all of six inches high, but he'd had great fun with it anyway. We spent the afternoon looking around Son Bou's fascinating little gift shops, buying more little trinkets and holiday T-shirts. Tori found a beautiful little necklace in a jewellery store that she fell in love with. It was a colourful round Mandala stone, encased in silver with a black leather cord. She begged and pleaded with me to buy it for her, which, seeing as it was her birthday, naturally I did. The fact was, I would've bought it for her *anyway,* but I never let on to that. She fell in love with it the minute I tied it securely around her neck. Later that evening the four of us walked into Tori's *'very favouritest restaurant in the whole wide world',* Son Bou's famous Hawaiian Bar, where I'd already pre-booked a table. Both kids jumped up into one of the bamboo double-cushioned basket-style seats, that were hanging suspended from the roof joists by strong metal chains, and swung there gently whilst sucking lavishly adorned fruit mocktails through colourful four foot long plastic straws. The food wasn't exactly first class, but the setting, surrounded by wicker peacock chairs, vases full of ornate feathers, and tame parrots and cockatiels screeching noisily from giant bamboo cages, was really quite stunning, and the atmosphere was simply electric. One of the things that Tori loved the most was the fact that all the young girl waitresses wore rollerblades, and swished around the place at high speed, snatching up empty glasses and replacing them with full ones as they passed by, often before you'd even asked! We all sat, and swung, and greatly enjoyed our meals, listening to the sounds of an old Spanish guy sat on a high stool over in the far corner, playing guitar, and attempting to sing Hawaiian-ish-type songs. It was one of those *most* memorable evenings that not one of us will ever forget, regardless of the fact that we've returned many times since.

The following day, the last full day of our wonderfully sunny fun-filled fortnight, after an early home cooked English breakfast, I packed towels and clean clothes into a couple of beach bags, and the four of us set off along the rocky little coastal path towards Fornells Town, the kids dressed in just their swimming cossies, whilst wearing tough-soled water shoes. Around halfway there we stopped off at our usual little inlet for a swim in the sea. Tori picked her way carefully across the rocks, and gradually lowered herself into the water. Once she'd just about reached waist depth, entirely predictably I might add, Alex threw himself bodily from the top of the highest rock he could find, splashing into the water right in front of her, and soaking her from head to waist. She immediately screamed abuse at him, but it went completely unnoticed, he was somewhere deep down in the depths by then. I literally laughed my socks off, then threw off my T-shirt too, dived in and joined them. Helen sat on top of a rock at the water's edge, merrily snapping off photos with my little Olympus, whilst Tori swam around the surface, trying her best not to get her long flowing locks *too* badly drenched, and Alex and I dived for shells deep down on the sandy bottom. *Happy times indeed!* After drying ourselves off sometime later we continued on our way along the little rocky path into Fornells Town. Upon reaching the harbour we walked across to the top of the slipway. The first thing I noticed was that the harbour itself had been completely cleared of all debris. It appeared to be just as tidy and pretty as it had ever looked, and thankfully for us the toilet block had been fully reinstated. We used it to change into more suitable clothing, then walked across to the near end of the quayside. The fuel pontoon and the visitor's pontoons had all been replaced. *Good work Pedro!* Although sadly, the roof was still missing from the Restaurant Es Pla, which looked very much like it would remain closed for the remainder of that particular season. Other than that, Fornells Town was its normal, pretty, thriving, buzzing, gorgeous self, no different to the way we'd always known it during any other summer, and the long row of safely moored white painted fishing boats still sat there, proudly bobbing around, all looking as pristine as ever. We crossed the road that ran along the harbourside waterfront together, and began to read some of the menu boards located at the entrances to each of the long row of high-quality fish restaurants with steadily increasing interest. Eventually we settled on one that appeared to cater well for adults and children alike. I was pretty sure we'd all eaten in that particular one at some point previously anyway! We took our seats together, underneath a pretty little yellow and white striped sun parasol, at a table for four on the front sun terrace. A waiter came over immediately, and I ordered a large jug of sangria for Helen and myself, a Fanta naranja for Tori, and a coke for Alex. A few minutes later the drinks arrived, along with a small dish of olives and some bread. Helen and I sat there picking at the olives, savouring the sangria, and just people watching, whilst simply soaking up both the sunshine and the atmosphere. Needless to say both Tori and Alex necked their drinks in short shrift, then asked if they could please go buy ice-creams from the little van parked along the other end of the harbourside waterfront. I said they could, gave them a couple of euros each, and told them both, in no uncertain terms, to *mind the road, and stay well away from the water's edge!* Both of which I knew full well they'd sensibly comply with. Although I must admit, whilst Helen began looking through the menu with ever growing interest at the various assorted lobster dishes on offer, I simply kept my eyes on the kids. They were both good kids however, and I just sat and watched whilst they simply paid for their ice-creams, then ambled back slowly along the waterfront together, eagerly devouring them as they went. They both walked a little way beyond where we were sitting, then mingled in with a small crowd of tourists, with young children in pushchairs, who were throwing pieces of bread into the harbour to feed the fish, most of which were being stolen by a small flock of seagulls before the fish could even get anywhere near them. A few minutes later, after finishing their ice-creams, the kids crossed back over the road, and wandered back to our table. Alex sat down, and started looking at the kiddies section on one of the menus, but Tori turned to me excitedly and exclaimed,

"dad, dad, I've found something *really interesting!* Come take a look with me, *please?*"

"Okay, okay," I replied, standing up and grabbing a hold of her hand, "What is it my love? What have you found that's so interesting exactly? Over by the harbour is it? Come along then babygirl, let's go take a look-see."

I kept a tight hold of Tori's hand whilst she led me back across the road towards the harbour, despite the road generally being traffic-free anyway. She tugged enthusiastically at my arm, leading me back around to the place where, a few moments earlier, the other folks with their kids had been trying their best to feed the fish in the harbour. Tori stood in the centre of the walkway with her back to the water, and tugged gently at my arm again, pointing excitedly directly ahead of her. Fastened securely to the rustic black railings that ran along the right-hand end of the quayside, inbetween the walkway and the car park, was a large wooden notice board, with an assortment of colourful posters and adverts pinned all over it.

"Look dad, look at what that one says," Tori exclaimed, her eyes lighting up as she turned her pretty little face towards me. "Can we take one out sometime, *please?* Like, next time we come here, like half-term maybe? *Please dad, can we, please?"*

I stared closely at the specific poster that had so very obviously caught Tori's eye.

MOTORISED FOUR-PERSON FISHING BOATS FOR HIRE – SELF-DRIVE AROUND FORNELLS BAY

ONLY €15 PER HOUR OR €60 PER DAY - FUEL INCLUDED - JUST CALL AND ASK FOR MANUEL

'Hmmm…' I thought to myself!

ACKNOWLEDGEMENTS

Commercial

Bristol Marina. Euro Tunnel. EasyJet. RAC European Assistance. Autos Victoria. Menorca-Sun. Iberia Airways. Trasmediterranea Ferrys. Artistic Blinds. The Set Connection. Pedro's Boat Centre.

Personal

Martin Brown, for his constant patience in helping me to correctly format *Word*.

Lizzie Barrett, for a significant amount of editing and proof-reading.

Mandy Smith, Brian and Rita, for a most welcome and entirely unforgettable Christmas.

My father John Reason, for giving me the inspiration and courage to tackle life's adventures.

My daughter Michelle, for holding and managing the fort with such ability and professionalism.

My daughter Tori, for stating the bleeding obvious right at the end instead of before I started.

My son Alex, despite being only nine years old, for being there when I needed him the most.

And lastly, an extra special massive *THANK YOU* to my long-suffering but wonderful wife Helen, for her help, patience and tolerance during the majority of my crazy escapades, and her willingness to share her company with me, not only throughout them, but also throughout the rest of my life.

AUTHOR'S NOTE

I was *told* to write a book, by a great many people. Not least of whom were my GP, various medical consultants, my physiotherapist, my solicitor, my accountant, my mortgage advisor, my insurance broker, and by no means least my bank manager! So here it is, *The Phoenix,* my very first attempt, and potentially the first in a series? Maybe I should just let you, *The Reader,* make that call for me!

I could certainly write a great deal more, I've definitely had more than my fair share of *Momentary Lapses of Reason;* albeit I'd endeavour to make the rest significantly shorter than this one! Nevertheless, I have a more than adequate repertoire of life's little mishaps over the years indelibly stamped deep within my memory, along with a seemingly new found urge to put pen to paper.

That aside, despite my tragically long list of life's mistakes and errors of judgement, the truthful fact still remains to this very day that I harbour only one single regret. That being, you may or may not be surprised to learn, the simple fact that I never got to see Freddie Mercury and Queen play live. Which just goes to show, our paths through life are all about learning, and not about regrets.

Very shortly after Freddie's tragic death I made a big point of attending my all time favourite band's best ever performance, namely Pink Floyd's awesome *Pulse* show at Earl's Court in 1992. The point I'm trying to make is that we should only ever live to regret something if we make the same mistake twice. Once is simply a learning curve. Twice is pure stupidity. And if you're smart enough to learn from other people's mistakes, then maybe you can go through life with no regrets whatsoever.

There are many lessons to be learned from the mistakes that I personally made that prompted me to pen this true story. I won't detail them, if you're clever enough you should easily be able to work them out for yourself.

And when you have, hopefully, you'll manage to avoid making the same mistakes that I have. Which, in itself, makes the telling of my own story all the more worthwhile.

Anyway, if you happen to have enjoyed my very first effort, then please could you email a massive thumbs-up to my publisher. Or if you'd prefer that I stopped, well, just come and find me, snatch this damned pen out of my hand, and let me crack on with something entirely different instead.

Thank you.